AMERICAN EXCEPTIONALISM?

Also by Rick Halpern

DOWN ON THE KILLING FLOOR: Black and White Workers in
Chicago's Packing Houses

Also by Jonathan Morris

THE POLITICAL ECONOMY OF SHOPKEEPING IN MILAN

American Exceptionalism?

US Working-Class Formation in an International Context

Edited by

Rick Halpern
Lecturer in American History
University College London

and

Jonathan Morris
Lecturer in Modern European History
University College London

First published in Great Britain 1997 by
MACMILLAN PRESS LTD
Houndmills, Basingstoke, Hampshire RG21 6XS and London
Companies and representatives throughout the world

A catalogue record for this book is available from the British Library.

ISBN 0–333–62810–1

First published in the United States of America 1997 by
ST. MARTIN'S PRESS, INC.,
Scholarly and Reference Division,
175 Fifth Avenue, New York, N.Y. 10010

ISBN 0–312–17470–5

Library of Congress Cataloging-in-Publication Data
American exceptionalism? : US working-class formation in an
international context / edited by Rick Halpern and Jonathan Morris.
p.   cm.
"This book arises out of the 1995 Commonwealth Fund Conference
held at University College London and the series of roundtable
discussions held by the seminar on Comparative Labour and Working
Class History at London's Institute of Historical Research"—P.   .
Includes index.
ISBN 0–312–17470–5 (cloth)
1. Working class—United States—History—Congresses.
I. Halpern, Rick.   II. Morris, Jonathan, 1961–   .
HD8066.A727 1997
305.5'62'0973—dc21   97–5320
                                                                             CIP

This book is printed on paper suitable for recycling and made from fully managed and
sustained forest sources.

10   9   8   7   6   5   4   3   2   1
06   05   04   03   02   01   00   99   98   97

Printed in Great Britain by
The Ipswich Book Company Ltd
Ipswich, Suffolk

Contents

Acknowledgements

This book arises out of the 1995 Commonwealth Fund Conference held at University College London and the series of roundtable discussions held by the seminar on Comparative Labour and Working Class History at London's Institute of Historical Research. We would like to thank all those who attended and contributed to those sessions. Special thanks are extended to the University College London Graduate School for its support of both endeavours. The conference also received financial assistance from the British Academy, the David Bruce Centre for American Studies at the University of Keele, the History Faculty of Cambridge University, the *Journal of American Studies* and the Institute of United States Studies at the University of London. We also would like to thank the various members of the Commonwealth Fund Committee, Nazneen Razwi, Rachel Aucott and Simon Renton for their advice and assistance.

Notes on the Contributors

Peter Alexander received his PhD from the University of London and was a postgraduate fellow at London's Institute of Commonwealth Studies. Currently, he is a Research Fellow at St Antony's College, Oxford, where he is working on a comparative study of miners in Alabama and the Transvaal.

Robin Archer is Fellow in Politics at Corpus Christi College, Oxford. He is the author of *Economic Democracy: The Politics of Feasible Socialism* (1995) and currently is working on a book about the failure of the American union movement to establish a labour party.

James Barrett teaches American and comparative labour history at the University of Illinois at Urbana-Champaign. His earlier works include *Steve Nelson, American Radical* (1981) and *Work and Community in the Jungle: Chicago's Packinghouse Workers* (1987). He is completing a biography of the American communist William Z. Foster and working on a book of essays dealing with the identities and personal lives of immigrant workers in the United States during the twentieth century.

Robert Gregg teaches American History at the Richard Stockton College of New Jersey. He is the author of *Sparks From the Anvil of Oppression: Philadelphia's African Methodists and Southern Migrants* (1993) and numerous articles on African-American history.

James Grossman is Director of the Dr William M. Scholl Center for Family and Community History at the Newberry Library, Chicago. He is the author of *Land of Hope: Chicago, Black Southerners, and the Great Migration* (1989) and, most recently, *'A Chance to Make Good': African Americans, 1900–1930* (1997). Currently he is working with Kathleen Neils Conzen on a project entitled 'Race and Citizenship: The Life and Death of Robert Cromwell'.

Rick Halpern is Lecturer in American History at University College London. He is the author of *Down on the Killing Floor: Black and White Workers in Chicago's Packinghouses* (1997) and co-author (with Roger Horowitz) of *Meatpackers: An Oral History of Black Packinghouse Workers* *and Their Struggle for Racial and Economic Equality* (1996). Currently he is working on a study of racialised labour in the sugar industry.

Roger Horowitz is Associate Director of the Center for the History of Business, Technology, and Society at the Hagley Museum and Library in Wilmington, Delaware. He is the author of *'Negro and White, Unite and Fight!' A Social History of Industrial Unionism in Meatpacking* (1997), and co-author (with Rick Halpern) of *Meatpackers: An Oral History of Black Packinghouse Workers and Their Struggle for Racial and Economic Equality* (1996). His current research concerns the effect of military service on working-class formation.

Ira Katznelson is Ruggles Professor of Political Science and History at Columbia University. His most recent books include *Liberalism's Crooked Circle: Letters to Adam Michnik* (1996), and (co-edited with Pierre Birnbaum) *Paths of Emancipation: Jews, States, and Citizenship* (1995). He is finishing a book about the making and character of post-New Deal American liberalism.

Neville Kirk is Reader in Economic and Social History at Manchester Metropolitan University. He is the author of *The Growth of Working Class Reformism in Mid-Victorian England* (1985) and *Labour and Society in Britain and the USA* (1994). He is currently writing a book on labour in modern Britian, and developing his comparative research focus upon labour and society in Britain, the United States, and Australia, 1880–1940.

Jonathan Morris is Lecturer in Modern European History at University College London. His publications include *The Political Economy of Shopkeeping in Milan* (1993) and various articles on Italian and European history. He has co-edited (with Robert Lumley) a collection of essays on *Liberal Italy and the 'Mezzogiorno'* (1997). Currently he is working on a comparative study of the politics of the European petite bourgeoisie in the twentieth century.

John Pollard is Professor of History at Anglia Polytechnic University. He is the author of *The Vatican and Italian Fascism, 1929–32: A Study in Conflict* (1985). He is currently working on a biography of Pope Benedict XV (1914–22).

David Roediger teaches working-class history and chairs the American Studies Program at the University of Minnesota. His recent books include

Towards the Abolition of Whiteness: Essays on Race, Politics, and Working Class History (1994) and (co-edited with Martin Blatt) *The Meaning of Slavery in the North* (1997). He is at work on an edited volume of African-American thought and writing about whiteness in the twentieth-century US.

Leslie Woodcock Tentler is Professor of History at the University of Michigan at Dearborn. She is the author of *Wage-Earning Women: Industrial Work and Family Life in the United States* (1979) and *Seasons of Grace: A History of the Catholic Archdiocese of Detroit* (1990).

Michael Zuckerman is Professor of History at the University of Pennsylvania. His many publications include *Peaceable Kingdoms: New England Towns in the Eighteenth Century* (1970) and *Almost Chosen People: Oblique Biographies in the American Grain* (1993).

1 The Persistence of Exceptionalism: Class Formation and the Comparative Method

Rick Halpern and Jonathan Morris

A true historical perennial, American exceptionalism shows no signs of losing its emotive power. Despite the institutionalisation of social history and the growth of rigorously comparative fields of enquiry, exceptionalism continues to beguile, frustrate, and excite students of the American past. Declared dead at periodic intervals, this is a corpse that continually springs back to life, calling forth defenders and detractors from successive generations of historians.

In recent years scholars have devoted greater attention to American exceptionalism than at any time since the 1950s. At first glance, this resurgence of interest is surprising. Given the collapse of the Soviet Union and the conclusion of the Cold War, the decline of labourism throughout Western Europe, and the rolling back of social democracy in Scandinavia and elsewhere, one reasonably might assume that exceptionalist arguments are now obsolete, outmoded ideological tropes no longer required in a world that has moved beyond *Pax Americana*. Yet this has hardly been the case. Books and articles dealing with exceptionalism form a small growth industry in academic publishing on both sides of the Atlantic that shows little sign of slowdown or stagnation in the immediate future.[1]

The vast majority of these recent publications engage with the problem of exceptionalism by seeking to isolate or reaffirm specific variables that render American historical development distinctive: the frontier, the federal party system, liberal individualism, high levels of social mobility, constant immigration, religious pluralism, race, untrammelled capitalist expansion, etc.[2] In doing so, they employ an exclusively internal reference in which the exceptional label is asserted or proclaimed; it does not emerge through a process of rigorous comparison with other cases.

Probably the best example of this mode of reasoning is Louis Hartz's classic *The Liberal Tradition in America* – a book that champions America's lack of a feudal past as the key to its twentieth-century politics, thereby

1

explaining via absence rather than through history. Without a hereditary aristocracy or a dispossessed proletariat, Hartz argued, American history was destined to unfold in a unique way. 'Born equal', Americans did not have to wage a revolution against privilege and property. Class-based ideologies and modes of political organisation held no appeal to them because they were irrelevant to American conditions. Instead of mobilising along lines of class, from the very outset Americans have been keen Lockean individualists – albeit unconscious ones – whose pragmatic politics have always been quintessentially liberal.[3]

Hartz, of course, was not the first commentator to consider the impact of a weak or absent feudalism upon American historical development, nor was he making a novel departure in suggesting a clean break with the dynamics of European society. Struggling to come to terms with American politics and assess the future of the socialist movement there, no less a dialectician than Karl Marx struck a positively Hartzian note when he observed in 1857 that 'bourgeois society did not develop on the foundation of the feudal system, but developed rather from itself . . . this society appears not as the surviving result of a centuries-old movement, but rather as the starting point of a new movement'.[4] But whereas Marx was endeavouring to place US development *within* history so as to render it intelligible, Hartz posited an America outside history, outside time itself.[5]

In the field of labour and working-class history, Werner Sombart's classic formulation – 'Why Is There No Socialism in the United States?' – has contributed in no small measure to a similar sort of ahistorical reasoning. Again, absence rather than presence is seen to hold the key to American distinctiveness. The lack of a sufficient degree of 'class consciousness', characterised by the failure to establish a labour party, renders intelligible both the relative weakness of early twentieth-century trade unionism in the US as well as the uncontested dominance of the two major parties. Of course, this framework precludes all sorts of interesting and important investigations into actual working-class politics, radicalism, organisation, and activity. As Eric Foner has trenchantly observed, in order to be historically relevant the 'Sombart question' must be rephrased: instead of asking about the reasons behind the absence of a European-style socialist or social democratic politics, scholars need to enquire about the contours and content of American socialism – 'why it once rose and fell' – as well as the persistence and power of other forms of indigenous radicalism.[6]

The 'new labor history' emerged in the 1970s with a programmatic and militantly revisionist agenda. Setting out to locate a working class that largely had been omitted from the historical literature and to document its struggles, the first wave of scholarship was written in a heroic vein.[7]

Locked in combat with both broad exceptionalist asssumptions and the economic reductionism of the 'Wisconsin School',[8] these historians ironically found themselves trapped within the same framework that lay beneath the arguments of Hartz and others. If the proponents of exceptionalism found no evidence of class conflict, then the labour historians would uncover a history of struggle that rivalled that of any European proletariat. If the Hartzians could see no evidence of viable socialist politics, then the new history would unearth a heretofore hidden record of popular practice. Although freed to write about *presences* in the American past, they sought to fill in the already outlined empty places marked off by their predecessors.[9]

Although implicitly comparative, most of this scholarship avoided serious and sustained consideration of European cases. Indeed, comparison most often served as a stylistic device – almost a rhetorical flourish – that allowed the process of revision to proceed. The most celebrated of these early 'comparisons' (and justly so), Alan Dawley's *Class and Community: The Industrial Revolution in Lynn*, illustrates these points. Concerned with the exploration of indigenous labour radicalism, Dawley looked to the history of the English working class to explain the distinctive features of the 'equal rights' tradition in the US. Noting that workers' struggles for economic rights merged with the campaign for direct political representation in early nineteenth-century England, Dawley identified the separation of these two currents of protest in America as holding the key to understanding workers' consciousness. His vital point about the mediating impact of political culture upon ideology is well taken – and, indeed, has been sustained and elaborated upon by numerous scholars. Yet, the comparison with England is really little more than an observation, a three paragraph intervention that sets up the book's most oft-cited quotation, 'the ballot box is the coffin of class consciousness'.[10]

Certainly, US labour historians have not dodged the problem of exceptionalism. More recently than Dawley, Sean Wilentz attempted to refute the traditional exceptionalist portrait of the American working class by arguing, in effect, that the language of artisan republicanism that emerged during and in the decades that followed the Revolution signalled the emergence of just the sort of class-based ideology that Sombart, Hartz and others found to be wanting in the United States. His essay provoked a lively but inconclusive exchange. While critics and allies alike agreed with Wilentz that theories of American exceptionalism resting on ahistorical and essentialist assumptions were unhelpful, few queried his sweeping generalisations about English and European socialism.[11] If, as Wilentz contended, with the decline of the artisan system of labour a peculiarly American form of class consciousness arose, then few scholars rose to the next logical task of actually comparing American republican ideology with, say, Chartist politics in England or republican socialism in France.[12]

A genuinely comparative approach to these sorts of questions would treat differences between cases as a problem for investigation – that is, as a starting point for enquiry rather than a final judgement. In the field of labour history, Aristide Zolberg has succinctly posed a question that can guide this sort of comparative study of class formation: 'If capitalism is of a piece, why is the working class it called into life so disparate?' Accordingly, actual empirical research and writing should seek to isolate and define both 'logics of difference' and 'logics of similarity' between cases.[13]

If precious few labour historians have adopted this approach, amongst exceptionalists, Seymour Martin Lipset has come closest to employing it, accepting that 'any effort to deal with Werner Sombart's question of "Why is there no socialism in the United States?" inherently must be comparative'. However, in all of his work, Lipset's aim is to affirm the validity of American exceptionalism. Although he considers other cases in a fairly full way, his ultimate aim is to demonstrate, in his own words, that 'the United States is qualitatively different from all other countries'.[14] For those interested in understanding variations in the making of proletariats (or bourgeoisies for that matter), Lipset's unit of analysis – 'the nation' – is too large and homogenising to be of much use. The 'working class' is at the same time smaller than 'the nation', and, because class formation is a dynamic process, more complex and trickier to define. As a result, Lipset's work is more successful at valorising national differences than analysing historical processes.

One could reasonably argue that there is little point in adhering to the vocabulary of exceptionalism when studying class formation. Some historians have gone as far as to suggest that the very term 'exceptionalism' should be stricken from the lexicon of class formation; others have forwarded the more moderate position that study should now move 'from exceptionalism to variability'. After all, each case will exhibit particularistic features setting it apart from all others. As Zolberg has it, the answer to the question 'How Many Exceptionalisms?' is 'as many as there are cases under consideration'.[15]

This does not mean to suggest that comparative history is a futile exercise simply because all cases can be said to be in some ways distinctive and none may be termed truly 'exceptional'. On the contrary, comparative analysis can be particularly powerful if we focus our enquiry upon a *constellation* of factors. Instead of seeking to privilege a single variable – be it the frontier or liberal ideology – and assigning to it overarching explanatory power, an approach that considers a number of elements and their relationship to each other can delineate a logic of distinctiveness *within* rather than outside of a comparative framework.

In practice, this requires adherence to certain basic methodological principles. The notion of a normative case must be abandoned and roughly equal attention should be devoted to all cases under consideration. Consequently, questions should be framed that are applicable to all cases rather than commencing with an enquiry arising from one case and not necessarily germane to the others. Thus, a 'why didn't they do that' question becomes a 'how did they do that' question: 'Why Is There No Socialism in the United States?' gives way to 'How Are Working Class Dispositions Formed?'. From this starting point critical enquiry can proceed to concrete analysis.[16]

In framing such enquiries, it is particularly important that reductionism be avoided. To utilise the strength of socialist politics as an index for working-class consciousness, as exceptionalists have done, is dysfunctional. It avoids consideration of other manifestations of class awareness, and sidesteps serious analysis of the content of consciousness itself. A more complete model, such as that suggested by Ira Katznelson, employs a multi-layered notion of class, one that encompasses economic structures, social and cultural patterns, *mentalités*, and capacities for collective action.[17] Within such a framework, discrete cases could resemble each other at the structural level while exhibiting striking degrees of dissimilarity at the level of class capacities. This allows not only for an understanding of each instance of class formation in its own terms, but exploration of the connections between them as well as evaluation of the arguments about the sources of their distinctiveness.

Exceptionalist formulations are far from unique to US history, and can themselves be made the subject of a comparative analysis. The same basic features that characterise the American example can be perceived in nearly all cases. The 'peculiarities' of a nation's (and usually in these discourses the notion of nation is an important feature of the analysis) history are again defined by absence, rather than presence: why does the country lack certain features, not why does it possess them? Amongst labour historians and those on the Left, these absences are defined in terms of failure – notably the failure to establish a genuinely socialist movement and/or government. Of course, it is these same features which account for the celebrations of the 'exceptional' character of a people amongst historians on the Right. Implicit in all these arguments is the existence of a 'normal' path of development from which the 'exceptional' nation has deviated, as suggested in the question 'why isn't *y* *x*?'

Sombart's query about the absence of socialism in the United States, for instance, crudely translates into the question 'why isn't America Germany?' After all, at the time he was writing, Germany possessed the strongest working-class movement in Europe, as was shown in 1913 when the Socialist Party became the largest single party in the Reichstag (the lower house of the German parliament). Yet German history since Sombart hardly followed a normal pattern. In the attempt to explain the horrors of 1933–45, historians frequently reverted to the notion of a special German path, the *Sonderweg*, whose course ran right through the years in which Sombart was writing.[18]

The strength of the Socialist Party at that time was illusory, they argue, because of the severely restricted role of the Reichstag within the German polity. Germany was an empire in which the chancellor was responsible to the sovereign, not a liberal democracy in which the government had to answer to parliament. Its structures were the creation of an astute aristocrat, Bismarck, who had unified the country through treaties and warfare. Consequently the country lacked the constitutional arrangements that might have developed out of a bourgeois revolution. Exceptionalists blame the absence of parliamentary democracy on the rejection of liberalism by the German middle classes following the events of 1848.[19] Although driving the rapid industrialisation that brought Germany close to overtaking Britain by 1914, the bourgeoisie had remained subservient to the political dominance of the Prussian aristocracy in contrast, *Sonderweg* historians argue, to the situation on the other side of the North Sea. As Ralf Dahrendorf effectively asked, 'Why wasn't Germany England?'[20]

Why not indeed? England, after all, was the first industrial nation, the cradle of the processes that Marx believed would transform the political situation throughout the developed world. It was a parliamentary democracy, and possessed strong liberal and labour movements. Yet while historians of Germany contrast the failure of its middle class to accept democracy with the 'normal' disposition of the English bourgeoisie who, they believed, supplanted the aristocracy with this weapon, so British historians have taken to asking why the labour movement of the country showed little disposition to support the Marxist doctrines developed by continental working-class political parties, chief amongst them the German SPD. Explanations of this have ranged over the lack (once again) of an actual moment of bourgeois revolution which might have redrawn the constitutional framework, the fragmented character of the apparently broad-ranging labour movement, its ideological and cultural inheritance from the artisan radicals who, as E.P. Thompson famously pointed out, were the primary makers of the English working class, the 'interclass' nature of many protest movements in the nineteenth century that bred a 'popular liberalism' reflected in the vocabulary of the participants, and, conversely, the lack of a middle-class intelligentsia within the leadership of the labour movement that might have persuaded it of the need to pursue projects for the establishment of an alternative set of political arrangements, alongside those for the satisfaction of economic demands within the existing system.[21] Whatever answer they favour, it is clear that these analysts believe there is a need to explain the 'peculiarities of the English'.

These exceptionalist discourses all point to the need to analyse cases through conscious informed comparisons, rather than in isolation against presumed 'norms' of historical development. One of the most telling points in the critique of German exceptionalism launched by the British historians David Blackbourn and Geoffrey Eley was that not only was Germany not England, England was not England either in that the liberal democracy posited by German historians bore little resemblance to a land where the suffrage remained restricted and the unelected House of Lords continued to protect the position of the privileged.[22] A more effective way to proceed is to return to the method we have previously outlined of contrasting the constellation of factors in each individual case.

At first the exceptionalist discourses about Britain, Germany and the United States may seem very different. The German case is concerned with the politics of the bourgeoisie, the British with those of the working class, whilst the American case essentially denies the existence of a working-class politics, and, to some extent, the formation of this class in the first place. Yet they all are essentially concerned with class relations and the various structures that these can assume. One obvious reason that the German middle classes were less enthused about liberal democratic structures than their British counterparts, for instance, was that they knew that these would increase not the power of their own political representatives but that of the Socialists. In nineteenth-century Britain, prior to the formation of the Labour Party in 1906, it was precisely through the use of such instruments that the bourgeoisie (or even, at times, the gentry) had been able to join with sections of the working classes to pursue its battles through numerical strength.

Furthermore, all the cases highlight the need to investigate the forms of political expression generated amongst classes as explicable in terms of dispositions generated through lived experience, including that of political and constitutional structures, alongside reference to economic position. Supposed deviations from 'normality' should not be seen as indicative of a 'false' or manipulated consciousness, but as arising from an objective assessment of opportunities. Popular liberalism amongst the British working class made as much sense as democratic illiberalism amongst the

German bourgeoisie. For that matter, the lack of opportunity within the German system made the SPD commitment to alternative arrangements easy to sustain, whereas in France, the revolutionary country *par excellence*, which after 1871 enjoyed both universal manhood suffrage and parliamentary sovereignty, the Socialist movement was divided into a plethora of parties, many owing more to political thinkers other than Marx, and which, despite some participation in government, achieved little in terms of the 'classical agenda' of working-class movements.

Finally, one should note the importance of periodisation in these cases. The exceptionalist discourse seeks to establish and explain an enduring difference that defines a nation's path through history. Yet those continuities in German history that have been cited in an attempt to explain 1933–45 are of little help in understanding the Weimar Republic, or the history of the two Germanies since the Second World War. Similarly the singularities of British working-class politics in the nineteenth and early twentieth centuries are far less striking for the post-1945 period.

Our objective in this book then is to utilise comparison in an attempt to tease out the particular constellation of factors affecting working-class formation and politics in the United States. The essays that follow engage with the exceptionalist discourse either through direct comparison, or by examination of those features of the American case that have been labelled distinctive.

The book opens with two re-evaluations of the historiography of American exceptionalism. In a free-wheeling essay, Michael Zuckerman explores both the resurgence of exceptionalist writing in recent years and considers the ideological dimension of this tradition. This is followed by Ira Katznelson's reflections on the changing political dispositions of the American working class in relation to adjustments in the 'grammar of liberalism'. This allows for a periodisation of class formation which transforms it from an 'exceptional' outcome into a historical process. The final article in this section returns to the classic 'Sombart Question'. Robin Archer considers the evolution of labour politics in the United States and Australia, two settler societies that exhibit a number of similar (and hence comparable) traits.

The connections between liberalism and working-class politics is examined in detail in the second section. Roger Horowitz shows how the labourist possibilities evident in the 1930s faded as liberalism expanded its scope and constituency. The consciousness formed among working-class soldiers in the Second World War facilitated the state's introduction of a restricted welfare system in which benefits were justified through reference to military service rather than universal entitlement. Challenging

Katznelson, Neville Kirk's piece examines workers' dispositions in Britain and the United States between the 1880s and the 1920s. He argues that the presence in both cases of a vibrant idiom of liberalism masks antagonistic class dynamics that were asserted through strong worker collective action and identity.

Indisputably, two variables which help account for the distinctive nature of the American working class are its heavily Catholic composition within a governing Protestant culture, and the role played by racial and ethnic divisions in restricting a vision of class solidarity. The first of these is charted in two articles on working-class Catholicism in the United States and Italy by Leslie Tentler and John Pollard respectively. In the Italian case, elite and subaltern classes shared the same religion, thus hindering the harnessing of Catholicism to the construction of class identity. In America, by contrast, Catholicism fostered a sense of group awareness which overlapped for most of the late nineteenth and twentieth centuries with working-class and political (though non-socialist) identities. These identities were further consolidated through the ethnic community's construction of grass roots parochial institutions, in contrast to Italy where the Catholic hierarchy imposed them from above.

Many historians have seen the issue of race as forming the greatest barrier to solidarity within the American working class. Until very recently, though, this has been a shorthand for colour, with 'race' functioning as a synonym for African-American. James Barrett and David Roediger employ a more complex and nuanced conception, however, one in which racial identity is constructed and ever-changing rather than given and static. Exploring the ways in which European immigrants 'became white', they chart the vocabulary of inclusion and exclusion in early twentieth-century America, showing both how employers sought to racialise the workforce and how workers came to understand the world and their class position through the distorting prism of 'race'. In the next article, James Grossman adds a spatial dimension to the ideology of race, mapping how southern ideas about social order revolved around the place of dependent, that is black, labour in the region. In contrast to Barrett and Roediger, he sees 'race' as an 'integral element of social structure and relations of production rather than merely an artefact of class formation, a set of ideas, a psychological problem or a cultural flaw'.

The final two pieces are explicitly comparative and focus upon the United States and South Africa. This field has produced a wealth of comparative literature in recent years, the vast bulk of which focuses upon the origins and implementation of segregation and apartheid. Most of this scholarship begins from the assumption that both countries are best seen as racially-ordered societies.[23] In contrast, Peter Alexander commences his investigation from the assumption that they are class-based societies, allowing him to acknowledge that during the Second World War both labour movements were able to significantly transcend racial obstacles to class solidarity. In the last contribution Robert Gregg also breaks with conventional forms of comparison, not least in pointing out the salient question of actual connections between cases under comparison. Eschewing the use of national units, he considers the imperial dimension in comparative history as he explores such apparently disparate phenomena as African Methodism, populism, and prostitution. Ironically, while exceptionalism is in many ways an imperialist formulation, it is Gregg's imperial vantage point that enables him to see beyond it.

NOTES

1. See, for instance, Byron E. Shafer, ed., *Is America Different? A New Look at American Exceptionalism* (Oxford, 1991); Jack Greene, *The Intellectual Construction of America: Exceptionalism and Identity from 1492 to 1900* (Chapel Hill, 1993); Kim Voss, *The Making of American Exceptionalism: The Knights of Labor and Class Formation in the Nineteenth Century* (Ithaca, 1993); and Seymour Martin Lipset, *American Exceptionalism: A Double Edged Sword* (New York, 1996).

2. The classic statement on the frontier is Frederick Jackson Turner, *The Significance of the Frontier in American History* (New York, 1963); for the federal structure of US politics, see Theodore J. Lowi, 'Why Is There No Socialism in the United States? A Federal Analysis', *International Political Science Review*, 5 (1984); and for social mobility see Stephan Thernstrom, *Poverty and Progress: Social Mobility in a Nineteenth Century City* (Cambridge MA, 1964); see also his 'Working Class Mobility in Industrial America', in Melvin Harris, ed., *Essays in History and Theory* (Cambridge MA, 1970). For the liberalism formulation, the foundation text is Louis Hartz, *The Liberal Tradition in America: An Interpretation of American Political Thought Since the Revolution* (New York, 1955); but see also Daniel J. Boorstin, *The Genius of American Politics* (Chicago, 1953). For immigration, the most provocative argument is found in Aileen S. Kraditor, *The Radical Persuasion, 1890–1917: Aspects of the Intellectual History and the Historiography of Three American Radical Organizations* (Baton Rouge, 1981); see also Gerald Rosenblum, *Immigrant Workers: Their Impact on American Labor Radicalism* (New York, 1973). The consequences of overwhelmingly Catholic immigration are taken up in Mike Davis, 'Why the US Working Class is Different', *New Left Review*, 123 (1980) reprinted in his *Prisoners of the American Dream* (London, 1989). A sweeping argument

about race and American distinctiveness is Michael Goldfield, 'The Color of Politics in the United States: White Supremacy as the Main Explanation for the Peculiarities of American Politics from Colonial Times to the Present', in Dominick LaCapra, ed., *The Bounds of Race: Perspectives on Hegemony and Resistance* (Ithaca, 1991).

3. Hartz, *Liberal Tradition*, esp. 35–66; a recent rebuttal, employing the same categories but grounded in detailed research into legal history is Karen Orren, *Belated Feudalism: Labor, the Law, and Liberal Development in the United States* (New York, 1992). If Hartz found in liberal hegemony a cause for celebration, the author of the other key text in this branch of the exceptionalist canon, Richard Hofstadter, regarded it as cause for anguish; Richard Hofstadter, *The American Political Tradition and the Men Who Made It* (New York, 1948).

4. Karl Marx, *Grundrisse: Foundations of the Critique of Political Economy* (London, 1973), 884; this passage continues, rife with exceptionalist tropes: 'where the state in contrast to all earlier national formations, was from the beginning subordinate to bourgeois sovereignty, to its production, and never could make the pretence of being an end-in-itself; where, finally, bourgeois society itself, linking up the productive forces of an old world with the enormous natural terrain of a new one, has developed to hitherto unheard-of dimensions and with unheard-of freedom of movement, has far outstripped all previous work in the forces of the conquest of nature, and where, finally, even the antitheses of bourgeois society appear only as vanishing moments'.

5. This point is developed by Daniel T. Rodgers, 'Exceptionalism' (paper delivered at the Scuola Superiore di Studi Storici, Universita di San Marino, June 1995), 18–19. Rodgers writes: 'Without a feudal past, the inner, dialectical engine of history had no purchase in America. No Robespierre, no de Maistre, no Marx, no Goebbels, no Stalin, only (in the shorthand Hartz affected) an eternal, changeless Locke. Other nations went through the throes of the twice-born, but the Americans, by the chance conditions of their founding, had slipped free of the underlying motor of historical change itself. Starting differently, they were fated to be eternally the same: eternally different from everyone else.'

6. Eric Foner, 'Why Is There No Socialism in the United States?', in Jean Heffer and Jeanine Rovet, eds, *Why Is There No Socialism in the United States?* (Paris, 1983), 55–65, quotation 56. Recent scholarship on the American socialism, let alone the larger radical tradition, is too voluminous to note here; three works exemplify this line of enquiry: James Green, *Grass Roots Socialism: Radical Movements in the Southwest, 1895–1943* (Baton Rouge, 1978); Mari Jo Buhle, *Women and American Socialism, 1870–1920* (Urbana, 1981); and especially Nick Salvatore, *Eugene V. Debs: Citizen and Socialist* (Urbana, 1982). See also Paul Buhle's provocative but idiosyncratic study of the interaction between indigenous radicalism and European socialism, *Marxism in the United States: Remapping the History of the American Left* (London, 1987).

7. See, for instance, Jeremy Brecher, *Strike!* (New York, 1972); and Paul Faler, 'Working Class Historiography', *Radical America*, 3:2 (March–April 1969).

8. The labour economists at the University of Wisconsin who pioneered the field of US labour history in the early twentieth century adopted an institutional approach that focused almost exclusively upon unions and collective bargaining. Downplaying social forces, and unconcerned with social and cultural history, they produced a history of the labour movement that championed its 'job consciousness' and resistance to radical ideologies. See John R. Commons *et al.*, *History of Labor in the United States*, 4 vols (New York, 1926); the theoretical underpinnings of this approach were made explicit by Selig Perlman in *A Theory of the Labor Movement* (New York, 1928). See also Maurice Isserman, '"God Bless Our American Institutions": The Labor History of John R. Commons', *Labor History*, 17:3 (Summer 1976). For an assessment of the 'new labor history's' revisionism, see David Brody, 'The Old Labor History and the New: In Search of an American Working Class', *Labor History*, 19 (1979).

9. For caustic, and exaggerated, treatment of this dynamic see Michael Kazin, 'Struggling with Class Struggle: Marxism and the Search for a Synthesis of US Labor History', *Labor History*, 28:4 (Fall 1987).

10. Alan Dawley, *Class and Community: The Industrial Revolution in Lynn* (Cambridge MA, 1976), 70–72 (quotation 70). See also Alan Dawley, 'E.P. Thompson and the Peculiarities of the Americans', *Radical History Review*, 19 (Winter 1978–79).

11. Sean Wilentz, 'Against Exceptionalism: Class Consciousness and the American Labor Movement', *International Labor and Working Class History*, 26 (Fall 1984), and responses in the same issue, as well as Steve Sapolsky, 'Response to Sean Wilentz's "Against Exceptionalism"', *International Labor and Working Class History*, 27 (Spring 1985). See also Sean Wilentz, 'Artisan Origins of the American Working Class', *International Labor and Working Class History*, 19 (Spring 1981), especially the concluding comments on page 20; and Wilentz, 'Artisan Republican Festivals and the Rise of Class Conflict in New York City, 1788–1837', in Michael H. Frisch and Daniel J. Walkowitz, eds, *Working-Class America: Essays on Labor, Community, and American Society* (Urbana, 1983).

12. For precisely this sort of comparison by a historian of France, and one in which Wilentz's argument fares rather poorly, see B.H. Moss, 'Republican Socialism and the Making of the Working Class in Britain, France, and the United States: A Critique of Thompsonian Culturalism', *Comparative Studies in Society and History*, 35:2 (April 1993). See also the piece by the German historian Friedrich Lenger, 'Beyond Exceptionalism: Notes on the Artisanal Phase of the Labour Movement in France, England, Germany and the United States', *International Review of Social History*, 46 (1991).

13. Aristide R. Zolberg, 'How Many Exceptionalisms?', in Ira Katznelson and Aristide R. Zolberg, eds, *Working-Class Formation: Nineteenth Century Patterns in Western Europe and the United States* (Princeton, 1986), 397.

14. Lipset, *American Exceptionalism*, 78, 18 (quotes); his most sustained comparison is found in *Continental Divide: The Values and Institutions of the United States and Canada* (New York, 1990).

15. Sapolsky, 'Response to Sean Wilentz', 35; George Fredrickson, 'From Exceptionalism to Variability: Recent Developments in Cross-National Comparative History', *Journal of American History*, 82:2 (September 1995); see also James E. Cronin, 'Neither Exceptional Nor Peculiar: Towards the

Comparative Study of Labor in Advanced Society', *International Review of Social History*, 38 (1993); Zolberg, 'How Many Exceptionalisms?', 455.

16. For elaboration upon these considerations, see John Breuilly, *Labour and Liberalism in Nineteenth Century Europe* (Manchester, 1992), 1–5; and Theda Skocpol and Margaret Somers, 'The Uses of Comparative History in Macrosocial Inquiry', *Comparative Studies in Society and History*, 22:2 (1980).

17. Ira Katznelson, 'Working-Class Formation: Constructing Cases and Comparisons' in Katznelson and Zolberg, *Working-Class Formation*, 14–19.

18. See, amongst many, Hans Ulrich Wehler, *The German Empire, 1871–1914* (Leamington Spa, 1985); Fritz Fischer, *From Kaiserreich to Third Reich: Elements of Continuity in German History* (London, 1986); and Barrington Moore, Jr, *Social Origins of Dictatorship and Democracy: Lord and Peasant in the Making of the Modern World* (Boston, 1966).

19. The essence of the crudely exceptionalist position is advanced in A.J.P. Taylor, *The Course of German History: A Survey of the Development of German History Since 1918* (London, 1945).

20. Ralf Dahrendorf, *Society and Democracy in Germany* (London, 1979), 1–16; see the more precise reformulation in David Blackbourn and Geoffrey Eley, *The Peculiarities of German History: Bourgeois Society and Politics in Nineteenth Century Germany* (Oxford, 1984), 7.

21. For the classic debate on English exceptionalism, see Perry Anderson, 'Origins of the Present Crisis', *New Left Review*, 23 (January–February 1964); Tom Nairn, 'The English Working Class', *New Left Review*, 24 (March–April 1964); Nairn, 'The Nature of the Labour Party', *New Left Review*, 27/28 (September–October/November–December 1964); E.P. Thompson, 'The Peculiarities of the English', in Ralph Miliband and John Saville, eds, *Socialist Register*, 2 (London, 1965), 311–36. Thompson's classic work on the artisanal origins of the labour movement is, of course, *The Making of the English Working Class* (Harmondsworth, 1968). The recent debates on the interrelationships between language, popular liberalism and class formation were initiated by Gareth Stedman Jones, *Languages of Class: Studies in English Working Class History 1832–1982* (Cambridge, 1983). See more recently, Dorothy Thompson, *The Chartists: Popular Politics in the Industrial Revolution* (New York, 1984); Eugenio Biagini and Alistair Reid, eds, *Currents of Radicalism: Popular Radicalism, Organised Labour and Party Politics in Britain, 1850–1914* (Cambridge, 1991); Patrick Joyce, *Visions of the People: Industrial England and the Question of Class 1840–1914* (Cambridge, 1991). The more recent debates have been incorporated into an exploration of 'Why was there no Marxism in Great Britain?', in Ross McKibbin, *The Ideologies of Class: Social Politics in Britain 1880–1950* (Oxford, 1990), 1–41.

22. Blackbourn and Eley, *Peculiarities of German History*, passim.

23. George M. Fredrickson, *White Supremacy: A Comparative Study in American and South African History* (New York, 1981); John W. Cell, *The Highest Stage of White Supremacy: The Origins of Segregation in South Africa and the American South* (Cambridge, 1982); Stanley B. Greenberg, *Race and State in Capitalist Development: South Africa in Comparative Perspective* (Johannesburg, 1980); and most recently Fredrickson, *Black Liberation: The Comparative History of Black Ideologies in the United States and South Africa* (New York, 1995).

2 The Dodo and the Phoenix: A Fable of American Exceptionalism

Michael Zuckerman

Americans have always been adamant about their own exceptionality. So there may be some paltry paradox in confessing that I have never been an ardent exponent of the doctrine of American exceptionalism.

Not that I have ever doubted or disputed it. On the contrary. I never invested in it emotionally because I always took it for granted.

From my earliest undergraduate reflection on American civilisation down to this day – or down, at least to the day before yesterday – I scarcely gave exceptionalism a passing thought. All I learned in all those years was to temper my unthinking assumption of the notion with an equally unthinking appropriation of Lincoln's poignant qualification of it, when I took his lovely line about Americans as almost chosen people for the title of a book of my essays.

But recently I have been doing some reading. And I have been finding, to my astonishment, that there is a lot to read. There has been, lately, a remarkable torrent of writing on American exceptionalism. I count two conferences on the subject in Paris and another in Oxford. I count a forum on exceptionalism in the *American Historical Review* and another on the topic in the *American Quarterly*. I count three presidential addresses on the theme to leading American historical associations. I count leading articles and articles by leading scholars in leading journals, and books by major figures besides. There has been no such rush of pontification on the issue since the decade of the dawn of the Cold War. It is not easy to see what new beast is slouching towards Bethlehem, or why.[1]

Taken together or taken separately, these writings are a dismayingly incoherent assemblage. If my own long, thoughtless attachment to the dogma of exceptionalism is an embarrassment, the recent literature itself and its considered commitment to the doctrine are a mortification.

Take, for example, a pair of essays by the celebrated social scientist Daniel Bell. Take first the first of them, written twenty years ago in the shadow of Vietnam, to announce 'the end of American exceptionalism'.[2]

Bell recognised that declaration of the demise of the doctrine required a specification of its substance. But he never bothered with the particularity and precision he recommended. He simply set forth a farrago of disconnected conceptualisations and incompatible quotations.

He began with an invocation of the 'unprecedented opportunities of [the American] continent' and 'a peculiar and unrepeatable combination of historical circumstances'. But he concluded, somehow, with his own insistence that these explicitly historical elements 'added up to' an idea of exceptionalism as exemption from history. 'America would, in the trials of history, get off "scot free".'[3]

With that contradiction installed at the core of his conception, he hastened to heap a motley mélange of other incoherent elements on his definitional pile. All of the first set of them were manifestly false, both historically and in 1975: that the country had 'a common political faith' which would obviate 'ideological vicissitudes and divisive passions', that it was 'entirely a middle-class society' which would preclude decadence, that it was 'a liberal society' which would 'escape the disaffection of the intelligentsia' and 'the resentment of the poor', and that it was a different, democratic sort of 'paramount power' in the world which would exercise its hegemony differently, democratically.[4]

A few pages later, he asserted an altogether incongruent exceptionalism expressive of a sense of self-appointed mission to save the world and exemplified in the appeal of the redeemer-president, Woodrow Wilson, to the redeemer-nation, America, to lead the League of Nations. (Bell was sublimely unperturbed that Americans spurned Wilson's idealistic summons and then, a generation later, willingly followed a more pragmatic president into the United Nations, an organisation which Roosevelt deliberately declined to depict in prose 'soaked in the rhetoric of redemption'.) And a few pages after that, summarising the sources of the society's exceptionalism that were no more, Bell enumerated yet another array, randomly related to those he had discussed before: land, equality, space and security, economic abundance, the two-party system, and constitutionalism.[5]

Bell's recitals of the aspects of exceptionalism that had ceased to obtain by 1975 were as diverse and disordered as his accounts of the elements of exceptionalism itself. And they were the more bewildering because, as often as not, they posited collapse where his prior accounts had not predicated exceptionalism in the first place. Thus Bell fretted that 'the belief in American exceptionalism has vanished with the end of empire, the weakening of power, the loss of faith in the nation's future'. Thus he worried that 'the social stability of the country – the meaning of American exceptionalism – has been weakened'. Thus he lamented that 'nature and religion have vanished' and that the 'sense of destiny has been shattered'.

Thus he moaned that the 'molds have been broken. There is no longer a Manifest Destiny or mission. We have not been immune to the corruption of power. We have not been the exception. . . . Our mortality now lies before us.'[6]

Yet even as he conceded that the United States had become 'a nation like all other nations', Bell clung to the consolation of his conviction that Americans were, somehow, still an anointed people. If they could not be outside history, as his first formulation required, they could have a special history. Their very history could confer upon them a dimension of invincible distinctiveness: 'We have, *in looking back*, a unique history, a history of constitutionalism and comity.'[7]

As a kind of coda to this first incoherent essay, Bell set conditions for the reclamation of a cohesive country: a 'moral credibility whose essential condition is simple honesty and openness' in politics, a 'conscious commitment . . . to forgo any hegemonic dream' (even the dream of 'being the moral policeman of the world') in foreign policy, and a 'policy of inclusion' with its corollary of allowing 'disadvantaged groups . . . priority' in domestic social policy.[8]

So take now the second of Bell's essays on exceptionalism, published in 1991 in the aftermath of George Bush's triumphant policing of the Persian Gulf. By then it was clear that the national leaders on whom Bell had called in 1975 had rejected every one of the conditions he had set. They had proven themselves even more obsessed with secrecy and security than their predecessors, and they had demonstrated a wilful and often unrepentant readiness to lie to Congress. Bell himself acknowledged the 'tissue of lies, webs of deceit, [and] rhetorical excesses of self-righteousness' in their regimes. They had shown themselves ardent to police Nicaragua, Lebanon, Grenada, and Panama before they lit upon Saddam Hussein as a pretext to undo the 'Vietnam syndrome' and restore their prerogatives around the globe. They had abandoned the disadvantaged and the cities in which they lived and undertaken domestic social policies eventuating in the most sweeping redistribution of income in half a century, virtually all of it to the very rich.[9]

Did this dishearten Bell? Not at all. By 1991 he had discovered a 'Hegelian secret' of American life that enabled him to proclaim anew the exceptionalism he had dismissed in 1975.

The exceptionalism that he proclaimed now was no better defined than the one he denied before. Once again he declared 'the question of exemption' from the corrosive compounds of history 'the acid test of exceptionalism'. And once again he dismissed that test as soon as he declared it, multiplying other tests as fast as they occurred to him: 'being exemplary, a beacon among nations', or being 'the providential nation, the redeemer nation', or protecting 'human rights', or preserving a 'commitment to constitutionalism', or upholding 'enduring values of character'.[10]

As though he had never asserted the nation's fall from greatness as a flat descriptive fact fifteen years before, he now confessed merely a certain solicitude 'whether America can maintain its greatness'. As though he had not denied that the country possessed any 'common purpose' or 'common faith' – as though he had not seen 'only bewilderment' in their stead – in 1975, he now professed a certainty that America had 'a *saving grace* which makes us still exemplary to other nations'.[11]

When Bell did finally disclose his 'Hegelian secret', it had, of course, nothing whatsoever to do with this quasi-religious rhetoric, this leftover language from older essays, this sounding fervour signifying nearly nothing. The 'Hegelian secret' was that America is, or was, a 'complete *civil society*, perhaps the only one in political history'. It embodied itself outside any state apparatus, in 'individual self-interest and a passion for liberty' alone.[12]

The argument is so fatuous that Bell himself had not the temerity to try to sustain it. He no sooner set it forth than he retracted it. He not only conceded that America experienced a massive expansion of the state and of statism after 1930, he also contended that 'the problem of "the state"' impelled 'country after country' in recent years to turn to 'the idea of "civil society"' rather than "the state" as the primary arena of political activities'.[13]

The contention was as bizarre as the concession. The concession granted that America is no longer a 'civil society' at all, let alone the only one, and that it has not been for at least the last two generations. The contention allowed that places as profoundly different from each other as from the United States, places such as Poland and Italy, are now turning from the state to the civic sphere or, at any rate, problematising the prerogatives of the state.

But Bell was as indifferent to these difficulties as he was unembarrassed by his reversals and repudiations of his own prior pontifications. He simply celebrated his every contradiction as another 'twist in the long tale of American exceptionalism'. He could hardly have made plainer his preference for sententious incantation rather than responsible analysis.[14]

Bell's vacuous sonorities are far from exceptional in the literature of American exceptionalism. The subject has always tangled its interpreters in contradictions, even if it has not always entailed upon them a cavalier obtuseness to their inconsistencies and incoherences.

Alexis de Tocqueville himself oscillated between an imagination of American uniqueness and an assumption of American prefiguration of the European future. Some of his favourite informants pressed him to 'remember that there are no precedents' for American history, and he took their tutelage to heart. In one of his most widely cited aperçus, he observed that 'the great advantage of the Americans is that they have arrived at a state of democracy without having to endure a democratic revolution, and that they are born equal instead of becoming so'. In one of his most inane ones, he insisted that he could 'see the whole destiny of America contained in the first Puritan who landed on those shores'.[15]

And yet, for all its historical peculiarity, America attracted Tocqueville because he believed that he could see the destiny of Europe in it. 'In America', he averred, 'I saw more than America; I sought there the image of democracy itself . . . in order to learn what we have to fear or to hope from its progress.'[16]

And yet, for all its exemplary implication, America fascinated Tocqueville because he was convinced that it would remain a place apart even after the nations of Europe adopted its democracy. 'The position of the Americans is', he said, 'quite exceptional, and it may be believed that no democratic people will ever be placed in a similar one.'[17]

The conundrums of American exceptionalism confounded even the most rational and responsible analysis. They left even as brilliant a student of society as Tocqueville divided against himself.

Both before Tocqueville and after, both foreign and American observers exhibited the same confusions. They admired a country that was at once inimitable and inspirational. They celebrated a nation that had been granted a blessed dispensation from the ills that afflicted other nations and a nation that would be a model for all mankind. They exalted a society singular and universal in its significance.

Their exceptionalism devolved swiftly into universalism, and it did so from the first. David Ramsay, reflecting on the Revolution before it was even won, believed that the new nation would edify the Old World. America's 'noble example, like a wide-spreading conflagration, [would] catch from breast to breast and extend from nation to nation, till tyranny and oppression [were] utterly extirpated from the earth'. The 'cause of America' would become the 'cause of Human Nature'. Albert Gallatin, contemplating the consequences of independence while the ink was still drying on the Treaty of Paris, came to the same conclusion. The United

States would 'enlighten [Europe], serve her as a model, and perhaps contribute to the happiness of mankind in general'.[18]

Such vanity inevitably subverted the exceptionalism it extolled. If others could so readily follow the American example, there was nothing exceptional about that example. The very idea of the United States as a paradigm, even when tempered by recognition that the infant republic was not a paragon, entailed the obsolescence of exceptionalism. It took for granted that others would appropriate the life that Americans pioneered. More, it presumed that others would appropriate it because they were like Americans and wanted what Americans wanted.

In short, exceptionalism of the exemplary sort ran straight to its antithesis: an assumptive American universalism. Without ever seeming to notice that they did so, its expositors abandoned the logic of American uniqueness for a very different logic of American priority.

Other advocates of exceptionalism also unwittingly undid their endeavour without seeming to see. Unlike their countrymen, who took America for a model for the world to follow so as to 'be universally set free', these exceptionalists thought merely that America might provide a haven for the victims of the invincible oppressions of the *ancien régime*. Theirs was authentically an affirmation of freedom in one country. In Paine's immortal apostrophe, America was appointed by 'the Almighty' to be 'the asylum for the persecuted lovers of civil and religious liberty from *every part* of Europe'.

> Every spot of the old world is over-run with oppression. Freedom hath been hunted round the globe. Asia, and Africa, have long expelled her. Europe regards her like a stranger, and England hath given her warning to depart. O! receive the fugitive, and prepare in time an asylum for mankind.

But even the notion of America as refuge ran soon enough to its inversion in universalism. Even it presumed that others wanted the liberty that America had, though they were inept at achieving it. Even it refused to countenance the possibility that others actually wanted lifeways and limits that America did not offer.[19]

Still other perplexities plagued other exceptionalists. Some of them postulated America's providential escape from history. Others assigned its exceptionality exactly to its distinctive historical situation. Some of them, in a tradition that comes down to Daniel Bell, vested the essential part of the nation's peculiarity in its ideology: its constitutional faith, its conviction that membership is more a matter of shared attachment to a set of ideas than of shared experiences or shared genes. Others, in a tradition that goes back to Tocqueville, saw the crux of the country's uniqueness in its absence of ideology: its adamant priority on practice rather than theory, its active indifference to ideas.[20]

The tantalising issue of utopia enters here. Hosts of historians have noted the utopic aspect of American civilisation. From the first, American colonies were founded on visions of the recovery of an ideal past in an empty continent; through the nineteenth century, American communities were settled in romances of the establishment of an ideal future on the beckoning frontiers. But hosts of ordinary Americans have confounded those very visions. From the first, they have disdained to take them to heart; throughout American history, they have made the New World the graveyard of grandiose designs to create new commonwealths or remake men and women. Europeans regularly imagined America a society 'totally different' than their own. Americans as regularly spurned such imaginings and sought to be more like their European admirers.[21]

And hosts of historians have taken their side. Bell may have maintained, like others before him and since, that the United States was constituted in a conscious 'act of will' and that it continues to be constituted by popular attachment to a creed that confers the nation's existence. But an even more numerous school has insisted with Frederick Jackson Turner that 'American democracy was born of no theorist's dream' and that it 'came out of the American forest and . . . gained new strength every time it touched a new frontier'.[22]

Turner took a deep aversion to ideas, an unabashed anti-intellectualism, as a crucial component of the exceptionalism he spent his scholarly career trying to specify. And multitudes followed where he led. In the 1950s, the apogee of exceptionalist thinking, Daniel Boorstin, took that Turnerian insight to its apotheosis. In one of the two boldest and most important articulations of exceptionalism in a decade deeply devoted to the doctrine, Boorstin made antipathy to theory the inmost genius of America.[23]

And yet, in the other of those two epiphanal articulations, Louis Hartz held theory itself the deepest secret of American life. Hartz insisted that, in the United States, a particular complex of ideas that he called liberalism governed politics and set the shape of the possible more largely. Americans only seemed a-theoretical because they were wedded so completely to the theory of liberalism that they could not even see it, let alone extricate themselves from its icy grip.[24]

Boorstin and Hartz have come to be considered together as 'consensus' historians. In fact they shared almost nothing. Their variant versions of exceptionalism defied synthesis. The consensus of the one was unassimilable to the consensus of the other, ethically as well as substantively. Boorstin believed that the enlivening poverty of American ideation enriched American society. Hartz thought that the overpowering plenitude of American ideation impoverished American politics and made the nation pathetically provincial.

One of the few things the two did share was a conviction – a conviction exceptional among exceptionalists – that America had no lessons to teach the world, no model to hold before it, no redemption to offer it. Boorstin was a conservative chauvinist, Hartz a radical cosmopolitan, but they were united in their disinclination to do ideological battle on America's behalf in that first fervid flush of the Cold War. America had 'nothing in the line of a theory that can be exported to other peoples of the world', Boorstin warned. 'The question is not whether our history has given us something to "export"', Hartz concurred, 'but whether it has given us the right thing.' For Hartz the question had 'to be answered in the negative'.[25]

Boorstin and Hartz were among the few conscientious objectors of their age. Other exceptionalists such as David Potter enlisted eagerly, and so, almost without fail, did pundits and polemicists outside the academy. Henry Luce, arguably the most influential business intellectual in modern America, proclaimed the twentieth century 'the American Century'.[26]

But Luce could no more specify the American century than anyone else had ever coherently analysed American exceptionalism. Challenged publicly to spell out what his fine phrase might mean, he 'hesitated', then 'mumbled . . . about some of us having been burnt, long ago, at that fire'. After a course of remedial reading, he pronounced himself 'no longer afraid to "redefine" the American Century'. But, as his biographer said, 'he never did so'.[27]

American exceptionalism is a subject that reduces smart people to prattle. It did in the first decade of the Cold War, and it does so in the first decade of the end of the Cold War. It teases. It tantalises. At its best it evokes a kind of vacant poetry. At its worst it invites a kind of vapid bibliographic commentary like Michael Kammen's recent survey of the 'slippery subject'.[28]

Kammen is a historian of distinction, just as Bell is a sociologist of deserved renown. But exceptionalism diminishes them and finally defeats them. It reduces Kammen to writing a prose so dense with deadening abstraction that he could be mistaken for the 'card-carrying social scientist' he swears he has 'never been'. It catches him in contradictions, snarls him in non sequiturs, and ultimately empties his argument of all substance.[29]

Kammen canvasses an astounding array of recent work on exceptionalism and posits in it a pair of intriguing reversals. Over the past half-century, historians studying the subject passed from eager enthusiasm to 'profound skepticism'. Over the same span, 'tough-minded social scientists' went from wariness to easy acceptance. Despite a disposition to side with historians, Kammen declares himself in the camp of the social scientists who 'comfortably resuscitated and reaffirmed' the 'gnarly' notion of American exceptionalism. 'In this instance, respecting this particular topic', he finds them 'more persuasive'.[30]

But the basis for his finding is impossible to extract from his essay. He no sooner announces his convincement than he concedes that the country has 'not had a singular mode or pattern of exceptionalism', only 'a configuration of situations that are not static'. It is, he grants, sounding like a latter-day Luce speaking in modern Academese, 'both difficult and dangerous to conclude that the United States as a whole, over an extended period of time, is different from all other cultures with respect to some particular criterion'.[31]

In other words, he commends American exceptionalism even as he denies any definable American exceptionality and indeed any definable America. No particular pattern pertains to the whole place over the whole period of its existence. Nothing remains static for long. One mode succeeds another, and one 'regional exceptionalism' supplants another within the ineffable American exceptionalism. There are 'configurations of situations', whatever that may mean.[32]

And the conceptualisation does not get sharper when Kammen gets down to cases. He takes David Hall's pioneering examination of popular religion in early New England as corroboration of American exceptionalism because Hall's comparison of American and English puritanism 'leaves the reader with a clear sense of important deviations based upon variables that ranged from the environment to social values'. The deviations of a deviant religious sect in America from a deviant religious sect in England cannot afford a compelling demonstration of American exceptionalism. In the absence of any more extensive, let alone systematic, comparison, they can be suggestive at best, in much the way that the deviations of, say, Irish from Italian Catholicism or Japanese from Chinese Buddhism can be suggestive.[33]

He takes David Reynolds' brilliant study of the American literary renaissance of the nineteenth century for another evidence of exceptionalism

because Reynolds' reinterpretation discovers 'distinctly American characteristics' in 'authors who wished to find literary correlatives for the horrific
or turbulent aspects of perceived reality in the new republic'. But the departure of certain schools of American writers from certain norms of nicety
maintained by their equivalent schools of English writers, at a certain
moment in time, cannot sustain the argument for exceptionalism either. In
truth, the only exceptionalism it can suggest is utterly incomparable with
the exceptionalisms that constitute the rest of the essay. Horror and turbulence may actually be elements of American exceptionality, but they play
no part in the literature of the subject, since they seem to be in sufficient
supply in the annals of other societies too. They disappear as instantan-
eously and inexplicably as they appear in Kammen's survey.[34]

He takes Kim Voss's illuminating investigation of unionised workers in
the 1890s for another indication of exceptionalism because Voss's account
of organised labour's opposition to mass immigration lends itself to an
inference of American identity at the expense of transnational or class
attachments. But the opposition of a modest minority of working people
to the influx of vast masses of immigrants cannot be construed so simply
as exceptionalist either. And even if it could, it would still leave altogether
unspecified the substance of that putative sense of American identity.[35]

Kammen cares as little about a coherent specification of such sense
of identity as he cares about his inconsistency in invoking seventeenth-
century puritan propriety and nineteenth-century novelistic impropriety as
equal evidence of American exceptionalism. His best 'affirmative ideological' formulation of American identity is the one he takes from Harry
Overstreet: 'it is the high distinction of America to have been the first
nation in civilized history to welcome different cultures and to give them
free scope to participate in the building of a new nation'. Voss's exclusionary labourers and Overstreet's inclusive new nation alike exhibit American exceptionalism to Kammen's satisfaction.[36]

Kammen is an equal-opportunity exceptionalist. He welcomes any evidence of American idiosyncrasy, no matter how egregiously it differs from
any other. It is enough for him that, according to Voss, Samuel Gompers
discriminated between the 'legitimate working class' and the great mass of
American working people and thereby justified 'a wider gap between skilled
and unskilled workers [in America] than in other countries'. Such a gap
does truly demonstrate an American distinctiveness, and never mind that
the distinctiveness it demonstrates makes America *less* democratic and
more hierarchical than Europe. By that point in the piece, Kammen is just
collecting scraps and shards of difference and cramming them into his
bibliographic grab-bag, indifferent to the logic of their aggregation.[37]

He concludes so badly because he begins no better. The definition of exceptionalism that he advances near the outset – 'the notion that the United States has had a unique destiny and history' – is itself too vague to be of much use. But before he settles on it – before he even finishes the sentence in which he propounds it – he seems to sense that it carries him further than he cares to go. So he qualifies his first innocuous formulation, abandoning the portentousness of destiny and the precision of uniqueness and demanding merely that the history has 'highly distinctive features or an unusual trajectory'.[38]

If it is hard to think of a society on the face of the earth that would fail to meet this 'more modest' standard, that is doubtless a consummation that Kammen finds congenial. He has no stomach for the jingoism at the marrow of the exceptionalist impulse. He rejects the assumptions of superiority to and exemption from the human condition that have driven that impulse from the first. When he asks, rhetorically, what we have learned or can conclude from his encyclopaedic reconnaissance, he hastens to answer that 'we are obliged to acknowledge the swiftly spreading perception that "every country is different", and that each society or culture is exceptional in its own way(s)'. With friends like Kammen, exceptionalism needs no enemies.[39]

Carl Degler recognises as Kammen does not that romantic relativism refuses more than it affirms of exceptionalism. He spells out explicitly that he means to steer clear of 'the specter of American exceptionalism' in asserting merely that 'Americans differ in some important ways from people of other nations'. But his rejection of the rank chauvinism of his peers and predecessors carries costs of its own. In declining to claim too much, he claims too little. In allowing that 'each nation is unique or exceptional', he levels the landscape and strips it of all urgency. His valedictory counsel – 'Let a hundred histories be written' – is as insipid as it is inevitable.[40]

Richard Rose catches the fatuousness of Degler's defensive formulation and exposes its fallacy besides. He admonishes that 'if every country is exceptional, there are no general rules'. If 'typologies can be developed in which each country [is] awarded a category of its own', then generalisation is rendered impossible even as uniqueness itself is reduced to absurdity. More than that, if uniqueness is an honorific to be accorded to every nation, then every nation has something in common with every other nation after all, 'namely, a unique national pattern' of development.[41]

Historians as well as social scientists see that this will not do. Joyce Appleby, among others, insists that exceptionalism ought not be redefined as difference because 'all nations are different'. Exceptionalism has, historically, referred to something much more. Only denatured definitions that forfeit the essence of the idea give up its projection onto a people of 'qualities that are envied because they represent deliverance from a common lot'.[42]

But even historians as comparatively careful as Appleby get sucked into the miasmic incoherence of exceptionalist discourse when they return to more pristine, powerful postulations. Like so many before her, Appleby conflates figures of archetype and asylum. In the very same sentence, she instances exceptionalism by quoting a pair of late eighteenth-century French observers, one hoping that the United States might be 'the model' for 'the human race', the other praying that the new nation might prove a refuge from fanaticism and tyranny 'for all the peoples of Europe', as though their visions could be reconciled with one another.[43]

In the vortex of exceptionalist excess, Appleby also adds other confusions all her own to the conversation. Attempting to account for the historical origins of the notion, she finds them in her favoured time and among her favoured people. In the 1790s, 'America's most undistinguished citizens' embraced exceptionalism as an American faith.[44]

According to Appleby, 'ordinary Americans' in that decisive decade found 'their voice, their cause, and their strategy for prevailing at the polls'. Following Jefferson's opposition to the 'undemocratic tendencies' of the Federalists, they not only carried the day in the election of 1800 but also precipitated a Federalist 'withdrawal from politics' which left 'the issue of national purpose' for 'common folk' to define. 'Uneducated men', given to a 'rambunctious politics' of 'egalitarian bombast', took over 'responsibility for creating a national identity'. They found 'affirmation of their values in the celebration of what was distinctively American'. The 'open opportunity, . . . unfettered spirit of inquiry, destruction of privilege, [and] personal independence' – the exceptionalism – that had long aggravated their betters now 'played to their strengths'. The values that informed those long-standing conditions of American life could be taken at the Jeffersonian juncture to establish 'a reciprocity between American abundance and high moral purpose' and to infuse it with civic significance.[45]

It is an appealing picture, perhaps, and artfully drawn. But it never happened as Appleby avers. The old elites no more abdicated en masse than the new men were all a radical rabble. Federalists such as Noah Webster and their spiritual descendants such as William Holmes McGuffey provided American children of the nineteenth century with the principal part of their education as American citizens. Republicans and Democrats such as Jefferson's fellow planters increasingly fettered freedom of speech in the South as they fortified the privileges of the slave-owning elite.

Appleby's exegesis of the strange career of American exceptionalism discloses her own dim awareness that its origins were not as she alleges. Torn between her keenness to claim an exceptionalism she admires for the Jeffersonians she adores and her hankering to blame an exceptionalism she dislikes on the contemporary elites she abhors, she sketches a truthful narrative that gives the lie to her first glowing construction.

Appleby draws on Benedict Anderson to draw a distinction between the realities of social relations in the infant republic and the rhetoric that created 'the imagined community that forms a nation'. She argues that, 'during the nineteenth century, ordinary white Americans ignored the actual insignificance of their nation's political existence and propelled their republic discursively into the vanguard of the march of progress'. But she offers no evidence to support the assertion that the promulgation of the imagined community was the work of the masses, and she offers more than she can comfortably admit to support the inference that it was not.[46]

Exactly because she posits a disjunction between 'actual insignificance' and discursive consequence, Appleby invites the supposition that the advancement of the imaginary was the work of privileged rhetoricians – 'the propagandists of American democracy', as she calls them – and not of scrabbling pioneers or struggling artisans and mechanics. Exactly because she intimates that the forging of American identity was a work of the head rather than the hand or the broad back, she invites obvious questions: to whom would the privileged rhetoricians be attached by birth and upbringing? By whom would they be published and paid? By whom would their works be reviewed and read?[47]

Such questions are inescapably succeeded by others as inconvenient for her argument when she assigns the task of 'democratizing [American] social values' to 'the country's history books'. How did her darling commoners control the writing, production, and distribution of those history books? Who, exactly, provided the history that promoted the myths of exceptionalism? Was an aristocratic Catholic like Matthew Carey in Philadelphia an ordinary American? Or was a Brahmin like George Ticknor in Boston? Or, for that matter, was an Episcopal minister like Mason Weems, who studied theology in London?[48]

Appleby's case for commoner control of the enterprise of the imaginary, already shaky on its face, collapses completely when she enunciates 'three insistent themes' of exceptionalism in the United States. All three of them – 'the autonomy of the individual with its accompanying disparagement of dependence; the clean slate with its implicit rejection of the past; and the concept of a uniform human nature with its ascription of universality to particular social traits' – protected and promoted the privileges of elite white males and discredited the customs of common folk. All three of them played a profoundly conservative part in profoundly partisan ideological contests over the course of the nineteenth century and into our own time. All three of them now stand as bulwarks against the 'multicultural agenda' that Appleby unabashedly espouses.[49]

Appleby's commitment to populist democracy inflects both her infatuation with the Jeffersonians and her critique of the exceptionalism she attributes to the Jeffersonians. But her acceptance of the imperative of exceptionalism infects her analysis of everything else. The three insistent themes that supply the substance of American exceptionality are exactly the same, on her account, when exceptionalism is the expression of ordinary people and when it is the instrument of the elite. The three themes remain unchanging even as exceptionalism passes from being a very good thing to a very bad one. By the time it is the instrument of the elite, the lives of ordinary Americans are quite 'buried' in its 'comfortable illusions'. A new social history is necessary to retrieve the experience of the majority of Americans, long 'muffled' by the exceptionalism of 'the Boston Brahmins who formed the caste of gentlemen historians' who, Appleby finally admits, formed our history.[50]

I could go on, because the scholarly swamp stretches on – I have not even discussed the deliciously doubled oxymorons of John Higham – but I have gone on too long already. Suffice it to say that the subject of exceptionalism sheds little glory on those who take it up, and that those who take it up shed little light on the subject.[51]

With a dry delicacy that is all too rare in this discourse, Byron Shafer says all that needs to be said. Summarising seven papers presented by seven American authorities to a symposium on American exceptionalism at Oxford a few years ago, Shafer remarks on how resolutely they resisted coherent summary. Exceptionalism 'never was; it once was, but is no more; new versions have substituted for old; it continues on, unchanged in its essence'. Plainly people are willing to pronounce upon the topic – especially if they are subsidised to do it by the British – and equally plainly the topic is incorrigibly unproductive. Shafer makes no effort to redeem the mutually vitiating variety of the arguments. As he wryly acknowledges, any effort to generalise on the basis of the symposium papers must 'testify more to imagination than to comprehension, more to impetuousness than to common sense'.[52]

What, after all, is there to say? All social systems have their own peculiarities, and all have external relations with other systems that compel commonalities. Between any two systems and within any set of systems, it is always possible to find both differences and similarities. We fetishise the one and forget the other at our peril.

So why do grown men and women get so worked up? Why don't scholars leave exceptionalism to the politicians, among whom florid pomposities, oracular rhetorical gestures, and flat-footed contradictions pass as a native tongue? Why do otherwise able analysts persist in making fools of themselves? What is so important about this issue, and why is it so important now? Why is exceptionalism the burden of so many books such as this one in the past few years? Why is it the subject of such a profusion of forums, anthologies, articles, and addresses in the same brief span?

One well-known notion of cultural development proposes that we see things that are central to the culture only as they cease to be central. Like the lush roses of late summer, they come to their fullest bloom as they fade and die. On that logic, the extensive attention that so many scholars are now giving to exceptionalism intimates that it is losing its command of the culture.

Kammen himself ultimately, bewilderingly, admits as much. 'The rather lengthy period in which the concept . . . seemed compellingly persuasive . . . is now', he says, 'over.' America's distinctive characteristics have grown 'notably less exceptional' as the twentieth century has advanced, and 'the burden of exceptionalism' has, if anything, 'passed to Japan'. American exceptionalism now matters only to a few academic antiquarians 'who seek to understand the *historical* dynamics of American culture'.[53]

Others concur. Laurence Veysey calls exceptionalism a phenomenon of 'certain relatively brief periods of the increasingly remote past'. He sees 'the real trend of American history' in 'the loss of whatever distinctiveness the society once possessed', and he dismisses whatever uniqueness remains as inconsequential 'except as a curiosity'. Peter Temin too finds images of wonderment at American uniqueness 'fading like an old photograph'. He sets out to study them 'before they disappear completely'.[54]

Exceptionalism is little more than an exercise in nostalgia now. Its essential issues are no longer ours. Exceptionalists celebrated America's distinctive democracy; since the Second World War we have deliberately dismantled a great deal of the apparatus of that democracy in order to manage our empire more efficiently. Exceptionalists vaunted American values of fairness; since Ronald Reagan's ascension to the presidency on the backlash against blacks and women, Bill Clinton's Democratic Leadership Council has explicitly begged Democrats to eliminate the very word fairness from the party's vocabulary and to speak instead of economic growth. Exceptionalists made much of American opportunity and justice; since the 1970s, as Jonathan Kozol demonstrates so poignantly, school officials across the country won't even talk the talk, let alone walk the walk.[55]

The very frame of reference of exceptionalism is no longer really ours. Almost two decades ago, Laurence Veysey ran and read, suggesting that the nation-state – the object of all exceptionalism – might be both too small and too large a unit for scholars to study. Too small because the 'texture of life' in developed capitalist countries grew 'increasingly uniform', arguing convergences that transcended separate nations. Too large because the idealised homogeneity of the nationalistic endeavour ill-fit the agenda of blacks and ethnic subculturists who demanded to be 'regarded as self-determining entities' and treated as 'fit subjects for legend-making on their own', and of feminists who insisted that women had to be reckoned into the national character as well as men. Before most other students of the subject, Veysey understood that in the modern period 'the most compelling differences' concerned 'groups of people defined by ethnicity, wealth, sex, age, or political or cognitive predisposition, not by nationality'.[56]

In the years since Veysey's pioneering piece appeared – years of the globalisation of capital, communication, and commerce and of an extraordinary exacerbation of the 'culture wars' in the United States – his insights have been confirmed and compounded. As Gary Gerstle observes, a 'communications revolution' has 'rendered national identity increasingly irrelevant to corporate welfare' and made 'capitalist vitality' far less dependent than it had been in the past 'on the support of nation states and of nationally defined markets'. Promotion of exceptionalism has been an elite project in the past, but it does not promise to be one in the future. The new elites do not need the patriotic loyalty that their old ideology inspired, and transnational elements of these new elites begin to find it an impediment to their operations and aspirations. At the same time, a grass roots revolt has left national affairs and attachments increasingly irrelevant to the middling masses. Exceptionalism offered them an identity that they found fulfilling in the past, but it does not provide them emotional satisfactions any more. The new suburbanites and city folk alike search for personal gratifications outside politics and in far smaller, more intimate spheres than the nation. As globalisation diminishes the elite's need for nationalism and personalisation dampens democratic interest in it, the definition of the nation ceases to be anyone's project.[57]

Certainly it is not the project of the young. The youth of America see so little significance in citizenship that fewer than 17 per cent of them between the ages of 18 and 24 have voted in recent elections. Focus group interviews with representative samples of young people reveal that they have 'extremely negative' perceptions of politicians, that they see no connection between issues they care about – drugs, homelessness, child abuse – and government policies, and that they 'do not see political participation as a way to address . . . problems'. Their disconnection from civic concern is so complete that, when asked what makes America unique, they fall silent. Hesitantly, reluctantly, one of them offers: cable TV. The others murmur and nod agreement.[58]

In a culture in which the rising generation can see nothing distinctive but a few dozen extra options on the TV, exceptionalism is obviously obsolete. As Saul Bellow once said, 'Occasionally I worry about what's happening to culture in the United States, but on other days I think there is no culture in the United States, and there's no point worrying about it.'[59]

And yet, as Veblen used to say. And yet . . .

The notion of American exceptionalism never did depend on empirical evidence. It was always impervious to the experience of the masses of Americans. It was from the first an ideological construction: of a fortunate minority in the New World, of yearning intellectuals in the Old. It was, as a succession of commentators have seen, a 'deception', an expression of 'national hubris', a veritable 'mirage in the West'.[60]

Daniel Bell maintained that American certitude of moral superiority dissipated in the dismal quagmires of south-east Asia. To conjure such loss of innocence, he had to ignore all the losses of innocence that had preceded it: in the Mexican War, the Gilded Age, the Spanish–American War, and more. Michael Kammen tied the retreat from exceptionalism to the crisis of political morality of the mid 1970s and to the shocks of Vietnam and Watergate that destroyed our illusions of distinctive virtue.

To do so, he had to ignore Twain and Lincoln and a hundred others who had already destroyed those illusions a hundred times over. Americans – especially Americans who ought to know better and indeed do know better – do not redeem the corruptions they discover in themselves. They simply 'disappear' them.[61]

In 1988 Jack Greene published a sweeping synthesis of early American history that was understood by perceptive reviewers to have 'destroyed American exceptionalism, or most of it, for the colonial period'. In 1993 Greene himself turned his back on that understanding. In a study that argued wide belief in the idea of American exceptionalism in the seventeenth and eighteenth centuries, he demanded of 'modern analysts' that they take such belief 'seriously'.[62]

In 1972 Sydney Ahlstrom published a magisterial synthesis of American religious history that pronounced the 'painful and tumultuous close' of 'the Puritan epoch in America's spiritual history'. The idea of America as 'a Chosen Nation and a beacon to the world' was, according to Ahlstrom, 'expiring'. In the quarter century since, an evangelical resurgence has invigorated the very chauvinism Ahlstrom supposed moribund. At the very least, that resurgence suggests the resilience of religious exceptionalism. On a more expansive interpretation, it intimates its invincibility.[63]

For that matter, in 1893 a young historian from Wisconsin worried about the end of the frontier and the concomitant closing of the first chapter – the exceptionalist chapter – of American history. Two generations of American historians, and more than a few social philosophers and policy-makers, took Frederick Jackson Turner's fears to heart and accepted a transition they took to be imperative from individualism to co-operation. In the half century since the New Deal, a renewed insistence on the fundamentality of exceptionalist individualism and its unbroken ascendancy in American life has dominated discussion of the American character, as though Turner and his problem never even existed.[64]

A friend of mine in Philadelphia distributes cigarettes for a major tobacco manufacturer. His work is pretty predictable. He makes his rounds week after week, and his sales are essentially stable week after week. Only one irregularity intrudes on his placid schedule. Every once in a while, in one of his areas or another, a billboard goes up for a rival brand of cigarettes. It is no ordinary billboard. It is a boldly arresting outline of a rugged cowboy, the Marlboro man, and it towers forty feet above its billboard base. Every time it appears, my friend's sales in that zone plummet.

In measurable market share, Philadelphians respond to this icon of individualism, though in all the vast city there is not a single ranch, not a single herd of cattle, not a single crew of cowboys. Americans resonate to the rhetoric of individualism though in all the land less than 7 per cent of us are self-employed or own our own enterprises. Our conviction of our exceptionality may be obsolete, and incoherent, but we have not given it up. We are just waiting – perhaps better, as Byron Shafer says, searching – for its 'next incarnation'.[65]

NOTES

1. Ira Katznelson and Aristide Zolberg, eds, *Working-Class Formation: Nineteenth-Century Patterns in Western Europe and the United States* (Princeton, 1986); Jean Heffer and Jeanine Rovet, eds, *Why Is There No Socialism in the United States?* (Paris, 1988); Byron Shafer, ed., *Is America Different? A New Look at American Exceptionalism* (Oxford, 1991); Ian Tyrell, 'American Exceptionalism in an Age of Intellectual History', with a critique by Michael McGerr, 'The Price of the "New Transnational History"', and a rejoinder by Tyrell, *American Historical Review*, 96 (1991), 1031–72; John Higham, 'Multiculturalism and Universalism: A History and Critique', *American Quarterly*, 45 (1993), 195–219; Carl Degler, 'In Pursuit of an American History', *American Historical Review*, 92 (1987), 1–12; Akira Iriye, 'The Internationalization of History', *American Historical Review* 94 (1989), 1–10; Joyce Appleby, 'Recovering America's Historic Diversity: Beyond Exceptionalism', *Journal of American History* 79 (1992), 419–31; Daniel Bell, 'American Exceptionalism Revisited: The Role of Civil Society', *The Public Interest* 95 (Spring 1989), 38–56; Richard Rose, 'How Exceptional Is the American Political Economy?', *Political Science Quarterly*, 104 (1989), 91–115; Michael Kammen, 'The Problem of American Exceptionalism: A Reconsideration', *American Quarterly*, 45 (1993), 1–43; Richard Curry and Lawrence Goodheart, eds, *American Chameleon: Individualism in Trans-National Context* (Kent, OH, 1991); Jack Greene, *The Intellectual Construction of America: Exceptionalism and Identity from 1492 to 1800* (Chapel Hill, 1993); Kim Voss, *The Making of American Exceptionalism: The Knights of Labor and Class Formation in the Nineteenth Century* (Ithaca, 1993); David Wrobel, *The End of American Exceptionalism: Frontier Anxiety from the Old West to the New Deal* (Lawrence, KA, 1993).
2. Daniel Bell, 'The End of American Exceptionalism', *The Public Interest*, 41 (1975), 193–224.
3. Bell, 'End of Exceptionalism', 197.
4. Bell, 'End of Exceptionalism', 197.
5. Bell, 'End of Exceptionalism', 202, 207–22.
6. Bell, 'End of Exceptionalism', 197, 229, 222, 205.
7. Bell, 'End of Exceptionalism', 222.
8. Bell, 'End of Exceptionalism', 223.
9. Daniel Bell, 'The "Hegelian Secret": Civil Society and American Exceptionalism', in Shafer, *Is America Different?*, 56–7.

10. Bell, 'The "Hegelian Secret"', 48, 50–1, 56–7.
11. Bell, 'The "Hegelian Secret"', 48; Bell, 'End of Exceptionalism', 211; Bell, 'The "Hegelian Secret"', 56–7. Such conceptual carelessness and substantive meandering go back still further; see Daniel Bell, *The End of Ideology: On the Exhaustion of Political Ideas in the Fifties* (rev. ed., New York, 1962), 13, 32, 37–8, 58–60, 65–6, 98–9, 112–13, 115, 117–18.
12. Bell, 'The "Hegelian Secret"', 60, 61.
13. Bell, 'The "Hegelian Secret"', 66–8.
14. Bell, 'The "Hegelian Secret"', 70.
15. James Schleifer, *The Making of Tocqueville's Democracy in America* (Chapel Hill, 1980), 59; Alexis de Tocqueville, *Democracy in America*, ed. Phillips Bradley (New York, 1945), II, 101, 301. See also Tocqueville, *Democracy*, I, 14.
16. Tocqueville, *Democracy*, I, 15.
17. Tocqueville, *Democracy*, II, 38.
18. Robert Brunhouse, ed., 'David Ramsay, 1749–1815: Selections from his Writings', *Transactions of the American Philosophical Society*, n.s., 55, part 4 (1965), 188; Greene, *Intellectual Construction*, 141.
19. Greene, *Intellectual Construction*, 173; Thomas Paine, *Common Sense*, in *The Thomas Paine Reader*, ed. Michael Foot and Isaac Kramnick (New York, 1987), 84, 81, 93. In regard to liberty even more than in regard to anything else, America was obviously no asylum from persecution for African-Americans. On the contrary, as William Pinckney admitted, it was 'an eternal grave for the liberties of themselves and their posterity'. Greene, *Intellectual Construction*, 187. Exponents of exceptionalism rarely take slavery as the touchstone of New World novelty that it was.
20. Sam Smith, *Shadows of Hope: A Freethinker's Guide to Politics in the Time of Clinton* (Bloomington, 1994). Smith added acerbically that, in our own time, antipathy to ideology has been the inanition more than the genius of American politics: Bush's notorious difficulties with 'the vision thing', Clinton's plaguing problems with truth and consistency that led one Arkansas wag to observe that, all by himself, 'Bill Clinton *is* a presidential debate'. But the embrace of ideology has been even more debilitating: Reagan's contempt for the Congress and the Constitution, the attrition of popular trust in the government. In 1964 over 60 per cent of a representative sample of Americans told pollsters that they could trust the government to do what was right. Three decades later, only 10 per cent reported a comparable confidence, and more than half of the precipitate plunge had occurred in the years of the 'Reagan revolution'. Smith, *Shadows of Hope*, 17, 89–90.
21. Greene, *Intellectual Construction*, 54–5, 58, 61; quotation at 143.
22. Bell, 'End of Exceptionalism', 198; Frederick Jackson Turner, *The Frontier in American History* (New York, 1920), 293.
23. Daniel Boorstin, *The Genius of American Politics* (Chicago, 1953).
24. Louis Hartz, *The Liberal Tradition in America* (New York, 1955); see also Louis Hartz, *The Founding of New Societies: Studies in the History of the United States, Latin America, South Africa, Canada, and Australia* (New York, 1964).
25. Boorstin, *Genius*, 1; Hartz, *Liberal Tradition*, 305.
26. Henry Luce, 'The American Century', *Life* 10:7 (17 February 1941), 61–5.

27. Robert Elson, *The World of Time, Inc.: The Intimate History of a Publishing Enterprise. Vol.2, 1941–1960*, Duncan Norton-Taylor, ed. (New York, 1973), 19.
28. Kammen, 'Problem of Exceptionalism', 2.
29. Kammen, 'Problem of Exceptionalism', 2.
30. Kammen, 'Problem of Exceptionalism', 2.
31. Kammen, 'Problem of Exceptionalism', 3.
32. Kammen, 'Problem of Exceptionalism', 3.
33. Kammen, 'Problem of Exceptionalism', 14; David Hall, *Worlds of Wonder, Days of Judgment: Popular Religious Belief in Early New England* (New York, 1989).
34. Kammen, 'Problem of Exceptionalism', 17; David Reynolds, *Beneath the American Renaissance: The Subversive Imagination in the Age of Emerson and Melville* (New York, 1988).
35. Kammen, 'Problem of Exceptionalism', 28; Voss, *Making of Exceptionalism.*
36. Kammen, 'Problem of Exceptionalism', 11.
37. Kammen, 'Problem of Exceptionalism', 28.
38. Kammen, 'Problem of Exceptionalism', 6.
39. Kammen, 'Problem of Exceptionalism', 6, 24. For Kammen's explicit embrace of 'the spirit of Herder's relativism', see 26.
40. Degler, 'Pursuit', 235, 236; Degler, reply to Laurence Veysey, *American Historical Review* 92 (1987), 1082.
41. Richard Rose, 'Is American Public Policy Exceptional?', in Shafer, *Is America Different?*, 188; Rose, 'How Exceptional?', 94, 96. For another exposition of the absurdity of infinite exceptionalism, see Aristide Zolberg, 'How Many Exceptionalisms?', in Katznelson and Zolberg, *Working-Class Formation*, 400–1, 454–5. For another gibe at the logic of Deglerian relativism, see Laurence Veysey, 'The Autonomy of American History Reconsidered', *American Quarterly* 31 (1979), 466–79.
42. Appleby, 'Recovering Diversity', 419.
43. Appleby, 'Recovering Diversity', 419. For the identical confusion in another recent work on exceptionalism, see Greene, *Intellectual Construction*, 173. For a different confusion identically compacted into a single sentence, see Tyrell, 'American Exceptionalism', 1031.
44. Appleby, 'Recovering Diversity', 422.
45. Appleby, 'Recovering Diversity', 422–4.
46. Appleby, 'Recovering Diversity', 424.
47. Appleby, 'Recovering Diversity', 424.
48. Appleby, 'Recovering Diversity', 425.
49. Appleby, 'Recovering Diversity', 426–9.
50. Appleby, 'Recovering Diversity', 427, 428.
51. Higham, 'Multiculturalism', 196–7.
52. Byron Shafer, 'What Is the American Way? Four Themes in Search of their Next Incarnation', in Shafer, *Is America Different?*, 222, 233.
53. Kammen, 'Problems of Exceptionalism', 32.
54. Veysey, 'Autonomy', 476, 477; Peter Temin, 'Free Land and Federalism: American Economic Exceptionalism', in Shafer, *Is America Different?*, 71.
55. Smith, *Shadows of Hope*, esp. 19; Jonathan Kozol, *Savage Inequalities: Children in America's Schools* (New York, 1991).

56. Veysey, 'Autonomy', 475, 457–8, 474.
57. Gary Gerstle, 'The Limits of American Universalism', *American Quarterly* 45 (1993), 234–5; see also Bell, 'The "Hegelian Secret"', 68. On the 'culture wars', see James Hunter, *Culture Wars: The Struggle to Define America* (New York, 1991).
58. *People for the American Way Forum* (Fall, 1988), 8.
59. Emory Elliott, *Revolutionary Writers: Literature and Authority in the New Republic, 1725–1810* (New York, 1982), 3.
60. Greene, *Intellectual Construction*, 209; Ian Tyrell, rejoinder to Michael McGerr, 'The Price of the New "Trans-National History"', *American Historical Review* 96 (1991), 1070; Durand Echeverria, *Mirage in the West: A History of the French Image of American Society to 1815* (Princeton, 1957).
61. Bell, 'End of Exceptionalism', 179; Kammen, 'Problem of Exceptionalism', 11.
62. Jack Greene, *Pursuits of Happiness: The Social Development of Early Modern British Colonies and the Formation of American Culture* (Chapel Hill, 1988); Greene, *Intellectual Construction*, 5–6, 17.
63. Sydney Ahlstrom, *A Religious History of the American People* (New Haven, 1972), 967–8.
64. Wrobel, *End of Exceptionalism*.
65. Shafer, 'What Is the American Way?'

3 Working-Class Formation and American Exceptionalism, Yet Again
Ira Katznelson

I should like to revisit the approach to American exceptionalism and working class formation I cultivated in work published in the 1980s when I sought to understand why working-class identities, dispositions, and collective action at work and away from work in the United States diverged so starkly; far more so than in Britain, France, or Germany where there was a greater congruence between the rhetoric, demands, and organisational efforts of workers across the work–home divide. While the American split between patterns of class formation in workplaces outside the home and in residential communities provided my main object of analysis, I also probed a number of subsidiary historical puzzles. These included: the failure of ante-bellum artisans to transfer their leadership, language of class, or holistic consciousness to the country's newly developing proletariat; the combination of a relatively high degree of wage-oriented labour militancy at places of work with reformist, non-militant political integration as citizens via the mechanism of cross-class political party participation in working-class urban neighbourhoods; and the comparative difficulty America's workers had in forming and sustaining strong national working-class organisations.[1]

At a theoretical level, I was concerned to contribute an analytical approach to comparative and historical studies of working-class formation. Though my work was strongly materialist, I wanted to transcend the analytical constraints and teleological proclivities of the class-in-itself/for-itself problematic drawn from orthodox Marxism that then dominated the field. I rejected linear attempts to infer class ideologies, discourses, institutions, and activities from class structure or relations of exploitation; and I refused a definition of the content of class formation fixed by theoretical or political expectations. As an alternative, I proposed we think about class in capitalist societies 'as a concept with four connected layers of theory and history: those of structure, ways of life (not limited to the workplace), dispositions, and collective action'.[2] I further suggested that a state-centred approach, especially if deployed in tandem with other

36

possibilities rather than simply as an alternative to traditional class analysis, could help account for variations between national cases, especially at the last two levels. By employing this set of tools, I tried to draw the American case into the ambit of systematic comparison and go beyond conventional understandings of American exceptionalism.

Such treatments typically have taken the form of counterfactualism, what Margaret Somers appropriately has called an epistemology of absence.[3] Somewhere – either in our theoretical imaginations or in actual historical examples – there is thought to exist a standard of normalcy which the United States has failed to achieve. The world's most important capitalist country lacks an assertive proletariat. Originally debated as a challenge within the framework of its ideology by the American Communist Party shortly after its founding, this apparent paradox became a historiographical staple. The puzzle of the distinctiveness of working-class formation in the United States thus was charged from the outset by a not always visible lineage characterised by a theoretical and political fusion of expectation and frustration. It focused less on actual conditions or behaviour than on deviations from an expected trajectory of class consciousness and the transcendence of capitalism. Haunted by the non-appearance of an appropriately formed working class, much of the scholarly Left has been convinced that if only the impediments interfering with the natural course of history could be identified and removed all would be well. America would cease to be exceptional. As a corollary, historians of the working class have been tempted to recapture every detail of working-class struggle (and to reinterpret non-class struggles in class terms) in order to demonstrate that the American working class is inherently no different from any proletariat under capitalist conditions. The result has been a doleful duet of disappointed abstract theory and romanticised empiricist behaviourism joined together by an insupportable set of assumptions about American exceptionalism. By now, surely, we know that there is no single historical norm against which to measure all working-class history and that each instance of agitation and resistance is not commensurable.

Of course, I was not alone in mounting such arguments a decade ago. When Eric Foner revisited Werner Sombart's famous question, 'Why is there no socialism in the United States?',[4] he, too, attacked the presumption that the rise of socialism is 'normal' and he questioned the degree to which differences between various European and American experiences of class formation have been qualitative or permanently fixed. The key flaw in the exceptionalist problematic, Foner observed, is the directness of the links it fashions among the social structure, ideologies of class, and political parties. 'What needs to be explained is the coexistence in American history of workplace militancy and a politics organized around non-ideological parties appealing to broad coalitions, rather than the interests of a particular class.' Why there is no socialism thus transmutes into 'a problem of explaining the disjuncture of industrial relations and political practice in the United States'. Further, he maintained, the extent to which American patterns diverged from those found in Europe varied both by period and as a result of shifts in the dispositions and behaviours of members of the working class over time in all the western capitalist countries.[5]

Sean Wilentz similarly argued that the time had come to move beyond the exceptionalist problematic. He urged not that we disown our understanding that the American experience has been different but that we break with the idea that these differences constitute a radical break either with other histories or with what good theory predicts. Rather, we should become more historical and more comparative: 'One important departure might be to undertake a truly comprehensive comparative history of American labour, one that is as open to analogies between events and movements in this country and those abroad as it is to the differences.'[6] Like Foner, he also insisted that a focus on the *not* present should be replaced by a focus on the array of moments and events that actually were existent.

These calls for a more thoroughgoing historical and historicised consideration of American working-class formation, including the imperative of specifying a richly textured set of objects of analysis grounded in the substantive experience of the United States (rather than the actual or imagined happenings elsewhere judged by non-historical standards), left open how this programme might be accomplished. Foner and Wilentz, however, did help clear ground and focus attention on important characteristics of the American regime, including the qualities of its liberal ideology. Foner rightly observed that the most popular candidates identified within the exceptionalist problematic to account for the failure of the American working class to perform its 'natural' role – including ethnic and racial diversity, repression, electoral participation as the death-knell for class consciousness, and internal failings within the socialist movement itself – either are not unique to the United States or represent barriers so high that they infirm any possibility of class-based understandings and mobilisations. Instead, he insisted that the new social history's findings about working-class mutuality, community, and subcultures based on class and ethnicity should be deployed to put to rest any simple notions of working-class complicity and to set aside the complementary consensus argument that American workers have been so enclosed from the start within a dominant individualist and property-oriented liberal ideology that their ability to think and act autonomously has been fatally compromised. In complementary fashion Wilentz stressed the variety of ways in which workers actually resisted capitalist relations of property and exchange through the deployment of democratic and republican strains of American values,[7] calling as well for 'a thorough reconsideration of what is usually accepted as a monolithic "bourgeois" liberalism – with a fuller appreciation of the ways in which American liberal political ideas could acquire distinctly anticapitalist ... connotations, from the late eighteenth century on'.[8]

Both Foner and Wilentz, in short, thought the project of analysing American working-class formation, while transcending the troubled assumptions and ways of working of the exceptionalist approach, had to critically travel the roadway of liberal hegemony associated, above all, with *The Liberal Tradition in America* by Louis Hartz.[9] With this recommendation, it soon will be clear, I strongly agree; yet with the Foner/Wilentz approach to such an effort I differ in a number of important respects. When it is suitably revised and conditioned, I think there is more power in Hartz's one-dimensional claim then they would admit. Where they focus mainly on liberalism as a procapitalist ideology, I treat liberalism primarily as a political doctrine. In consequence, I think we need to attend both to distinctive features of the American regime and to the cluster of rules, conventions, and institutions that have governed the ties between civil society and the state in the United States. This cluster of issues is decisive for the realisation of Foner's call for a more conditional and contingent approach to the ties joining class, society, and politics.

My other main difference with Foner and Wilentz concerns their downgrading of theory in favour of history. More and better history, alas, is no substitute for bad theory. What studies of working-class formation have missed badly is what Robert Merton once labelled theories of the middle-range which can serve as guides to inquiry located between the grandeur of epochal history and focused work on detailed cases;[10] that is, conceptual schemes close to rather than distant from the particular configuration of American politics and society.

This essay revisits these themes and further pursues this approach to theory primarily by rethinking the role I assigned to the state in shaping working-class formation. I treated the state, I noted recently, 'almost as a deus ex machina that descended on capitalist class relations to shape outcomes of class formation' without anything like sufficient appreciation of the ways in which states, in interaction with the substantially, but not entirely, distinctive zones of the economy and civil society, both constitute those domains and are constituted by them. 'It is the ... insufficient account of the terms and institutions governing these ties', I concluded, 'that constitutes [my] most significant evasion.'[11] I want to address this insufficiency by renovating the way I developed a state-focused approach and by indicating the relevance of this reconceptualisation to the empirical issues that drew me to studies of working-class formation in the United States in the first place.

I proceed by making an argument with two related clusters of assertions. First, though it is necessary to say a decisive good-bye to the most common forms of American exceptionalism, studies of the American working class stand to benefit nonetheless from an appreciation of the distinctive institutional and political context for class formation established by America's contested but hegemonic liberalism. My position, albeit with a family resemblance to that of Louis Hartz, is distinguished from his by my rejection of treatments of liberalism as a fixed entity beyond dispute, or as the only legitimate ideological player in American history. But with a nod to Hartz, suitably revised, I suggest a shift in angle of vision away from the state as such to the character of the rules and institutions that govern the transactions between the state and civil society. This, of course, has been the hallmark concern of political liberalism from its founding in early modern Europe as a doctrine of religious toleration and as a guide geared to restrain predatory rulers and find ways to represent diverse interests inside the state. In liberal regimes, the domain of interactions between state and civil society is that of citizenship. Like liberalism more generally, citizenship is never fixed or uncontested. Two issues regularly recur: the range of individuals deemed eligible to participate (hence also the rules of inclusion and exclusion) and the terms (in rights and institutions) of their linkage to the political system.

Second, by conceptualising American liberalism not as an unchanging being but as a boundary condition whose content has been shaped and reshaped, to varying degrees, by working-class agency at key moments of transition in the country's political development, I argue that working-class history can be re-integrated into larger schemes for the periodisation of American development from which they have been severed to an uncomfortable degree. Key break points when the organisational design, institutional ensemble, public policies, and normative claims of the state all are up for grabs have been times when these issues of belonging, inclusion, and linkage became relatively open and then were durably settled for extended periods. If 'exceptionalism' connotes comparison, so, too, does the approach I advocate, but with a difference. Rather than conduct what might be called variable-specific exercises that search for key factors (mobility, prosperity, the frontier, ethnic diversity, state repression and so on), I argue in favour of a relational approach focusing on large-scale processes not unique to the United States but which have been configured singularly as a result of their patterns of interaction with the unusual qualities of the country's semi-liberal regime.

TRANSCENDING EXCEPTIONALISM, RETHINKING LIBERALISM

It is hard to think of a text more influential yet more maligned than Hartz's; or, indeed, one more deserving of appreciation and deprecation. Hartz made the claim that the most important underlying force in American history, the standing and power of its political liberalism, was constituted by the non-appearance of feudalism on American soil. Lacking an adversary, he argued that the contractual, individualist, and constitutional liberalism identified most closely with John Locke gained free sway in the United States and quickly came to possess the power to snuff out either pre- or anti-liberal impulses of various kinds. Though hardly a celebrant of these qualities, Hartz claimed that meaningful stories about the American regime must be contained inside the boundaries of this exceptional history and situation.

Hartz targeted the limitations imposed by uncontested liberalism on discourse, ideology, and policy in the United States as well as the historiographical provincialism caused by an unreflective enclosure inside liberalism's meta-framework. *The Liberal Tradition in America* insisted the United States is distinctive in the universe of western countries because its liberalism has been ascendant and constitutive. American history has been marked by remarkable continuities, to the point of non-progression. As a country without a feudal past and the fissures of class which struggles about feudalism generated elsewhere, the United States has had little room for fundamental conflict, competing ideologies, or moments of genuine uncertainty and turnabout. Hartz's analytical non-narrative, anti-history version of American exceptionalism thus constituted a refusal to credit the significance of multiple ideologies or changes to the regime because liberalism's dominion is total.

Hartz's assertions about 'the moral unanimity' of American liberal society are not compelling because he overstates the uncontested quality of America's 'nationalist articulation of Locke'.[12] Like many other critics, Foner and Wilentz were on target in asserting Hartz had failed to give adequate recognition to the country's multiple political traditions, including the full range possessed by members of the working class; Hartz clearly also undervalued conflicts concerning the deep illiberalism of race.[13] Notwithstanding these flaws, there remains a great deal of power in his analysis, but only if we reread his claim (probably against his own intentions) about the status of liberalism as an assertion about liberalism as a boundary condition embodying norms of speech and action. A boundary condition, David Greenstone has observed, is 'a set of relatively permanent features of a particular context that affect causal relationships within it' even as it remains subject to dispute.[14] As just such a boundary condition, liberalism in America has been dominant but not unchanging or unchallenged. The content of liberalism's grammar of rules – its bundle of institutions and norms – was not settled once and for all; hence Hartz's label of Lockean liberalism is misleading to the extent it suggests a static set of limits rather than multiple possibilities. Unfortunately, Hartz made no provision for contests about the substance of American liberalism's grammar, preferring to underscore continuities and consensus with regard to the basic features of the regime.

To be sure, he did not rule out considerations of change; he only wanted to put them in their place. He wrote:

> So one cannot say of the liberal society analysis that by concentrating on national unities it rules out the meaning of domestic conflict. Actually it discovers that meaning. . . . You do not get closer to the significance of an earthquake by ignoring the terrain on which it takes place. On the contrary, that is one of the best ways of making sure that you will miss its significance. The argument over whether we should 'stress' solidarity or conflict in American politics misleads us by advancing a false set of alternatives.[15]

This defence of his emphasis on the ties that bind American politics and render it a politics of non-development is logically impeccable, but it advances a false set of alternatives by the manner in which it locates continuity and change. *Contra* Hartz, the character of the liberal frame as a boundary condition itself has been the object of conflict, mounted both from within and outside the liberal tradition. By treating liberalism as unchanging, Hartz promoted the reduction of studies of change to processes wholly within an imputedly fixed grammar, thus eliding the fact that conflict about institutions and basic systems of meaning have been recurring features of American political development.[16]

Precisely at moments when struggle about liberalism's rules has been most robust – the moments spanning the Founding, the Civil War, and the New Deal – the multiple traditions which exist in the United States, including republicanism, communitarianism, protestantism, and populism, as well as diverse bases of ascriptive Americanism including nationalism, nativism, patriarchy, and racism have been deployed as resources by contestants fighting about the kind of liberalism the United States should possess. Once we introduce conflicts over liberalism's grammar at key moments of indeterminacy into the story of American political development, the contradiction between the claim that the United States is the West's most durably liberal regime and the view from the inside stressing cacophony and conflict is revealed as artificial. Like Tocqueville, Hartz was quite correct to underscore how liberalism has been fundamental to the American experience as a boundary condition. The central values of the liberal tradition, including equal respect of persons as citizens (coupled with an irreducible individualism and a doctrine of rights), consent, toleration of a plurality of beliefs and ways of life, and a demarcation of separate public and private spheres, as well as the central institutional arrangements of western liberalism, including representative democracy and markets,[17] have been far more continuous, instantiated features in the United States than elsewhere in the West. What Hartz undervalued, however, was the extent to which these durable regime features themselves have defined spheres of vigorous contestation in constitutional jurisprudence, the politics of social movements, electoral mobilisations, and recurring discord about language and culture.

Hartz's failure to target struggles concerned with liberalism's grammar helped produce an unproductive dichotomy between scholars who focus on processes and change within a putatively constant liberal order, and critics who think Hartz's fixation on liberalism is a form of ideological celebration and urge, instead, an amplified focus on American disharmonies, divergent idioms, diverse passions, and disparate ideologies. I dissent from both positions. I am entirely unpersuaded that plurality and conflict infirm Hartz's key insight about the comparative standing of American liberalism, just as I strongly reject his essentialised view of the liberal tradition. Rather, like Greenstone, I think there is far more analytical and normative profit in focusing on American liberalism as a contested boundary condition.

This shift in orientation has implications for the tropes of disappointment and romance which have characterised the historiography of working-class formation. Hartz's story, in one form or another, has been an integral part of the litany of frustration and chagrin at the failure of the working class to become a proletariat. That possibility, Hartz told us (in marxisant fashion) was excluded from the start. The reconsideration I propose, however, leaves ample room for challenge and contention. But not so much space as the extravagant tendency which has identified oppositional tendencies to virtually every instance of conflict between workers and relevant others. It is in this regard that Hartz's insistence that conflict be inserted within a determinative terrain of norms, conventions, and institutions is telling. Aggregating stories of struggle does not add up to a coherent tale of class formation.

Even revised as a boundary condition, however, a focus on liberalism as the master tool of American political development, hence as a frame for our understanding of working-class formation, is inadequate unless it is joined to other large-scale processes about which Hartz was rather too silent – especially those of state formation and racialised labour systems – which were fundamental to contests about liberalism's institutions and norms in the United States. Although neither process was distinctive to the United States, each was essential to the constitution of liberalism as a contested boundary condition. I return to this theme below.

The most basic conflicts about liberalism as a boundary condition in American life have been concerned with three interrelated issues: the institutional structure of the American state (including its territorial extensiveness, the character of its federalism, and the powers it can exercise); the nature of the body of citizens in civil society eligible to participate in American political life (relevant issues include barriers of property, race, nationality, and gender); and the rules and institutions which govern the ties between this state and these citizens. These linkages, of course, are the very stuff of liberal political theory and practice.

It is thus not the state as such but the terms of these transactions that have been vital to the history of working-class formation in the United States. The patterning of political participation and representation has been the object of enormous conflict between sections, parties, races, and classes. In turn, at any given time, connections between group and class experiences, on the one side, and identities and proclivities for collective action, on the other, are conditioned by just this institutional and normative topography. Class formation and institutional–political arrangements are mutually constitutive.

It is a matter of some chagrin, therefore, that the overwhelming thrusts in labour and working-class history in recent years have been concerned either with traditional materialist analysis focusing on questions of production and workplace struggle or, in a postmodern turn, with matters of language and identity treated with great openness and flexibility. The first orientation, as noted, has been closely aligned with the teleology, and frustration, of the class-in-itself/for-itself model and with economism; while the second tends to skirt not only the materiality of production but of political structures and arrangements, preferring to find power relations everywhere (thus running the risk of locating them nowhere in particular). The turn away from formal politics and the rules of the game has the effect of directing studies of class formation away from the terrain in which members of the working class, in fact, were urgently engaged: in struggles about local government; in battles about the content of public policy; in combat about rules and rights concerning unions; in skirmishes about immigration; in contests about the political participation of blacks, women, and Asians; in clashes about the very institutions of liberal political life itself; in short, in engagements concerned with the material and normative content of citizenship. If, in most other western countries, basic political conflicts have revolved around the axis of liberalism versus an *ancien régime*, in the United States they have concerned the terms of liberalism as a boundary condition. By connecting the history of working-class formation to the larger regime story, it becomes possible not only to more systematically study working-class history but, in turn, to deploy the analysis of class to impugn studies of liberal citizenship which elide issues of inequality and power. What the study of class formation offers political analysis is the chance to recognise 'the significance of the differential character of experiences of citizenship' and 'the desirability of placing differential experiences within a context which acknowledges class and intra-class divisions, incorporation, and exclusion'.[18]

In part, this approach to working-class formation and American exceptionalism counsels a return to the forgotten institutional aspects of Sombart's account of the absence of socialism in the United States. He is best remembered, of course, for his treatment in Section Two of *Why is There No Socialism in the United States?* of the comparative affluence of America's working class. But it is Section One on 'The Political Position of the Worker' that is the text's neglected gem. Its discussions of the political machine, the monopoly and character of the two major parties, and 'the position of the American worker in the state' are outstanding instances of historical institutionalism aimed at showing how the comparatively open and responsive American system (at least for white men) has shaped working-class sensibilities, language, and activity. These factors are best deployed, however, not (as Sombart does) to explain why the 'natural' trajectory of working-class consciousness was interrupted in America, but as an invitation to take seriously the range of liberal political institutions, rules, conventions, and relationships which have provided the particular political milieu of American political life which has shaped working-class formation as a contingent process.

WORKING-CLASS FORMATION AND THE PERIODICITY OF AMERICAN POLITICAL DEVELOPMENT

This post-Hartzian orientation to liberalism and working-class formation suggests an opportunity to closely connect labour and working-class history to more general programmes for the periodisation of the American past because of the connections it invites linking class formation and more general dynamics of American political development. In this respect, I should like to argue that the approach to periodisation best capable of advancing these links neither is comparative in the manner of Hartz's work (which contrasts America to a counterfactual 'Europe') nor is it internalist in the routine of most studies of the United States by political scientists which operate wholly inside an American framework and which often assume, without question, Hartz's claims about the fixed hegemony of liberalism in American life. Rather, I advance what might be called a relational approach to periodisation which situates and interrogates the American experience from the perspective of processes and events not exclusive to itself at those moments when conflicts about liberalism's grammar have been most intense.

Just this kind of focus, I argue, invites us to grapple with alterations to public policy which transform rules and institutions in response to electoral and other domestic perturbations at times of such grand crises as war and economic depression, and to consider the impact of such changes on working-class history. From this prospect, the periodisation of American political development should be concerned above all with the substance of liberal institutions and norms without being confined to the American case alone. This programme of research would treat periodisation as an opportunity to ask whether critical moments in American political development have coincided with such moments elsewhere, and to inquire about relationships among countries grappling with broadly common challenges. It also provides us with the chance to inquire about how the particularities of working-class agency helped shape outcomes at such moments when the contours of the regime's institutional and normative liberalism were relatively open; and, in turn, how the resolution of conflicts at such moments of change shaped the subsequent development of the American working class.

The relational approach to periodicity I have in mind is indebted above all to Karl Polanyi's provocative attempt in *The Great Transformation* to make sense of the rhythms of nineteenth- and twentieth-century western history. He was concerned above all with the status of liberalism understood as a contested doctrine and as a set of institutions, just the themes I suggest have been missing from studies of working-class formation more generally.

As is well known, Polanyi treated the elaboration of markets, especially labour markets, as defining characteristics of modern liberal orders. Only when labour as well as land and capital was commodified was 'the great transformation' complete. Polanyi tells this story, culminating in a dark view of the world crisis of the 1930s and 1940s, as a tale characterised by three overlapping moments: the establishment of liberal institutional orders in the early decades of the nineteenth century, with England being the pioneer case; a long period spanning the middle of the nineteenth century, well into the 1880s, when a global liberalism of free trade and the gold standard underpinned the domestic elaboration of markets and representative democracy; and a subsequent period of crisis for liberalism, created by the coexistence of contradictory processes including the functioning of markets and market rationality, on the one side, and the utilisation of the instruments of representative institutions to produce public policies geared to protect individuals, groups, and society as a whole from the consequences of market arrangements on the other.

Polanyi thus ordered the history of much of the nineteenth and twentieth centuries in the West by distinguishing, first, a moment when state action made markets possible by securing the conditions needed for their functioning; second, a moment of relative success for such regimes; and, third, a moment when the imperatives of markets and citizenship sharply clashed. As a social democrat by conviction but a realist about markets, international arrangements, and the possibilities of anti-liberal regimes and violence, Polanyi yearned for a fourth moment, of the type that actually did come to characterise the West in the immediate post-war years, based on what John Ruggie has labelled 'embedded liberalism'. This prescription was different in kind from earlier liberal policy regimes in the manner in which it made international economic relations compatible with domestic stability. 'This was the essence of the embedded liberalism compromise: unlike the economic nationalism of the thirties, it would be multinational in character; unlike the liberalism of the gold standard and free trade, its multilateralism would be predicated on domestic interventionism.'[19]

With the exception of the New Deal, which he thought to be an auspicious archetype promising an exit from the impasse of liberal capitalism, Polanyi had nothing specific to say about the United States but his text is resonant with implications for thinking about the periodisation of American history and its ties to the history of the working class. He insisted that liberal political and economic institutions are authoritative products of state action, not facts of nature; that liberalism cannot be considered exclusively at the national level but has critical underpinnings in international geopolitics and political economy; and that the fate of liberalism in any single country is entailed in liberalism's providence more generally. Though it makes little sense to mechanically apply Polanyi's arrangement of western history to the United States, his scholarship helps us fruitfully rethink our questions and categories of analysis by prodding the reconstruction of American history as concerned substantively with liberalism's rules. In the United States, Polanyi's first period was marked by the establishment of the rules of property and contract necessary to a liberal market economy; his second by the triumph of a domestic political economy privileging a robust capitalist industrialisation under the aegis of a Republican Party committed to 'a political economy in which central state power could sweep aside regional and local barriers to the development of a national capitalist market and directly assist in the construction of the physical and financial infrastructure necessary for that market';[20] his third by the insufficiency of liberal policy repertoires to sustain liberty and prosperity simultaneously; and his anticipated fourth by the renewal of liberal democracy by way of the policy innovations of embedded liberalism.

It would take quite some time, and a good deal of effort, to construct what might be called a Polanyian periodisation of American history focusing on the development of modern liberal doctrines and institutions, but the elements are not hard to discern. So, too, are the advantages of a Polanyian approach as compared both to Hartz's story of non-development and to the wholly internalist accounts which have become the conventional stock-in-trade for students of periodisation. Polanyi's approach makes the provisional constitution of liberalism the object of explanation, and it identifies processes and crises not specifically tied to any single country but which are central elements of the political development of each.

The macroscopic processes Polanyi stressed at the domestic and international levels, however, are insufficient for the United States. For there are two other large-scale sets of processes about which he was silent – those of state formation and racialised labour systems – which were fundamental to contests about American liberalism's institutions and norms. Although neither process was distinctive to the United States, each was essential to the constitution of liberalism as a contested boundary condition.

Liberalism in the Lockean version has had a dual orientation to the modern state. Even as it has sought to find ways to limit untrammelled state power, it has recognised the state as the essential requisite of security and self-governance and as the central instrument of a series of welcome differentiations: between god and history, between rulers and the state, between property and sovereignty, and between the state and the separate private spheres of civil society and the economy. Liberalism, in short, has been premised on a statist institutional framework. But statebuilding has not come easily in the West. Through processes far more coercive than consensual, state formation was marked in Europe after feudalism by the disappearance of scores of once viable political units as a far more limited number of national states replaced systems of fragmented sovereignty and tribute-making empires.[21] None of the European state units we take for granted today, whether those of Germany, the United Kingdom, Italy, Poland, the Netherlands, or even France, was unmarked by fierce contests over sovereignty understood as a claim to rule over determinate people and territory. Certainly, core features of the American experience – including its federalism and contests over states rights, the ties that have (or have not) fastened the South with the rest of the Republic, and boundary disputes with other sovereign states to the north and the south and with aboriginal peoples to the west – have been elaborated in a complex history of American state formation whose elements are not markers of a singularly exceptional past but of distinctive resolutions to challenges of statebuilding shared by western countries after feudalism.

Further, the United States, as the largest slave society of the first half of the nineteenth century, possessed a liberalism which came to terms with the deepest of illiberalisms. As part of a global political economy integrated by the slave trade, commodity production by unfree labour, and imperial domination, it was not alone in grappling with the complex ties, at the levels of ideas and institutions, connecting and justifying freedom for some and exclusion for others based on colour. It is inconceivable that an account of American liberalism as a boundary condition could elide issues of race. Yet to incorporate them effectively requires a more supple insertion of the racialised American story within a larger global framework concerned with slavery and anti-slavery, a better periodisation of slavery and racial subordination, and a consideration of the terms of political incorporation experienced by post-emancipation people of colour.

The grand break points of crisis and restructuring in American history have come when uncertainties have been unusually pronounced in the three dimensions of political economy, sovereignty, and race simultaneously; that is, when the three time lines of processes which transcend the borders of the United States have coincided in such a way as to produce a very high degree of uncertainty about the substantive content and commitments of American liberalism. I suggest that we seek a balance between Polanyian-style macroanalysis geared to identify the contested grammar of liberalism's institutions, rules, and values in a relational context and an approach to working-class formation focusing on the patterning of dispositions and collective action at just such contingent and contested moments. For it is just at those times when deep policy and electoral change coincide that the content of liberalism as a boundary condition is directly addressed; in turn, it is at these junctures (such as the Civil War–Reconstruction and the New Deal–Second World War periods) that the character of the American working class has been most plastic and consequential.

Within mainstream American political history, the main efforts at periodisation have been aimed at demarcating distinctive party systems based on
oscillations of electoral stability and change. Even though this work has
been geared from the start to inform our understanding of policy change,
it has focused far more on elections and partisanship as such. As Richard
McCormick has observed, 'the Key–Schattschneider–Burnham insight that
critical elections were critical because they had something to do with governance' has been 'largely absent' from the next generation of scholarship
that sought to place realignment theory on a more systematic, scientific
basis.[22] Instead, the core of the attempt to demarcate types of elections and
party system eras should be the enhancement of our understanding of large-
scale changes to the contours of American liberalism. 'The justification
for arranging political experience in this way', Joel Silbey recently has reminded us, 'relates to the kind of society that predominated in each era,
and to the kinds of political institutions, norms, and behavior that were
paramount in each.' These 'norms, rituals, and routines', he avers, 'provided
the constraints within which involved Americans went about their political
activities'.[23]

Most scholars of periodisation have considered critical elections to be
the motor of significant changes in public policy. In an important work
published some fifteen years ago, Jerome Clubb, William Flanigan, and
Nancy Zingale suggestively turned such work on electoral realignment on
its head by arguing that electoral behaviour in the United States has been
quite stable and that most interruptions to this stability have proved to be
only short-term perturbations. More enduring partisan change, they show,
has come about only when startling voting results quickly were followed
up by policy changes which secured the realignment in partisanship and
caused it to last. Thus, it is the making of policy, not voting as such, that
constitutes the more fundamental process, and the reason we think of a
small number of key moments as genuinely pivotal. From this perspective,
elections and voting behaviour are assigned the task of making policy
alterations possible, but the central force of the argument is that policy
alterations concerned with the content of ties between the state and the
economy and the state and civil society compose the significant stuff of
political change.[24] Changes in public policy – especially large-scale changes
at moments of high indeterminacy – are especially significant as indicators
of basic shifts in ties between societal actors and the state. Their transactions are mutually constituted: actors are 'affected by the rules and institutions through which they act. But the impact of rules and institutions
depends on who tries to use them for what purposes.'[25]

States often are assessed as either weak or strong, autonomous or permeable, capable or insufficient. But what matters even more is the understanding that 'issues of state capacity are not just questions of the instruments of governance, but of the content of governance. . . . What is at stake is not the strength of the state as such but the character and orientation of its capacities.'[26] Shifts in policy and in state organisation and ability go hand in hand. In the United States, such alterations imply modifications to the boundary conditions of liberalism.

Thus, what is suggested by this approach is a focus on the connections linking electoral and policy realignments at those 'open moments when system creating choices are made'.[27] Such intervals of indeterminacy are times when the boundary conditions of politics are renegotiated and reset. Recast, the idea of periodic realignment, stripped of its scientistic aim to discover law-like regularities and concerned not only with elections but with non-incremental changes to the character of transactions between the state and society and the state and the economy, provides a hinge linking domestic actors and institutions to the larger environment constituted by relational ties to other states, economies, and societies. A meaningful periodisation of American history thus requires not only the kind of supple attention to liberalism's grammar that neither Hartz nor students of realignment have provided, but also a decisive farewell to American exceptionalism.

THE STATE IN ITS PLACE

The state as a concept and object of analysis has lived a doubly insecure life in the United States inside the discipline of political science (and the cognate field of political sociology). Except as a unit of federalism, the term is not part of the ordinary language of political life. Both the liberal traditions and republican traditions of political thought so important to American ideology and discourse not only have been uneasy about the term but have insisted on treating public institutions of rule and coercion as extensions of civil society and the consent of citizens. Government is a civic association. Building on this normative perspective, many political analysts have insisted the American state is no more than one such association among many.[28] By the late 1960s, this view had become dominant. The entry on 'The State' in the 1968 *International Encyclopedia of the Social Sciences* thus declared that the once fashionable notion that the state defines the main focus of political science as a discipline 'no longer corresponds . . . to the theory and practice of contemporary political scientists'.[29]

At just this moment, a group composed mainly of younger scholars opened an effort to restore the state to its traditional central place. They had political and analytical motivations. During an epoch characterised by the war in Vietnam fought by a conscript army and a massive civil rights revolution both enabled and repressed by different institutions of government, they stressed how the United States manifestly possessed a significant state. Like all modern territorial sovereign states, this one was distinguished from other civic associations by its indivisible claims of sovereign control over people and places; by the coercive inclusiveness of its ensemble of institutions; and by its distinctive normative vision of what constitutes a good political regime. Based on this premise of structural distinctiveness, an influential movement to return political studies to the state transformed many agendas for research (at just the moment, ironically, when historians of the same generation were turning from political to social history from below).[30]

Both Aristide Zolberg and I identified broadly with this scholarly development. In our *Working Class Formation* we sought in part to help transform studies of this subject by placing variations to the character of the French, German, and American state at the centre of our explanations for why dispositions about class and patterns of collective action by working people differed so much in these three cases in the nineteenth century. As historically-oriented political scientists, we invited other political scientists and a group of estimable historians to join with us to see how far state-focused causal narratives could take us.

Quite far, I still think, but not quite far enough. The main barriers inherent in our work, I now believe, concern the silences which I have sought to address above. The first of these might be called the problem of the borderland between state and society. The state is not just a significant macrostructure that is strong or weak, centralised or decentralised, autonomous or penetrated, stable or unstable (the dichotomies which the new statist literature made central to its analyses, as did we). It possesses a distinctive and contested institutional topography geared to intertwine with members of civil society. Because the state possesses such infrastructural capacities, what matters a great deal are the terms of its transactions across the state/society divide: who gets to be a citizen, how they participate, how their interests are represented, what categories of social action are recognised as legitimate, which forms of identity the party system organises, among other key issues. These are not simply state- *or* society-centred matters, but questions of relationships and exchanges. This domain of transactions, of course, is the site of the most important contests about the grammar of liberalism. A focus on the state itself thus proves insufficient. Rather, a shift in attention both to the moments when conflicts about liberalism as a boundary condition have been most robust, and to the content of such battles at times of contention, promises to incorporate while transcending the gains achieved by restoring the state to a pride of place in political analysis.

This modification to the axis of political analysis also has the welcome effect of promising to grapple with a second key problem in my work (undertaken alone or in partnership with Zolberg) on the state and the working class. There, the state appeared as a fixed set of structures which shapes and conditions working-class experiences, discourses, and actions; but it did not appear as responsive to working-class agency. The state was treated as a cause; working-class thought and behaviour as effects. As a partial truth, this is a permissible construction, but its limits are palpable. If we focus instead on the content and moments when liberalism and its institutions have been most contested, we can see not only how working-class formation has been shaped by the organisation of state–society transactions, but also how their terms have been affected by the agency of working-class people. Working-class formation, from this vantage, is not an outcome (whether typical or exceptional) but a process.

Indeed, it is a process with three main elements: the relationship of working people to the material conditions of their lives, at work and away from work; the symbolic and discursive manner in which they come to map and remap these experiences; and the terms and quality of the ties they forge and have forged for them linking their lives as citizens to the state. Labour and working-class historians traditionally have placed their bets on the first of these conditions, working loosely or tightly within the confines of historical materialism. Recently, a focus on the second, emerging primarily from students of gender, has joined and challenged this materialism. Alas, the third focus – on political relationships and on liberalism as a contested boundary condition – has not established a comparable role in contemporary labour studies and often is treated either as hopelessly old-fashioned or as something of a sell-out to dominant interests. This is more than an unwelcome elision or an unreasonable calumny. For the relative absence of work in this genre diminishes the other two projects as well.

NOTES

1. Ira Katznelson, *City Trenches: Urban Politics and the Patterning of Class in the United States* (New York, 1981); Ira Katznelson, 'Working Class

Formation and the State: Nineteenth Century England in American Perspective', in Peter Evans, Dietrich Rueschmeyer, and Theda Skocpol, eds, *Bringing the State Back In* (Cambridge, 1985); Ira Katznelson, 'Working Class Formation: Constructing Cases and Comparisons', in Ira Katznelson and Aristide Zolberg, eds, *Working Class Formation: Nineteenth-Century Patterns in Western Europe and the United States* (Princeton, 1986).

2.	Katznelson, 'Working Class Formation', 14.

3.	Margaret Ramsay Somers, 'Workers of the World, Compare', *Contemporary Sociology* 18 (May 1989), 325.

4.	Werner Sombart, *Why is There No Socialism in the United States?* (White Plains, 1976) [original edition, *Warum gibt es in den Vereinigten Staaten keinen Sozialismus?* (Tubingen, 1906)].

5.	Eric Foner, 'Why is There No Socialism in the United States?', *History Workshop* 17 (Spring 1984), 59, 60.

6.	Sean Wilentz, 'Against Exceptionalism: Class Consciousness and the American Labor Movement, 1790–1920', *International Labor and Working Class History* 26 (Fall 1984), 5.

7.	This, of course, is a main theme of Wilentz's *Chants Democratic: New York City and the Rise of the American Working Class, 1788–1850* (New York, 1984).

8.	Wilentz, 'Against Exceptionalism', 5.

9.	Louis Hartz, *The Liberal Tradition in America: An Interpretation of American Political Thought Since the Revolution* (New York, 1955).

10.	Robert K. Merton, *Social Theory and Social Structure* (Glencoe IL, 1949), 9.

11.	Ira Katznelson, 'The "Bourgeois" Dimension: A Provocation About Institutions, Politics, and the Future of Labor History', *International Labor and Working-Class History* 46 (Fall 1994), 19–20.

12.	Hartz, *Liberal Tradition*, 10–11.

13.	For a recent critique along these lines, see Rogers M. Smith, 'Beyond Tocqueville, Myrdal, and Hartz: The Multiple Traditions in America', *American Political Science Review* 87 (September 1993).

14.	J. David Greenstone, *The Lincoln Persuasion: Remaking American Liberalism* (Princeton, 1993), 42, 45.

15.	Hartz, *Liberal Tradition*, 20.

16.	Greenstone, *Lincoln Persuasion*, 242.

17.	For discussions of the core features of liberal doctrine, see Ronald Dworkin, 'Liberalism' and 'Why Liberals Should Care about Equality', in Dworkin, *A Matter of Principle* (Cambridge MA, 1985); Charles Larmore, 'Political Liberalism', *Political Theory* 18 (August 1990); and Jeremy Waldron, 'Theoretical Foundations of Liberalism', *The Philosophical Quarterly* 37 (April 1987).

18.	M.L. Harrison, 'Citizenship, Consumption, and Rights: A Comment on B.S. Turner's Theory of Citizenship', *Sociology* 25 (May 1991), 209.

19.	John Gerard Ruggie, 'International Regimes, Transactions, and Change: Embedded Liberalism in the Postwar Economic Order', *International Organization* 36 (Spring 1982), 209, 210.

20.	Richard Franklin Bensel, *Yankee Leviathan: The Origins of Central State Authority in America, 1859–1877* (New York, 1990), 10.

21. See Charles Tilly, ed., *The Formation of National States in Western Europe* (Princeton, 1975); and Tilly, *Coercion, Capital, and European States, AD990–1990* (Oxford, 1990).
22. Richard L. McCormick, 'The Realignment Synthesis in American History', *Journal of Interdisciplinary History* XIII (Summer 1982), 92.
23. Joel H. Silbey, 'Beyond Realignment and Realignment Theory: American Political Eras, 1789–1989', in Byron E. Shafer, ed., *The End of Realignment: Interpreting American Electoral Eras* (Madison, 1991).
24. Jerome M. Clubb, William H. Flanigan, and Nancy H. Zingale, *Partisan Realignment: Voters, Parties, and Government in American History* (Beverly Hills, 1980).
25. Peter Gourevitch, *Politics in Hard Times: Comparative Responses to International Economic Crises* (Ithaca, 1986).
26. Ira Katznelson and Bruce Pietrykowski, 'Rebuilding the American State: Evidence from the 1940's', *Studies in American Political Development* 5 (Fall 1991), 301–2.
27. Gourevitch, *Politics in Hard Times*, 34.
28. For an example, see Frederick Mundell Watkins, *The State as a Concept in Political Science* (New York, 1944).
29. Frederick Mundell Watkins, 'The State', in David Sills, ed., *International Encyclopedia of the Social Sciences*, vol. 15 (New York, 1968), 155.
30. For important summaries of these efforts, see Stephen Krasner, 'Approaches to the State: Alternative Conceptions and Historical Dynamics', *Comparative Politics* 16 (January 1984); and Peter B. Evans, Dietrich Rueschemeyer, and Theda Skocpol, eds, *Bringing the State Back In* (New York, 1985).

4 Why Is There No Labor Party? Class and Race in the United States and Australia

Robin Archer

Political parties based on the labour movement have become electorally important in every advanced capitalist country. Every one, that is, except the United States. The standard explanations for this American exceptionalism rely on comparisons between the United States and Europe. But many of these explanations look much weaker when the United States is compared with Australia. For in the late nineteenth century, compared with Old World Europe, Australia had many of the same New World characteristics as the United States. And yet Australia produced one of the world's earliest and most electorally powerful labour parties.

It is often argued, for example, that the United States was a 'land of opportunity' in which the possibility of prosperity removed the incentive for working-class mobilisation that existed in Europe. But in the late nineteenth century the standard of living for Australian workers was at least as high or even higher, and the country was frequently referred to as a 'working-man's paradise'.

It is also often argued that the early introduction of universal manhood suffrage for whites meant that workers did not have to mobilise politically as they did in Europe, where many workers were denied the vote. But the early introduction of universal manhood suffrage for whites was also a feature of the Australian political system.

And it is often argued that mass immigration to the United States flooded the labour market and undermined the kind of unions that would have had an interest in establishing a labour party. But, relative to its population size, the three-fold population increase in Australia between 1860 and 1890 almost matched the four-fold increase that took place in the United States during the same period.

However, not all of the standard explanations for the failure to establish a labour party in the United States are undermined when the United States is compared with Australia. In particular the general thrust of those explanations which focus on class organisation and racial hostility are actually reinforced, although comparison with the Australian experience highlights the significance of some frequently overlooked aspects of these factors.

In this chapter I want to reassess these explanations for American exceptionalism: in each case considering them in light of the Australian experience. First I will consider the importance of class organisation, paying special attention to the organisational structure of the union movement. Then I will consider the role of racial and ethnic hostilities. In the process I hope to show that it is the *interaction* between these factors that helps to explain why a labour party was established in Australia but was not established in the United States. The chapter will focus on the period around the late 1880s and early 1890s because it was in this period that the Australian Labor Party was established and that the American labour movement came closest to establishing a similar party.

In each case the immediate background against which these initiatives took place was similar. In the early 1890s both countries suffered their worst depression of the nineteenth century, and a series of major industrial confrontations took place which left the unions completely defeated. But in each case the response of the union movement was different. After some initial vacillation, the American Federation of Labor (AFL) rejected the arguments in favour of independent labour politics and an alliance with the agrarian-based populist movement at its conference in 1894, and opted instead for AFL President Samuel Gompers' vision of a nonpolitical 'pure and simple' unionism. The Australian unions, on the other hand, responded by vigorously following up on what had earlier been rather tentative plans to establish labour parties in each of the different self-governing colonies.

The first of these was established in New South Wales in 1890 (well before any similar initiatives in Britain).[1] In its first electoral test the following year, the new party won 22 per cent of the votes and 25 per cent of the seats, leaving it holding the balance of power. Labor parties also began to build support in other colonies, and, after its establishment in 1901, in the new federal parliament. By 1899 the Queensland Labor Party was able to form a minority government – the world's first labour government – although it only lasted for six days. In 1904, and again in 1909, Labor was able to form longer lasting minority governments in the federal parliament. And by 1910 the federal Labor Party came to power with a majority in its own right.

In the 1890s, the United States (along with Britain and Germany) was one of the three most advanced industrial countries in the world. It had a large industrial working class, many of whom were concentrated in huge enterprises which employed large numbers of unskilled and semi-skilled workers. The organisations of the working class, however, were still dominated by the 'closed' craft unionism which had its roots in an earlier artisanal form of production. In other countries – notably Britain, which had a long tradition of craft unionism similar to that in the United States – a 'new unionism' emerged in the late 1880s, which organised unskilled and semi-skilled workers into large 'open' industrial and general unions.[2] But no similar development took place in the United States. Not, that is, until the 1930s. With the brief exceptions of the Knights of Labor and the American Railway Union, unskilled and semi-skilled workers were largely left outside the union movement.

A number of commentators connect the absence of a labour party in the United States to the absence of this 'new unionism'. They argue that these new unions had both the motivation and the resources to engage in independent political activity.[3] The new 'open' unions had the motivation to engage in political activity because, unlike 'closed' craft unions, they could not hope to control the supply of particular skills, and so they had a greater need for political intervention in order to achieve their goals. They had the motivation to engage in *independent* political activity because their inclusive recruitment strategy fostered a class consciousness which encouraged members to see politics in class terms. The new 'open' unions also had the resources to engage in independent political activity because their large memberships could potentially be translated into large numbers of votes, and because these votes were often geographically concentrated and so could be translated into parliamentary seats.

These arguments seem to be borne out by the British case where the rise of the Independent Labour Party is closely connected with the rise of the new unionism.[4] American evidence also shows that the few unions within the AFL that were open to unskilled and semi-skilled workers were far more likely to support independent political activity than the closed craft unions which dominated the union movement.[5]

Does the Australian case also support the claimed connection between the formation of labour parties and the new unionism? Overall, the answer is 'yes'.

In the 1870s, and even more so in the 1880s, the Australian union movement expanded beyond its original craft base to include large numbers of unskilled and semi-skilled workers. This Australian version of the 'new unionism' grew rapidly on the waterfront, on the railways, in mining, and in the pastoral industry. The formation of the Amalgamated Shearers' Union in 1886 was a particularly important development because of the pivotal role which the export of wool played in the Australian economy.

At the beginning of the 1880s most Australian unionists would have been deeply apprehensive about the idea of forming a political party.[6] But the new unions (and the intellectuals that supported them) played a central role in changing this attitude. It was these unions that pushed the issue of political representation forward in the late 1880s as part of the proposal for a centralised labour federation.[7] It was these unions that were at the centre of the industrial struggles of the early 1890s which cemented union support for the formation of a Labor party. And it was these unions, and especially the shearers' union, that provided the organisational base which enabled the fledgling Labor Parties to sustain themselves after the first flush of success.[8]

Comparison between New South Wales and Victoria also confirms the importance of the new unionism. In Victoria the new unions were less influential than in New South Wales and urban craft unions remained dominant well into the 1890s. The union movement in Victoria did establish a Labor Party, but they were slower to do so than their New South Wales counterparts, and the party they established was little more than a wing of the Liberal Party until the 1900s.[9]

So the Australian case supports the claim that the weakness of a 'new unionism' that was open to unskilled and semi-skilled workers is an important factor in explaining the failure of the American union movement to form a Labor Party. But, arguably, the Australian example tells us more than this. For, in Australia, the new unionism took a particular form. As in other countries, the impetus to form open unions was strong in the mining, maritime, and railway industries.[10] But, in Australia, it was another industry – the pastoral industry organised by the shearers' union – which provided the most important base for the new unionism and the new labour politics.

As we have seen, the shearers' union – which amalgamated in 1894 with the smaller shed-hands' union to form the Australian Workers' Union (AWU) – played an important role in the establishment of independent labour politics. But it was able to do this not only because it was the leading proponent and most important example of the new unionism, but also because it was able to forge an alliance between rural workers and small farmers (or 'selectors') which brought a large section of rural population under the influence of the union movement.[11]

Although highly urbanised compared with other countries, both Australia and the United States still had large rural populations. These rural populations were politically important both because of their size and because of the ideological significance of the yeoman ideal.

The shearers' union exercised an influence over the two largest sections

Table 4.1 Geographical Distribution of New South Wales Labor Seats

	1891	1894	1895	1898	1901	1904	1907
Rural	13	5	5	8	11	13	14
Urban	16	5	7	5	10	6	10
Mining	6	5	7	7	4	6	8
TOTAL	35	15	19	20	25	25	32

Note: The 1895 and 1898 totals include seats won at later by-elections.
Source: Raymond Markey, *The Making of the Labor Party in New South Wales* (Sydney, 1988), 189.

of the rural population. The majority of its members were itinerant workers. But the union also organised large numbers of shearer-selectors: small farmers who took seasonal work as shearers in order to supplement their income. Something like 35 per cent of the shearing workforce were selectors or their sons.[12] These shearer-selectors often played an important organisational role because their land gave them a permanent base in the countryside all the year round.[13]

In short, the shearers' union not only brought rural workers into the otherwise largely urban union movement, but it also forged an alliance between workers and small farmers. The electoral significance which this composite constituency of workers and selectors had for the early Labor Party can be seen from Table 4.1 which shows the proportion of Labor's seats that were held in rural areas.[14]

In contrast, in the late 1880s and early 1890s, the American labour movement failed to capitalise on the burgeoning discontent of populist farmers and build the kind of farmer–labour alliance that might have sustained an independent political party. Rural labour remained largely non-unionised and Samuel Gompers emphasised the gap between small farmers and those attempting to unionise rural labour in order to explain why the AFL leadership opposed union involvement in the populist People's Party. Gompers' argument was not without merit. For even in the midwest heartland of labour-populism, farmers frequently sought to stymie union efforts to organise the rural labourers which they sometimes employed.[15]

But it is too simple to merely juxtapose small farmers with rural labour, since, in both countries, many farmers and their sons were also periodically labourers. Whereas these farmer-labourers were principally organised around farmer-based interests in the United States, they were principally organised around employee-based interests in Australia. In this way, at least for a time, the shearers' union bridged the gap between workers and farmers by integrating small farmers into the institutional framework of the labour movement.

Why was this possible in Australia, but not in the United States? In large measure the answer lies in differences in the structure of the rural economy. Three factors stand out. First, the nature of the pastoral industry and its dominant position in the economy fostered unionisation by bringing large numbers of shearers together for a few months of the year under conditions similar to those in big industrial enterprises.[16] Second, the relative failure of the Selection Acts of the early 1860s, which (like the 1862 Homestead Act in the US) had sought to create a large class of yeoman farmers, gave the bushworkers a numerically dominant position in rural Australia which they did not enjoy in the US.[17] And third, although tensions did exist between selectors and landless bushworkers, these were overshadowed by tensions between both of these groups and the large landholders (or 'squatters') who were both the main employers of rural labour and the traditional antagonists of those seeking to unlock the land in the interests of small farmers.[18]

Analogous factors were not wholly absent from the rural economy in the United States. Seasonal work in the corn and wheat belt brought large numbers of rural workers together in some areas. There were many more landless rural labourers than the traditional image of rural America acknowledges.[19] And cattle kings and railroad barons provided a common enemy to homesteaders and rural labour alike.

Nevertheless it is difficult to identify a group of workers in a similar position to that of the shearers. Perhaps cowboys on the large cattle ranches would qualify. But the era of the open range had already passed by the middle of the 1880s, and, in any case, American cowboys were more like Australian overlanders and stockmen.[20] The overlanders and stockmen played a central role in the mythology of the Australian bushworker, but they did not form a base for union organisation. Perhaps those employed in the seasonal harvesting of corn and wheat shared some of the characteristics of the shearers.

Arguably, however, it was the railway workers who were in the best position to play a role analogous to that of the shearers as the social vanguard for the labour movement in rural America. Railway workers were located in all the main rural centres, and the railway barons were a common enemy to small farmers and workers alike. The railway workers did indeed produce a brief explosion of new unionism in their industry, and a closer comparison of the American Railway Union (ARU) and Amalgamated Shearers' Union would be well worth pursuing.[21] But railway employment was not seasonal and so, even if the ARU had survived, it would not have been able to bring small farmers into the institutional framework of the labour movement.

In summary, Australian unions developed a more inclusive form of unionism than their American counterparts. In New South Wales, where the Labor Party was first established, around 20 per cent of the workforce was unionised by 1891: a very high figure for the time. There was a similar membership density in Victoria. Moreover, unlike in the United States, the industrial defeats of the early 1890s reinforced the importance of an inclusive recruitment strategy in the eyes of leading unionists.[22]

The Australian union movement was inclusive in two different ways. As in other countries, the success of the new unionism fostered an intra-class alliance between skilled and unskilled members of the working class. But unlike in other countries, the particular form which the new unionism took in the pastoral industry also fostered an inter-class alliance between workers and farmers. Neither of these developments took place in the United States. The American labour movement's failure to establish a worker-farmer alliance under its own aegis, can (at least partly) be explained by differences in the structure of its rural economy. But the failure to establish an alliance between skilled and unskilled workers has still to be explained. There were certainly differences in the structure of American and Australian industry: industrialisation was far more advanced in the United States. But this should have helped rather than hindered the new unionism.

One way to explain the failure of the new unionism in the United States is to focus on the immigrant origins and ethnic heterogeneity of its population. In particular, it has been argued that since ethnic divisions between the various communities of old and new immigrants overlapped with divisions between skilled and unskilled workers, they tended to reinforce the exclusive craft-focus of the established unions and inhibit the formation of more inclusive industry-based unions.[23]

Indirectly, therefore, ethnic heterogeneity undermined the possibility of establishing a labour party by undermining the capacity to establish an inclusive union movement. But ethnic heterogeneity also directly undermined the possibility of establishing a labour party by providing an alternative basis for political mobilisation which cut across class loyalties. Even where workers had been mobilised on a class basis at the workplace, they frequently continued to base their political loyalties on their ethnic affiliation.[24]

At first sight the Australian case seems to foreshadow problems for these arguments. For, as in the United States, the Australian population has (since white settlement) been built on immigration, and its ethnic composition

Table 4.2 Change in Source of Immigration to the US from Europe, 1860–1930

Period	Total Admitted	Northern & Western Europe	Southern & Eastern Europe
1861–70	2 314 824	2 031 624 (87.8%)	33 628 (1.4%)
1871–80	2 812 191	2 070 373 (73.6)	201 889 (7.2)
1881–90	5 246 613	3 778 633 (72.0)	958 413 (18.3)
1891–1900	3 687 564	1 643 492 (44.6)	1 915 486 (51.9)
1901–10	8 795 386	1 910 035 (21.7)	6 225 981 (70.8)
1911–20	5 735 811	997 438 (17.4)	3 379 126 (58.9)
1921–30	4 107 209	1 284 023 (31.3)	1 193 830 (29.0)

Source: Samuel Eliot Morison, Henry Steele Commager, and William Leuchtenburg, *The Growth of the American Republic*, vol. 2, 7th edn (New York, 1980), 108.

has played a central role in political life. However, contrary to first appearances, a closer comparison of ethnic and racial consciousness in the United States and Australia tends to reinforce the importance of these arguments, although it sometimes does so in unexpected ways.

In the discussion that follows I will first consider ethnic differences between Europeans, where by 'Europeans' I mean both European immigrants themselves and those descended from European immigrants. I will then consider relations between Europeans and Chinese. And finally I will consider relations between Europeans and blacks.

There were important differences in the ethnic composition of the European population in the United States and Australia in the 1890s. In the United States, immigration during these years increasingly came from a new source. As Table 4.2 shows, until about 1880, immigration was principally from northern and western Europe, with the largest numbers coming from Britain, Ireland, and Germany. Thereafter, immigration from these countries declined rapidly and 'new immigrants' increasingly came from southern and eastern Europe, with the largest numbers coming from Italy, Austria-Hungary, and Russia.

By contrast, although there were a small number of Italians and others in Australia in the 1890s, immigration from southern and eastern Europe only became a major factor much later.[25] Moreover, while there had been some immigration from Germany, the vast majority of immigrants came from Britain and Ireland.[26] Thus Australians in the 1890s were overwhelmingly 'Anglo-Celts' who could trace their origins to the United Kingdom. There were, however, important ethnic differences within this group. In particular, more than a quarter of the population were Irish Catholics.[27]

In the United States, the growth of southern and eastern European immigration in the 1880s and 1890s was accompanied by the growth of a politically salient 'nativist' hostility on the part of both the American-born and many of the 'old immigrants' from northern and western Europe. But this antagonism was not an inevitable, 'objective' consequence of the presence of different ethnic groups. Rather it came about because of the 'subjective' significance which people attributed to these ethnic differences: what we could call for short their 'ethnic consciousness'.

It is possible to argue that the kind of ethnic consciousness that was prevalent throughout the English-speaking world in the late nineteenth century did indeed make ethnic hostility inevitable once large numbers of southern and eastern Europeans began to migrate to America. The widespread need to justify colonial expansion and dispossession, and the popularisation of Social Darwinism and other 'scientific' theories about the racial superiority of Anglo-Saxons and their Nordic and Germanic 'cousins' could be cited to support this argument.[28] And if the argument is accepted, then the simple fact that Australia's European population was relatively ethnically homogeneous may indeed help explain why a labour party could be established there but not in the United States.[29]

However, it is also possible to offer an alternative explanation: one that emphasises, not an international (Anglo-Saxon) ethnic consciousness, but, rather, a peculiarly American one. For the origins of the intra-European ethnic antagonisms which plagued the US working class in the late nineteenth century can be traced to powerful ethno-religious antagonisms earlier in the century. The mass immigration to the United States following the European crop failures of the 1840s was accompanied by a Protestant nativist reaction against immigrant (especially Irish) Catholicism. And this earlier nativism fed into and fed the nativism of the late nineteenth century. In particular the populist movement drew heavily on the cultural tone of nativist evangelical Protestantism, and, as a result, alienated many new immigrant and Catholic workers.[30]

Comparison with Australia helps to bring out the peculiarly American character of this ethno-religious consciousness. For the intra-European ethnic composition of the United States in the mid nineteenth century was not so different to that of Australia. And yet ethno-religious antagonisms were less powerful in Australia. Although there is no doubt that they *were* present, they did not come to dominate working-class loyalties as they did in the United States.[31]

Part of the explanation for this difference lies in the different role which religion played in the founding of the two societies. The religious vocation of the 'Pilgrim Fathers' gave Protestantism a central role in defining America's identity and the terms of its ideological disputes. In contrast, Australia's convict origins made it difficult for anyone to claim that the country embodied a special religious mission: least of all a Puritan Protestant one.[32]

So it is possible to argue that it was not simply the ethnic heterogeneity of its potential constituency that undermined the establishment of an American labour party, but rather a deeply-rooted tradition of ethnoreligious consciousness.

Of course antagonism between Europeans was not the only source of ethnic antagonism. There was also a common racial antagonism among Europeans towards those who were not of European descent. In particular there was vitriolic hostility towards Chinese immigrants in both countries. In both cases this hostility first came to prominence during the gold rushes of the 1850s which took place on the west coast of the United States and in south-east Australia.[33] Although there were a large number of Chinese diggers in certain districts, overall, they were never more than a small percentage of either country's population. And, as Table 4.3 shows, once the gold rush was over, that percentage continually declined.

Despite this, from the late 1870s onwards, anti-Chinese agitation came to occupy a central place on the political agenda of both labour movements. This development was given a major boost around the same time by the California Workingmen's movement which grew out of a meeting called to support the 1877 railway strike in the United States and by the popular movement against Chinese immigration which supported the Australian seamen's strike of 1878.[34] In each case opposition to competition from Chinese labour merged with general racial objections to the Chinese *per se*.

By the beginning of the 1900s, Gompers could summarise the AFL's position in a pamphlet entitled *Meat vs. Rice: American Manhood vs. Asiatic Coolieism: Which Shall Survive?*, and the Australian Labor Party, loudly proclaiming its fear of 'racial contamination', had made the maintenance of 'White Australia' its first and foremost objective.[35]

The common presence of this highly charged racial consciousness raises

Table 4.3   Chinese Population: California, Victoria, and New South Wales, 1860–81

		California	Victoria	NSW
1860–61	Chinese	34 000	24 724	12 986
	% of total pop.	9	4.59	3.7
1870–71	Chinese	49 000	17 795	7 208
	% of total pop.	8.6	2.4	1.4
1880–81	Chinese	75 000	11 795	10 141
	% of total pop.	7.5	1.4	1.3

Source: Andrew Markus, *Australian Race Relations, 1788–1993* (Sydney, 1994), 71.

a paradox: for while in Australia it was compatible with and in fact helped to facilitate the emergence of a labour party, in the United States it had quite the opposite effect.

In Australia racial consciousness helped to facilitate the establishment of the Labor Party both directly and indirectly. Indirectly, it helped to facilitate the formation of the Labor Party by helping to consolidate some of the earliest and most important examples of the new unionism. In key unions like those of the seamen, the miners, and the shearers, anti-Chinese mobilisation played an important (though by no means the only) role in consolidating industry-wide organisation.

Unlike craft unions, the new unions could not rely on the control of a monopoly of skills in order to exercise power in the labour market. As a result they were more reliant on mobilising popular support and political pressure to make industrial gains. Racial consciousness helped the new unions to do this because it made it easier for them to present their grievances as part of a concern which commanded broad cross-class support. In 1878, for example, the recently formed seamen's union went on strike against the employment of Chinese labour at below union rates by the largest shipping company in Australia.[36] Because of the anti-Chinese aspect of the dispute, the seamen rapidly gained support not only from other unions, but also from large public meetings backed by middle-class politicians, and even eventually from government. As the union itself noted in a retrospective assessment, it was this broad base of support which enabled it to effectively win the dispute and enjoy a subsequent period of 'stability and solidarity'. Other unions were quick to learn the lesson.[37]

Racial consciousness also directly helped to consolidate electoral support for the fledgling Labor Party in the second half of the 1890s and beyond. From 1896 onwards, the Labor platform called for the 'total exclusion of undesirable alien races'.[38] And in the first debate on immigration policy in the federal parliament in 1901, the Labor leader made it clear that, while Labor's support for the 'White Australia' policy was 'tinged with considerations of an industrial nature', the *main* reason for this support was 'the possibility and probability of racial contamination'.[39] Racial consciousness had a strong grip on all classes. By presenting itself as the most fervent advocate of a 'White Australia', and by outbidding its opponents in its commitment to racial purity, the Labor Party was able to appeal successfully to a broad cross-class electoral coalition and reinforce its credentials as a national rather than a sectional party.[40]

It is important not to overstate this point. Neither the new unions nor the Labor Party were established with racial goals as their principle objective. Indeed in the early 1890s (when the Labor Party was established) racial issues were well down on the labour movement's agenda.[41] In part this was because the organisational security of the unions became the movement's central concern in the wake of repeated industrial defeats, and in part it was because legislation prohibiting Chinese immigration had already been achieved. Nevertheless, anti-Chinese rhetoric remained popular and in the late 1890s it returned to prominence and played an important role in consolidating support for the Labor Party.

Why was the equally vociferous anti-Chinese agitation in the United States unable to have a similar effect? Some argue that the responsiveness of the US political system to organised labour's anti-Chinese demands led the unions to desist from undertaking independent political action.[42] But comparison with Australia does not bear this out. For if the American political system was responsive, the Australian political system was even more so. In particular, union-backed campaigns against Chinese immigration had much greater and more rapid success in achieving changes in government policy than they did in the United States. In any case the significance of greater political responsiveness is itself open to question. For it has been argued that in Australia, far from discouraging union involvement in politics, the success of anti-Chinese campaigns served actually to encourage it by demonstrating that political intervention could be successful.[43]

A more promising explanation for the effect of anti-Chinese sentiment in the United States focuses on the way in which this racial consciousness interacted with ethno-religious consciousness to redefine the meaning of nativism. Once the racial logic of anti-Chinese agitation had been widely accepted (and it was accepted within the labour movement across the board), it could be used to reignite and relegitimise nativist antagonisms by defining them in racial rather than religious terms. In particular racial antagonism could be extended by analogy to the new immigrants from southern and eastern Europe.

This is in fact what happened in the 1880s and 1890s. Italians, Slavs, and others were increasingly characterised as 'continental Chinese'.[44] Like the Chinese, they were condemned not only for low-wage 'coolie' competition and for supposed 'slavish' sycophancy towards employers, but also for being 'unassimilable' and somehow morally and physically 'degenerate'. Characteristics that were originally attributed exclusively to immigrants from China were transposed to southern and eastern European immigrants. We can trace this process by following the changing assumptions underpinning immigration policy. Responding in part to union pressure, the federal government first excluded Chinese labourers, then contract labour, then imposed a literacy test, and finally ended up explicitly restricting the immigration of various categories of Europeans.[45]

The overall effect of these developments was to weaken the old antagonism between Protestants and Catholics and to strengthen a new antagonism between old and new immigrants.[46] Old immigrant Catholics from Ireland and Germany – many of whom were prominent unionists – were now redefined as natives in opposition to new immigrant Catholics and Jews from southern and eastern Europe.

This in turn reinforced the solidarity of the skilled AFL craft workers, most of whom could trace their origins to northern and western Europe. But it simultaneously strengthened the cleavage between them and the unorganised, unskilled new immigrant workers from southern and eastern Europe. In short, the emergence of racial nativism strengthened the intraclass divisions between skilled and unskilled workers which were hampering the emergence of a more inclusive unionism. It thereby undermined the prospects for the establishment of a labour party.

Whereas, in Australia, racial hostility towards the Chinese reinforced a class-wide solidarity between skilled and unskilled workers (and even enabled the labour movement to appeal beyond its class base to farmers and the urban middle class), in the United States it gave new life to nativist hostilities which divided the working class.

Antagonism towards blacks was also prevalent in both countries, but, again, it had different effects in each case. In the United States, the black population stood at about 7.5 million in 1890 or about 12 per cent of the total population.[47] But, before the great internal migration that began during the First World War, nine out of ten blacks lived in the South, and the vast majority of these were tenant farmers or sharecroppers.[48]

Officially, there had never been any slavery in Australia. But there was a group of people whom contemporaries thought of as occupying an analogous position to that of African-Americans. These people were known as 'Kanakas': Melanesians from the South Pacific islands who worked on sugar plantations in Queensland. In legal terms Kanakas were brought to Australia as indentured labourers on three-year contracts, though in fact some were kidnapped (a practice known as 'blackbirding') and many others must have had little understanding of what was being proposed. Altogether some 62 000 Kanakas were brought to Australia before the trade was ended by the Federal parliament in 1901, although there were never more than 11 500 in the country at any one time.[49] In 1891, for example, Kanakas were less than 2 per cent of the Queensland population, although they were a much larger percentage of the population in cane-growing districts.[50]

In some ways the situation of the Kanakas was more like that of Chinese contract labourers in America than it was like that of African-Americans. But contemporary Australian whites saw Kanakas as racially inferior to the Chinese, and they also saw them as representing the emergence of a feudal plantation economy in the Australian 'Far North' similar to that which had existed in the American 'Deep South'.[51]

As with Chinese immigrants, the attitude of the Australian labour movement towards the Kanakas was unremittingly hostile. And as with the anti-Chinese campaign, the campaign against Kanaka labour helped the movement both to solidify its class-wide support and to appeal beyond it. This effect was particularly important in Queensland, though the campaign was taken up, and had an effect, throughout Australia. Some sense of just how important it was can be gleaned from Labor's reaction to its by-election victory in the the seat of Bundaberg in 1892. 'Bundaberg goes White' was the headline in the Queensland *Worker*.[52]

American unions, on the other hand, in contrast with their uniformly hostile attitude towards the Chinese, adopted a more ambivalent attitude towards blacks. The main reason for this ambivalence was the ideological legacy of the Civil War and Reconstruction which, for a time, went some way towards delegitimising hostility towards African-Americans. The influence within the labour movement of socialist activists, especially those influenced by Marxism, also had some effect.[53]

AFL policy towards blacks illustrates this ambivalence. Formally, the AFL refused to allow unions which excluded blacks to affiliate with it. On the ground, however, the AFL soon came to accommodate the reracialisation of politics that built up momentum in the 1890s. In 1890 the AFL refused to admit the Machinists' Union because its constitution excluded blacks. But in 1895 the machinists were admitted in a compromise that allowed them to continue to exclude blacks in practice so long as there was no mention of this fact in the constitution. In reality, then, unions were free to decide their own policy towards blacks. In some cases, notably in the industry-wide United Mine Workers (and, for a time, in various unions in New Orleans), black and white workers worked together in the same union. But in most cases, segregation of black unionists or their exclusion from the labour market altogether became the norm.[54]

In the early 1890s, then, the main difference with Australia was not an absence of hostility towards blacks, but an absence of a sure sense that this hostility was legitimate.[55] How did this hostility and the ambivalence about it affect the prospects for the establishment of a labour party?

In the South, hostility towards blacks undermined the prospects for a labour party both by creating divisions within the working class which weakened the prospects for a more inclusive new unionism, and by creating divisions between black tenants and sharecroppers and white yeoman farmers, which weakened labour's potential allies in the populist movement. In effect, racial hostility against blacks served as the southern counterpart to the revival of racial nativism in the North.[56]

In the heartlands of unionism in the North however, blacks were only a small percentage of the working class. Accordingly, anti-black hostility had little direct effect on either the prospects for a new unionism or the prospects for labour populism. In principle it was possible for blacks to come north and compete with white workers – indeed employers sometimes recruited southern blacks as strike breakers – but by and large blacks were excluded from the northern labour market in the 1890s.[57]

In this context, it could be argued that it was ambivalence about hostility towards blacks (rather than the hostility itself) which had the more important effect on the prospects for establishing a labour party in the North, because it was this ambivalence that precluded the possibility of an Australian-style attempt to use racial consciousness to strengthen both the class-wide solidarity of white workers and the cross-class appeal of the labour movement.

However, the effect of anti-Chinese racism (about which there was no ambivalence) suggests that, even if the legitimacy of anti-black racism had been hegemonic, it would not have been able to produce an Australian-style 'inclusive' labour movement. The widespread anti-black sentiment that did exist in the North simply further fuelled the rise of racial nativism and the intra-European hostilities which that fostered. Indeed, arguably, hostility towards blacks provided a model of racial logic that helped to facilitate the rise of anti-Chinese racism in the first place. For example, in California, anti-Chinese sentiments served as a proxy for Southern sympathies and hostility towards blacks.[58]

In essence, then, racial hostility towards blacks had a similar paradoxical effect to racial hostility towards Chinese. In Australia it bolstered the new unionism and strengthened cross-class support for the fledgling Labor Party. Whereas in the United States it bolstered a new nativist hostility amongst Europeans in the North, and directly inhibited solidarity between whites and blacks in the South. However, in the United States, attitudes towards blacks were less certain than they were in Australia. In Australia, hostility towards Kanakas and hostility towards slavery went hand in hand. In the United States, the struggle against slavery left a legacy which cast doubt on the legitimacy of hostility towards blacks.

So why is there no labour party in the United States? Clearly a comprehensive explanation would involve a wide range of factors, including, perhaps, factors which have not been considered here: factors like the role of state-backed repression, the nature of the political system, and the impact of individualist ideologies. But comparison with Australia suggests that, whatever other factors may be involved, the interaction of class organisation and racial consciousness is central to any such explanation.

For when the United States is compared with Australia, the failure of the new unionism emerges as the principle proximate cause for the failure of the union movement to establish a labour party in the United States. In Australia, as elsewhere, the new unions showed that they had both the motivation and the resources to engage in independent labour politics. In addition, in Australia, one of their number was able to provide a bridge between the union movement and aggrieved small farmers: just the group with whom the American unions most needed to form an alliance.

The structure of the economy explains in part why American unions were unable to facilitate an inter-class alliance with small farmers, but it cannot explain their failure to facilitate an intra-class alliance between skilled and unskilled workers. Comparison with Australia suggests that this is best understood as resulting from the impact of ethnic and racial antagonisms.

Racial hostility was a powerful force in both countries. But it had very different effects on class organisation. In Australia, hostility towards Chinese and Melanesian immigrants helped to consolidate the new unions by providing them with a popular rallying cry which enabled them to mobilise cross-class support. Racial hostility also directly helped to consolidate the fledgling Labor Party by enabling it to reinforce its credentials as a national party and to appeal beyond the working class to small farmers and the urban middle class.

In the United States, by contrast, hostility towards Chinese immigrants and blacks melded with an earlier tradition of ethno-religious nativism to produce a new racial nativism which set the old immigrants from northern and western Europe against the new immigrants from southern and eastern Europe. Since the cleavage between old and new immigrants tended to coincide with the cleavage between skilled and unskilled workers, this new nativism strengthened the intra-class cleavage between skilled and unskilled workers and hampered the emergence of a more inclusive unionism. It thus undermined the prospects for the establishment of a labour party.

NOTES

1. In Britain, the Independent Labour Party was established in 1893, and the union-based Labour Representation Committee (the forerunner of the Labour Party) was only established in 1900.
2. Eric Hobsbawm, 'The Making of the Working Class, 1870–1914' in Hobsbawm, *Worlds of Labour: Further Studies in the History of Labour* (London, 1984).
3. Gary Marks, *Unions in Politics: Britain, Germany, and the United States in the Nineteenth and Early Twentieth Centuries* (Princeton, 1989), 45–8, 204–10.
4. Henry Pelling, *The Origins of the Labour Party, 1880–1900* (Oxford, 1954); and Pelling, *A History of British Trade Unionism* (London, 1963).
5. Marks, 206–7.
6. Robin Gollan, *Radical and Working Class Politics: A Study of Eastern Australia 1850–1910* (Melbourne, 1960), 94.
7. Gollan, 94–8, 106–8.
8. Raymond Markey, *The Making of the Labor Party in New South Wales 1880–1900* (Sydney, 1988), 182–192; Greg Patmore, *Australian Labour History* (Melbourne, 1991), 76–80.
9. Gollan, 129, 139–44. Note, however, that the Victoria unions behaved more like the British than the American unions. Like the British unions, they did not eschew political activity *per se*. On the contrary, they had a long-standing alliance with the Liberal Party. But they were cautious about independent political activity.
10. Russell Ward, *The Australian Legend* (Melbourne, 1958), 212.
11. The shearers' union was a self-conscious advocate of the 'new unionism'. See the various statements of its secretary, W.G. Spence, in Noel Ebbels, *The Australian Labor Movement 1850–1907* (Sydney, 1983), 119–21.
12. J.A. Merritt, 'W.G. Spence and the 1890 Maritime Strike', *Historical Studies* 15 (April 1973), 595.
13. This was especially so in the eastern areas where the largest concentrations of selectors were to be found; Markey, 57–67, 141–4.
14. Markey, 189.
15. Philip S. Foner, *History of the Labor Movement in the United States*, vol.

2 (New York, 1955), 305–8; and Paul W. Gates, 'Frontier Estate Builders and Farm Laborers' in Hofstadter and Lipset, eds, *Turner and the Sociology of the Frontier* (New York, 1968).

16. Gollan, 101, 103–4.
17. Markey, 56.
18. Ward, 196–9.
19. See Gates, 'Frontier Estate Builders'; and Fred A. Shannon, 'Post-Mortem on the Labor-Safety-Valve Theory' in Hofstadter and Lipset, *Turner and the Sociology of the Frontier.*
20. Ward, 10.
21. Like the shearers, the ARU had a strong political orientation. After the 1894 Pullman strike the remnants of the union formed the Social Democratic Party which was the forerunner of the American Socialist Party. Had the union survived its industrial defeats, the leaders of the AFL would have had to deal with it, as they pragmatically did with other socialist and industry-based unions. The role of railway union leader Eugene Debs in the labour-populist movement suggests that the ARU might then have been able to play a similar role to the shearers in establishing and consolidating a labour party. Foner, 276, 323.
22. In contrast, many American union leaders saw a retreat to traditional craft unionism as a prerequisite for organisational survival; see Martin Shefter, 'Trade Unions and Political Machines: The Organisation and Disorganization of the American Working Class in the Late Nineteenth Century' in Ira Katznelson and Aristide Zolberg, eds, *Class Formation: Nineteenth-Century Patterns in Western Europe and the United States* (Princeton, 1986). For New South Wales, see Gollan, 132–3; and Markey 139–40, 318. For Victoria, see Patmore, 56. For the impact in Australia of the defeats of the 1890s, Markey, 164–6; and Ebbels, 150–2.
23. Gwendolyn Mink, *Old Labor and New Immigrants in American Political Development* (Ithaca, 1986); Mike Davis, *Prisoners of the American Dream* (London, 1986).
24. Ira Katznelson, *City Trenches: Urban Politics and the Patterning of Class in the United States* (New York, 1981).
25. First in the 1920s when the United States began to restrict immigration, and then, on a much larger scale, after the Second World War. See Charles Price, *Southern Europeans in Australia* (Melbourne, 1963), 9–11 and James Jupp, *Immigration* (Sydney, 1991), 69–81.
26. Jupp, 127.
27. Jupp, 31; Manning Clark, *Select Documents in Australian History 1851–1900* (Sydney, 1955), 667.
28. Richard White, *Inventing Australia* (Sydney, 1981), 66–72.
29. For evidence of the hostility towards southern and eastern Europeans that undoubtedly existed in Australia see Ward, 224; Markey, 293–4; Jupp, 52, 69–70; and Verity Burgman, 'Capital and Labour: Responses to Immigration in the Nineteenth Century' in Ann Curthoys and Andrew Markus, eds, *Who Are Our Enemies? Racism and the Working Class in Australia* (Sydney, 1978), 28.
30. A.T. Lane, *Solidarity or Survival? American Labor and European Immigrants, 1830–1924* (New York, 1987), 9–32; Davis, 38–40.

31. Andrew Parkin, 'Ethnic Politics: A Comparative Study of Two Immigrant
     Societies, Australia and the United States', *Journal of Commonwealth and
     Comparative Politics*, 15:1 (March 1977), 25–7. For anti-Catholic sentiments
     among the political elite see the speech by Henry Parkes in Clark, 248–9;
     and the *Age* editorial in Graeme Davison, 'Unemployment, Race and Pub-
     lic Opinion: Reflections on the Asian Immigration Controversy of 1888'
     in Andrew Markus and M.C. Ricklefs, eds, *Surrender Australia? Essays in
     the Study and Uses of History: Geoffrey Blainey and Asian Immigration*
     (Sydney, 1985), 106. For popular anti-Catholic sentiments see Andrew
     Markus, *Australian Race Relations 1788–1993* (Sydney, 1994), 89 on gold-
     field prejudice; and Patmore, 79 on the opposition by the Victorian miners'
     union to state aid for Catholic schools.

32. Other factors which help to explain the lesser influence of ethno-religious
     antagonism in Australia include the timing of population movements and
     residential patterns. In Australia, Catholics and Protestants settled the coun-
     try more or less simultaneously, whereas in the United States, Catholics
     arrived in a long-established Protestant society. In Australia, Catholics and
     Protestants lived in the same residential communities (and, to a lesser extent,
     inter-married), while in the United States, ethnically distinct communities
     were the norm.

33. Andrew Markus, *Australian Race Relations*, 59–72, and Markus, *Fear
     and Hatred: Purifying Australia and California 1850–1901* (Sydney, 1979),
     1–44.

34. Mink, 81–8; Ann Curthoys, 'The Seamen's Strike of 1878' in Curthoys and
     Markus, *Who Are Our Enemies?*, 48–65.

35. Samuel Gompers and Herman Guttstadt, *Meat vs. Rice: American Manhood
     vs. Asiatic Coolieism: Which Shall Survive?* (Washington, 1902); Brian
     McKinlay, *Australian Labor History in Documents*, Volume 2, *The Labor
     Party* (Melbourne, 1990), 28; and Ebbels, 222, 234–6.

36. Curthoys, 'Seamen's Strike, *passim*.

37. Ebbels, 155–6. In 1885, similar action by the seamen's union – this time
     linked to the demand for wage rises and a closed shop – initiated another
     wave of anti-Chinese mobilisation which peaked at the end of the 1880s; see
     Markey, 288–9. The shearers also linked their 1891 campaign for a closed
     shop to agitation against the employment of Chinese cooks and shedhands;
     for details, see Markus, *Australian Race Relations*, 170–6.

38. Ebbels, 217–19, 222; McKinlay, 28.

39. Ebbels, 234–5.

40. Ray Markey, 'Populist Politics: Racism and Labor in New South Wales
     1880–1900' in Curthoys and Markus, *Who Are Our Enemies?*, 76–7; Markey,
     Making of the Labor Party, 295–6.

41. Markus, *Australian Race Relations*, 176–222.

42. Mink, 100, 113–14.

43. Markey, *Making of the Labor Party*, 285, 289.

44. Lane, 69, 85. There is some evidence of a similar transposition in Australia
     in the 1890s; see Curthoys and Markus, xii, 73, and 84, and Markus, *Fear
     and Hatred*, 259. However, this took the form of sporadic outbursts and did
     not involve the labour movement in any sort of organised campaign.

45. Mink, 108–10. See the complementary argument in Bob Carter, Marci Green,

and Rick Halpern, 'Immigration Policy and the Racialisation of Migrant Labour: The Construction of National Identities in the USA and Britain', *Ethnic and Racial Studies* 19:1 (January 1996).

46. Mink, 53, 76–7.

47. William Cohen, *At Freedom's Edge: Black Mobility and the Southern White Quest for Racial Control, 1861–1915* (Baton Rouge, 1991), 93; Samuel Eliot Morison, Henry Steele Commager, and William E. Leuchtenburg, *The Growth of the American Republic*, vol. 2, 7th edn (New York, 1980), 859.

48. Stephen Thernstrom, *A History of the American People*, 2nd edn (San Diego, 1989), 673, 679; Cohen, 78–108.

49. Patmore, 196–9; Jupp, 44, 47.

50. Doug Hunt, 'Exclusivism and Unionism: Europeans in the Queensland Sugar Industry 1900–10' in Curthoys and Markus; Humphrey McQueen, *A New Britannia: An Argument Concerning the Social Origins of Australian Radicalism and Nationalism*, 3rd edn (Melbourne, 1986), 36.

51. This connection between a liberal concern with the conditions for a free society of equals and a racist concern with the exclusion of certain groups is one of the dominant motifs of late nineteenth-century thought in Australia, both within the labour movement and amongst middle-class progressives.

52. Markus, *Fear and Hatred*, 207–22; McQueen, 38.

53. Although the influence of Marxism was much weaker in the United States than it was in Continental Europe, it was still much stronger than it was in Australia; see Albert Metin, *Socialism Without Doctrine* (Sydney, 1977). Note, however, that debates within the Socialist Party of America in the early twentieth century showed that the influence of Marxism alone was no guarantee of immunity to racist attitudes; see Sally Miller, 'Socialism and Race' and Charles Leinenweber, 'Socialism and Ethnicity' both in John H.M. Laslett and Seymour Martin Lipset, eds, *Failure of a Dream? Essays in the History of American Socialism* (Berkeley, 1984).

54. Foner, 195–204, 345–61; Mink, 96–7; Alexander Saxton, *The Rise and Fall of the White Republic: Class Politics and Mass Culture in Nineteenth Century America* (London, 1990), 300–3; and David Montgomery, *The Fall of the House of Labor: The Workplace, the State and American Labor Activism* (Cambridge, 1987), 107–9. For the UMWA see Herbert Gutman, 'The Negro and the United Mine Workers' in his *Work, Culture and Society in Industrializing America* (New York, 1976); and Rick Halpern, 'Organized Labour, Black Workers, and the Twentieth Century South: The Emerging Revision', *Social History* 19:3 (October 1994).

55. Although, interestingly, there was even occasional evidence of this ambivalence in Australia. The 1895 rules of the shearers' union, which usually had a particularly strident attitude towards racial issues, specifically exempted American Negros (along with Aborigines and Maoris) from its bar on coloured membership. See Markey, 'Populist Politics', 77; and Markus, *Fear and Hatred*, 175–6.

56. C. Vann Woodward, *Origins of the New South, 1877–1913* (Baton Rouge, 1951); Davis, *passim*.

57. Cohen, 97–101, 109.

58. Mink, 104; Saxton, 294–6.

5 It Is 'the Working Class Who Fight All the Battles': Military Service, Patriotism, and the Study of American Workers[1]

Roger Horowitz

In the Canton, Ohio speech which resulted in his imprisonment, Eugene Debs explained that he opposed American involvement in the First World War because it is 'the working class who fight all the battles, the working class who make the supreme sacrifices, the working class who freely shed their blood and furnish the corpses'. Debs was merely restating, in his especially eloquent manner, the classic Marxist position, that wars between nations were not in the interest of workers as they would be the ones to fight and die in a conflict that was neither of their making nor to their benefit.[2]

Debs emphasised the devastation experienced by workers as soldiers; but he paid less attention to the lingering effects of military service on those who returned from battle. This is also the case in traditional American historiography on war and the working class. Generally books which discuss workers during wartime consider only their role on the home front; in the typical narrative (including my own on meatpacking), they disappear from the story once they enter the armed forces, and reappear several years later, as if military service was simply a parenthesis in their lives. Books written about soldiers from the perspective of military history generally eschew class analysis; their story begins with induction into the military and ends with demobilisation. Some important work in progress has started to bridge the arbitrary divide between labour history and the social history of the soldier. It is time for historians to recognise that the military experience has been a central influence on the process of working-class formation, especially among men.[3]

Consider the periodicity of American wars from a generational perspective. Military personnel in Vietnam often had fathers who had served during the Second World War and/or Korea. Among Second World War soldiers born in America, many had fathers who fought in the First World War. The veterans of the Great War were themselves only one or two generations distant from Civil War soldiers. The native-born Civil War veterans easily could be children of participants in the war of 1812, and grandchildren of combatants in the American Revolution. For American men from the labouring class, participation in the military was a recurring, periodic experience stretching back to the creation of the Republic.

The regularity of military participation by American workers does not mean they had similar experiences or drew similar conclusions. In his important article, 'The Social History of the American Soldier', Richard H. Kohn reminded us that 'the most pernicious myth of all is that there has ever been a prototypical American in uniform'. While as historians we naturally search for typicality, the variation in character of American wars, as well as the enormous changes in American society since independence, should warn us against overly ambitious levels of generalisation concerning the effect of military service on workers. Moreover, inside each war were a multitude of different experiences. Whether one fought as a rifleman in an infantry battalion or served as a trucker in a service unit had an enormous impact on the actual content of the experience of being a soldier. To grasp the simultaneously pervasive and highly variegated character of military service, we need to develop a set of analytic tools to understand how it shaped the American working class in a particular historical moment.[4]

I will pursue this investigation in two stages. First I will suggest some categories and techniques we can use to understand the effect of participation in the military on men from working-class backgrounds. Then I will look at the case of the Second World War to assess the influence of military service on the outlook of GIs as they returned to civilian life.

UNDERSTANDING THE MILITARY EXPERIENCE

A useful starting point for understanding the military experience is Reid Mitchell's notion of it as a 'coming of age' episode. In his analysis of Civil War soldiers, Mitchell explores how military service 'in itself was a sign of coming into manhood – it meant accepting a man's duties to defend his home and country'. While particular conceptions of what it meant 'to be a man' have to be contextualised historically, soldiers and sailors consistently operated in an all-male fraternity in which women were not only not equals, but outsiders. The process of male bonding entrenched particular notions of manliness for those who went through the crucible of a war.[5]

While Mitchell employs this 'coming of age' notion primarily to explore masculinity, it also can be used to explicate other aspects of working-class formation shaped by military service. Participation in the armed forces became a permanent reference point for soldiers and sailors, to which other experiences were related and compared. Of course, how workers applied this frame of reference was affected by many other factors, including their lives prior to induction, the actual experience in the war itself, and what they encountered during demobilisation. Nonetheless, military service was an episode in their lives which left a permanent residue of experiences, relationships, and opinions, from which former GIs drew upon selectively to understand their needs, and the conflicts they faced, in post-war society.

In addition to influencing notions of manliness, military service also affected the development of ethnic and racial identities among American workers. Here, the periodic character of American wars interacted powerfully with recurring cycles of immigration, and the repeated recomposition of the American working class. The Civil War was an important crucible of Americanisation of recent Irish immigrants, while the First World War and especially the Second World War played a similar role for the later generation of eastern European ethnics. Ethnic assimilation, however, was not matched by similar lessening of racial barriers inside the military except in exceptional situations, usually combat. Consequently, in war the very decline of ethnic identity could accentuate race consciousness, and awareness of membership in a racial group, among whites and non-whites.[6]

Military service also seems central to understanding the powerful tug of nationalism on the American working class. Patriotic appeals, of course, permeated the home front during wars through government propaganda, popular culture, and the mobilisation for war production. The cultivation of patriotism by the government, business, and the media, while true, is only part of the story. The powerful appeal of patriotism to American workers also grew out of their own personal experiences with military service. Patriotism profoundly influenced American workers during wartime partly because it had an immediate and personal meaning. As Debs recognised, workers were the military's main source for foot soldiers. Moreover, following the war these workers had a special relationship with the state by virtue of status as veterans, and not as workers. Allegiance to the nation by working-class veterans thus received a powerful stimulus from the experience of war, and the aftermath of special economic and social programmes only available to them as former members of the military fraternity.[7]

To explicate the content of these 'coming of age' experiences for GIs, we can draw on many of the concepts employed to study the civilian working class. After all, most chores performed by enlisted men in the military are working-class tasks, whether cleaning a barracks, repairing equipment, or typing reports. Consequently, we should consider military service a variation of the work experience, with attendant issues of cohesion, division, authority, community, and recreation.

Military service is a special form of the work experience, especially during wartime, because soldiers are obliged to kill, and to place themselves in situations where they can lose their lives. Turning civilians into soldiers capable of ending the lives of others is a special challenge of supervisory authority unique to the military. While not all soldiers have to kill, they are all engaged in an operation in which killing the enemy is a common objective and placing their own mortality at risk is part of the job. Much of the initial indoctrination process of the new recruit was designed to make the internal psychological changes necessary for him to accept a morality that was fundamentally at odds with civilian life. From the moment he joined, the new recruit learned that his only role was to obey orders; he no longer existed as an individual with the right of personal choice. Stripping individuality from a soldier was the key step towards teaching him to accept death, both of his enemy and himself. As one American infantrymen explained, he was trained to view himself as the 'chattel' – the property – of his society, and was therefore as dispensable as the ships and other 'chattels' owned by the military. This same soldier explained that 'everything' taught to him 'was one more delicate step along the path of the soldier evolving towards the acceptance of his own death'.[8] The same process trained the soldier to kill, and taught that killing was not an immoral crime, but a moral and heroic act, sanctioned by the institution of which he was a part.

The danger of death, and importance of killing, makes the problem of authority especially troubling in a military organisation. To a certain extent officers faced the same dilemma as supervisors in a factory or office – how to make people perform particular jobs correctly and efficiently. In theory the military solved this problem by establishing a rigid hierarchy where the chain of command allowed a central staff to control its forces in an authoritarian manner. The dilemma, however, is that soldiers had to be motivated to fight, and to fight well under the confusing conditions of actual combat. As Stephen Ambrose observes, discipline alone isn't sufficient, 'because discipline relies on punishment, and there is no punishment the army can inflict on a front-line soldier worse than putting him into the front line'. Consequently, maintaining military discipline was a complex problem, and one not solved by the creation of a rigid command structure.[9]

Indeed, the very special demands on soldiers and sailors gave them the authority, and power, to render very harsh judgements on their superiors, especially over aspects of discipline and military life which bore little obvious relevance to the task at hand. Soldiers particularly objected to 'chickenshit', – the annoying minutiae of military discipline which had no intent other than instilling habits of obedience. Resentment against chickenshit in the American army easily spilled over to more general criticism of special privileges enjoyed by officers. The military tried to create a hard and clear separation between officers and enlisted men as part of the effort to enforce discipline. This meant separating them – creating a different system of residences, mess halls, food, special reserved seats in military theatres, separate hospital wards, and even latrines for the officers, and a better set of privileges. The satirical cartoons of Bill Mauldin, which appeared in the enlisted soldier's paper *Stars and Stripes*, reflected the dissatisfaction of GIs with these rules of obedience and deference. In one especially famous drawing, Mauldin depicted two officers contemplating a sunset, while one says to the other: 'Beautiful view. Is there one for the enlisted men?' Mauldin explained the cartoon's popularity among soldiers by observing that the American military during the Second World War was a 'citizen army' which had in it 'men who in civil life were not accustomed to being directed to the back door and the servant quarters'.[10]

The power of soldiers and sailors to not perform their job well closely parallels the power of workers on the job. Just as the production of goods or provision of services are never as absent of human initiative as management would like, the essential initiative of soldiers on the battlefield was beyond the control of the formal command structure. In his powerful book on D-Day, Stephen Ambrose paints a convincing picture of the chaos that destroyed the elaborate plans of the Allied command for Operation Overlord. Tides and currents disrupted the initial landings on the Normandy shore, and poor surveillance made soldiers unprepared for the tough hedgerow fighting inland. In the confusion, it took the initiatives of 'NCOs [noncommissioned officers] or junior officers or, in some cases, privates' to continue the assault. In such a context, military discipline is an inadequate method for making soldiers perform their tasks.[11]

To explain the cohesion and motivation of enlisted men, sociologists and psychologists have identified a process of 'small-group cohesion' which creates especially tight bonds among GIs. One soldier called these groups 'entities', and explained that these entities of 'threes and fours' were the 'core elements within the families that were the small units'. Often this process of bonding was replete with rituals of maleness, such as drunken recreation and fights, and those of gangs, especially the special insignias, symbols, and styles of dress which distinguished one unit from another. Under the pressure of extraordinary experiences, small group cohesion encouraged a closeness between men that soldiers described very simply as love. Motivation in war, then, came not from a nominal allegiance to military authority, but from a solidarity with one's comrades, from a mutual obligation to defend each other, and to live up to the military fraternity's code of manliness.[12]

These small 'entities' in military units bear a striking resemblance to Stan Weir's concept of the closely-knit 'informal work group'. Weir explained that while working in factories, he repeatedly noticed the existence of an 'informal work group with a life of its own, its own informal leadership, discipline, and activity'. Labour historians have explored how these work groups emerge out of the organisation of production, where the joining of workers in common tasks creates natural bonds, and how in particular moments these groups form the basis for shop floor struggles and union formation. This comparison should not be overdrawn; obviously the stakes are lower in an auto plant's paint department than an infantry platoon. Yet the heightened importance of the small group in the military only accentuates the potential for the group's 'leadership, discipline, and activity' to profoundly influence its members.[13]

It is worth reflecting how the military form of Stan Weir's informal work group could generate new attitudes as well as reinforce historic prejudices. The exclusively male context made manliness central to the bonding experience and generally buttressed ideas that women and men were fundamentally different, with different roles to play in society. The separation of blacks from whites in the military had a comparable effect, reinforcing notions that the races were different, and that black men were inferior and not as 'manly'. At the same time, the process of male bonding also could generate tolerance for men who performed their 'jobs' well but were in some ways different or unusual. This was an especially important means for men of immigrant backgrounds to prove their 'Americanism' and to influence native-born whites to accept them as equals. Allan Berube has even documented that among the tough Marines engaged in the brutal Pacific war during the Second World War, the intense male bonding of the informal work groups stimulated tolerance for homosexuality.[14]

The above argument directs us to look at the actual context and experience of war, and the manner in which military service provided a stimulus for new sets of ideas at the same time as it may have inculcated traditional ideologies. To consider the effects of one such war, let us turn now to the case of the Second World War.

WORKING-CLASS ENLISTED MEN AND THE SECOND WORLD WAR

It is surprising how the labour and social history literature on the critical period immediately after the Second World War has largely ignored the intense political struggle to win the allegiance of returning servicemen. The lack of attention is especially unfortunate if we consider the size and influence of the veteran population. Sixteen million GIs returned home between 1944 and 1946. This included 75 per cent of all men who were between the ages of 18 and 27 in 1945. Many soon married, formed families, became involved in their unions, local politics, and communities. Their actions in turn influenced other workers who stayed home, but who valued and respected the aspirations and outlook of these veterans, and more often than not were related to someone who was in the military. There is no doubt that veterans shared a 'rights consciousness' born of the legitimacy of their aspirations after several years overseas, risking death to support their country's democratic ways. Yet the debate over the content of their rights has remained opaque, even though it was critical to the reconstruction of post-war society.[15]

To begin with, the framework of military service was central to the outlook and rhetoric of enlisted men and veterans as they discussed the transition from war to peace in America in the mid-1940s. Typically, combat veteran J. Porter Reilly led off his letter to President Harry Truman by stating, 'I spent almost five years proudly wearing the uniform of our Army'. Using rhetoric common among recently demobilised soldiers, Reilly legitimised his comments by relating his extended combat duties in the European theatre and his belief that, while at war, he 'knew why we fought'. He also confided, in another theme common among veterans, that returning home and finding 'America was different' had left him 'shocked and bewildered', especially as civilians did not see 'eye to eye' with the warriors who had won the war. Given new courage by Truman's recent State of the Union speech, he pledged, along with 'millions of men like myself', to support the president in 'the toughest campaign we've known'.[16]

Embedded in Reilly's brief letter are themes that informed veterans' politics in the immediate aftermath of the war. Like many former soldiers, Reilly claimed a special relationship with the American nation because of his military service and personal sacrifice. His dissatisfaction with a chaotic civilian world was mollified by the potential for a strong state signified in Truman's speech. Reilly even viewed the assertion of authority by the federal government on domestic issues in military terms, as another 'campaign' in which former soldiers would once again rally to their commander in chief.

Letters from men like J. Porter Reilly provide valuable insights into the aspirations and politics of active and demobilised military personnel in the aftermath of the Second World War. These documents must be used with caution. They can only be taken as illustrative of veterans' attitudes, the way veterans conversed on these issues, and not as measures of public opinion. They are difficult to quantify and classify, but contain persistent motifs that helped define public discussion over the shape of American society and responsibilities of the federal government after the war.[17]

A defining feature of these letters was the way GIs from working-class backgrounds wove their anger at economic and social inequality into the wartime discourse of patriotism. One former sailor bitterly complained it was 'shameful' that while 'we can produce so lavishly in time of war, we cannot produce and raise the standard of living in time of peace'. A small raise secured by his union had been consumed by taxes and higher food prices. Linking his entitlement as a veteran with the grievances of his class, he wrote to President Harry Truman that 'I, as an American who did his duty in the armed forces, believe we are entitled to a better standard of living in peacetime than in wartime'.[18]

For this sailor, as with many other GIs from modest backgrounds, service in the military had earned them the right to government policies and patterns of community and family life that would allow them to participate, as civilians, in the bounty of American life. The creation of a successful war machine by the federal government encouraged veterans to project a similar guiding role for it after hostilities ended. 'It will be difficult to convince the returning servicemen that a nation which can equip the greatest war machine in history', warned Sergeant Bernard W. Lohbauer, 'cannot offer him the opportunity to achieve security.' Proposals along these themes ranged from utilising deserted army barracks to house veterans' families to the creation of federally-funded corporations which would bankroll co-operative business ventures.[19]

These sentiments led many soldiers to favour a wide range of social democratic policies. Reflecting these sentiments, Private First Class Norman P. Salz pointed out that the military had naval and army colleges which taught how to kill. Why not devote similar resources, he wondered, to the construction of medical colleges which would 'keep us alive in peacetime'. A former railroad worker, stationed at Fort Riley, Kansas, pointed out that 'the average GI wouldn't have an anxious thought about his future' if America had socialised medicine and guaranteed job security. Other veterans linked government provision of jobs to programmes like the Tennessee Valley Authority, and the construction of good, modern housing in slum areas that would benefit all citizens, not just veterans.[20]

Contemporary polls indicate that these letters reflected widely-held sentiment among veterans for government initiatives after the war. A survey of veterans in December 1944 by the Military Research branch of the Army found that a large majority favoured direct government measures to provide employment. In 1946, a *Fortune* poll revealed that a similar proportion supported federal efforts to create adequate housing, including direct involvement in home construction.[21]

At the same time, these social democratic ideas were thoroughly imbricated with the gendered aspirations of male veterans to establish stable families. Servicemen, deeply anxious over gender relations in civilian life, expected assistance in their efforts to form traditional families headed by male breadwinners. These concerns are not hard to understand. In 1945, a majority of servicemen were single, and many married men had wed under the unnatural conditions of war. While unmarried men worried whether they would ever have a chance to form a family, husbands alternated between fear that they would be killed and anger over widespread rumours of unfaithful wives and 'golddiggers' who married soldiers simply to receive dependant allotments. In one plaintive reflection of this anxiety, a soldier appealed to Eleanor Roosevelt for help so that he and his buddies could learn 'if our women are true to us' as 'we are very handicapped being overseas'. While the male fraternity of the Army cultivated heightened concerns over manliness, the physical separation of women created a culture in which fear of female independence had a fertile soil.[22]

In even their most progressive visions of post-war America, veterans linked their access to post-war employment with a subordinate status for women. Sergeant J.W. Grooms wanted women to leave their wartime jobs so they could 'make a job and a happy home' for returning servicemen. In a wry summary of their vision, thirteen enlisted men in France sent *Yank* a 'Bill of Rights' to govern the post-war home. It provided for men keeping the paycheck, having nothing to do with the kitchen, and wearing 'the pants in the family'. Another GI warned that allowing women to remain in industry after the war would make America a 'second-rate power', produce a 'double-dose of the roaring twenties', and result in the 'largest juvenile delinquency problem the nation has every faced'. Masculine fears of the uncertainty of future civilian life translated easily into a search for tradition, and for the family as the bedrock on which the former warriors could rebuild their lives.[23]

Social democratic inclinations among working-class veterans were mitigated, and ultimately undermined, by being based on rights linked with military service, rather than national citizenship. It was ironic that the very 'rights consciousness' which inspired the expansive visions of the post-war state allowed veterans to claim, and to settle for, an American welfare state which awarded such benefits only to them, and imperfectly at that, through the Servicemen's Readjustment Act, better known as the GI Bill of Rights. The special status of veterans, which gave them so much authority, also served as a defensive strategy when the potential for broad society-wide social measures seemed either destabilising to soldiers of conservative inclination or too remote a possibility for those who still clung to expansive visions of what could be accomplished in America.

We can trace the contours of these sentiments in three distinct but interrelated episodes in the immediate aftermath of the war. First I shall look at how a rail strike and price controls provoked sharp debate over the state's relationship with the economy and civil society. Second, I will explore the way veterans' demands for government measures to address the housing shortage helped generate a struggle over the extent of federal initiatives to guarantee the satisfaction of basic human needs. And finally, I will identify divisions along racial lines among returning veterans, and how they graphically exposed disagreements among soldiers as to what they had been fighting for.

STATE AND SOCIETY IN POST-WAR AMERICA: THE VETERANS' DEBATE

Controversies over the powers of labour and business immediately after the war forced veterans to think concretely about the relationship between state and society in post-war America. In general terms, veterans judged both business and labour by their contribution to national interests, and the subordination of narrow sectoral objectives to the greater good of America.

Among the many veterans sympathetic to labour organisations, most assigned unions a relatively delimited space in the post-war world as primarily economic institutions. Servicemen like Private Leon G. Jackson saw them primarily as a necessary means to advance their standard of living. 'If labor was treated fair and given a fair wage', he wrote to Truman in January 1946, 'they would not be striking.' As a person from the 'laboring class . . . all I desire upon return to civilian life is a decent living and fair working conditions to support my family'. Absent from veterans' letters was any expanded notion of a role for labour in the operation of industry and government regulation, as was being offered at the time by CIO leaders Philip Murray and Walter Reuther.[24]

Returning soldiers who criticised unions generally emphasised their own poverty, and contrasted their sacrifice to strikes at home which hurt the war effort and hindered veterans' efforts to establish civilian lives. Veteran Robert Cole wrote to Truman that he faced loss of his furniture and home because of a strike, and feared that his wife and soon-to-be-born child would suffer from 'the uncomforts of starvation'. Cole recommended drafting strikers so they could gain a 'fox hole perspective' and learn how to support their families on $50 a month. His concerns reflected how soldiers earned considerably less pay than industrial workers; packinghouse workers received over $150 a month at the time this GI penned his complaint. Cole's criticism of unions thus stressed their selfishness – how they only benefited more privileged segments of the working population, rather than the most needy and deserving, especially veterans.[25]

Business occupied unstable terrain in the veterans' picture of the post-war period. While overwhelmingly supportive of the private enterprise system, servicemen nonetheless criticised the 'selfish' efforts of firms to use patriotism to sell goods and to make money at the expense of national interests. One 'flabbergasted' sergeant stationed in France sent *Yank* a Lord & Taylor advertisement which unabashedly addressed itself to 'the hero who stuck to the home front'. The ad promoted a 'dashing battle-jacket done in soft tweeds' which was cut with 'Army attention to detail, and set for a full post-war life on links and country lanes'. Appalled at the elitism and shirking of manly duty depicted in the ad, the sergeant sarcastically recommended that the firm create a selection of awards and ribbons 'for those battle-scared home front heroes'. Another veteran linked the profit motive with outright disloyalty. Explaining that he was the son of a steelworker as well as 'just returned from war', Joseph Norris wrote to Truman, 'I did not voluntarily go to war because I upheld the right of industrialists to sell steel to Japan for the destruction of China and for use on me and my buddies'. American business still had to prove to veterans like these that it was patriotic, and would act in a manner that benefited national, as opposed to selfish, interests.[26]

Two interrelated controversies in 1946 forced veterans to think concretely about the place of labour and business in post-war America. In May 1946 a strike by two rail unions, which threatened to paralyse the nation's transportation system, ended only after President Harry Truman ordered workers to return to their jobs or face induction into the military. In an overlapping crisis, post-war inflation led to a nationwide struggle over price controls, climaxing in October 1946 when Truman relaxed ceilings on meat prices. The rail strike and price control controversies posed sharply the extent of the power exercised by the post-war state, and its relationship with labour and business. National concerns pervaded all sides of the debate, as veterans argued over the appropriate powers of the government in the post-war American democracy 'which we were fighting for'. Class also was ever-present in the conversation among veterans – but only rarely a defining element.[27]

After Truman forced the railroad unions back to work in May 1946, veterans – and other Americans – deluged the president with letters debating his threat to draft strikers. Most veterans who expressed sympathy for the rail strike, while animated by working-class concerns, generally emphasised the compatibility of the strike with national interests and ideals of the recent war. 'I lost many buddies for the principle that the democratic form of government is right and best', Robert Bloch wrote to Truman in a carefully argued letter. Bloch, like several other veterans, used legitimacy conferred through military service to contend that use of the army against strikers was inappropriate, and indeed an 'insult' to men 'taught to pride themselves for wearing this very uniform'. The rhetoric of class, however, remained present, if secondary, in these letters. A veteran who spent 34 months overseas related his 'bitterness' to Truman over the government's suppression of the rail strike as 'it was the people of the United States, and not the "Economic Royalists" whom we defended'. And some called for strong, social democratic measures against the rail companies to end the crisis. Henry Miller, who signed his letter 'Ex soldier/Ex prisoner of war/Ex Democrat', called on Truman to operate the companies as public utilities. These veterans, clearly animated by working-class resentments, nonetheless relied most heavily on nationalist language to express opposition to Truman's action. They also tended to be a young cohort whose formative experiences were in the military, having volunteered or been drafted in their teens.[28]

Among the strike's supporters, it is notable that a substantial minority tended to incorporate the rights of labour and the traditions of the New Deal into their rhetoric. While nationalism among younger men was reflected in appeals to universal icons of the American nation, such as the Constitution, Abraham Lincoln, and America's democratic traditions, this more politicised group used Franklin D. Roosevelt and the New Deal as their reference point. The men in this category tended to be older, in their late twenties and thirties, whose formative experiences were in the crucible of the Great Depression. Veteran Iver Chilson, a Democrat for thirteen years, labelled Truman's statements 'a comfort to big business and a dire warning to all the working people of the U.S.' and promised to 'do all I can to bring back the principles for which I fought'. Another called Truman a 'fink for the railroads' and promised to take electioneering skills honed supporting Roosevelt and apply them to defeat Truman. Despite expression of working-class sensibilities, these veterans nonetheless still drew heavily on America's courageous conduct during the war as the most telling counterpoint to the president's alleged capitulation. Jack Bernard clinched his attack on Truman's failures by thundering he had served in the army for three years 'in a war made necessary because weaklings like you and Neville Chamberlain preferred to compromise with power'. And he pointedly linked Truman's 'appeasement' with attacks on labour by closing his letter with the refrain from the popular union song, 'Which side are you on?'[29]

Critics of the rail strike – and thus supporters of Truman's harsh tactics – almost universally recalled their military experience in the strongest terms, and assailed the strike in nationalist language as 'an attack on humanity and our very country that we have fought hard to preserve'. Yet, as with the pro-strike veterans, class nonetheless infiltrated the rhetoric. Eugene Bassett, who had done 'every conceivable job' before going into the service and losing both legs in European combat, complained about the high wages of rail workers compared to his earnings in various unskilled occupations. He recommended jail for union members who 'refuse to go to work for Uncle Sam' rather than inducting them into the military, because the 'army is to[o] good for them'. These letters also typically drew on wartime rhetoric to label union leaders dictators or war criminals. Reflecting attitudes probably formed among soldiers during the 1943 coal strikes, John L. Lewis was attacked by name more often than the heads of rail unions, even though he had nothing do to with the strike in question.[30]

The twin rhetorical reservoirs of military service and national interest also set the terms of the fractious debate among veterans over price controls. Proponents of controls leveraged their legitimacy as veterans to propose a strong government stand against the deleterious effects on the nation of price inflation. After Truman ended price controls on meat in October 1946, one veteran despaired 'that the government which we fought for so well, which only needs to call out for help and 15 000 000 veterans will respond, is so weak . . . [against] selfish interests'. Some veterans called for seizure of cattle-raising facilities, special sessions of Congress to adopt stricter measures, and other unstated 'immediate action' to ensure the availability of goods at reasonable prices and 'to demonstrate that no industry was stronger than our government'. As former soldiers, they urged the government to not shrink from using strong measures to curtail the powers of business, and to achieve objectives of material benefit to the great majority of patriotic citizens.[31]

The most uncompromising letters linked resentment at ending price controls with a more prevalent sense of betrayal of America's war objectives. 'Those of us who had the duty of actively participating in the recent fight for the liberty of the world have been both disillusioned and angered by the willingness of our representatives to throw away the victory which cost so much', Joseph Ambrose wrote to Truman in 1947. In a few cases, the perceived betrayal of national objectives contributed to a sharper sense of class differences in America. One former sailor, who claimed he first voted for Roosevelt while on route for Great Britain, bemoaned the acquiescence to a 'selfish minority' signalled by ending meat price controls. 'Does that mean all we learned about democracy was bunk?' he asked Truman. 'Does the majority bow to the wishes of a financially powerful minority?' He promised to 'join the union tomorrow' to ensure that the people of the country could enjoy 'peace and the good things of life'.[32]

While many veterans may have agreed with this sailor that the 'common people' would fare poorly without price controls, they generally did not deploy these notions in a class-structured 'map' of post-war social conflicts. Instead, veterans portrayed themselves as the most aggrieved group. Irving Harris vociferously attacked the 'money bags' who had killed the Office of Price Administration, and linked the ability to pay higher prices with shirking military service. 'Not all of us were able to stack away money while the war was on!!!!!!!!!!' he emphatically told Truman in October 1946. Veterans typically framed resentment at economic difficulties as objections to the obstacles they encountered to use of benefits accorded by the GI Bill of Rights. One disabled veteran attending a state college grudgingly endorsed price controls and rationing 'to assure a fair distribution between those people with a large income and those with a very small one'. Struggling to support himself and his wife on student veteran allotments, he warned that if prices rose, 'people like myself are going to discontinue their search for education and seek employment in factories'. In case Truman didn't get the point, he added, 'That is something that cannot happen.' In both cases, their central complaint was not receiving adequate compensation in peacetime for service in the American military.[33]

Veterans who opposed price controls also debated this issue in terms of national interest and military service. But they alluded to different elements of that experience, especially a dislike for the regimentation of military life and the alienation from the normative framework of civilian life which they endured as soldiers. Throughout the war, soldiers had railed against 'chickenshit' – the many arbitrary rules governing military service – as a violation of their rights as Americans. While granting the necessity for a strict line of command, GIs chafed at the many social privileges accorded commissioned officers which seemed to have no other role than entrenching 'caste' distinctions more appropriate to a 'Prussian Army' than an American one. As the war ended, many GIs spontaneously offered proposals for democratising the military. These sentiments peaked in January 1946, when American GIs in the Pacific and Europe openly defied military discipline and demonstrated against the slow pace of troop demobilisation.[34]

Drawing on this anti-authoritarian strain, former soldiers portrayed price controls as a continuation of government powers which did not belong in the post-war world soldiers had sought to preserve. 'If you think the American people will follow you into a war economy and control over our every move you are wrong', veteran Robert Barden warned Truman in 1947. Some veterans linked this argument to other disturbing disruptions in the nation's cultural fabric they encountered upon returning home. Since returning from the military, 'I have found in this community that you have to know the proper person to get many different items', I.N. Carr complained to Truman from Jefferson City, Tennessee, 'and it appears that there is often involved some form of bribery'. For the sake of the 'morals of our people' he recommended lifting price controls.[35]

While veterans differed over the rail strike and price controls, their arguments negotiated shared concepts and drew on shared themes. Suffusing their arguments was nationalism and veterans' special affiliation with the nation. Veterans generally judged business and labour by their contribution to national interest, and used characterisations of 'selfishness' as the ultimate epithet. Among veterans there were significant differences concerning the appropriate character of state regulation of commerce and labour. But even advocates of aggressive state intervention framed their arguments in national, and not class, terms.

In contrast to the debates among veterans over the appropriate extent of state regulation of labour, business, and commerce, housing was an area in which support for federal initiatives ran deep. If there was a place in which social democratic aspirations would find the most fertile soil, here it was. In this area, it was the decentralised structure of the post-war American state and political alliance in Congress between the Republican Party and conservative southern Democrats that was a more significant obstacle to social democratic possibilities than the sentiments of veterans.

Veterans' specific need for housing interacted with a national housing crisis to generate unusually deep sentiment for strong federal measures. Sometimes veterans' ideas were more fantastic than programmatic, such as Norman Gerard's proposal that the federal government finance 'a beautiful New City, a Memorial City, Peace City or Victory City' whose construction would benefit industry, house veterans, and 'fight this unemployment the same way we fought the war'. More practically, veterans repeatedly called for government initiatives to use military bases and surplus government property for federally-sponsored veterans' housing. It seemed logical to Private John Miller, when he wrote to President Roosevelt in January 1944, that bases located 'practically in every state of the union', possessing 'the basic fundamentals for housing developments' such as sewers and utilities, can be 'readily converted to low-cost housing developments'. As the housing crisis worsened after the war's end, even leaders of state Veterans of Foreign Wars chapters wrote to Truman urging use of military base facilities to house veterans. Unlike the arguments over price controls and labour unions, veterans seemingly called with one voice for strong federal initiatives on housing.[36]

The federal government did respond to pressures from veterans. The Lanham Act and the Federal Temporary Re-Use Housing Program provided for conversion of facilities on government property for housing – just as veterans were demanding. For a short time, the impact was considerable. One-third of all new dwelling units made available in 1946 came from these programmes. However, nothing on the scale of sustained state-sponsored action contemplated by veterans appeared. These two programmes were defined as temporary measures, and the housing industry vigorously resisted expansion of direct federal initiatives to build permanent housing. Not long after the Republican Party swept the November 1946 election, Congress terminated the temporary conversion programmes.[37]

Appeals by veterans to use non-military surplus property for housing also fell on deaf ears. The federal agencies in charge of reconversion prioritised disposing of government assets as quickly as possible, rather than using them to satisfy social needs. Veterans contested these practices by contending they had special rights to federal property formerly used in wartime. In one incident, the American Legion post in Poughkeepsie, New York, led a coalition of veterans' groups (including the liberal American Veterans Committee) in a protest against the sale of Reconstruction Finance Corporation (RFC) property 'for private speculative purposes'. RFC Chairman John D. Goodloe curtly dismissed the protests, as 'diversion' of the land 'to temporary housing purposes would severely impede the sale of the property' and went ahead with the sale to a private developer.[38]

Public rental housing fared no better in reconversion politics. Despite the preference of many veterans for scarce rental accommodations (at least half, according to government surveys), the building of public housing as a proportion of the building of all housing fell from 1.2 per cent in 1946 to a minuscule 0.4 per cent in 1947. The 1949 National Housing Act corrected this slide, but most housing under its provisions was built for low-income residents in major cities, and consistently contributed less than 10 per cent to the nation's housing supply throughout the 1950s.[39]

Frustrated by the limitations of state initiatives, veterans had little choice but to turn to the private housing market, assisted by the GI Bill. Under its provisions veterans could purchase homes with virtually no down payment and receive federal loan guarantees for the remaining amount up to (by 1950) $7500. These benefits had a considerable impact on the fortunes of former soldiers. By 1956, almost 4 million veterans had taken advantage of these guarantees.[40]

The outcome of agitation for housing by veterans – where there was the broadest support for strong federal measures – indicates how the political structures of the post-war American state inhibited expansion of the welfare state. Decentralising the administration of federal housing programmes through state and municipal agencies fragmented struggles for housing by veterans into innumerable local protests that did not have the capacity to alter fundamental government policy. Requiring veterans to secure government-backed loans through private lenders precluded concerted political challenges to the preferences and prejudices of banks and realtors. And by forcing veterans into the private housing market, federal housing policies exacerbated the separation between special veterans' benefits and those available to the non-veteran population, as well as the many cleavages within the veteran population itself.

Race was the most potent source of divisions among veterans over housing, and indeed many of the benefits afforded under the GI Bill. The entitlement of black veterans under that measure conflicted with the limits of Jim Crow in the South and traditions of racial separation in the North. A 1946 study by the American Council on Race Relations found that minority veterans rarely had access to the emergency veterans' housing programmes, and were restricted to residential areas that generally did not qualify for federally-guaranteed loans under the GI Bill.[41]

A poignant appeal to Truman by partially-disabled black veteran Herman Woodard indicates how racial obstacles in housing remained unchecked by the GI Bill. Although he had left a skilled job in a cement plant and his family to give 'my country the best of my service', he now faced homelessness. The Nashville Housing Authority had served eviction papers on Woodard, allegedly for earning more than permitted in public housing, and he was unable to purchase a home under the GI Bill. In Nashville real estate agents reserved the 'nice new houses built all over town' for white veterans, and only made available 'old ragged houses in the white settlements to colored people for double what they are worth'. Moreover, white veterans had no trouble obtaining government-guaranteed loans for 100 per cent of a home's purchase price, while blacks had to provide at least $1000 for a down payment. Buttressing his argument by including real estate advertisements that reflected these discriminatory policies, Woodard concluded by appealing for Truman to investigate how 'they really are hard on the Negro Veterans here'.[42]

Woodard's contrast between patriotic service in the war and restricted post-war opportunities was replicated in many other letters by black veterans. 'We had the right to enter service we had the right to go overseas and fight and die', black veteran Frank Saunch wrote to Truman in 1945. 'It was all to help protect this Great Nation the USA don't you think we deserve more rights and privileges just like everyone else.' Black veterans often linked general statements such as these with specific grievances. In one case, a group of black veterans complained to Truman that the Los Angeles City Council had refused to grant them a franchise to operate a taxi cab co-operative, even though they had fulfilled the same requirements as a successful company composed of white veterans. 'We fought for our country and are proud of it. Now we would be so grateful to be able to earn a honest living like any respectable man', they stated simply.[43]

In making these complaints blacks routinely contrasted the country's wartime democratic rhetoric with the existence of legal racial discrimination in America. A few went as far as one black sergeant who wrote to Eleanor Roosevelt that the 'colored soldier in the south someday is going to wake up and forget about the rules of Democracy it will no doubt cost a lot of lives, but I hope to God I'll be able to give mine for a real cause'. More commonly black servicemen made the essential, and irrefutable, observation that Jim Crow was inconsistent with American war propaganda. 'If we are fighting for Democracy why not begin Right here in Mississippi?' one soldier said. And they repeatedly predicted that the expected victory over the Axis 'prescribes the doom' of racial barriers in America.[44]

The contrast between the war's democratic rhetoric and American racial practices also influenced white servicemen. The uncomfortable parallel between the racial policies of Nazi Germany and the American South frequently stimulated discomfort among white GIs, especially when an incident brought this dilemma into sharp relief. White soldiers were outraged when black Corporal Rupert Trimmingham complained in *Yank* that he had been barred from a southern restaurant because of his race, while German POWs received a courteous welcome. One southern soldier wrote that it was a 'disgrace' and asked 'are we not waging a war, in part, for this fundamental of democracy?'[45]

For white soldiers who had contacts with blacks in combat situations, racism seems to have been considerably moderated. 'I have fought from D-Day to VE-day with Negro soldiers', wrote a sergeant from Mississippi, who credited one black GI with saving his life. If Americans planned to forgive the Germans after the war, 'why not let the Negro race have what they fought for?' A disabled service man wrote to Truman that, as a veteran who had fought with blacks, 'I *know* the colored service men did their best . . . to protect the interests of our country and the good old stars and stripes'. Based on what he knew of the treatment of blacks in the South, he appealed for Truman 'to just set your foot down'. However, sympathy among white veterans for blacks rarely translated into support for social equality. Typically, this veteran hastened to add that he still believed 'in negroes keeping their place'. Comments such as these indicate that even white veterans inclined towards legal equality for blacks still preferred to retain a social distance between the races.[46]

As the limited support for civil rights by even this sympathetic veteran indicates, the issue of the rights of black veterans exposed divisions among former soldiers and sailors over the pertinence of the military experience to the implementation of peacetime policies. Among some white veterans, opposition to black rights was facilitated by the pattern of segregation in the Second World War military which generally placed blacks in service divisions that replicated their subordinate place in the domestic labour market. One veteran wrote to Congressman John Rankin that he opposed civil rights measures for blacks because of his experiences with the conduct of black labour battalions overseas, especially during the Okinawa invasion where some 'went on a sit down strike' and had to be replaced by white sailors. Another told Harry Truman that he had 'eaten, slept, and worked with negro troops' in Europe and felt no prejudice towards blacks 'as long as I don't have to eat with them, work with them, live with them'. For these men, the military experience had only provided more evidence to support racial separation.[47]

Far more typical among racist whites, however, were letters which simply denied that military service entitled blacks to anything at all. Its only relevance was the tendency to encourage improper attitudes and behaviour among blacks. 'This talk of giving the Negro social rights is slowly leading to a race war', a soldier complained to Eleanor Roosevelt in 1944. He warned that as a result of fraternisation between black soldiers and English women, 'many of them think they will return to the states & run around with our sisters or girl friends. That's when the war will start.' Most letters opposing civil rights echoed this theme that ending segregation would lead to social equality and miscegenation. 'Would you like for your daughter to arrive at home . . . with a negro escort?' southern veteran Charles Ross asked Harry Truman rhetorically. 'Would you welcome a negro man and his wife to your home to have dinner with you and your wife?' These GIs saw preservation of existing race relations as one of the things they had fought for, and any alteration of barriers between black and white as a threat to establishing stable civilian lives.[48]

The demobilisation process heightened these fears, as it was unclear how including black GIs under government programmes for veterans would affect race relations. In one case, white veterans in Merigold, Mississippi mobilised against the effort of a nearby black town to have a black Veterans Administration hospital built there. Mississippi Congressman John Rankin apologetically explained that he wanted to put an 'all-negro hospital' in the state 'so as to take care of negro veterans without sending them to our white hospitals'. In view of the protest, though, he promised to find another location.[49]

For these former soldiers, their military service had earned white men the right to the perpetuation of the American system of racial segregation. They interpreted military service as part of a patriotic duty linked to old American traditions, not the particular overtones of the struggle against fascism in the Second World War. One southern veteran even went so far as to refer to his grandfather 'wearing the grey' of the Confederacy to certify himself as a patriotic American with the right to define the character of post-war society. Racial fears, and the white supremacist attitudes it fed, thus constituted a major impediment to the construction of post-war social democratic measures in which national citizenship defined access to social benefits.[50]

CONCLUSION

Not long before the fighting ended Langston Hughes wrote a poem which spoke to the contested meaning of the war's legacy. In 'Will V-Day be Me-Too Day?' Hughes asked:

> Here in my own, my native land
> Will the Jim Crow laws still stand?
> Will Dixie lynch me still
> When I return?
> Or will you comrades in arms
> From the factories and the farms,
> Have learned what this war
> Was fought for us to learn?[51]

Despite its optimistic hopes for the war's aftermath, Hughes' poem also acknowledged the conflict among former soldiers over what the Second

World War had accomplished. Without doubt their rhetorical appeals to national interest, certified through military service, had enormous resonance in domestic politics. These calls, however, tended to obscure underlying disagreements over which national traditions were validated by America's conduct in the Second World War. Was it a war against fascism and intolerance, a war to secure equal opportunity for the 'common man', a war to protect individuals from government control of private life, or a war to ensure the preservation of old American traditions? The talk about national interests thus became articulated with other elements of soldiers' identities, especially race and class. It was easy to maintain a facade of agreement among the veterans until the particular conflicts of the immediate post-war years exposed the fissures among former combatants.

We know the outcome of these arguments. Veterans proved willing to accept a restricted welfare state that benefited them far more than most Americans. Government benefits were a due reward for service, not citizenship. In this manner, the nationalist line of argumentation that underlay pro-statist arguments in veterans' rhetoric mitigated against 'labourite' politics among working-class veterans, as well as support for broadly based social democratic policies in post-war America.

The experience of Second World War soldiers indicates how 'working-class Americanism', to adopt Gary Gerstle's phrase, was powerfully influenced by military service.[52] Wartime left a patriotic frame of reference deeply burned into veterans, and the many millions touched by them through family ties. This indicates the great importance of appreciating the complex legacy of the military experience among the veterans who subsequently went to work at wage labour. Explicating the impact of military service requires that we attend to the actual experience of war, and its affect on notions of masculinity, race, nation, and social class among enlisted men. We can no longer consider military service an unimportant parenthesis in the lives of American workers. It certainly was crucial to them.

NOTES

1. This paper was made possible by support from the Franklin and Eleanor Roosevelt Institute, the Harry S. Truman Library Institute, the American Council of Learned Societies, and the Hagley Museum and Library. To a

great extent it was inspired by the methodology and work of Judy Barrett Litoff and David C. Smith. The paper draws on approximately 600 letters; only those directly quoted or referred to are cited. Abbreviations in the endnotes refer to the following manuscript collections:

HT OF Harry Truman papers, Official File, Harry S. Truman Library, Independence, Missouri.; HT PPF Harry Truman papers, President's Personal File, Harry S. Truman Presidential Library, Independence, Missouri.; ER Eleanor Roosevelt papers, Franklin D. Roosevelt Library, Hyde Park, New York; FDR PSF Franklin D. Roosevelt papers, President's Secretary's File, Franklin D. Roosevelt Library, Hyde Park, New York; FDR OF Franklin D. Roosevelt papers, Official File, Franklin D. Roosevelt Library, Hyde Park, New York; RC Record Group 233, US House of Representatives papers, House Committee on World War Veterans Legislation 79th Congress, Legislation Reference Branch, National Archives. Generally known as the Rankin Committee, as it was chaired by Mississippi Democrat John Rankin; UPWA United Packinghouse Workers of America papers, State Historical Society of Wisconsin, Madison, Wisconsin.

2. Jean Y. Tussey ed., *Eugene Debs Speaks* (New York, 1970), 261.
3. Roger Horowitz, *'Negro and White Unite and Fight': A Social History of Industrial Unionism in Meatpacking, 1930–1990* (Urbana, IL, forthcoming 1997); Peter Karsten, *Soldiers and Society: The Effects of Military Service and War on American Life* (Westport, CT, 1978); Lee Kennett, *G.I.: The American Soldier in World War II* (New York, 1987); Samuel A. Stouffer, *The American Soldier* vols I–IV (Princeton, 1949); William Skelton, 'Soldiers as Workers, The Old Army Experience, 1820–1860', paper presented at the October 1994 Social Science History Conference; Thomas A. Moore, 'Unions and Veterans: A History of Veteran Status and Membership in the Labor Movement after World War II' (unpublished PhD dissertation, Wayne State University, in progress).
4. Richard H. Kohn, 'The Social History of the American Soldier: A Review and Prospectus for Research', *American Historical Review* 86:3 (June 1981), 560.
5. Reid Mitchell, *The Vacant Chair: The Northern Soldier Leaves Home* (New York, 1993), 12.
6. Warren Wilkerson, *Mother, May You Never See the Sights I Have Seen: The Fifty-Seventh Massachusetts Veteran Volunteers in the Army of the Potomac, 1864–1865* (New York, 1990); David Power Conyngham, *The Irish Brigade and its Campaigns* (New York, 1994, originally published 1867); Lawrence Federick Kohl, ed., *Irish Green and Union Blue: The Civil War Letters of Peter Walsh* (New York, 1986).
7. Stephen Skowronek, *Building a New American State: The Expansion of National Administrative Capacities, 1877–1920* (New York, 1982); Theda Skocpol, *Protecting Soldiers and Mothers: The Political Origins of Social Policy in the United States* (Cambridge, MA, 1992); David Ross, *Preparing for Ulysses: Politics and Veterans During World War II* (New York, 1969); Edwin Amenta and Theda Skocpol, 'Redefining the New Deal: World War II and the Development of Social Provisions in the U.S.', in Margaret

Weir *et al.*, eds, *The Politics of Social Policy in the United States* (Princeton, 1988).

8. Quoted in John Ellis, *The Sharp End: The Fighting Man in World War II* (New York, 1980), 15.
9. Stephen E. Ambrose, *Band of Brothers* (New York, 1992), 157. These dynamics are closely examined in Leonard V. Smith, *Between Mutiny and Obedience, The Case of the French Fifth Infantry Division During World War II* (Princeton, 1994).
10. Paul Fussell, 'Chickenshit: An Anatomy', in *Wartime: Understanding and Behavior in the Second World War* (New York, 1989); Bill Mauldin, *Up Front* (New York, 1991, orig. published 1944), 179, 184.
11. Stephen E. Ambrose, *D-Day, June 6, 1944: the Climactic Battle of World War II* (New York, 1994), 342.
12. Quoted in Ambrose, *Band of Brothers*, 19.
13. Stan Weir, 'The Informal Work Group', in *Rank and File*, Alice and Staughton Lynd, eds (Princeton, 1973), 196.
14. Allan Berube, *Coming Out Under Fire: The History of Gay Men and Women in World War Two* (New York, 1990).
15. John Modell and Duane Steffey, 'Waging War and Marriage: Military Service and Family Formation, 1940–1950', *Journal of Family History*, 13:2 (1988), 196–7.
16. J. Porter Reilly to Harry Truman, 3 January 1946, HT PPF 200, Box 265.
17. On the use of letters, see William M. Tuttle, Jr, *'Daddy's Gone to War': The Second World War in the Lives of America's Children* (New York, 1993), x–xii; Craig M. Cameron, *American Samurai: Myth, Imagination, and the Conduct of Battle in the First Marine Division, 1941–1951* (New York, 1994), 17; Judy Barrett Litoff and David C. Smith, *Miss You: The World War II Letters of Barbara Woodall Taylor and Charles E. Taylor* (New York, 1990), x–xi; Regina Kunzel, 'Pulp Fiction and Problem Girls: Reading and Rewriting Single Pregnancy in the Postwar United States', *American Historical Review*, 100:5 (December 1995), 1465–87.
18. R.J. Engomar to President Truman, 3 January 1946, HT PPF 200, Box 262.
19. Sergeant Bernard W. Lohbauer, *Yank*, 31 August 1945; John A. Miller to the President, 16 January 1944, FDR OF 4351, Box 3; Anonymous letter in *Yank*, 16 November 1945; United Enlisted Veterans of America resolution, 21 February 1946, RC HR 79A-F38.2; Parke W.W. Masters to the President, 19 May 1944, FDR OF 4361, Box 3; Joseph Scott to C.H. McDaniel, 7 August 1946, HT OF 190-A; 'Veterans Cooperative Industries Plan' by Sergeant A.W. Roitel, RC HR 79A-F38.2.
20. Norman P. Salz to Eleanor Roosevelt, 7 May 1944, ER 1793; Pvt. Robert M. Brewer, *Yank*, 31 May 1945; Charles Beverly, Sgt Ralph Shaw, and Cpl Robert Hayden, *Yank*, 4 May 1945.
21. *Fortune*, April 1946, 266, 268; Stouffer, *The American Soldier*, II, 638.
22. See *Yank*, 19 May 1944 for discussion of the allotment issue; M. Mandel to Eleanor Roosevelt, 11 May 1944, ER 1789.
23. J.W. Grooms, *Yank*, 22 December 1944; 'GI Bill of Rights', *Yank*, 4 May 1945; J.R. Young, *Yank*, 22 December 1944.
24. Leon G. Jackson to Harry Truman, 5 January 1946, HT PPF 200, Box 268;

Nelson Lichtenstein, 'From Corporatism to Collective Bargaining: Organised Labor and the Eclipse of Social Democracy in the Post-War Era', in *The Rise and Fall of the New Deal Order, 1930–1980*, Steve Fraser and Gary Gerstle, eds (Princeton, 1989), 122–52.

25. Robert A. Cole to Harry S. Truman, 4 January 1946, HT PPF 200, Box 267. Auto workers pay from Bureau of Labor Statistics table in UPWA papers Box 196, folder 7.

26. G.J. Winner, *Yank*, 10 March 1945; Joseph D. Norris to President Truman, 3 January 1946, HT PPF 200, Box 264.

27. Frank McClure to Truman, 27 May 1946, HT PPF 200, Box 286.

28. Robert Bloch to Truman, 27 May 1946, HT PPF 200, Box 294; Irving Chapman to Truman, 28 May 1946, HT PPF 200, Box 294; Henry Miller to Truman, 27 May 1946, HT PPF 200, Box 297.

29. Iver Chilson to Truman, 26 May 1946, HT PPF 200, Box 293; Kenneth Born to Truman 26 May 1946, HT PPF 200, Box 294; Jack Bernard to Truman, 28 May 1946, HT PPF 200, Box 294.

30. Eugene Bassett, 28 May 1946, HT PPF 200, Box 287; Bill Barrett to Truman, 24 May 1946, HT PPF 200, Box 287; Roy Anderson to Truman, 27 May 1946, HT PPF 200, Box 286; Robert Marlow to Truman, 27 May 1946, HT PPF 200, Box 286.

31. J.L. Dunlay to Truman, 14 October 1946, HT PPF 200, Box 303, quotes one and three; Norman Garmezy to Truman, 15 October 1946, HT PPF 200, Box 303; Sol Gorelick to Truman, 14 October 1946, HT PPF 200, Box 303; Jean Jeffords, *et al.*, to Truman, 30 June 1947, RC HR 79A-F38.1. Veterans like Philip Levitas also reminded Truman of his attack on the rail strike a few months earlier for resisting the authority of the government. 'Pray, tell me is there a much clearer sit-down strike against all the people of this land' than withholding meat, Philip Levitas to Truman, 14 October 1946, HT PPF 200, Box 303.

32. Joseph Ambrose to Truman, 18 November 1947, HT PPF 200, Box 303; Haskell Wexler to Truman, n.d., HT PPF 200, Box 303.

33. Irving Harris to Truman, 14 October 1946, HT PPF 200, Box 303; Keith King to Truman, 18 November 1947, HT PPF 200, Box 307. This was a common theme in the letters of veterans trying to attend school in 1946 and 1947. One veteran councillor in a Los Angeles Junior College wrote to Truman in November 1946, 'We have more students dropping from school for necessity of obtaining a living existence than for any other reason.' Stuart E. Marsee to Truman, 18 November 1946, HT PPF 200, Box 307.

34. Fussell, 'Chickenshit', 79–95; Research Branch, War Department, 'Survey of Soldier Opinion: United States Army Forces in the Middle East', FDR PSF, Box 91; Anthony F. Petritz, *Yank*, 16 November 1945; P. J. Restivo, *Yank*, 10 August 1945; On the January 1946 protests, see Steven Ashby, 'Shattered Dreams: The American Working Class and the Origins of the Cold War, 1945–1949' (unpublished PhD dissertation, University of Chicago, 1993), 125–72.

35. Robert Barden, Jr to Truman, 17 November 1947, HT PPF 200, Box 307; I.N. Carr to Truman, 15 October 1946, HT PPF 200, Box 302.

36. Norman Gerard to John Rankin, 19 August 1945, RC HR 79A-F38.1; John

Miller to Franklin D. Roosevelt, 16 January 1944, FDR OF Box 3; M.L. Welty to Truman, 29 June 1945, HT OF 345; Joe Deenabury to Truman, 12 January 1946, HT OF 345.

37. US Department of Labor, *Construction and Housing, 1946–1947*, Bureau of Labor Statistics Report No. 941 (Washington DC, 1948), 19–21; US Department of Labor, *Nonfarm Housing Starts, 1889–1958*, Bureau of Labor Statistics Bulletin 1260 (Washington DC, 1959).

38. Paul Samuels to William Hassett, 19 June 1947 and John Goodloe to Samuels, 30 June 1947, HT OF 63 Miscellaneous, Box 368. See in the same box Robert S. Eberly to Truman, 2 March 1947; Francis Ahearn to Truman, 13 May 1947.

39. *Construction and Housing, 1946–1947*, 22, 17; *Nonfarm Housing Starts, 1889–1958*, 32–4.

40. David Ross, *Waiting For Ulysses: Politics and Veterans During World War II* (New York, 1969), 272.

41. American Council on Race Relations, 'Survey of Community Veterans Information Centers', 29 March 1946, HT OF 190-L; Kenneth T. Jackson, *Crabgrass Frontier: The Suburbanization of the United States* (New York, 1985), 204–15; David H. Onkst, '"First a Negro . . . incidently a Veteran": Black World War Two Veterans and the G.I. Bill of Rights in the Deep South, 1944–1948', paper presented at the October 1995 'Aftermath' conference at the Hagley Museum and Library, Wilmington DE.

42. Herman Woodard to Truman, 16 April 1948, HT OF 63 Miscellaneous, Box 369.

43. Frank Saunch to Truman, 5 March 1948, HT PPF 200, Box 312; Eastside Taxi Cab Veterans Association to Truman, 1 February 1947, HT OF 190A.

44. Grady O. Shank to Eleanor Roosevelt, 14 January 1945, ER 1799; Sgt Richard Lacy to Eleanor Roosevelt, 27 May 1944, ER 1788; Arthur Russell Teasdale, 'Why I Fight', 29 July 1944, ER 1994.

45. Henry S. Wooten, Jr, *Yank*, 9 June 1944.

46. Willie Jones, *Yank*, 14 September 1945; V.J. Campbell to Truman, 12 March 1948, HT PPF 200, Box 309.

47. Edward Foster to John Rankin, 23 July 1945, RC HR 79A-F38.2; Truman Hinshaw to Truman, 18 February 1948, HT PPF 200, Box 313.

48. Edward John Cass to Eleanor Roosevelt, 4 July 1944, ER 1784; Charles Ross to Truman, 13 April 1946, HT PPF 200, Box 314.

49. J.E. Rankin to I.C. Rayner, 27 June 1945 and attachments, RC HR 79A-F38.2.

50. Henry Lee to RC, 21 June 1945, RC HR 79A-F38.2.

51. Arnold Rampersand, ed., *The Collected Poems of Langston Hughes* (New York, 1994), 304.

52. Gary Gerstle, *Working-Class Americanism: The Politics of Labor in a Textile City, 1914–1960* (New York, 1989).

6 The Limits of Liberalism: Working-Class Formation in Britain and the United States
Neville Kirk

THE LIBERAL 'TURN'

In the wake of the collapse of Stalinism in eastern Europe, the increasing globalisation of capital and its attendant social relations, the defeats and retreats of labour-movement collectivism and Social Democracy, and their accelerated accommodation to the rule of 'The Market', democratic and market-based liberalism, whether of the deregulated or 'social-market' based variety, has become all the rage in western political and academic circles. This observation holds true for both those besuited and stridently ascendant 'rational-choice' theorists who dominate many of the international conferences of political scientists and economists and, ironically, for many of those subscribing to the more sceptical, anti-systemic and relativist tenets of post-modernism. Modern-day liberalism, complete with its proclamations in favour of the natural qualities of (largely unfettered) individualism and competition, market-embeddedness and the pursuit of the 'main chance', the individual maximisation of pleasure, flexibility, and choice, the minimisation of individual pain, and the superior claims of the 'self' over the 'social', has become the new master narrative of the late twentieth century.

As deconstructionists have been quick to remind us, and as historians have long known, words can and do take on a variety of meanings within different contexts, over time and in the minds of diverse individuals and social groups (the epistemological status of the 'modernist' historian's identification of *key* meanings of words is not the immediate point at issue). Within this context it is imperative to consider the ways in which the words liberalism (as political theory) and Liberalism (as political ideas and a political movement) have recently been employed by those historians in the United States and Britain who share two central propositions: that attention to the tenets of liberal political theory holds a rich and largely undiscovered

store of benefits for the labour historian; and that liberal ideas in both countries and the politics of radical Liberalism in Britain have been factors of
major, if academically neglected, importance among nineteenth- and early
twentieth-century workers and organised labour movements.

Of special note in the American context has been the work of Ira
Katznelson. In his article 'The "Bourgeois" Dimension: A Provocation
About Institutions, Politics, and the Future of Labor History', Katznelson
argues that a (re)turn to the study of politics and institutions, with special
reference to the issues of the specifications of state power, the nature and
roles of the law and political parties, and the 'linkages between the state
and the capitalist economy and between the state and civil society' might
'help jump-start a field facing problems of self-definition'.[1] For example,
the 'neglected' and 'underappreciated', 'liberal' and non-teleological ('even
if doggedly atheoretical') work of Henry Pelling is viewed by Katznelson
as providing 'a potentially rich source of nourishment for any return to
the study of politics', in that 'it is integrated . . . by a central, unwavering
theme: the quest to understand how the labour movement in Britain . . . has
forged institutional ties of representation, influence, and negotiation with
the state within a broadly liberal framework of rights and citizenship'.
And, 'today within labor history there is no single body of work as accomplished as Pelling's that takes seriously a relational approach to the ties
between the state and the working class via an analysis of their institutions
considered in a larger regime framework'.[2]

Katznelson does accept the argument that, if judged by the overall standard of its empirical work, then labour history *cannot* currently 'be judged
to be in a state of scholarly crisis'. However, notwithstanding these empirical strengths, political defeats for the Left and the welcome advent of
feminist and other concerns with forms of identity beyond class have,
according to Katznelson, stripped labour history of its 'unitary theoretical
grounding', and effectively toppled both class as the master narrative of
modern history and 'the credibility of a forward march for labor'. As a
result, there has occurred a 'loss of elan, directionality, and intellectual
purpose'.[3] Katznelson judges the restricted and often mutually aggressive
dualisms characteristic of recent and ongoing debates between 'traditional
materialism' and post-modernism to be highly unproductive and damaging
to the discipline. And,

> these alternatives also are politically debilitating because they make
> labor history either hostage to the fate of problematical movements and
> political tendencies or eradicate the specificities of class structure and
> agency altogether.[4]

In Katznelson's opinion, labour history can move out of the current impasse and recover its sense of purpose and direction by two means: honest, open and *productive* engagements on the part of different approaches and methodologies; and, crucially, the attainment of a new synthesis which brings together the material, discursive, institutional, political and cultural dimensions of people's lives. Thus,

> I do not counsel the abandonment of history done on materialist premises nor do I suggest we reject out of hand the postmodern turn. Rather, I urge they be kept in useful tension and that they both should be joined in a relationship with once-hegemonic but now-less-fashionable polit- ical, institutional, and state-focused themes within labor history. I should like these elements to join issues of class and identity to provide the third main pillar for labor history.[5]

Similarly, in outlining his future liberal agenda for labour history, Katznelson is not counselling the uncritical adoption of either the self- proclaimed past and present tenets of liberalism or liberal/Liberal politics. Pluralism and openness, as opposed to closure and narrow partisanship, are the defining characteristics of Katznelson's manifesto. He declares,

> My aim is not to propose a lurch away from labor history's other pre- occupations, nor is it to endorse a particular kind of liberal politics; my aim is to note that an engagement with liberal theory that is both open- minded and skeptical might produce a two-way process of interrogation in which questions drawn from liberal theory could inform the research of labor historians and the resources possessed by labor history could be utilized to critically interrogate liberalism's claims.[6]

We might suggest at this point that Katznelson's fashionable commit- ments to openness, scepticism and the 'multi-factor' approach to historical study amount to little more than traditional liberal pluralism, complete with its somewhat 'weak' tendencies to prize description over analysis (as epitomised in the work of Pelling) and to shy away from the necessary attempt on the part of the historian to arrange a variety of factors into some order of causal priority. And we might also wish to question both the novelty of Katznelson's proposed agenda for labour historians, and the extent to which, historically, liberalism has been able adequately to ad- dress and embrace the concerns and experiences of workers.[7]

Before proceeding to a more detailed elaboration of these criticisms, it is, however, first of all necessary to investigate liberalism's historical 'claims', in terms of its stock of political ideas, in both the United States and Britain. Within this context Katznelson suggests that, just as liberal theory offers the labour historian a range of questions and perspectives which can be applied fruitfully to the study of the past, so attention to the historical record of liberalism, as a set of political ideas and movements, can serve to enrich and broaden our knowledge and understanding of workers' and labour movements' political choices and allegiances. For example, as shown in the work of Pelling and more recently in that of Eugenio Biagini and Alastair Reid, radical–liberal ideas, and particularly such ideas as expressed in the radical or 'advanced' wing of the British Liberal Party, enjoyed massive support among working people in Britain during the nineteenth and early twentieth centuries. What is more, claims Katznelson (and Biagini and Reid), both the full popular appeal of nineteenth-century liberal and Liberal ideas in Britain and the 'tightly, if problematically, intertwined' relations between the socialist and liberal traditions in 'much of the West', have been 'vastly underplayed' by labour historians, and especially by those labour historians operating within materialist, class-based frameworks of analysis.[8]

Historically, observes Katznelson, liberal ideas have *not* stood as a pure-and-simple synonym for the kind of current de-regulated or even 'social-market' capitalisms referred to at the beginning of this chapter. The present cannot be read into the past in such simplistic and narrow ways. Katznelson thus makes reference, albeit in far too cursory a manner, to the richness of liberalism as a stock of historical ideas. Liberalism, we are informed, has signified, especially within the context of US history, commitments to 'economic markets and representative democracy'; to citizenship, and equal rights; to the toleration of individual choice and freedom in matters of life style and values; to procedural and civil rights designed to safeguard individual choice and freedoms against the undue power and influence of the state, other individuals and interest groups; and to the achievement of a fair balance between the rights and duties of citizenship and individual, community- and state-based needs.[9] Such liberal commitments, it is *implied* (for Katznelson does not explicitly detail or substantiate this view) have exerted an enduring hegemonic influence upon ideological and political discourse in the United States, and have accordingly, if variably, embraced large numbers of Republicans, Democrats and even third-party and other challengers to the *status quo*. Katznelson does make brief reference to some of the historical tensions and conflicts *within* liberalism, such as its 'tendency to mask questions of inequality and social power' and 'privilege grounded in the class structure and patriarchy'. But such tensions are not adequately pursued. And we are given the distinct impression that liberalism, at least in the United States, has possessed in the past, and continues to demonstrate, in-built systemic checks and correcting mechanisms designed successfully to 'manage the tensions inherent in a liberal order'.[10]

In sum, Katznelson's dominant emphases upon the largely pluralistic, consensual, stable and non-coercive nature of US liberalism are manifest. Functionalism, rooted in the successful and largely harmonious production and reproduction of US liberalism, lies at the core of his analysis. We might also suggest that the current malaise of the Left and organised labour in the US and Europe and the loudly proclaimed 'victories' of market-based liberal capitalism have also been more influential in setting Katznelson's agenda than he leads us to believe.

Whereas Katznelson's treatment of the historical content of liberalism in the United States lacks adequate empirical substantiation, the nature and content of nineteenth-century British liberal thought and of popular Liberalism have been well documented by a number of historians, including seminal contributions by Brian Harrison and Patricia Hollis, John Vincent and Peter Clarke.[11] Within this context the recent work of Jon Lawrence, Miles Taylor, Alastair Reid and Eugenio Biagini (all trained in the historical profession at Cambridge University, and greatly indebted to the inspiration and guidance of Gareth Stedman Jones) has been of particular importance.[12] Indeed, Katznelson's article draws considerable strength not only from the work of Pelling but also from their 'pathbreaking' endeavours.

Biagini's and Reid's 'central thesis' is that 'there was a substantial continuity in popular radicalism throughout the nineteenth and into the twentieth century', as expressed in the view that 'those who were originally called Chartists, were afterwards called Liberal and Labour activists'.[13] Reaching its apogee between the 1860s and 1880s in the progressive or 'advanced' wing of Gladstonian Liberalism, popular radicalism demonstrated continuity in a number of abiding commitments and causes: 'for open government and the rule of law, for freedom from intervention both at home and abroad, and for individual liberty and community-centred democracy'.

Some of these themes were voiced in popular slogans like 'anti-corruption' and 'fair play', usually directed against familiar 'parasites' like the landed aristocracy, financiers and the established Church. And some of them were embodied in a vision of the ideal citizen-patriot who would be independent of both government pressure and excessive party loyalty . . . Within this broad tendency there were differences over how far government ought to be *by* the people, but demands for the extension of the franchise were one of the most outstanding continuities in the main stream, and radicalism in general was democratic in its commitment to government *for* the people and with their consent, and to the prevention of tyranny through the constitutional separation of powers.[14]

Drawing upon a long historical pedigree – from 'Renaissance humanism', the 'Calvinist project for the Reformation of the Church' through to the seventeenth-century 'Puritan Revolution' and the eighteenth-century 'country' opposition – radicalism, and especially radical liberalism, put down genuinely popular roots. In the nineteenth century, claim Biagini and Reid (along with Stedman Jones and Patrick Joyce)[15] radicalism spoke more the language of personal and collective 'independence', of 'individual and community self-determination' (as being 'vital to the survival of liberty'), of accountable, popular government, and of 'the people', the 'producers' and 'humankind' than those of class-based exploitation in production and the alienated and isolated proletarian cast adrift in a deregulated market sea. By the 1860s Liberalism sought to embrace the 'independent minded', 'improving', 'self-helping', 'respectable' and 'morally-earnest' of all classes who believed in a capitalist economy 'tempered by the rule of law' and notions of 'fairness' and reciprocity between employer and employed. Opposition to authoritarian and militaristic rule, combined with commitments to limited and cost-conscious government (consistent with efficiency and 'fairness'), free trade and reductions in taxation, and all manner of 'progressive' political and social causes (such as enhanced civil and religious liberty, educational and public-health improvement schemes and, in some cases, votes for women and feminism) were also widely claimed to be special radical and Liberal attributes.[16] Making due allowance for hyperbole on the part of Liberal claims to represent the will of 'the people', and the considerable purchase of the Conservative Party on the allegiances of sections of the very same 'people',[17] the genuinely popular nature of Victorian Liberalism cannot be doubted.

Biagini and Reid thus share with Katznelson a historical view of liberalism markedly at odds with that peddled by Margaret Thatcher, Ronald Reagan and their acolytes. Thus:

> Popular radicals and intellectual liberals alike stressed that individual liberty had a meaning only within the collective identity provided by local self-governing units, and in this way Victorian liberalism was also clearly quite different from the dogmatic individualism which has been championed by the 'New Right' in the 1980s, frequently under the banner of 'Victorian values'.[18]

In contrast, however, to Katznelson's call for labour history to become more pluralistic and eclectic in character, Biagini and Reid's work, along with that of Lawrence and Stedman Jones, challenges fundamentally the continued right of a materialist historical interpretation to be at the heart of the labour historian's future agenda. As against the materialist argument that class feeling (of a predominantly economic kind) and discontinuity were central to developments in nineteenth- and early twentieth-century popular political consciousness and behaviour – as seen in the 'making' (1790s to 1830s) of class and the growth of Chartism; the 'unmaking' (1840s to 1870s) and the ascendancy of liberal radicalism; and the 're-making' (1880s to 1900s) and the revival of socialism and the birth of the Labour Party – Biagini and Reid offer a very different interpretation of events and processes. Radical ideas and languages are claimed to be largely continuous and inter-class, based in character throughout the period in question. Materialist and other[19] emphases upon discontinuities between Chartism and Liberalism and Liberalism and the birth of the Labour Party, supposedly rooted in the experiential conflicts of class and wider social and political experiences, are downplayed and/or denied. Just as radicalism remained pretty much of a coherent whole throughout the period, so, we are told, did workers' notions of class and class conflict remain limited. Important differences rooted in occupation, skill, geographical 'place', sectionalism and culture and cross-class political and other ties persisted with great force to deny the validity of Marx's prediction that the proletariat would become more united and revolutionary. Furthermore, as demonstrated in the close ties between Chartism and Liberalism, and in the case of early twentieth-century Progressivism, radicalism was largely successful in responding to and accommodating periodic increases in class consciousness among workers. Whatever changes did take place in politics, such as the decline of Chartism and the birth and growth of the Labour Party, are, claim Biagini and Reid, to be explained primarily in political rather than materialist ways. Much in keeping with the traditions of historical scholarship at Cambridge University, Biagini and Reid thus lay claim to the primacy of politics and political ideas, as opposed to the material or 'social' factors, in the historical process. Labour historians should set their future agendas accordingly.[20]

Finally, Biagini, Reid and other contributors to their edited volume on *Currents of Radicalism* place a 'strong emphasis' upon the 'continuity of radicalism' into the twentieth century, and the continued relevance and appeal of radical liberal ideas (such as 'individual liberty' and 'local democracy') to the Labour Party and its supporters up to the Second World War and beyond. Indeed, it is provocatively suggested by Biagini and Reid that much of the party's outlook in the twentieth century has in effect been radical liberal rather than socialist in character (despite the frequent and misleading resort to the language of 'socialism' on the part of Labour leaders); and that all those concerned with Labour's future wellbeing would be well advised to take due prescriptive note of this fact.

If from this point of view the Labour party begins to look like the major party of twentieth-century radical liberalism, it is not as a result of some decline from the ideals of its founders, or of some deficit in their political thought, but rather of an understandable commitment to a political tradition which has proved its effectiveness in both theory and practice over a long period of time. . . . it seems to us that the Labour party's ability to play a leading role in broad progressive movements in the future will be strengthened if it becomes more restrained in its tendency to legitimise its policies primarily in relation to 'socialism', and if it develops more self-consciousness of, and more pride in, its relation to currents of radicalism.[21]

In contrast to Katznelson's declared aim of *not* endorsing 'a particular kind of liberal politics', Biagini and Reid are therefore keen to advertise their perceived virtues of radical liberalism, in terms both of its past history and its current partisan political relevance. In addition to arguably providing historical sustenance to the views of progressives, such as Tony Blair, the 'committed' work of Reid, Biagini and other members of the 'Cambridge School' has utilised present political concerns to enable us to think more openly and imaginatively about workers' and organised labour's varied pasts.

LIBERALISM: STRENGTHS

The present author welcomes the initiatives of Katznelson and Reid and Biagini and their colleagues at Cambridge. If allied to recent calls to integrate more fully gender, race and ethnicity into the subject matter of labour history,[22] these initiatives will broaden and enrich our understanding of the workers' past in relation to questions of identity, diversity, continuity and discontinuity, ideological orientation, political allegiance and inter-class ties and alliances. Furthermore, in laying a claim to the popular importance and durable appeal of liberal ideas in *both* the United States and Britain, Katznelson is mounting a fundamental challenge to the notion of American 'exceptionalism'. It is the striking similarity of British and US workers' allegiance to liberal ideas and *not* the differences beloved of proponents of exceptionalism – of liberal, 'business-unionist' US workers being out of step with the socialist class consciousness of their continental European and British counterparts – which emerges as a central conclusion from consideration of the texts of Katznelson and Reid and Biagini.[23] Indeed, as observed above, Biagini and Reid are very keen to downplay the class conscious, socialist, and perhaps even labourist, as opposed to the 'progressive', often cross-class and radical-liberal traditions and credentials of British workers. Finally, Biagini's and Reid's work can help (certainly) to sharpen and (possibly) to advance debates concerning the relative importance of material and political factors in the development of history.

LIBERALISM: WEAKNESSES

The welcome offered is, however, by no means unqualified. A number of nagging doubts and questions exist. For example, in their haste to question the 'traditional' labour historian's (admittedly narrow) focus upon socialism and Labour politics and to present an alternative case in favour of a hegemonic liberalism are not Reid, Biagini and Katznelson in danger of erecting a new and unsatisfactory paradigm of 'exceptionalism', in which liberalism is seen as the 'norm' for workers, and socialism and other ideas as being of lesser significance or even 'deviant'? If so, then the familiar weaknesses of the classic US model of exceptionalism – of insufficient attention to complexity, diversity, context and to historical actors' own frameworks of reference and value systems, and the false positing of a 'normal', and often linear and teleological, model of working-class experience, development and consciousness – are in danger of being repeated.

Furthermore, the liberal ideas outlined by Katznelson, Biagini and Reid frequently assume an enduring, general, and in some instances almost timeless character and significance, and are not sufficiently *contextualised* in terms of time, place, changeover time and the social world. This is particularly the case with Katznelson's article. Biagini and Reid do, of course, focus particularly upon nineteenth- and early twentieth-century Liberalism and radicalism. But all three authors tend falsely to assume that liberal ideas, such as the 'people' and 'democracy', carry largely unchanging and consensual *meanings* across long periods of time. One does not have to be a deconstructionist to appreciate the fact that the meanings of words and ideas are elusive, often contested, and subject to change. And when we place liberal and other words and ideas within the wider context of workers' lives – into engagement with material and other structures, and to relate saying to doing, thought to action and conscious to unconscious levels and consequences – then we begin to develop a more complete understanding of the complex and contradictory character of reality. Some of the tensions and contradictions within liberalism and Liberalism suddenly begin to emerge. Other, competing, allegiances, such as Chartism, Conservatism and socialism come into play, and can be understood within perfectly rational frameworks of reference. And question marks can be set against the demonstrable capacity of liberalism adequately to express or 'capture' the central concerns in workers' lives at particular points in time.[24]

Neither are a number of other issues and goals satisfactorily resolved or met. Katznelson, for example, asserts rather than demonstrates the importance of liberalism to US workers. Remarkably, he also shows precious little familiarity with the work of a long line of labour historians in Britain and the United States which, contrary to the claim of Katznelson (which is in turn based upon an uncritical acceptance of Eley's and Nield's 1980 thesis), has manifestly *not* ignored the role of politics in workers' lives, including the three-cornered relationship between workers, their institutions and the state. For example, relations between the Chartists and the state and Labour and Liberalism have hardly constituted neglected topics in social and political history.[25] Similarly, Biagini and Reid pass too easily and quickly over the question of political and other discontinuities in modern British labour history, the complex and contradictory inner workings of class, and the tensions within Liberalism and limits of its popular appeal. Indeed, it is with the last two issues – that of class and the closely interrelated question of the limits of liberalism – that the rest of this chapter concerns itself.

We begin with a survey of some of the key tensions and conflicts, often class-based in character, between, on the one hand workers and workers' movements and, on the other, liberals and Liberals in Britain and the United States before the 1880s. We then proceed to our central concern: a demonstration of the profound, if fluctuating, influence of class feeling or consciousness on the part of workers in *both* countries between the 1880s and 1920s. The main conclusions to be drawn from this demonstration are that the profundity of class both exposed the limits and weaknesses of liberal ideas and Liberalism, and flatly contradicts an absolute notion of US 'exceptionalism'. Nevertheless, we must also note that during the period from the 1880s to the 1920s as a whole, class demonstrated a more durable, if less spectacularly combustible and militantly radical, presence in Britain than in the US. By the mid 1920s the strong growth of the British Labour Party is to be contrasted with the serious decline of independent labour and socialist politics in the US. In addition the trade union movement and general working-class solidarity were much weaker in the United States than in Britain.

These instances of labour movement and class divergence between the two countries during the 1920s have led some historians to embrace a notion of American exceptionalism, as dating from that decade.[26] But this chapter offers a more qualified conclusion. The massive revival of class in 1930s America, reaching its climax in the successful 'new unionist' upsurge under the umbrella of the CIO, combined with the national reversal of the British Labour Party's fortunes in the 1930s and the hegemonic success of Conservatism, do not lend themselves easily to the claims of exceptionalism. Simultaneously, however, the Labour Party did 'rise' at the expense of the Liberals; collectivism, of a predominantly reformist kind, increasingly characterised the British labour movement; and socialist influences remained, *pace* Biagini and Reid, significant if limited. Reformism and labourism, as opposed to radical liberalism or a transforming socialism, had become the dominant characteristics of organised labour in late 1930s Britain. In the United States class continued to inform workers' lives in significant ways, especially at work. But the post-Depression revival (however limited) of consumerism, combined with the Democratic Party's accommodation to and protection of the gains of the CIO, and sustained pressure to conform to the standards of 'Americanism', effectively denied American labour its political independence and ensured that liberalism would continue more effectively than in Britain to survive the challenges of worker collectivism and class consciousness.

Class

Before moving to a consideration of class and the limits of pre-1880s liberalism it is necessary briefly to alert the reader as to the usage of class employed by the author. The term class is employed in a 'Thompsonian' manner, to refer to both structure and consciousness, conditioning and agency, and their complex *interactions*. In opposition to reductionist accounts of class, Edward and Dorothy Thompson have argued that class structure is anchored firmly in, but is by no means confined solely to, the material conditions and structures of life. For example, political and cultural structures and conditions can, and often do, bear the strong imprint of class. Furthermore, whereas the 'material' can be observed to set limits to and exert (often considerable) pressures upon consciousness, the latter is not predetermined or 'given', in any simple, unmediated sense, by the former. In turn consciousness – embracing language, ideas and action – shapes and changes inherited structures. Workers' class consciousness manifests itself in their articulation of shared or common interests – as expressed in (especially independent) institutions, ideas, norms and values, and ways of life – and opposition to the interests and ideas of other groups and social classes. As Dorothy Thompson has suggested, class feeling thus involves, 'both a positive sense of identification and a negative hostility to superior classes'.[27] In what follows we are concerned more with the extent to which workers expressed class consciousness rather than with class structure.

THE LIMITS OF LIBERALISM: PRE-1880S

As argued by Lawrence, Biagini and Reid, there were indeed elements of continuity in the vocabulary of radicalism in Britain between the second and third quarters of the nineteenth century. Words such as reform, respectability, self-help and independence, and 'producerist' opposition to 'Old Corruption' and aristocratic privilege enjoyed enduring, if varied, degrees of support across class lines. But the emphasis of these scholars upon the continuous and consensual nature of political and cultural ideas provides us with a very partial sense of a much more complicated, and often far less harmonious, social reality. Ideas are insufficiently set within a world being fundamentally transformed by capitalist industrialisation and political revolution and counter-revolution. And we suggest that (especially) during the 1830s and 1840s (and in some instances much earlier) inter-class commitments to a common 'producerist' and 'respectable' radicalism were severely strained, and in many cases torn apart, by the mushrooming presence of class conflict and class consciousness. As claimed by Dorothy and Edward Thompson and Eileen Yeo, the meanings and practices of radicalism multiplied and splintered in contested and increasingly 'classed' ways.[28]

Selected references to the many ways in which largely class-based economic, political and cultural experiences of the 1830s and 1840s were productive more of working-class independent radicalism than inter-class-based radical liberalism may serve to demonstrate the force of our argument. In terms of economic experiences,[29] the period from the late eighteenth century to the mid-nineteenth century witnessed the greatly accelerated development of industrial capitalism, characterised by full-blown commodity production, more intensive and extensive proletarianisation, and profit maximisation and cost minimisation. During this period of rapid change the 'customary' economy of 'fair' wages, prices and surpluses and 'honourable' masters and artisans, possessing mutual obligations as well as rights, was subjected to full-frontal attack by the new political economy.

The latter, complete with its ideological baggage of 'laws' and 'natural truths' concerning the 'rational' pursuit of self-interest and unrestricted individualism and gain, attempted to substitute the impersonal 'laws of the market' and the cash nexus for the more traditional regulations and 'moral' norms of customary practice. In addition, the transformation of labour proceeded apace: employers sought to introduce new patterns of working, discipline, authority and power into their enterprises and to wrest 'real' control over the labour process from their 'artisanal' employees.

To be sure, a number of qualifications and cautions must be incorporated into this general picture of fundamental, rapid and profoundly disruptive economic change. For example, industrial capitalist development proceeded unevenly within and between rural and urban areas and across processes of production carried on in factories, workshops, households and fields. Furthermore, the 'harsh' and 'unnatural' tenets of the new political economy were sometimes softened in practice (as demonstrated in the case of the early industrial paternalists); and industrialisation by no means had uniformly adverse effects upon the conditions of life of the 'working class' or 'classes'. Similarly, poverty and exploitation did not *begin* with the Industrial Revolution and the spread of 'machinofacture'. Contrary to its self-proclaimed virtues of reciprocity and fairness, the traditional 'moral order' did experience conflicts at the workplace, often triggered off by the 'dishonourable' practices of 'exacting' (if unrepresentative) 'capitalist' employers.[30] Nevertheless, artisans and other workers did increasingly express the viewpoint that exploitation and oppression within the workplace had greatly *intensified* as a direct result of capitalist transformation. Complaints multiplied concerning lack of independence and control at work, diminished opportunities for the achievement of occupational mobility and the benefits of material and mental culture, and greatly enhanced insecurity, poverty, proletarianisation and the breakdown of 'traditional' structures and relationships at work, in the home and in the community. And such complaints informed many of the popular and working-class protest movements which mushroomed during the first half of the nineteenth century.

Economic grievances formed a significant part of an increasingly widespread, sharp, and class-based (if predominantly non-revolutionary socialist) critique among workers of the new political economy and inter-class radicalism. For example, such seemingly diverse and unconnected workers as London and Birmingham artisans and Lancashire cotton operatives came together in Chartism to challenge the harmonious inter-class assumptions of 'producerism'. These disaffected workers identified the widespread and rapid growth of 'dishonourable' 'capitalist' employers (as opposed to 'traditional' 'masters'), intent upon the conscious exploitation of workers (by means of 'buying cheap and selling dear'), and the rejection of the norms and practices of 'custom' and 'morality' in favour of taking full, 'de-regulated' advantage of expanding market opportunities. What is more, contrary to the claim of Stedman Jones, these capitalist employers were increasingly perceived to be less isolated 'bad apples' than the 'true' representatives of an increasingly dominant and 'unnatural' economic *system*, rooted in class conflict and oppression. The 'hypocrisy' of the reforming, liberal-minded and Liberal employers of the Anti-Corn-Law League was singled out for special criticism by O'Connor and several other Chartist leaders. Thus, many future Liberal 'tribunes of the people', such as John Bright, were taken to task by the Chartists for preaching freedom, equality and independence in the abstract while practising 'tyranny' and worker dependence in their own workplaces; and opposing factory legislation, strikes, and trade unionism and other forms of collective worker organisation and independence.[31]

This experientially-based critique of capitalist employers formed part of the wider, and in many ways *de-facto* anti-capitalist social programme implicit for many Chartists in the demand for universal manhood suffrage. As James Epstein has recently observed,

> for many working people the demand for democratic citizenship implied, at the very least, arresting the emergent force of industrial capitalism: regulation of factory hours, repeal of the new Poor Law, some form of state intervention to guarantee a 'fair' wage for labour, a redistribution of land, and a balance between the claims of agricultural and industrial production ... *the rejection of prevailing notions of political economy defined a fundamental difference between Chartists and middle-class radicals ... Chartists refused to shake loose the social from the political.*[32] [emphasis added]

Therein lay many of the economic underpinnings of Chartism's independent class-based character and its differences and conflicts with the ideas of middle-class radicals and reformers. In effect, Reid, Biagini, Lawrence and Stedman Jones have greatly understated the importance of the 'economic' to Chartism, and its class-based influences upon Chartist ideology and language. In the process necessary attention to the interactions between the political and other dimensions of the movement has been eschewed. An unduly narrow and reductionist politico-linguistic interpretation of Chartism has in effect been substituted for the equally narrow and unsatisfactory economic reductionism characteristic of some of the more 'traditional' approaches.[33]

Furthermore, when we turn to a consideration of the political experiences and ideas of the Chartists, matters are far less straightforwardly consensual than members of the 'Cambridge School' would have us believe. It is true that the Chartists often did prefer to make tactical political alliances with middle-class reformers and radicals than with Whigs and Tories. The radicals were generally seen to be more friendly towards the reforming aims of the Chartists than were either the openly reactionary Tories or the 'deceitful' Whigs. But, as Dorothy Thompson and other historians of Chartism have clearly demonstrated, there were strict limits to the extent of co-operation. Middle-class radical commitments to a further extension of the suffrage and the cause of 'progress' did *not* in the vast majority of cases signal support for or involvement in Chartism.[34] Although the demand for the vote had a long radical pedigree and hardly constituted, in itself, 'a revolutionary threat to British society', it did, when set within the *context* of independent, militant, and class-conscious Chartism, present a serious threat to the perceived fundamentals of aristocratic and bourgeois society. What the propertied classes feared, writes Thompson,

> was the lack of respect for property, the lack of respect for authority, and the lack of dignified behaviour which they perceived in these Chartist demonstrations, as well as their avowed purposes.
>
> There were, indeed, a certain number of radicals among the middle classes who supported in principle the idea of manhood suffrage. But these middle-class politicians never made common cause with the Chartists for more than a fleeting moment.[35]

Unable to control the Chartists and offer them the 'benefits' of political and economic tutelage, and totally unwilling to approach the Chartists as political and social equals, the vast majority of middle-class people, including reformers and Liberals, did not, therefore, share a common political culture of radicalism with working people. As Thompson observes, 'Those middle-class men who became Chartists were held to have deserted the interests of their class as surely as were those working men who became spokesmen for the Anti-Corn-Law League, or who wrote attacks on trade unionism.'[36] Finally, the vast cultural gulf between the classes in 1830s and 1840s Britain, combined with middle- and upper-class attitudes of condescension, fear and hostility towards the labouring people, reinforced feelings of class separation and consciousness.[37] In such ways did class-based identities and languages take root in political, social and cultural experiences as well as in the material aspects of life.

It is, of course, the case that during the mid-Victorian years Chartism declined, that radical liberalism became the 'official' creed of the labour movement, and that class conflict ebbed. However, as most recently observed by Margot Finn, the transition from Chartism to Liberalism was less easy and untroubled than suggested by Reid and Biagini. Different, indeed conflicting, responses within radicalism and Liberalism to questions concerning the extent of further suffrage reform, strikes, trade unionism, 'economy' versus 'expenditure', state intervention versus *laissez-faire*, control of political and voluntary organisations and initiatives, and popular support for continental nationalist causes ensured that 'the history of mid-Victorian radicalism was centrally informed by the perception of class relations'.[38] The undoubted class-based reconciliations achieved within Liberalism involved concessions and accommodations on the part of *both* working- and middle-class radical constituencies. And, to an extent largely ignored in the accounts of Biagini and Reid, the shelving of Chartism's threatening tone and social programme, combined with mid-Victorian working-class movements' increasing 'respectability', 'responsibility' and more limited vision, constituted factors of fundamental importance to the successful growth of inter-class radical liberalism.[39] As we will observe in due course, the revival and development of independent labour's social programme and growing economic and social conflicts towards the end of the nineteenth century once again placed serious question marks against the continued ability of Liberalism adequately to meet working-class demands.

In the pre-1880s United States those liberal ideas outlined by Katznelson – 'economic markets and representative democracy', citizenship and equal rights, personal and community-based independence, opposition to a centralised state, and the safeguarding of individual freedoms, opportunity and choice – certainly commanded widespread popular support. As active citizens and ardent protectors of the modern world's first republic, native-born white male artisans and their immigrant counterparts from northern and western Europe constituted important supporters of the 'free labor' and 'equal rights' platforms adopted by the ante-bellum Whigs, Republicans and Democrats.[40]

However, as in Britain, liberal ideas and popular political attachments to the mainstream parties did not exercise undisputed sway among workers. As splendidly illustrated by Bruce Laurie, Sean Wilentz, Steven Ross and other 'new' labour historians, class was of mounting importance to artisans and others during the decade from the late 1820s to the late 1830s.[41] Albeit generally less widespread and advanced than in Britain, the process of capitalist transformation and its adverse effects upon the workplace-based independence, control, status and living standards of some artisans was a factor of fundamental importance to the growth of trade unionism and labour radicalism during the 1830s. Artisans contrasted the 'European' or 'alien' upsurges in wage-earning dependency and economic insecurity with the 'republican' promises of mobility and independence. The very notion of active American citizenship was perceived to be at risk. As in Britain, popular perceptions of a sharp decline in 'moral' concerns and relationships within the workplace, combined with the growth of 'dishonorable', 'capitalist' employers, the 'bastardisation' of several crafts and the rule of the cash nexus underpinned the impressive rise in trade union membership and conflict at the workplace which took place during the mid 1830s. And growing dissatisfaction with the ability or desire of the existing political parties, courts and other agencies of the state favourably to respond to and safeguard workers' interests led to popular 'turns' to the Workingmen's Parties and other examples of independent political action from the late 1820s down to the 1840s. As Amy Bridges has declared, although both Whigs and Democrats did succeed in gaining the votes of many workers during the 1830s, neither 'succeeded in winning the allegiance of the labour movement'. Independence and a distinctive political culture 'characterised large and important sections of the Jacksonian working class'.[42] And, as argued most forcibly by Wilentz, in the face of the perceived 'capture' of key political and economic institutions of the republic by 'monopolistic', 'aristocratic', 'unproductive', 'parasitical' and 'tyrannical' interests, radical workers in New York City and elsewhere increasingly imparted class-based and anti-capitalist inflexions and meanings to the languages of 'producerism' and republican citizenship.[43]

In such ways did American workers demonstrate their early anti-exceptionalism and class consciousness. In company with their British counterparts they were coming to the conclusion, subsequently famously expressed by Marx in *Capital*, that liberal emphases upon freedom and equality in the market-place – seemingly 'a very Eden of the innate rights of man' – acted as an ideological mask for exploitation and inequality.[44]

To be sure, we must be careful not to exaggerate both the extent and depth of class among American workers during the 1830s. Workers formed identities and attachments beyond, and in some instances antagonistic to those of class. Capitalist transformation and industrialisation proceeded unevenly and exerted a variety of both positive and negative effects upon workers. And experiments in independent politics were invariably short-lived, often falling victim to mainstream political parties increasingly skilled in the arts of co-optation and accommodation. Finally, from the 1840s down to the Civil War era a mixture of economic depression, racial, ethnic and other ethnocultural divisions, the politics of national unity, and the

continued promises of mobility, independence and improved living standards for some (especially for sections of the white, native-born working
class) placed severe limits upon the appeals of class and collectivism.
During the 1850s the labour movement did show limited signs of recovery
from the disasters of the 1840s. But on the eve of the Civil War the US
working class and the labour movement were respectively more divided
and weak than their counterparts in Britain.[45]

During the 1860s and 1870s the limits of liberalism were more clearly
and consistently revealed.[46] Notwithstanding the continued mass appeal of
the Democrats and Republicans, the immediate post-bellum years in the
North saw a revived labour movement commit itself to the principle of
independent labour politics. In the South the desires of free black people
for personal and collective independence, for control over their labour and
ownership of land flatly contradicted bourgeois expectations that freedom
for black people would equal the freedom to earn a wage and sell their
labour power to capitalist employers. During the mid-1870s depression
and the massive industrial conflicts of 1877 the languages of producerism
and the 'people' retreated in the face of the marked growth of conscious
perceptions and articulations of class. As clearly shown by David Montgomery, the state also assumed increasingly coercive and class-based powers
in order to 'police working people to suit the . . . market economy'.[47] Legislation was enacted to punish 'idleness' and push people into the labour
market, and popular customs suppressed or 'tamed' in order better to
facilitate the process of capital accumulation. The authority of the employer within the workplace was underwritten by statute and 'new rulings
at common law', while, conversely, 'customs and usages of the trade that
ran counter to an employer's rules or practices enjoyed no legal sanction'.
The practices of trade unions were attacked by militantly and (for the
most part) chronically anti-union judges as 'coercive', 'conspiratorial' and
'unnatural' interferences with the free flows of commerce and the 'pecu-
niary interests' and 'exchangeable value' of a company's business. The
economy as a whole was increasingly 'insulated from democratic control'.
And, as seen in its treatment of the 'Rising' of 1877, the state resorted to
the services of growing numbers of policemen, the National Guard and the
army in order to teach workers their due subservience at the workplace.
As we will see in more detail in the following section, labour relations in
the US were increasingly characterised by degrees of violence and official
repression and coercion generally unmatched in the 'Peaceable Kingdom'
of Britain.

Herein lay the far less consensual, neutral and pluralistic sides of the
American liberal state and ruling bloc: capital accumulation and the

employer's 'right' to absolute mastery in the workplace were to be guaranteed at all costs. It is highly significant that attention to the repressive and coercive measures frequently utilised by 'liberal' federal and state governments, judges and employers in their dealings with workers barely figures in Katznelson's idealised account. In truth the blessings of liberal capitalist democracy to male American workers were decidedly mixed. As Montgomery observes, just as the advent of democracy 'hastened the destruction of onerous forms of personal subordination to masters, landlords, and creditors', so 'the doctrine of the "free market" . . . enshrined rules established by employers in the legal definition of the wage contract . . . [and] justified severe restriction of the use working people could make of their democratic rights and powers through their own collective initiatives or through governmental action'.[48] And liberalism was by no means consistently or fully equipped to handle the system's fundamental contradiction between the assumed natural spontaneity and harmony of the workings and relations of 'the market' and the necessary enforcement of and unending instruction in and negotiation of such market-based ways and habits. In sum, as astutely perceived by Gramsci, contradiction, class conflict and constant renegotiation as to the 'rules of the game' lay at the heart of the the consolidation of liberal capitalist hegemony.[49]

THE LIMITS OF LIBERALISM: 1880S TO 1920S

The outer limits and internal limitations of liberalism were perhaps exposed most markedly in both Britain and the United States in the period from the 1880s to the mid 1920s. Given the centrality of class to both this process of exposure and the widespread popular resorts to extra-Liberal political options, it is necessary to firmly document the growth of class consciousness during this period. Particular emphasis will be placed upon the facts that the constituencies of the labour movement and class grew significantly, and that workers on both sides of the Atlantic acted and thought in increasingly independent ways and expressed their hostility to other social groups and classes.

In terms of Britain, it is first of all important to note that the constituency of the labour movement demonstrated clear, class-based advances over its mid-Victorian counterpart. In the post-Chartist years organised labour, and especially the trade union movement, was dominated by the craft, skilled and more regularly employed workers. The domination of trade unionism by coal and cotton lay in the future; and the vast majority of the 'non-respectable' poor were increasingly shunned by many self-helping, 'respectable' labour-movement 'pukes'. However, between the 1870s and early 1920s organised labour's base was greatly enlarged. As James Hinton has observed:

> Between the 1870s and the First World War a mass labour movement was formed in Britain. Trade union membership grew from about half a million in the mid-1870s to over four million by 1914 . . . Membership of the co-operative movement grew . . . from about 600,000 in 1880 to over three million by 1914. Trades Councils . . . spread rapidly over the whole country . . . The formation of the Labour Party in 1900 gave further expression to this sense of a working-class movement. By 1912 more than half the total trade union membership was affiliated to the Labour Party . . .[50]

There were important limitations to organised labour's embrace – as reflected in its continuing inability adequately to relate to the needs of women and large sections of the poor. But the emergence of a mass-based, durable and officially-recognised labour movement was a factor of the utmost significance. By 1920 the British labour movement was, by international standards, in an enviably strong position. Trade union density stood at the extremely impressive level of 45 per cent. The 'labour unrest' of 1910–14 had seen a successful conclusion to the 'new-unionist' upsurges begun in the 1870s, and Britain was in the grip of a massive wave of radical post-war militancy. Liberalism was in manifest decline. Furthermore, the Labour Party was beginning its rise to national influence and power. A mass-based movement, rooted in mutualism and class pride and independence, had superseded the aloof, 'aristocratic' creation of the mid-Victorian period. In sum, organised labour had become a powerful, independent force in the land which could not easily be either ignored or smashed by the establishment.

Second, workers and the labour movement between the 1880s and the 1920s acted in increasingly independent ways and sharpened greatly their consciousness of class, of differences and conflicts between 'Us' and 'Them'. Notwithstanding the continued importance of popular Conservatism, important ideological affinities between the young Labour Party and 'advanced' Liberals, and, as argued by Duncan Tanner and others, the extremely complex and varied relations between socialists, Labourites and Progressives throughout Britain, the outstanding political fact of this period lay in the emergence and growth of the Labour Party as an independent political organisation.[51] Up to 1914 and beyond the Labour Party was relatively weak. But by 1920 few among the newly-created mass electorate could doubt that the party had become an established fact of national political life. In effect, and despite the continuation of divided political allegiances within the working class, the pattern of politics which had characterised much of the Victorian period – of worker confinement within the two party system of the Liberals and Conservatives – had come to an end. As Hobsbawm and others have noted, revolutionary socialism and syndicalism enjoyed limited constituencies in Britain. But their positive effects upon labour activists, and the latter's influence within 'the movement', were far greater than numbers alone would suggest. Measured by the standards of Marxism-Leninism, British workers' aims and attachments, as reflected in their 'labourism', constitutionalism, mild socialism, mutualism, collective solidarity and allegiance to 'those of our kind' were modest and limited. But testimony to their growing strength was seen in the 'Rise of Labour' within early twentieth-century British society.

Reid, Biagini, Tanner and others have highlighted important ideological continuities and general accommodations between Labour and Liberalism. But the birth of the Labour Party and organised labour's heightened independent stance and presence cannot satisfactorily be reduced to the narrow range of political and organisational factors emphasised by these scholars and by Pelling. The resistance of local Liberals to the selection of working-class candidates, national Liberal reluctance to pay MPs, and especially the effects and general implications of the Taff Vale case (which held the Amalgamated Society of Railway Servants financially liable for the actions of its members) did undoubtedly have an important influence upon labour's independent 'turn'.[52] But, as pioneeringly argued by Hobsbawm, and as confirmed by many local studies, wider and deeper political, material and cultural influences were at work in a number of instances and localities.[53]

'Old' Liberalism was frequently unable to come to terms with 'new' unionism, industrial conflict and demands for the eight-hour day and the right to work. And, notwithstanding its collectivist garb and its undoubted successes at the parliamentary level, 'New Liberalism' generally failed to assimilate the growth of 'class' politics (the revival and development of the social programme of the Chartists), especially at the municipal level. Thus,

From Scotland to South Wales there arose, albeit unevenly, areas of disagreement which, while not generally manifest in the political deals of Westminster and in national voting patterns, nevertheless were of major importance in modifying and transforming local political cultures, allegiances and, increasingly, voting preferences. . . . these were the key issues which, time and time again, variously moved workers to champion independent labour representation in preference to Liberalism.[54]

In terms of the wider political, social and economic canvas, Hobsbawm has identified developments in material and cultural life which further heightened senses of class and independence among workers.[55] For example, the crisis of late nineteenth-century competitive capitalism, complete with its downward pressure on price levels and profit margins, induced many employers to increase the 'squeeze' upon labour. Taylorism and other management initiatives (such as the 'open shop') designed to transfer 'real' control from workers to employers undoubtedly proceeded far more slowly and with less force in Britain than in the US. Similarly, the vast and safe markets of empire cushioned British capital, and to some extent British labour, against the worst effects of intensified international competition. But international economic developments, coupled with domestic changes – employers more intent upon asserting their mastery over the workplace, reducing craft privileges and controls, 'driving' workers, opposing 'new' unions and attempting to use 'responsible' trade union officials to 'police' agreements and discipline 'troublemakers' – severely tested the accommodation between labour and capital achieved during the third quarter of the nineteenth century.

From the Great Depression onwards class feeling was also stimulated by the growth of an increasingly common, or 'traditional' way of life among workers. As Hobsbawm has suggested, marked increases in urbanisation, class-based residential segregation, factory production, commercialised patterns of leisure, the demand for semi-skilled labour, regular and better paid employment, and in living standards for the 'masses', combined with the growing white-collar wedge between the skilled and the middle class proper, the adverse pressures upon some of the craft and skilled, and the narrowing of wage differentials, produced an increasingly standardised and separate working-class culture. Diversity and conflicts – revolving around gender, ethnicity, religion and so on – by no means disappeared.[56] But the validity of Hobsbawm's case never rested upon assumptions of total unity or flat uniformity. What Hobsbawm did argue convincingly was that (much in the manner of E.P. Thompson for the 1790s to 1830s period) those forces conducive to the development of class-based solidarity increasingly overshadowed those productive of divisions and conflicts.

The horizons of the skilled worker were . . . increasingly bounded by the world of manual labour, and those of the less skilled even more so. . . . What all this amounts to is a growing sense of a single working class, bound together in a community of fate irrespective of its internal differences.[57]

In comparison with the highly differentiated working class of the post-Chartist period Hobsbawm's 'traditional' working class was highly united, independent and class conscious.

As seen in accelerated workplace conflicts and worker militancy, in the growing numbers of workers and occupations involved in labour insurgencies and the labour movement, in the mounting importance of independent labour and socialist politics, and in the widespread development of class-based cultures and values, the United States also witnessed intensified and more widespread class consciousness from the 1880s down to the early 1920s. To be sure, by the mid-1920s the American labour movement was much weaker than its British counterpart, generally lacked its 'new' union base, was controlled by an increasingly conservative AFL and had not created its own political party. But we must be wary of reading the evidence in terms of exceptional, static, narrowly institutional and success-orientated criteria. As the scholarship of the 'new' labour history has shown, beyond the 'Rise of the AFL' and narrow 'craft' unionism lies a fascinating, rich and complex history largely ignored or underplayed by practitioners of the 'old' labour history.

In terms of workplace conflict and militancy, the historian of the relatively 'Peaceable Kingdom' of Britain is immediately taken aback by the sheer magnitude, frequency and bloody character of conflicts between, on the one hand, workers and petty producers and, on the other hand, capitalists and 'monopolists' in the United States from the post-bellum years down to the early 1920s. The reader's attention can be drawn to the following key examples: endemic conflict and black opposition to continued white supremacy and class rule (to being forced into 'wage slavery') in the post-bellum South; chronic agrarian 'unrest' between 1865 and 1896 climaxing in the Alliances and Populism; the forging of important links between rural and urban workers in the West, South and North and the frequent, if often troubled, attempts to break down racial, ethnic and gender-based divisions among these workers; the Great Strike of 1877, involving over 500 000 workers nationwide; the 'Great Upheaval' of 1884–6, embracing well over 1 million workers; the Homestead strike (1892); the Pullman strike (1894); the bloody conflicts in mining during the late nineteenth and early twentieth centuries; and the decade of mass strikes between 1910 and 1922, including what Montgomery has called 'the most continuous strike wave in the history of the United States' between 1916 and 1922, and the all-time high of union membership in 1920 (4 775 000, a density of 16.7 per cent). The events and factors of the first order of importance which reveal most starkly the violent, conflict-ridden and anti-collectivist labour relations side of a supposedly consensual and peace-loving US liberalism.[58]

It was in large measure in response to employer and state coercion in the workplace that American workers learned the limits of liberal individualism and the habits of collectivism and class. Such habits became more widespread and pronounced during the mass conflicts of the 1880s to 1920s period. Labour movement constituencies expanded massively, to include the non-skilled, immigrants, women and on occasion black workers, during the periods of mass struggle outlined above. Similarly we can observe several explosions of 'new' unionism, embracing these same non-craft-based constituencies, during the period in question. And these 'new' unions frequently provided radical alternatives (such as socialist-led industrial unionism) to the sectional 'prudential unionism' (to borrow Bruce Laurie's apposite description) of the AFL. In a wider context, workplace conflict and the chronic and powerful anti-unionism of employers, judges and some politicians provoked fierce debates about the nature of American democracy and the continued survival of cherished traditions of radical republicanism and equal rights. And in its 'tyrannical', 'un-republican', 'anti-democratic' and 'class-ridden European' attempts to control all aspects of life, corporate America met with massive popular opposition and helped unwittingly to bring about a variety of radical and revolutionary responses, ranging from the Knights of Labor, to Populism, syndicalism and socialism.

To be sure, workers' radical mass insurgencies and oppositions and their 'new' unions were often defeated by the combined forces of the state and corporate capital. And the 'new' unions generally lacked the staying power of their British counterparts. But the very existence of such radical oppositional forces, and the depth of their appeal, challenge fundamentally the truth of the 'exceptional' position that labour movements in the late nineteenth- and early twentieth-century United States were far more narrowly based and possessed far more of a 'business' mentality than their counterparts in Britain and Europe. As David Montgomery has conclusively demonstrated, before the 'triumph' of the AFL in the 1920s there existed many Houses of Labour in the United States.

A significant aspect of labour's multi-faceted character and in part radical, class-based appeal lay in the support given to attempts to create an independent political party of labour. As in earlier parts of the century, there were several attempts made – notably in 1877, 1886–8, the early–mid 1890s, 1906–8, and in the early 1920s – to create such a party. According to Leon Fink, labour's defeat in 1886 at the hands of the state and an 'anti-democratic Money Power' triggered 'what may still stand as the American worker's single greatest push for political power'. Adopting 'Working-men's', 'United Labor', 'Union Labor', 'People's Party' and 'Independent' tickets, or locally capturing one of the established parties, the Knights entered electoral contests in '189 towns and cities in thirty-four (out of thirty-eight) . . . states and four territories'. By 1888 this 'push for power' had come to an abrupt end, the victim of internal wrangling and divisions and successful co-optation and accommodation on the part of the main-stream parties.[59] But support for third-party and independent labour pol-itics resurfaced in the 1890s, most prominently in, respectively, Populism and in the AFL during 1893–4. In the latter case many AFLers cast their eyes across the Atlantic and sought to imitate the successful example of the ILP in Britain. During the years 1906–8 when organised labour was suffering acutely from the hostile attentions of the courts, the issue of par-tisan versus non-partisan political allegiance was once again opened up by the AFL leadership, albeit temporarily. Furthermore, as seen in the pre-1914 fortunes of the Socialist Party, there *did* exist considerable popular support for socialism in America, both inside and (especially) outside the AFL. As Eric Foner has reminded us, the American level of support com-pared favourably with similar support for socialism in Britain and much of continental Europe.[60] During the early 1920s labour movement activists once again vigorously discussed the advantages and disadvantages of an independent political 'turn'. But by the middle years of the decade the for-tunes of both the Socialist Party and independent labour politics were in sharp decline. Notwithstanding this latter fact, it is not the *absence* of moves to independent labour and/or socialism which demand explanation, as sug-gested by proponents of 'exceptionalism', but rather both the *frequency* and *shortlived* character of such moves.

Within popular radical movements linguistic constructions of the 'peo-ple' and the 'producers' continued to exert powerful appeals. But class-based concerns were often part and parcel of these 'anti-monopoly' constructions. And within the Knights of Labor, the early AFL and the socialist and syndicalist movements more discrete and sharply delineated notions of class – declaring, for instance, the antipathy between, on the one hand 'wage slavery' and, on the other, 'true' independence, virtue and citizenship – developed.

Such constructions were, in turn, rooted within a working-class world of family, neighbourhood, shared, if often grossly unequal, responsibili-ties and rewards on the part of the sexes, increasingly commercialised patterns of leisure and in which the values and practices of mutuality generally took precedence over acquisitive individualism. As in Britain, the growth of the factory and its demand for semi-skilled labour, the easing of wage differentials, and the intensification of class-based residential segregation, combined with middle- and upper-class attitudes of condescension and fear underpinned feelings of a separate workers' world. But, to a much greater extent than in Britain, ethnic and racial divisions, allied to 'the promise of social mobility' (especially for the native born) persistently bedevilled attempts to build solid and lasting class-based 'sub-cultures of opposition'.[61]

In these various economic, political, ideological and cultural ways American workers were displaying strong evidence of class. And in some respects – especially in their industrial militancy and solidarity, their opposition to the claims of corporate capital to legitimation and hegemony, their frequent resorts to political independence, and in their support for the Socialist Party – American workers were manifesting a more marked sense of class than their British (especially English) counterparts. After all, relations between labour and capital in Britain were, notwithstanding the pre- and post-war periods of 'labour unrest' and the militancy of Clydeside and South Wales, generally far less acrimonious and violent than across the Atlantic. And on the eve of the First World War the American Socialist Party appeared to be performing much better than the British Labour Party in terms of general levels of support and organisation and performance at the polls.[62]

The more inflammatory nature of class and social relations in the United States, as compared with Britain, was intimately related to the stages of development and characteristics of capitalism in the two countries. The more acute nature of the crisis of competitive capitalism in the late nineteenth-century US (as manifested in cut-throat business competition, falling prices, adverse pressures upon rates of profit and insufficient rates of productivity growth to offset negative economic indicators), and that country's more rapid, uncontrolled and disruptive transition from competitive to monopoly capitalism; the relative weakness of the cushion of formal empire and 'gentlemanly' practices for American capital; the far more aggressively individualistic ideologies and transforming strategies (centrally embracing the 'open shop' and Taylorism) of hegemonic US employers and their powerful, 'unrepublican' allies in the judiciary and other parts of the state machinery; and, despite periods of tension and conflict, the more settled, accommodating, and increasingly 'traditional' nature of British capitalism, complete with greater official acceptance of and negotiation with organised labour – all these factors combined to generate higher levels of conflict and turbulence in the United States.[63]

CONCLUSIONS

Our overview of key economic, political, social and cultural developments between the 1880s and 1920s lends itself to two conclusions. First, the growing influence of class, as manifested in strong worker collectivism and independence and the widespread adoption of actions and ideas conducive to a shared identity and common interests and antagonistic to those of other groups and classes, clearly exposed the deficiencies of liberalism in the United States and Liberalism in Britain. Second, the strong presence of class in the United States flatly contradicts the notion of American exceptionalism.

This is not, however, the end of the story. Notwithstanding the demonstrable presence of class in both countries in this period, we can observe the emergence of three important nationally-based differences during the 1920s: the much weaker presence of trade unionism in the United States; the far more fragmented nature of the US working class; and the successful development of the British Labour Party into a party of government as contrasted with the failures of independent labour and socialist politics in the United States.[64]

The first difference resulted in large measure from contrasts in the balance of social forces and employer and state strategies pursued in the two countries. Industrial manual wage earners comprised a significantly higher percentage of the labour force in Britain, and the trade union movement had received early recognition. In Britain, even in the wake of the 1926 General Strike, the state and employers sought to contain and 'educate' rather than eradicate the trade union movement. In the United States the more exposed and minority position of such workers, combined with the manifest post-bellum hegemony of a militantly anti-union bourgeoisie, supported by the courts and an increasingly coercive state machinery, made, as we have seen, for much higher levels of conflict at the workplace. Furthermore, by the mid-1920s state and employer opposition to the very existence of trade unionism (combined with the carrot of 'welfarism') had shown itself to be extremely successful. As Montgomery observes, we have the depressing post-1922 picture of 'beleaguered unions clinging to minority sectors of their industries, surrounded by a hostile open-shop environment and governed by ruthless suppression of dissent even within their own ranks'.[65] Defeated workers largely abandoned collective, union remedies for their ills and turned to more privatised strategies. Mounting ethnic and racial divisions and pressures to conform to mainly anti-radical and individualistic 'American' standards and values also seriously weakened the appeal of trade unions.[66] In 1920s Britain the working class was less fragmented and trade unionism more deeply rooted and resilient than in the United States.

The second difference issued in large measure from the marked rise in anti-black and anti-immigrant sentiments in 1920s America. Ensuing racial and ethnic conflicts and divisions did much to fragment the working class and to undermine the impressive labour solidarity which had characterised post-war radicalism and militancy in the United States. In an attempt to protect themselves many immigrant and black communities became introverted and defensive, while in a bid to gain 'respectability' some middle-class leaders of immigrant communities 'furiously waved the flag and adopted the "American Creed"'.[67] In addition we may note the increasingly differential character of the American working class in the 1920s as seen, for example, in the experiences of the more affluent, privatised and consumer-orientated skilled workers in the 'new' industries as opposed to the insecurity and poverty of many of those in the more traditional and depressed sectors of the economy. In 1920s Britain the experiences of workers were less differentiated and ethnic and racial conflicts far less pronounced.

The third difference owed much to the more flexible and accommodating nature of the political system in the United States, long experienced in dealing with and spectacularly successful in overcoming periodic radical third-party challenges and insurgencies.[68] Notwithstanding the affinities between Labour and Liberalism and the popular appeal of Conservatism in Britain, neither the Conservatives nor the Liberals displayed sufficient concessionary, accommodating and flexible powers to prevent the birth and growth of independent Labour. Furthermore, the American state was far less reluctant than its British counterpart to employ force successfully to smash radical political movements. And, in recognition of the partial validity of Katznelson's case, we must note the more successful appeal of the liberal ideas of individualism, citizenship (however ambiguous and diverse the meanings of 'Americanism' and 'Americanisation' might have been), equal rights, the rule of the market and consumerism to 1920s US workers and organised labour. Finally we may contrast both the more divided nature of the American labour movement with its more unified British cousin, and, crucially, the AFL leadership's continued opposition to independent labour politics and socialism as opposed to the official support of the British trade union movement for the Labour Party. In the 1920s socialism also enjoyed a more significant role within the labour movement in Britain than was the case in the United States.[69]

The developments of these differences have led some commentators to suggest that a qualified notion of US exceptionalism, dating from the

1920s, is valid. This chapter offers a more cautious conclusion. The mass militancy and greatly enhanced worker solidarity and radicalism of 1930s America, combined with the rise of the CIO, hardly support the case of exceptionalism. Moreover, in 1930s Britain the Labour Party did not continue its national 'rise', Conservatism ruled the roost, and working-class experience was increasingly differentiated along lines of residence, income, employment and lifestyle. In sum, the case of exceptionalism does not carry overall conviction. Simultaneously, however, the case in favour of the greater strength and resilience of liberalism in the United States may be more persuasive. After all, the inter-war and post-war US labour movements did, on balance, remain wedded to the mainstream politics of limited state welfarism and general intervention, opposition to socialism, citizenship versus class, and the rule of the market to a much greater extent than its 'labourist' and increasingly social-democratic British counterpart. It is with respect to the period from the 1930s onwards that Ira Katznelson's provocative thesis perhaps carries most weight and as such merits careful empirical investigation. Finally it is arguably the case that Biagini and Reid's notion of the longevity of radical liberalism in Britain assumes particular relevance less with reference to the history of the Labour Party between 1918 and the 1980s than with reference to the mid-1990s 'liberal turn' of Tony Blair.

NOTES

1. Ira Katznelson, 'The "Bourgeois" Dimension: a Provocation about Institutions, Politics, and the Future of Labor History', *International Labor and Working Class History* (hereafter *ILWCH*), 46 (Fall 1994), 10, 11, 15.
2. *Ibid.*, 21, 22.
3. *Ibid.*, 7.
4. *Ibid.*, 15, 9.
5. *Ibid.*, 9, 14.
6. *Ibid.*, 24.
7. See, for example, David Montgomery, 'From Scientific Socialism to Political Science?'; Mary Nolan, 'Is Liberalism Really the Answer?'; Sean Wilentz, 'Labor History: Out of Vogue?', *ILWCH*, 46, (Fall 1994).
8. Katznelson, 'The "Bourgeois" Dimension', 22; Eugenio F. Biagini and Alastair J. Reid, eds, *Currents of Radicalism: Popular Radicalism, Organised Labour and Party Politics in Britain 1850–1914* (Cambridge, 1991), especially Biagini and Reed, 'Currents of Radicalism, 1850–1914', 1–19; Biagini, *Liberty, Retrenchment and Reform: Popular Liberalism in the Age of*

130   *American Exceptionalism?*

Gladstone 1860–1880 (Cambridge, 1992); H. Pelling, *The Origins of the Labour Party 1880–1900* (London, 1954).

9. Katznelson, 'The "Bourgeois" Dimension', 21, 23–6.
10. *Ibid.*, 11, 23, 25.
11. Brian Harrison and Patricia Hollis, 'Chartism, Liberalism and the Life of Robert Lowery', *English Historical Review*, LXXXII (July 1967); John R. Vincent, *The Formation of the British Liberal Party 1857–68* (Harmondsworth, 1972); Peter F. Clarke, *Lancashire and the New Liberalism* (Cambridge, 1971).
12. Jon Lawrence, 'Popular Radicalism and the Socialist Revival in Britain', *Journal of British Studies*, 31 (April 1992), 163–86; Jon Lawrence, 'Popular Politics and the Limitations of Party: Wolverhampton, 1867–1900', in Biagini and Reid, *Currents*; Miles Taylor, *The Decline of British Radicalism 1847–1860* (Oxford, 1995); Biagini and Reid, 'Currents'.
13. Biagini and Reid, 'Currents', 1.
14. *Ibid.*, 5–6.
15. Gareth Stedman Jones, *Languages of Class: Studies in English Working Class History 1832–1982* (Cambridge, 1987, orig. ed. 1983); Patrick Joyce, *Visions of the People: Industrial England and the Question of Class 1840–1914* (Cambridge, 1991).
16. Biagini and Reid, 'Currents', 6, 8, 10, 11; Biagini, *Liberty*, 31–83, 139–91.
17. Lawrence, 'Class and Gender in the Making of Urban Toryism, 1880–1914', *English Historical Review*, CCCCXXVIII (July 1993), 629–52.
18. Biagini and Reid, 'Currents', 9.
19. It is interesting to note in this context that the recent work of Miles Taylor, a Cambridge University historian sharing the wish of Stedman Jones, Lawrence, Biagini and Reid to 'restore politics to the analysis of radical movements', does nevertheless posit a break in the radical political tradition during the late 1850s and early 1860s. See Taylor, *Decline*, 6, 338.
20. Lawrence, 'Popular Radicalism and the Socialist Revival'; Stedman Jones, *Languages of Class*, 90–178; Biagini and Reid, 'Currents', 16–17; Alastair J. Reid, 'The Division of Labour and Politics in Britain, 1880–1920', in Wolfgang J. Mommsen and Hans-Gerhardt Husung, eds, *The Development of Trade Unionism in Great Britain and Germany 1880–1914* (London, 1985), 150–65; A.J. Reid, 'Dilution, Trade Unionism, and the State in Britain during the First World War', in Stephen Tolliday and Jonathan Zeitlin, eds, *Shop Floor Bargaining and the State: Historical and Comparative Perspectives* (Cambridge, 1985), 46–74.
21. Biagini and Reid, 'Currents', 18–19.
22. See, for example, Sonya O. Rose, 'Gender and Labor History: the Nineteenth-century Legacy', *International Review of Social History*, supplement 1, 38 (1993), 145–62; David Roediger, 'Race and the Working-Class Past in the United States: Multiple Identities and the Future of Labor History', *ibid.*, 127–43.
23. For the pros and cons of the thesis of US exceptionalism see Sean Wilentz, 'Against Exceptionalism: Class Consciousness and the American Labor Movement, 1790–1920', *ILWCH*, 26 (Fall 1984), and the ensuing debates between Wilentz, Nick Salvatore, Michael Hanagan and Steven Sapolsky in *ibid.*, 26 (Fall 1984), 27 (Spring 1985) and 28 (Fall 1985). See also Aristide Zolberg, 'How Many Exceptionalisms?', in Ira Katznelson and Aristide

Zolberg, eds, *Working Class Formation: Nineteenth Century Patterns in Western Europe and the United States* (Princeton, 1986), 397–455; Eric Foner, 'Why is There no Socialism in the United States?', *History Workshop Journal*, 17 (Spring 1984); G. Friedman, 'The State and the Making of the Working Class: France and the United States, 1880–1914', *Theory and Society*, 17 (1988), 403–30; Friedrich Lenger, 'Beyond Exceptionalism: Notes on the Artisanal Phase of the Labour Movement in France, England, Germany and the United States', *International Review of Social History*, XXXVI (1991); Neville Kirk, *Labour and Society in Britain and the United States*, 2 vols (Aldershot, 1994): v. 1. *Capitalism, Custom and Protest 1780–1850*, 1–16; v. 2. *Challenge and Accommodation 1850–1939*, 367–9.

24. Kirk, *Challenge and Accommodation*, 173–264; Montgomery, 'From Scientific Socialism to Political Science?', 66.

25. See, for example, F.C. Mather, *Public Order in the Age of the Chartists* (Manchester, 1959); John Saville, *1848: the British State and the Chartist Movement* (Cambridge, 1987); Neville Kirk, *The Growth of Working Class Reformism in MidVictorian England* (Beckenham, 1985); Patrick Joyce, *Work, Society and Politics: the Culture of the Factory in Later Victorian England* (Brighton, 1980); Clarke, *Lancashire*; Vincent, *Formation*; David Howell, *British Workers and the Independent Labour Party 1888–1906* (Manchester, 1983); Frances E. Gillespie, *Labor and Politics in England 1850–1870* (Durham, North Carolina, 1927).

26. See, for example, Steven Sapolsky, 'Response to Sean Wilentz's "Against Exceptionalism"', *ILWCH*, 27 (Spring 1985), 35.

27. Dorothy Thompson, *Outsiders: Class, Gender and Nation* (London, 1993), 57; Anthony Giddens, *New Rules of Sociological Method: a Positive Critique of Interpretative Sociologies* (London, 1976) for an interesting and useful discussion of the interactions between agency and conditioning, action and structure.

28. Eileen Yeo and Stephen Yeo, 'On the Uses of "Community": from Owenism to the Present', in Stephen Yeo, ed., *New Views of Co-operation* (London, 1988); Eileen Yeo, 'Culture and Constraint in Working-Class Movements, 1830–1855', in E. Yeo and S.Yeo, eds, *Popular Culture and Class Conflict 1590–1914: Explorations in the History of Labour and Leisure* (Brighton, 1981); E. Yeo and S. Yeo, 'Some Practices and Problems of Chartist Democracy', in James A. Epstein and Dorothy Thompson, eds, *The Chartist Experience: Studies in Working Class Radicalism and Culture 1830–1860* (London, 1982); Dorothy Thompson, 'The Languages of Class', in *Bulletin of the Society for the Study of Labour History*, 52:1 (1987), 54–7; Edward P. Thompson, *The Making of the English Working Class* (New York, 1966), 7–14, 711–832.

29. For an outline of these economic experiences see Kirk, *Capitalism, Custom and Protest*, 19–81.

30. John Rule, *The Experience of Labour in Eighteenth-Century Industry* (Beckenham, 1981); John Rule, *The Labouring Classes in Early Industrial England 1750–1850* (London, 1987), 105–52, 253–378; John Rule, *Albion's People: English Society 1714–1815* (London, 1992).

31. Neville Kirk, 'In Defence of Class', *International Review of Social History*, XXXII (1987), especially 16–35; John Cole, *Rochdale Revisited: a Town and its People*, II (Littleborough, 1990), 41–4; John Cole, *Conflict and*

Co-operation: Rochdale and the Pioneering Spirit 1790–1844 (Littleborough, 1994), 29, 32–3. For a sympathetic treatment of Bright see Patrick Joyce, *Democratic Subjects: the Self and the Social in Nineteenth-Century England* (Cambridge, 1994), 85–146.

32. James Epstein, 'National Chartist Leadership: some Perspectives', in Owen Ashton, Robert Fyson and Stephen Roberts, eds, *The Duty of Discontent: Essays for Dorothy Thompson* (London, 1995), 37.

33. Kirk, 'In Defence', 46–7. For Chartism as the creed of hard times see, for example, Asa Briggs, *The Age of Improvement 1783–1867* (London, 1962), 394, 402–4.

34. Thompson, *Outsiders*, 29.

35. Dorothy Thompson, *The Chartists: Popular Politics in the Industrial Revolution* (Aldershot, 1986), 237.

36. *Ibid.*, 255.

37. *Ibid.*, 242–54.

38. Margot C. Finn, *After Chartism: Class and Nation in English Radical Politics 1848–1874* (Cambridge, 1993), 321; Theodore Koditschek, *Class Formation and Urban Industrial Society: Bradford 1750–1850* (Cambridge, 1990), 517–66; Peter F. Taylor, *Popular Politics in Early Industrial Britain: Bolton 1825–1850* (Keele, 1995), 151–80, 217–26.

39. Kirk, *Reformism*, Chs. 4 and 5; Finn, *After Chartism*, 306–23.

40. Kirk, *Capitalism, Custom and Protest*, 87–8, 109–11.

41. Bruce Laurie, *Artisans into Workers: Labor in Nineteenth Century America* (New York, 1989); Sean Wilentz, *Chants Democratic: New York City and the Rise of the American Working Class 1788–1850* (New York, 1986); Steven J. Ross, *Workers on the Edge: Work, Leisure and Politics in Industrializing Cincinnati 1788–1890* (New York, 1985).

42. Amy Bridges, 'Becoming American', in Katznelson and Zolberg, eds, *Working Class Formation*, 162; Bridges, *A City in the Republic: Antebellum New York and the Origins of Machine Politics* (Ithaca, 1987), 103–24.

43. Wilentz, *Chants*, 241–8, 263–71.

44. Karl Marx, *Capital: a Critique of Political Economy*, v. 1. *Capitalist Production* (London, 1970), 176.

45. Kirk, *Capitalism, Custom and Protest*, 147–91; Ross, *Workers on the Edge*, 67–216.

46. See, for example, Eric Foner, *Reconstruction: America's Unfinished Revolution 1863–1877* (New York, 1988); David Montgomery, *Beyond Equality: Labor and the Radical Republicans 1862–1872*, (New York, 1967); Philip S. Foner, *The Great Labor Uprising of 1877* (New York, 1977); Kirk, *Challenge and Accommodation*, 80–97, 208–17.

47. David Montgomery, *Citizen Worker: the Experience of Workers in the United States with Democracy and the Free Market during the Nineteenth Century* (Cambridge, 1995), 52–114.

48. *Ibid.*, 50–1.

49. Quintin Hoare and Geoffrey N. Smith, eds, *Selections from the Prison Notebooks of Antonio Gramsci* (London, 1971), 206–318.

50. James Hinton, *Labour and Socialism: a History of the British Labour Movement 1867–1974* (Brighton, 1983), 24.

51. For a summary of much of the large body of literature concerning Lib.–

Labism and the development of independent labour politics see Kirk, *Challenge and Accommodation*, 243–4, 256–60, 398 fn.176.

52. Biagini and Reid, 'Currents', 16–17.
53. Eric J. Hobsbawm, *Worlds of Labour: Further Studies in the History of Labour* (London, 1984), 176–213. See Kirk, *Challenge and Accommodation*, 259 for such confirmatory local studies. See Duncan Tanner, *Political Change and the Labour Party* (Cambridge, 1990), for an important (and Cambridge-inspired) dissenting voice.
54. Kirk, *Challenge and Accommodation*, 258–9.
55. Hobsbawm, *Worlds of Labour*, 184–194; Eric Hobsbawm, *Labouring Men: Studies in the History of Labour* (London, 1974 edition), 272–343.
56. Andrew Davies and Steven Fielding, eds, *Workers Worlds: Cultures and Communities in Manchester and Salford 1880–1939* (Manchester, 1992).
57. Hobsbawm, *Worlds of Labour*, 206–7.
58. For studies of mass protest between the 1870s and the 1920s see David Montgomery's magisterial *The Fall of the House of Labor: the Workplace, the State and American Labor Activism 1865–1925* (Cambridge, 1987), 257–464; Kirk, *Challenge and Accommodation*, 94–8, 115–54.
59. Leon Fink, *Workingmen's Democracy: the Knights of Labor and American Politics* (Urbana, 1983), xiii, 26–7; Ross, *Workers on the Edge*, 294–325.
60. Foner, 'Why is there no Socialism?', 60.
61. See, for example, Richard J. Oestreicher, *Solidarity and Fragmentation: Working People and Class Consciousness in Detroit 1875–1900* (Urbana, 1986).
62. Kirk, *Challenge and Accommodation*, 115–54, 219–44; Gary W. Marks, *Unions in Politics: Britain, Germany and the United States in the Nineteenth and Early Twentieth Centuries* (Princeton, 1989); Foner, 'Why is there no Socialism?'
63. Kirk, *Challenge and Accommodation*, 37–41.
64. *Ibid.*, 244–5, 300–31.
65. Montgomery, *The Fall*, 393–4, 406–10.
66. Notwithstanding Gerstle's important emphasis upon the many-sidedness and radical potential of the term 'Americanism'. See Gary Gerstle, *Working Class Americanism: the Politics of Labor in a Textile City 1914–1960* (Cambridge, 1989); Kirk, *Challenge and Accommodation* 152, 280–2, 302–3; D. Brody, *Workers in Industrial America: Essays on the Twentieth Century Struggle* (London, 1981), 63–4.
67. Kirk, *Challenge and Accommodation*, 153, 303–4; John J. Bukowczyk, 'The Transformation of Working-Class Ethnicity: Corporate Control, Americanization and the Polish Immigrant Middle Class in Bayonne, New Jersey, 1915–1925', *Labor History*, 25:1 (Winter 1984); Lizabeth Cohen, *Making a New Deal: Industrial Workers in Chicago 1919–1939* (Cambridge, 1990), 53–97.
68. Marks, *Unions in Politics*, 217; Foner, 'Why is there no Socialism?'; Kirk, *Challenge and Accommodation*, 173–264.
69. Kirk, *Challenge and Accommodation*, 323–31.

7 Present at the Creation: Working-Class Catholics in the United States

Leslie Woodcock Tentler

Although Protestants have always been a substantial majority in the United States, the nation's industrial working class has been heavily Catholic. By European standards, moreover, and especially in comparison with Italy and France, America's Catholic workers have as a group been remarkably disciplined in their religious practice. 'It is not our people who miss Mass on Sunday, refuse the sacraments and vote the Communist ticket', as Auxiliary Bishop Steven Leven reminded Curial conservatives at the Second Vatican Council. 'We have not lost the working class. They are the foundation and support of the Church.'[1] Like most 'American exceptionalists', Bishop Leven saw only in part: American Catholics by the 1960s were more disaffected than he evidently knew, while the situation in Europe – even in Italy – was more complex than his rhetoric allowed. Still, Bishop Leven for all his provincialism was clearly onto something, and not only with regard to religion.

This is not to deny the transnational aspects of working-class history in the United States, or the transnational aspects of Roman Catholicism. America's immigrant workers were players in an international economic drama, and their lives make full sense only in this context. Nor can American Catholicism be adequately understood without reference to the various Catholic cultures of Europe, or indeed of Asia and Latin America, and without reference to the transnational character of Catholic Church governance. But American realities matter too. A tradition of state neutrality with regard to religion, predominantly Protestant elites, a heavily immigrant and unusually heterogeneous working class – these make for a history that is in certain ways distinctive. The effects have been felt in the realm of politics as well as religion.

Despite the demonstrable religiosity of many working-class sub-cultures, however, historians of American labour have paid relatively little attention to religion, particularly as a positive force in working-class life. There has of late been some change in this regard, primarily under the influence of what is sometimes called the 'new religious history'. But the gulf between most labour historians and those who work mainly on American religion is still substantial. Even recent work in labour history fails for the most part to incorporate the insights of the 'new' historians of American Catholicism, while historians of Catholicism have had remarkably little to say about class.[2] Each group has much to learn from the other, as I hope to demonstrate.

The argument presented in this essay will necessarily be broad, ranging over numerous ethnic groups and a full century of American experience. I want to convey in general terms the central role that Catholicism played in the creation and sustenance of ethnic working-class communities in the United States. Certain of my arguments are applicable to religion *per se*; others pertain particularly to Catholicism, with its centralised and rigidly hierarchical teaching authority and its emphasis – of special importance in the context of American voluntarism – on the building and maintenance of separate institutions. I look first, and most extensively, at the significance of religion for the creation of ethnic identity in the United States. Then I consider the ways in which ethnic religiosity provided essential resources both for individual and family survival – psychic as well as economic – and for group mobilisation. Catholicism was not an invariably progressive force in family and community life: religious loyalties often reinforced parochialism and suspicion of 'outsiders', and worked against the equality and autonomy of women. But I will argue nonetheless for the largely positive effects of Catholicism in the lives of immigrant workers, their children and grandchildren. Religion provided them with perhaps their richest resources for shaping the world of everyday living, and with a potent counterweight to the dominant American ideology of competitive individualism.

The religious landscape of Catholic America has been a varied one. Ethnic groups differed with respect to religious practice, and in their attitudes toward the clergy. No one has yet found a diocese where Italians rivalled Poles in their enthusiasm for church- and school-building or their attendance at Mass. Variations within groups were even greater than those between groups. Women in every ethnic population were more likely than men to be regular in their religious practice, with young adult males almost invariably described by the clergy as especially resistant to religious discipline. In every generation, moreover, ostensibly 'Catholic' ethnics rejected the Church altogether, sometimes in favour of economic radicalism or, more commonly, secular nationalism. In certain ethnic populations – the Germans especially come to mind – nationalists and even economic radicals were plausible rivals to the clergy in the realm of moral authority.[3]

But despite a varied and uneven pattern of development, the Catholic Church in the United States was, even in the nineteenth century, a remarkably successful institution – or set of institutions, as it might more accurately be described. The Famine Irish, many of them virtually 'unchurched' upon arrival, were, as early as the 1870s, sufficiently disciplined to support a network of urban parishes, some of which included schools. Post-Famine immigrants used these same parishes to ease their transition to city living, and as support for their increasingly high standards of religious practice.[4] A similar pattern prevailed in other immigrant populations, though none – save perhaps South Italians – faced so daunting a process of transition as the Famine Irish. Even the Italians, however, were within the space of a generation supporting parishes of their own, and sometimes parochial schools as well. Their women and children, if not their men, were present at Mass in sufficient numbers to make the Church a central institution in the nascent ethnic community.[5] That Italians were far more likely than the Irish to be anti-clerical, that their religious practice was far less regular – this matters less, I think, than the shared experience of church-building and support, and the evolving connection between religion and ethnic identity.

As immigrants moved increasingly into the nation's industrial cities, the American Catholic Church took on an intensely urban character. A vibrant Catholic life could surely be found in ethnic farming hamlets, perhaps especially in the heavily German Midwest. But the Catholic institutional ghetto was in the United States a mainly urban phenomenon. Thus situated, Catholic elites moved with relative ease into politics, where they served as powerful brokers for their ethnic tribesmen and increasingly for their co-religionists generally. Its thorough integration into urban life gave the Catholic Church in the United States an aura of modernity, despite the anti-modernism of its teaching, and a sense of confidence with regard to the future. The contrast with France could not be more striking.

Equally striking were American trends with regard to men's religious practice. We do not have for the United States the kind of statistical data that scholars like LeBras and Cholvy have compiled for France, and our conclusions in this regard must be tentative. But recent work on the history of various American dioceses suggests that males from many ethnic backgrounds were gradually habituated to a relatively disciplined mode of religious behaviour. There were of course variations according to ethnicity: assimilation to a disciplined norm proceeded more readily among the Irish than the Italians, and was more central to Irish identity. And in every group, extreme poverty was a likely impediment to full participation in parish life. It is among the very poor that we are most apt to find the largest concentration of 'mission Catholics' – those who were lax with regard to weekly observance but willing, even anxious, to reaffirm a commitment to the church during parish-sponsored revivals.[6]

By the inter-war years of the twentieth century, however, the most resistant groups were remarkable by European standards for the levels of church adherence among adult males and the regularity of men's religious practice. The Holy Name Society brought thousands of working-class men to communion (and hence confession) on a monthly basis in cities like New York, Chicago and Detroit.[7] Indeed, the trend to a more frequent reception of the sacraments was apparent among many groups even in the nineteenth century. In the Diocese of Detroit, for example, growing numbers of men's church-sponsored benefit societies were by the 1890s requiring communion of their members at least four times a year.[8] This more disciplined practice did not necessarily mean that men gave full assent to Catholic teaching, or that they were untroubled with regard to belief. Catholic ritual practice had a significant social dimension in the ethnic working class: the regular reception of communion was an affirmation of responsible manhood, indeed of a patriarchal ethic, as well as a statement of faith. But their disciplined practice does suggest that many working-class males identified strongly with a system of communally-sanctioned values that found embodiment in the local church.

They did so, I would argue, largely because that local church was so genuinely popular an institution. (In this essential regard, the experience of America's Catholic immigrants differed fundamentally from that of urban migrants in Italy, or indeed in France.) The immigrant church in the United States was often a product of lay initiative: immigrant 'pioneers' to a particular locale, having organised themselves into mutual aid societies, eventually undertook to found a parish and underwrite the building of a church. Sometimes this happened without benefit of clergy, particularly in the case of Eastern Europeans for whom the supply of ethnic clergy was for many years inadequate. More typically, the laity proceeded in consultation with a priest, though he might be an itinerant whose ministry encompassed a number of nascent congregations. Priests played dominant roles in the formation of many Irish and Italian parishes, partly because of a greater passivity on the part of the laity. But even where priests took a leading role, the work of fund-raising fell squarely on the laity, as would the subsequent obligation of church and school support.[9]

One can hardly overstate the extent of the burden thus imposed on impoverished immigrants, or the opportunities thereby presented for the creation of a rooted community in alien surroundings. Fund-raising might be cause for popular resentment at the clergy, and thus of potential alienation from the church and the community it represented. But its usual effects were profoundly integrative. Fund-raising provided practice in group planning and co-operative action. It involved both sexes, with women typically taking the lead in the organisation of social events, while men collected door-to-door and donated their labour to excavate the church site, even to quarry and transport stone. And because church-building had as much to do with secular as religious purposes, it involved not only the devout but many who were lax in their practice, even altogether indifferent. For a great many immigrants, the first New World experience of large-scale collective action came in the context of parish creation.[10]

New immigrant populations were highly mobile and frequently dominated, in a numerical sense, by temporarily unattached young men, at least some of whom had previously been migrants in Europe. Many regarded themselves as temporary residents of the United States. In the circumstances, parish creation was not only a remarkable achievement but one with unusual potential for altering immigrant consciousness. To participate in building a church was to gain a stake in America. It meant identification with a particular locale and a particular group of 'countrymen' – not all of whom had necessarily been recognisable as one's countrymen in Europe. It meant revivifying in a New World context an ethic by which the individual subordinated himself to the purposes of the group. And church-building helped to heal the psychic wounds of migration: a church was visible reparation to one's ancestors for deserting home soil, as well as a promise of continued fidelity to ancestral values. For all these reasons, church-building was likely to lead to a heightened association between religion and an emerging ethnic identity.[11]

The building of churches did not of course mean an end to immigrant mobility, still less an end to division in local immigrant populations. Churches were themselves a frequent locus of conflict, in good part because they brought together more people than any other community institution. This was especially true of Catholic churches, where greater numbers were often conjoined to variety. Mindful of costs and typically committed to the spread of parochial schools, American bishops insisted that the ethnic boundaries of their 'national' parishes be defined as generously as possible. Catholics from Alsace, Bavaria and Westphalia were 'Germans' for purposes of parish formation, just as 'Tipperary men' and those from Cork were Irish, or Kashubs and Galicians were Poles.[12] (Only Italians seem regularly to have defeated their bishops' purposes in this regard. Detroit was by no means alone in its separate parishes for northerners and for migrants from the South and Sicily.) But regardless of conflict and continued high rates of population turnover, a church changed local life in fundamental ways. No other institution did so much to stimulate ethnic feeling and encourage ethnic consciousness.

This happened not only in the course of fund-raising and church-building. The conflicts so common to immigrant churches were occasions on which the immigrant community was mobilised, sometimes against an external enemy – most likely an 'Irish' bishop – but more often against itself. Divisive though this was in the short run, the larger effect of such conflicts was fundamentally integrative. Struggles over parochial governance or the requisites of a good pastor were often the means by which immigrants debated the nature and purpose of their American presence, and the context in which they articulated the possibility of embracing a new understanding of self. Such struggles drew their participants more deeply into the life of the church – and, by extension, into the life of the emerging ethnic group. And they were often the means by which settled and generally more affluent males contended for community leadership. 'The internal growth of the ethnic group . . . owes a great deal to struggle', as David Gerber reminds us.[13]

A church was also crucial for the badge of identity it provided even its least fervent members. The building itself staked a claim for the group to a modest piece of urban turf, no matter how ethnically mixed the inhabitants of that turf might be. (Since the establishment of an ethnic church almost invariably attracted an increased migration of the same ethnic population, we might reasonably regard the founding of churches as a kind of 'people's city planning'.) And if the presence of a church defined a 'Polish' or a 'German' neighbourhood, it also defined that church's members as 'Poles' and 'Germans', no matter what village or provincial identity they might have brought to the United States. This identity, moreover, applied equally to the more marginal members as well as the most devout. At the same time, a church represented a step toward America and toward the 'hyphenated' status of an ethnic. As American Protestants became increasingly diverse in the ante-bellum decades, church membership became an increasingly potent social marker. To build a church and acquire thereby a public religious identity was an 'American' act as well as a gesture of ancestral fealty. It was likewise an American act to carry one's ethno-religious loyalties into politics.[14]

The ethnic group was an important construct for a variety of reasons. It provided persuasive answers to pressing questions of personal identity, and made possible the institutions that afforded essential, if minimal, protections against the radical insecurity in which most immigrants lived. Those institutions, and especially the church, also worked to reinforce a demanding ethic of familial solidarity, which prior to the welfare state was crucial to survival for nearly all working-class families. That an ethnic identity could inhibit the realisation of a class identity is obvious, though even recent immigrants were quite capable of an elementary 'trade union consciousness'. But in the context of massive labour migrations, and perhaps especially in the extreme context of American heterogeneity, ethnic consciousness was generally a necessary antecedent to class consciousness. Ethnicity provided the means by which America's immigrants entered public life, there to contend with other 'ethnics' whose interests were sometimes congruent with their own, as well as the means by which they survived the corrosive effects of dislocation and poverty.

Thus insofar as the church facilitated the emergence of ethnic consciousness, it unwittingly facilitated the eventual realisation of a trans-ethnic, even a class, identity – though the extent of this realisation, like the consequences of it, depended on economic and political circumstances beyond the control of churchmen. Church life was also a principal source of the skills and values that class-based political action required. Immigrants honed their political skills in the parish as well as the local machine. Their support of such church-linked institutions as schools, orphanages and hospitals served to limit state power with regard to the group, and underwrote a potentially radical ideology of what we today call community control. And while Catholic teaching might reasonably be argued to have promoted resignation with regard to the things of this world, that same teaching provided workers with the basics of an economic morality. In the right circumstances, that morality could sustain Catholic workers in collective action and justify making common cause with religious 'outsiders'.

The immigrant church was from its very inception an arena for ethnic politics. Immigrant 'pioneers' vied for prestige in the process of parish formation, and sometimes parlayed their subsequent visibility into secular political careers. Most immigrant parishes supported a variety of social and devotional organisations, each of which typically featured a roster of elected leaders. Offices like these were a source of status in the ethnic community, and sometimes a springboard into politics.[15] And many immigrant parishes were at least partially governed by elected boards of lay trustees. Theirs was hardly a radical brand of democracy: trustees were disproportionately drawn from the more affluent reaches of the community, while women were almost invariably excluded from the ranks of electors. Still, labourers were sometimes chosen as trustees, especially in parishes for Eastern Europeans, and few immigrant parishes by the late nineteenth century linked suffrage in parish elections to the renting of a pew.[16] Parish politics thus mirrored the American secular variety in terms of inclusiveness. Some congregations of the break-away Polish National Catholic Church, founded in 1904, were sufficiently attuned to secular trends to extend the suffrage in parish elections to women.[17]

The extent of lay governance in the parish did vary according to ethnic group. Strong boards of lay trustees were most common in German and Eastern European parishes, which were also the parishes most prone to conflict with bishops and priests over lay prerogatives. Such boards were notably weaker, even absent entirely, in parishes composed primarily of Italians, Mexicans, or post-Famine Irish. Differences on this score had mainly to do with a group's pre-migration history: lay parish activism was common in Germany, much less so in Ireland.[18] American circumstances, however, nearly always enhanced the authority that laymen were able to exercise over parish affairs. Conscious that church support rested with them alone, ethnic parishioners were quite capable of democratising the ancient right of patronage – prompted, often, by laymen intent on eclipsing the clergy as ethnic community leaders. As an indignant Father Alphonse Bertele told the Bishop of Detroit in 1916, 'One of my former defunct trustees had the hardihood to tell me to my face: I don't see why a bishop or a priest would not do what the people expect him to do since they are paid by the people.'[19]

That priests were wholly dependent on voluntary contributions from the laity was a powerful check on clerical authoritarianism, even in those parishes where formal traditions of lay governance were weak. True, some priests cultivated an autocratic style, to which their extensive education and relatively comfortable style of life lent visible support. Tridentine theology, moreover, was emphatic in its understanding of the priest as an *alter Christus*, a quite literal mediator between God and humanity. A priest's symbolic authority was immense, and it was constantly reinforced by means of the liturgy and the deferent behaviour his presence usually commanded.[20] But insofar as the priest was an ethnic leader – insofar as he represented his group in the public eye – deference toward him was a complex thing. To honour one's priest was also to honour one's compatriots, and indeed to honour oneself. For it meant championing a way of being that the host society regarded with suspicion and sometimes with contempt.

Still, priests could not invariably count on deference, as the frequence and occasionally the violence of immigrant parish disputes makes clear. Successful pastoring was almost by definition a balancing act: no matter how aloof or forbidding a face he presented to the world, the priest who avoided trouble was the one who could negotiate with numerous and potentially fractious lay constituencies. This was perhaps an easier task among the Irish than the Poles, though Irish pastors had often to navigate the stormy waters of nationalist politics. But even the Irish were familiar with arguments that limited the sphere of a priest's authority while honouring his exalted status. The more colourful disputes over lay parish governance received a generous press, as did the distinction – common to nearly all disputes – between 'spiritual matters', over which priests were conceded sole jurisdiction by even the most radical lay leaders, and those many 'temporal matters' over which the laity claimed control.[21] The distinction, which survived an eventual decline in the vigour of lay governance, was not without its applicability to the clergy and secular politics, though priests in the United States were far less likely than those in most European nations to be politically active.[22]

The politics attendant on parish formation and the on-going life of the local church did more than provide a protected sphere in which electoral skills might be practised. They were also a part of the complex process by which peasant traditions of deference to elites were gradually undermined. This latter effect was doubtless enhanced as the ethnic community matured, and its more prosperous members increasingly moved beyond the area of first settlement. As cities like Detroit were more and more segregated by class as opposed to ethnicity, their Catholic parishes were increasingly defined by class, often coming in the process to have congregations that were ethnically mixed.[23] This is the primary context in which Catholicism itself evolved into a form of ethnicity – a process fuelled in probably equal parts by mobility and persistent anti-Catholicism.

In the circumstances, working-class parishioners may well have felt freer to enter fully into parish life and assume positions of leadership. True, strong boards of lay trustees were increasingly rare after 1920, as bishops in nearly all dioceses wielded ever greater administrative control.[24] More assimilated ethnics were less apt than immigrants to assert their putative rights with regard to parish governance, and less suspicious of episcopal authority – due, presumably, to their broadened horizons and diminished feelings of alienation. The perceived need for lay control may also have been lessened by more democratic recruitment to the priesthood and the adoption by many priests, mainly after the First World War, of a genial, quasi-egalitarian public style.[25]

But more assimilated ethnics were still heavily invested in the parish, and perhaps inclined in their youth to more active involvement than had been the case in an earlier generation. Young men were increasingly incorporated into parish activities after the turn of the century, as more and more parishes targeted this group via social clubs and athletics.[26] Growing numbers of parochial high schools were likewise centres of adolescent social life, especially in the 1920s and after.[27] The need to build and support such schools, moreover, and perhaps to replace the immigrant church with a larger and more sumptuous structure gave American-born ethnics their own opportunity to create institutions and thereby strengthen the community those institutions served. As they sacrificed in this cause, much as their parents and grandparents had done, they came to a revivified sense of 'ownership' with regard to the local church, and to an enhanced sense of agency. Certainly their American experience was wider than that of their immigrant forebears, and their lives were in consequence less bounded by the parish. But the local church was nonetheless for them a principal source of identity and pride, and an embodiment of values that often seemed threatened by a society that withheld both dignity and security from all but the most privileged members of the working class.

The continued importance of the church to American-born ethnics is evidenced by the proliferation of Catholic institutions in working-class communities in the late nineteenth century and after. Schools were by far the most numerous of these. The number of Catholic elementary schools in Chicago, for example, rose from 29 in 1880 to 87 in 1900 to 196 in 1920. In 1920 86 per cent of the city's parishes had an elementary school; the figure had risen to 93 per cent by 1930. Chicago's Catholic elementary schools enrolled nearly 28 per cent of the relevant school-age population in that latter year. Secondary schools developed more slowly, but in Chicago as elsewhere a fully articulated system of Catholic schools had begun to emerge by the close of the 1920s.[28]

Those systems were in part the result of episcopal pressure and clerical cajoling. But they were more fundamentally the result of lay commitment to alternative schooling. Working-class Catholics built schools as they built churches – through sacrificial giving and sometimes by means of donated labour. The cost of maintaining those schools was frequently borne by the parish as a whole, so as to minimise the burden of tuition on already-struggling parents.[29] (Such arrangements bespeak an admirable capacity for solidarity, and might properly be regarded as a form of sustained collective action.) It is true that by the 1890s pastors in Chicago, and in most other American dioceses, were directed to withhold the sacraments from parents who failed to send their children to available Catholic schools. But such draconian measures were simply incapable of enforcement, as the case of Chicago's Italians makes clear. No combination of pleas and threats from their bishop or pastors could persuade that stubbornly independent group to build and use parochial schools. Other groups could have resisted too, had they been so inclined.[30]

The commitment to alternative schools was partly rooted in an exaggerated fear of American individualism and materialism – twin threats to the family economy and ultimately to ethnic group survival. The clergy did much to fan these fears, and with obvious effect. (Where episcopal, and hence clerical, commitment to parochial schooling was weak at a critical juncture in a diocese's history, parochial schools typically appeared later and in relatively smaller numbers than in neighbouring dioceses. Boston is a case in point.)[31] The same fears helped to underwrite lay support of Catholic hospitals and such social service institutions as orphanages and homes for the aged poor.[32] But immigrants also learned from their own experience that American institutions were often hostile to immigrant values and priorities. Public schools rarely made provision for instruction in the ancestral tongue, and typically promoted an aggressive and wholly uncritical programme of Americanisation – as did various social welfare institutions. School and welfare personnel were often overtly contemptuous of Catholicism, especially prior to the First World War, and continued in the post-war years to oppose a familial ethic that endorsed early wage-earning for the young. Even sympathetic teachers and welfare workers were separated from the realities of the immigrant world by formidable barriers of language and class.[33]

In the circumstances, it was an act of resistance to build alternative institutions. Such institutions were shaped by the dominant values of the community that supported them, and worked to reinforce those values. This was especially true of schools. Few American dioceses before the First World War had anything approaching centralised school governance; some, like Detroit, had radically decentralised systems well into the 1930s.[34] Decentralisation meant that decisions about curricula and pedagogy rested mainly with the various teaching orders and the pastors who solicited their services. And ultimately with parents: no sensible pastor would recruit an order whose style and curricular goals were likely to antagonise even a portion of his parishioners. The burden of school support was so onerous, the public alternative so visibly at hand, that pastors had necessarily to accommodate parental priorities.

As for the sisters who taught in the schools, they typically came from backgrounds similar to those of their students. European-born religious were sometimes of higher social origin than their immigrant charges: this was the case, for example, with the first generation of Felician Sisters in Chicago and Detroit. American-born sisters, however, were often from working-class families. (The modest educational requirements for membership in most orders democratised the sisterhoods in terms of recruitment long before a similar trend was evident among the clergy.)[35] True, the eventual extent of a sister's schooling set her apart from the world she had known as a child. So did the rigidities of convent life. But she was apt, nonetheless, to retain an identification with the world from which she came. Religious orders recruited primarily in the communities they served and their cultures could not help but reflect this. The semi-cloistered sister, moreover, was for all her other-worldliness a potent symbol for Catholics of their distinctive identity.[36]

The communal orientation of Catholic schools in the decades around the turn of the century contrasts sharply with trends in public education. Urban school systems in these decades were increasingly bureaucratised and more and more in the charge of highly specialised 'experts'. By nearly every conventional measure, the quality of urban schools improved substantially in these years. But those same schools were increasingly beyond the direct control of parents.[37] Support for parochial schools thus brought for Catholics a measure of protection from the state, and a greater than usual degree of control over an important aspect of local community life. Ironically, many of the state-sponsored experts thus kept at bay thought of Catholic schools as the products, and bulwarks, of an authoritarian mind-set.

Catholics of course paid a price for their version of community control. They taxed themselves heavily to support their alternative institutions, and perpetuated their isolation from the larger American society. Their reluctance to support improvements in the public schools bred resentment on the part of non-Catholics, including those in the working class.[38] But these alternative institutions seem to have served their constituents well. What little research we possess with regard to the Catholic schools, for example, suggests that they may have facilitated academic achievement for working-class youngsters to a greater extent than their public counterparts.[39] (That they have this effect today for African-American and Hispanic students has been amply documented.)[40] The very existence of Catholic schools, moreover, was a monument to ethnic achievement – to the efficacy of collective action on the part of the poor and near-poor. As such, these schools – like other Catholic institutions – embodied a moral lesson that was not without its relevance for politics.

Still, it could reasonably be argued that Catholic institutional separatism, coupled with the conservatism of Catholic teaching, worked mainly to inhibit militancy – let alone radicalism – on the part of most Catholic workers. It is hard to quarrel with Kerby Miller's observation that the American Church, like its Irish counterpart, 'preached the twin gospels of respectability and resignation'.[41] But religious ideas and symbol systems are rarely unambiguous; there is ample room for contestation with respect to meaning. Counsels of resignation and respect for one's betters were received and assessed in a variety of circumstances and by men and women whose experiences did indeed change over time. Much depends on context.

Consider, for example, what we might call the gospel of internalised restraint. This was probably preached most insistently among the Irish, often in conjunction with total abstinence crusades.[42] But every ethnic group was subjected to vigorous condemnations of drunkenness, sexual impurity, and gambling (save in the cause of parish support). The manly ideal was disciplined family living and disciplined work on the family's behalf.[43] Such preachments bore with particular weight on poorer working-class men, and were surely a source of guilt and shame for many among them. It was middle-class males, after all, who seemed to embody the manly ethic most fully and to have reaped its putative rewards. One wonders, indeed, if the violence that sometimes accompanied parish disputes was not often rooted in anger at clerical moralism.[44]

But despite the psychic costs involved, the church's ascetic norms had legitimacy for many working-class men. (Women, it goes almost without saying, had far greater cause to endorse them.) For men like these, the gospel of internalised restraint was productive of pride as well as shame, of mastery as well as guilt, of identification with the church as well as resentment toward it. That gospel permitted, even encouraged, a sense of virtue in the absence of material success, for Catholics were regularly warned about the corrosive effects of materialism on faith and conduct.[45] Thus a working-class man could envision his life in terms of struggle and moral progress: he could endow it with a shape and meaning that his social immobility would otherwise have denied. And more than 'resignation' was involved: such a man would necessarily see himself as an active moral agent, as the maker of consequential choices.

Nor did he labour alone in this regard: a variety of men's parish societies lent public encouragement and support to an ethic of disciplined living.[46] So the self was redeemed at least partly in a collective context; there was redemption for one's fellows too, and indeed for the moral standing of one's ethno-religious group, whose capacity for independence and virtue had likely been matter of public dispute. An erosion of deference in the moral order is not an easy thing for historians to chart, nor are its public consequences simple to predict. But lacking a sense of their own moral respectability, the poor are not likely – in this or any other day – to develop a heightened political consciousness. Considered in this light, the moral rigorism to which working-class Catholics were heir might be seen as a double-edged sword – a source of liberation as well as repression. Catholic teaching on marriage is perhaps especially instructive in this regard. I refer here both to the indissolubility of marriage and the prohibition on contraception, though the latter may not have been preached with much frequency before the time of the First World War.[47]

Still, the teaching can easily look in retrospect to have been unrelievedly repressive, certainly for women but also for working-class men, who bore principal responsibility for family support. One might even be tempted to argue that working-class Catholics who remained in the church were schooling themselves in submission to cruel and irrational authority. Given current sexual assumptions, it is easy to ignore the obvious: that the teaching on marriage both reflected and reinforced the familial ethic so essential to survival among the poor. (Even the ban on contraception, at first glance no aid to such survival, had utility insofar as it reinforced the prohibition on any but marital sex.) Less obvious, but no less important, is the economic morality implicit in Catholic teaching on marriage and the family.

That teaching was essentially patriarchal, despite the restraints imposed on men's sexual behaviour. Men were the rightful family heads, and the proper sources of family support. (The working daughter was so familiar a figure in ethnic communities that her earning was rarely questioned. But wives were to remain at home.) The male family head was not without his tender side: he was to be a model of 'virile' piety, and devote the greater part of his leisure to the family. And he, like his wife, was to welcome new births as gifts from God.[48] Realisation of this family ideal required far higher wages and a greater degree of employment security than America generally afforded. Few Catholic workers, accordingly, were able to achieve it. But the family ideal, rooted as it was in religion, lent moral legitimacy to this higher standard of wages and job security. It gave religious content to the seemingly secular notion of an 'American' living standard. And it gave Catholics the right – indeed the obligation – to claim that standard as their own, even to struggle on its behalf with non-Catholic allies.

What this meant in political terms depended on the circumstances. Where economic and political realities were conducive to worker organisation, a religiously-rooted economic morality might well be the spark for mass worker action, and certainly a factor in sustaining it.[49] Even workers whose lives had been largely defined by ethnic loyalties could apply this morality in larger-than-ethnic terms. We would do well to examine the ostensibly secular rhetoric of the early CIO, to pick an especially apt example, for references to the values which underlay Catholic teaching on the family. The same morality, however, could under different political circumstances align Catholic workers with conservative, even reactionary, forces. Steve Rosswurm has argued that Catholic 'patriarchalism' contributed directly to the almost obsessive anti-Communism of many Catholic workers in the years after the Second World War, and thus to their waning support for economic radicalism.[50] Still, the 'family wage', for all its patriarchal bias, had not – indeed, has not – ceased to be a potentially radical concept. Given current circumstances, one can only regret its almost complete eclipse not only on the American Left but among the great majority of Catholics, for whom social mobility and assimilation to an individualist norm have eroded an ethic of communalism.[51]

The complex potential of ethnic Catholicism as a force in American working-class life cannot be fully appreciated without taking anti-Catholicism into account. Anti-Catholicism has of course been one of the most enduring and politically consequential of the nation's many bigotries. (That it has had so little appeal as a topic for historians of my own generation has largely to do, I suspect, with our inability to see today's mostly Catholic 'white ethnics' as anything but bigots themselves.)[52] Anti-Catholicism was clearly an impetus to political mobilisation among even nominally Catholic immigrants. The Famine Irish are the best example of this: suffering more from anti-Catholicism than any other group, particularly in New England and the Middle Atlantic states, they were swiftly recruited as voters to the wide-open ranks of the Democratic Party and developed a political elite of their own within the space of a generation. Subsequent post-Famine immigrants were incorporated into the local machine almost as soon as they were absorbed into the local parish – indeed, there were typically close connections between the two institutions. For the Irish at least, loyalty to the Democratic Party was for many generations nearly as compelling an aspect of their American ethnic identity as loyalty to the church.[53] If this was less true of other Catholic ethnics, those ethnics were nonetheless likely, based on their own experience of anti-Catholicism, to cling to their Democratic loyalties with close to religious intensity.

Their Democratic loyalties brought ethnic Catholics certain clear advantages. Involved willy-nilly in the business of coalition politics, Catholic voters helped to create a new American pluralism – though one that was based for a very long time on overtly racist assumptions. Afforded legitimacy in the political order, Catholic ethnics were eventually freed from the most onerous forms of economic discrimination. Belonging to a party that protected Catholic interests without being 'Catholic' itself, ethnics gained a confidence in American institutions that facilitated their eventual participation in, even leadership of, secular trade unions. (The separatist impulse in American Catholicism has, as in other Anglophone countries, been largely confined to those institutions that impinge directly on private life – to schools and social service institutions rather than unions and political parties.) Party loyalty thus helped to mitigate the social isolation and parochialism of various Catholic ethnic populations, even as that same loyalty was an ingredient in their evolving ethnic identities.

But Democratic loyalties also worked to inhibit economic radicalism among ethnic workers, and to impede the consolidation of independent working-class movements. The legacy of anti-Catholicism was critical in this regard. The Democratic Party was linked for most ethnics in an almost visceral way to the defence not simply of Catholic interests but of their own respectability and claim to full American citizenship. For this was precisely what the purveyors of anti-Catholicism denied – typically in pursuit of moral reforms whose sponsors tended to be both Republican and middle-class.[54] In the circumstances, Democratic loyalties could easily seem synonymous with working-class loyalty – as could a proud public identification with Catholicism. Generations of Democratic politicians played skilfully on this theme. The temporary emergence of a more class-based politics in the 1930s was accompanied, interestingly enough, by a marked and enduring decrease in popular anti-Catholicism. Religious wars continued in the post-Depression decades, and were at least sometimes surrogates for war between the classes. But American religious wars have not in recent decades been fought along confessional lines.[55]

Anti-Catholicism may also have worked to intensify the racism so central to American politics in the nineteenth and for much of the twentieth century. Anti-Catholicism in its crudest nativist form was itself a kind of racism. (The Irish, as David Roediger has pointed out, and later the Italians and Slavs, were initially regarded as other-than-white.) As Catholics mobilised in their own defence, they learned to play the 'race card' – to stake their claim to citizenship on their European origins. Political mobilisation, coupled with their growing numbers, enabled Catholic immigrants 'to insist on their own whiteness' – to lift a phrase from Roediger's important book.[56] Church leaders typically encouraged this mentality: few Catholic clergy in the nineteenth or early twentieth centuries argued against racism, while the Catholic press was for the most part conventionally racist in its news and editorial content.[57] Significant change in this regard came only in the 1930s, as the first real efforts at Catholic evangelisation among African-Americans began in the urban north, and a symbolic handful of Catholic schools and colleges lowered the colour bar.[58] Coincidentally perhaps, it was also in the 1930s that ethnic Catholics and African-Americans came to share loyalties to, and membership in, the CIO and the Democratic Party. Coincident or no, these new alliances were the prelude to a major shift in American racial politics.

Catholicism, then, has been a complex factor in the history of America's industrial working class. It provided a critical store of resources for the psychic – and indeed the economic – survival of countless immigrants, and for the on-going business of creating an ethnic identity. It was a force for group mobilisation, and hence for at least a defensive form of political empowerment. At the same time, Catholicism arguably worked to intensify division in the working class, certainly along confessional lines and even among those Catholic ethnics for whom religion underwrote a heightened group consciousness. Confessional and ethnic antagonisms, like racial hatred, were formidable obstacles to those who sought a genuinely class-based politics.

But above all else Catholicism in the American context was a genuinely popular creation. It was lay Catholics, the great majority of them working-class, who underwrote and sometimes literally helped to build the Catholic institutional ghetto – and did so voluntarily. America's Catholics were not unique in this regard: Catholic immigrants have been formidable institution-builders in the other Anglophone countries too. Nor should we ignore those many workers, especially in Belgium and Germany, who were active in Catholic unions and parties. They too were institution-sustainers if not always builders in their own right. But the American experience has been unusual in certain key respects. The heterogeneity of its Catholic population, the absence of a state church, the extent to which religion has underwritten group identity and been integrated into the nation's popular and political cultures – these make for a working-class history to which the religious factor must be central. By taking religion seriously, we enlarge our vision of working-class life and politics. We deepen our understanding of what Aristide Zolberg has called 'the most distinctive feature of the American outcome: the orientation of workers *qua citizens* overwhelmingly toward the political mainstream'.[59] We open up a new perspective on the dynamics of strikes and other forms of working-class protest, and on the ideological orientation of American unions.

Perhaps most important, taking religion seriously directs our attention to the community-building achievements of the nation's ethnic workers, and causes us to reflect on the meaning of those achievements. The institutions that Catholic workers built and sustained speak directly to their consciousness – to the values, hopes and fears of this largely marginal and inarticulate group. They speak as well to the often underestimated capacities of this group for collective endeavour and for resistance to the host society's priorities. One might plausibly argue that these institutions constituted a critique of industrial capitalism, at least insofar as they testified to the agency of ordinary men and women, and championed their family-centred values and priorities. If this 'world-in-opposition' was ultimately vulnerable to the host society's individualism, it was still while it lasted a remarkable creation and one that had major effect on the evolution of the American working class.

NOTES

1.   Quoted in Gerald P. Fogarty, *The Vatican and the American Hierarchy from 1870 to 1965* (Stuttgart, 1982), 394.

2.   I explore these themes more fully in 'On the Margins: The State of American Catholic History', *American Quarterly*, 45:1 (1993), 104–27. See also 'Looking Backward: Reflections on Workers' Culture and Certain Conceptual Dilemmas within Labor History', in Leon Fink, *In Search of the Working Class: Essays in American Labor History and Political Culture* (Urbana, IL, 1994), 183.

3.   The literature here is immense, but as examples of ethnic variations in religious practice see, for the Irish: David M. Emmons, *The Butte Irish: Class and Ethnicity in an American Mining Town, 1875–1925* (Urbana and Chicago, 1989), 95–103; Timothy J. Meagher, 'Irish, American, Catholic: Irish-American Identity in Worcester, Massachusetts, 1880 to 1920', in Timothy J. Meagher, ed., *From Paddy to Studs: Irish-American Communities in the Turn of the Century Era* (Westport, CT, 1986), 75–92 and (in the same volume) Ellen Skerrett, 'The Development of Catholic Identity Among Irish-Americans in Chicago, 1880–1920', 117–38; Kerby A. Miller, *Emigrants and Exiles: Ireland and the Irish Exodus to North America* (New York, 1985), 331–4, 526–34; Thomas E. Wangler, 'Catholic Religious Life in Boston in the Era of Cardinal O'Connell', in Robert E. Sullivan and James M. O'Toole, eds, *Catholic Boston: Studies in Religion and Community, 1870–1970* (Boston, 1985), 239–72; on the Germans: David A. Gerber, *The Making of an American Pluralism: Buffalo, New York, 1825–1860* (Urbana and Chicago, 1989), which also deals with the Irish; Kathleen Neils Conzen, *Immigrant Milwaukee, 1836–1860: Accommodation and Community in a Frontier City* (Cambridge, MA, 1976), 158–64; Jay P. Dolan, *The Immigrant Church: New York's Irish and German Catholics, 1815–1865* (Baltimore, 1975); on the Italians: Gary Ross Mormino, *Immigrants on the Hill: Italian-Americans in St. Louis, 1882–1982* (Urbana, 1986); Robert Anthony Orsi, *The Madonna of 115th Street: Faith and Community in Italian Harlem, 1880–1950*; John W. Briggs, *An Italian Passage: Immigrants to Three American Cities, 1890–1930* (New Haven, 1978), 193–6; Silvano M. Tomasi, *Piety and Power: The Role of the Italian Parishes in the New York Metropolitan Area, 1880–1930* (New York, 1975); on Poles: Dominic A. Pacyga, *Polish Immigrants and Industrial Chicago: Workers on the South Side, 1880–1920* (Columbus, OH, 1991); Robert A. Slayton, *Back of the Yards: The Making of a Local Democracy* (Chicago, 1986); Ewa Morawska, *For Bread with Butter: The Life-world of East Central Europeans in Johnstown, Pennsylvania, 1890–1930* (Cambridge, 1985), 107–9, which also deals with other Slavic groups; Joseph John Parot, *Polish Catholics in Chicago, 1850–1920* (De Kalb, IL, 1981); Leslie Woodcock Tentler, 'Who is the Church? Conflict in a Polish Immigrant Parish in Late Nineteenth-Century Detroit', *Comparative Studies in Society and History*, 25:2 (April 1983), 267–8; on Slovaks: June Granatir Alexander, *The Immigrant Church and Community: Pittsburgh's Slovak Catholics and Lutherans, 1880–1915* (Pittsburgh, 1987); M. Mark Stolarik, *Growing Up on the South Side: Three Generations of Slovaks in Bethlehem, Pennsylvania, 1880–1976* (Lewisburg,

PA, 1985), 44, 52–3, 74–82. Most of these studies deal with gender-based differences in religious practice, though sometimes only in passing. For a more sustained discussion, see Leslie Woodcock Tentler, *Seasons of Grace: A History of the Catholic Archdiocese of Detroit* (Detroit, 1990), 61, 64–6, 169, 172–5, 402–7. On secular–church rivalries over group leadership, see John Bodnar, *The Transplanted: A History of Immigrants in Urban America* (Bloomington, IN, 1985), 109–10, 156–66; for similar rivalries among the Germans, see Eric L. Hirsch, *Urban Revolt: Ethnic Politics in the Nineteenth-Century Chicago Labor Movement* (Berkeley, CA, 1990), 157–8; Richard Oestreicher, *Solidarity and Fragmentation: Working People and Class Consciousness in Detroit, 1875–1900* (Urbana, 1986), 51.

4. Skerrett, 'The Development of Catholic Identity Among Irish-Americans', in Meagher, *From Paddy to Studs*, 118; Miller, *Emigrants and Exiles*, 331–4, 526–34.

5. Mormino, *Immigrants on the Hill*, 153–164; Orsi, *Madonna of 115th Street*, 52–60, 65–7.

6. Paula M. Kane, *Separatism and Subculture: Boston Catholicism, 1900–1920* (Chapel Hill, NC, 1994), 100–1; Tentler, *Seasons of Grace*, 61–3, 172–6, 403–5; Hugh MacLeod, 'Catholicism and the New York Irish, 1880–1910', in Jim Obelkevich, Lyndal Roper and Raphael Samuel, eds, *Disciplines of Faith: Studies in Religion, Politics and Patriarchy*, (London, 1987), 344–6; Wangler, 'Catholic Religious Life', 263–4; Jay P. Dolan, *The American Catholic Experience: A History from Colonial Times to the Present* (Garden City, NY, 1985), 219–20; Jay P. Dolan, *Catholic Revivalism* (Notre Dame, IN, 1978) 131–4.

7. Kane, *Separatism and Subculture*, 23–4; Tentler, *Seasons of Grace*, 208–11, 403–4, 427–8; Wangler, 'Catholic Religious Life', 255, 258, 264; Dolan, *American Catholic Experience*, 233.

8. Tentler, *Seasons of Grace*, 66–7.

9. The literature on lay initiative is now very large. The seminal publications are Timothy L. Smith, 'Religion and Ethnicity in America', *American Historical Review* 83 (Dec. 1978), 1155–85, and 'Lay Initiative in the Religious Life of American Immigrants, 1880–1950', in Tamara K. Hareven, ed., *Anonymous Americans: Explorations in Nineteenth-Century Social History* (Englewood Cliffs, NJ, 1971), 214–49. For a summary of work prior to the mid-1980s, see Dolan, *American Catholic Experience*, chapter 6; see also Tentler, *Seasons of Grace*, 71–2, 220; Joseph J. Casino, 'From Sanctuary to Involvement: A History of the Catholic Parish in the Northeast', in Jay P. Dolan, ed., *The American Catholic Parish: A History from 1850 to the Present*, v. 1: *Northeast, Southeast, South Central* (New York and Mahwah, NJ, 1987), 12; Bodnar, *The Transplanted*, 150; on Germans, see Joseph M. White, 'Cincinnati's German Catholic Life: A Heritage of Lay Participation', *U.S. Catholic Historian*, 12:3 (Summer 1994), 6–8; Gerber, *American Pluralism*, 193; Dolan, *Immigrant Church*, 72–3; on Poles, see Tentler, 'Who is the Church?', 260–4; on Slovaks, see Stolarik, *Growing Up on the South Side*, 45–6; Alexander, *Immigrant Church and Community*, 36–7; Mark Stolarik, 'Lay Initiative in American-Slovak Parishes, 1880–1930', *Records of the American Catholic Historical Society of Philadelphia* 83:3–4 (Sept.–Dec. 1972), 151–8; on Eastern Europeans more generally, see

Morawska, *For Bread with Butter*, 106–7; on the dominant role of clergy among the Famine Irish and the Italians, see Ellen Skerrett, 'Sacred Space: Parish and Neighborhood in Chicago', in Ellen Skerrett, Edward R. Kantowicz and Steven Avella, eds, *Catholicism, Chicago Style* (Chicago, 1993), 143–5, 148–9; on Italians, see Mormino, *Immigrants on the Hill*, 153–4.

10. Tentler, *Seasons of Grace*, 76, 407; Gerber, *American Pluralism*, 152, 193; Alexander, *Immigrant Church and Community*, 32–3; Skerrett, 'Development of Catholic Identity', 123; Orsi, *Madonna of 115th Street*, 54; Stolarik, *Growing Up on the South Side*, 45–6; Tentler, 'Who is the Church?', 269.

11. Skerrett, 'Sacred Space,' 152–5; Gerber, *American Pluralism*, 190; John J. Bukowczyk, *And My Children Did Not Know Me: A History of the Polish-Americans* (Bloomington, IN, 1987), 40–1; Morawska, *For Bread with Butter*, 109–11; Orsi, *Madonna of 115th Street*, 54–5, 59–60, 64–7; Smith, 'Religion and Ethnicity', 1168–74.

12. Gerber, *American Pluralism*, 190; Dolan, *Immigrant Church*, 73–4; Tomasi, *Piety and Power*, 124.

13. Gerber, *American Pluralism*, 119; see also Bodnar, *The Transplanted*, 150–66; Tentler, 'Who is the Church?', 252–4.

14. R. Laurence Moore, 'The End of Religious Establishment and the Beginning of Religious Politics: Church and State in the United States', in Thomas Kselman, ed., *Belief in History: Innovative Approaches to European and American History* (Notre Dame, IN, 1991), 256–7.

15. White, 'Cincinnati's German Catholic Life', 11; Pacyga, *Polish Immigrants and Industrial Chicago*, 140–3; Robert Lewis Mikkelsen, 'Immigrants in Politics: Poles, Germans, and the Social Democratic Party of Milwaukee', in Dirk Hoerder, ed., *Labor Migration in the Atlantic Economies: The European and North American Working Classes During the Period of Industrialization* (Westport, CN, 1985), 288–9; Morawska, *For Bread with Butter*, 230–1.

16. White, 'Cincinnati's German Catholic Life,' 8–9, 16–17; Tentler, *Seasons of Grace*, 71–5, 219–21; Alexander, *Immigrant Church and Community*, 56–8; Dolan, *American Catholic Community*, 193–4; Dolan, *Immigrant Church*, 52. On the ante-bellum period, see Patrick Carey, *People, Priests and Prelates: Ecclesiastical Democracy and the Tensions of Trusteeism* (Notre Dame, IN, 1987).

17. Tentler, *Seasons of Grace*, 220–1; on the Polish National Catholic Church, see William Galush, 'The Polish National Church: A Survey of the Origins, Development and Mission', *Records of the American Catholic Historical Society of Philadelphia* 83:3–4 (Sept.–Dec. 1972), 131–49.

18. White, 'Cincinnati's German Catholic Life', 2–4; Miller, *Emigrants and Exiles*, 126; David A. Gerber, 'Modernity in the Service of Tradition: Catholic Lay Trustees at Buffalo's St. Louis Church and the Transformation of European Communal Traditions, 1829–1855', *Journal of Social History* 15:4 (Summer 1982), 655–84.

19. Bertele to Bishop John Foley, 16 February 1916, Archives of the Archdiocese of Detroit, St. Michael, Monroe parish file. See also White, 'Cincinnati's German Catholic Life', 9–10; Tentler, *Seasons of Grace*, 72–4, 218–24; Alexander, *Immigrant Church and Community*, 58–65.

20. Tentler, *Seasons of Grace*, 142; Robert E. Sullivan, 'Beneficial Relations:

Toward a Social History of the Diocesan Priests of Boston, 1875–1944', in Sullivan and O'Toole, eds, *Catholic Boston*, 206, 235; Thomas E. Wangler, 'Catholic Religious Life', 242–3.

21. Tentler, *Seasons of Grace*, 72–4, 219–21; Stolarik, *Growing Up on the South Side*, 52–3; Tentler, 'Who is the Church?', 266. The prolonged dispute discussed in this last-mentioned source provides a good example of extensive press coverage.

22. On this point see John H. Whyte, *Catholics in Western Democracies: A Study in Political Behaviour* (Dublin, 1981), 15–16 and *passim*. For an example of a political application of this logic, see Joshua B. Freeman, 'Catholics, Communists, and Republicans: Irish Workers and the Organization of the Transport Workers Union', in Michael H. Frisch and Daniel J. Walkowitz, eds, *Working-Class America: Essays on Labor, Community, and American Society* (Urbana, 1983), 275.

23. Olivier Zunz, *The Changing Face of Inequality: Urbanization, Industrial Development and Immigrants in Detroit, 1880–1920* (Chicago, 1982), chapters 3, 13 and *passim*.

24. James M. O'Toole, *Militant and Triumphant: William Henry O'Connell and the Catholic Church in Boston, 1859–1944* (Notre Dame, IN, 1992), especially 102–20; Tentler, *Seasons of Grace*, 425–6; Edward R. Kantowicz, *Corporation Sole: Cardinal Mundelein and Chicago Catholicism* (Notre Dame, IN, 1983), especially 49–83.

25. Tentler, *Seasons of Grace*, 149–50, 367, 375; Sullivan, 'Beneficial Relations', 205–6. Priests typically came from higher-status backgrounds than the mass of Catholics. But ordination became increasingly possible for men from modest backgrounds as various dioceses were increasingly able to underwrite high school training for prospective seminarians. See Joseph Fichter, *Religion as an Occupation: A Study in the Sociology of Professions* (Notre Dame, IN, 1961), 63–7 for data on the socio-economic origins of American seminarians in the 1920s.

26. Kane, *Separatism and Subculture*, 95–9; Tentler, *Seasons of Grace*, 200–11, 426–31; Miller, *Emigrants and Exiles*, 532–5; for parallel developments in American Protestantism, see Joseph F. Kett, *Rites of Passage: Adolescence in America, 1790 to the Present* (New York, 1977), 189–98.

27. Tentler, *Seasons of Grace*, 452–5; James W. Sanders, *The Education of an Urban Minority: Catholics in Chicago, 1833–1965* (New York, 1977), 13, 75–6. Boston, however, differed in this regard: see James W. Sanders, 'Catholics and the School Question in Boston: The Cardinal O'Connor Years', in Sullivan and O'Toole, eds, *Catholic Boston*, 140–1.

28. Sanders, *Education of an Urban Minority*, 4–5, 12–13.

29. Tentler, *Seasons of Grace*, 86–7, 90, 237; Sanders, *Education of an Urban Minority*, 86; Briggs, *An Italian Passage*, 196–7. The rising costs of educating sisters eventually caused most parishes to abandon free-tuition policies, but most continued to provide subsidies to families with children in the parish school.

30. Tentler, *Seasons of Grace*, 232–3, 237; Briggs, *An Italian Passage*, 193–203; Sanders, *Education of an Urban Minority*, 70.

31. Joel Perlmann, *Ethnic Differences: Schooling and Social Structure Among the Irish, Italians, Jews, and Blacks in an American City, 1880–1935*

(Cambridge, 1988), 68; Sanders, 'The School Question in Boston', 121, 123–8, 158–9; Sanders, *Education of an Urban Minority*, 21–3, 36.

32. Catholic hospitals were often founded in response to perceived Protestant hostility, but were markedly more ecumenical in their policies than orphanages. See Mary J. Oates, *The Catholic Philanthropic Tradition in America* (Bloomington, IN, 1995), 46–50 and Christopher J. Kauffman, 'Catholic Health Care: American Pluralism and Religious Meanings', unpublished paper, delivered at the Center for the Study of American Religion, Princeton University, June 18, 1994. See also Tentler, *Seasons of Grace*, 107–9; Susan S. Walton, 'To Preserve the Faith: Catholic Charities in Boston, 1870–1930', in Sullivan and O'Toole, eds, *Catholic Boston*, 67–119.

33. Morawska, *For Bread with Butter*, 268–70; William Issel, 'Americanization, Acculturation and Social Control: School Reform Ideology in Industrial Pennsylvania, 1880–1910', *Journal of Social History*, 12:4 (Summer 1979), 569–90; on the ideological content of American school textbooks in the late nineteenth and early twentieth centuries, see Daniel Rodgers, *The Work Ethic in America, 1850–1920* (Chicago, 1978), especially ch. 5; Sanders, *Education of an Urban Minority*, 21–6.

34. Tentler, *Seasons of Grace*, 92–4, 241, 248–9, 450, 454–8; Thomas W. Spalding, *The Premier See: A History of the Archdiocese of Baltimore, 1789–1989* (Baltimore, 1989), 329–30; Sanders, 'The School Question in Boston', 128, 130; Sanders, *Education of an Urban Minority*, 141–60.

35. Patricia Byrne, 'In the Parish but Not of It: Sisters', in Jay P. Dolan *et al.*, *Transforming Parish Ministry: The Changing Roles of Catholic Clergy, Laity, and Women Religious* (New York, 1989), 124; Patricia Byrne, 'Sisters of St. Joseph: The Americanization of a French Tradition', *US Catholic Historian*, 5 (1986), 270. Byrne also notes that 'indigenous American sisterhoods . . . did not, as a rule, form a separate servant class within their communities' (*ibid.*, 268).

36. On convent culture see Byrne, 'In the Parish', 128–32; for a good sampling of recent works on American women religious, see Margaret Susan Thompson, 'Cultural Conundrum: Sisters, Ethnicity and Adaptation of American Catholicism', *Mid-America*, 74 (October, 1992), 205–30; Mary J. Oates, 'Organized Voluntarism: The Catholic Sisters in Massachusetts, 1870–1940', in Janet Wilson James, ed., *Women in American Religion* (Philadelphia, 1980), 141–69; Mary Ewens, OP, *The Role of the Nun in Nineteenth-Century America* (New York, 1978).

37. Jeffrey Mirel, *The Rise and Fall of an Urban School System: Detroit, 1907–81* (Ann Arbor, 1993), ch. 1, especially 29–31; Ira Katznelson and Margaret Weir, *Schooling for All: Class, Race, and the Decline of the Democratic Ideal* (New York, 1985), 102–20; Issel, 'Americanization, Acculturation and Social Control', 571–4, 581–6; Diane Ravitch, *The Great School Wars: New York City, 1805–1973* (New York, 1974), 182–6; Marvin Lazerson, *Origins of the Urban School: Public Education in Massachusetts, 1870–1915* (Cambridge, MA, 1971), 242–5; Raymond E. Callahan, *Education and the Cult of Efficiency* (Chicago, 1964) argues for the continued vulnerability of school administrators to political pressure groups, but shows the dominant role played by business elites in shaping turn-of-the century urban schools.

38. Ken Fones-Wolf, *Trade Union Gospel: Christianity and Labor in Industrial Philadelphia* (Philadelphia, 1989), 73; Sanders, *Education of an Urban Minority*, 30–2.

39. Perlmann, *Ethnic Differences*, 76–81; Morawska, *For Bread with Butter*, 269.

40. James S. Coleman, Thomas Hoffer and Sally Kilgore, *High School Achievement: Public, Catholic, and Private Schools Compared* (New York, 1982), esp. 122–78; Andrew M. Greeley, *Catholic High Schools and Minority Students* (New Brunswick, NJ, 1982); James S. Coleman and Thomas Hoffer, *Public and Private High Schools: The Impact of Communities* (New York, 1987), esp. ch. 5.

41. Kerby A. Miller, 'Class, Culture, and Immigrant Group Identity in the United States: The Case of Irish-American Ethnicity', in Virginia Yans-McLcughlin, ed., *Immigration Reconsidered: History, Sociology, and Politics* (New York, 1990), 114.

42. Brian P. Clarke, *Piety and Nationalism: Lay Voluntary Associations and the Creation of an Irish-Catholic Community in Toronto, 1850–1893* (Montreal, 1993), 132–9; Edith Jeffrey, 'Reform, Renewal, and Vindication: Irish Immigrants and the Catholic Total Abstinence Movement in Antebellum Philadelphia', *Pennsylvania Magazine of History and Biography*, CXIII (July 1988), 407–31; Fones-Wolf, *Trade Union Gospel*, 73; Miller, *Emigrants and Exiles*, 533–5.

43. Kane, *Separatism and Subculture*, 81–2; Clarke, *Piety and Nationalism*, 146–7; Tentler, *Seasons of Grace*, 204–6; Dale Light, 'The Reformation of Philadelphia Catholicism, 1830–1860', *Pennsylvania Magazine of History and Biography*, CXII:3 (July 1988), 401–5; Jay P. Dolan, *Catholic Revivalism: The American Experience, 1830–1900* (Notre Dame, IN, 1978), 147–63.

44. Tentler, 'Who is the Church?', 241–4, 251–2.

45. Kane, *Separatism and Subculture*, 84–7; Miller, 'Class, Culture, and Immigrant Group Identity', 114–15; Meagher, 'Irish, American, Catholic', 80–1; Sanders, 'The School Question in Boston', 162–3; Wangler, 'Catholic Religious Life in Boston', 253; Dolan, *Catholic Revivalism*, 157–61.

46. Kane, *Separatism and Subculture*, 95–9; Tentler, *Seasons of Grace*, 204–11; Wangler, 'Catholic Religious Life', 255, 258; Dolan, *Immigrant Church*, 77.

47. Tentler, *Seasons of Grace*, 263–7, 478–83; John T. Noonan, *Contraception: A History of Its Treatment by the Catholic Theologians and Canonists* (Cambridge, MA, 1986), chapter 13.

48. Kane, *Separatism and Subculture*, 81; Colleen McDannell, 'True Men as We Need Them: Catholicism and the Irish-American Male', *American Studies*, 27:2 (Fall 1986), 19–35.

49. Lizabeth Cohen, *Making a New Deal: Industrial Workers in Chicago, 1919–1939* (Cambridge, 1990), discusses 'economic morality' in the working class, but fails to consider the role that religion played in this regard. Oestreicher, *Solidarity and Fragmentation*, includes the religious dimension, but addresses the theme from a slightly different perspective than I have done. See also Fones-Wolf, *Trade Union Gospel*.

50. Steve Rosswurm, 'The Catholic Church and the Left-Led Unions: Labor

Priests, Labor Schools, and the ACTU', in Steve Rosswurm, ed., *The CIO's Left-Led Unions* (New Brunswick, NJ, 1992), 129.

51. On this general point, see Daniel Patrick Moynihan, *Family and Nation* (San Diego, New York and London, 1987), 4–15.

52. The standard sources are still John Higham, *Strangers in the Land: Patterns of American Nativism, 1860–1925* (New York, 1963) and Ray Allen Billington, *The Protestant Crusade, 1800–1860: A Study of the Origins of American Nativism* (Gloucester, MA, 1963, originally published 1938).

53. Martin G. Towey, 'Kerry Patch Revisited: Irish Americans in St. Louis in the Turn of the Century Era', in Meagher, ed., *From Paddy to Studs*, 151; James M. O'Toole, 'Prelates and Politicos: Catholics and Politics in Massachusetts, 1900–1970', in Sullivan and O'Toole, eds, *Catholic Boston*, 16–17; Miller, *Emigrants and Exiles*, 328–31, 524–6; Douglas V. Shaw, 'Political Leadership in the Industrial City: Irish Development and Nativist Response in Jersey City', in Richard L. Ehrlich, ed., *Immigrants in Industrial America, 1850–1920* (Charlottesville, VA, 1977), 85–95.

54. Jo Ann Manfra and Robert Kolesar, 'Irishmen, Elites and Reformers: Behavioral Continuities in Nineteenth Century Anti-Catholicism', *Mid-America: An Historical Review*, 76:1 (Winter 1994), 27–52; Mikkelson, 'Immigrants in Politics', 228–9.

55. On this point, see Robert Wuthnow, *The Restructuring of American Religion: Society and Faith Since World War II* (Princeton, NJ, 1988).

56. David R. Roediger, *The Wages of Whiteness: Race and the Making of the American Working Class* (London and New York, 1991), 137.

57. In the ante-bellum period, see *ibid.*, 140; for the late nineteenth and early twentieth centuries, see Tentler, *Seasons of Grace*, 494–7; Dolan, *American Catholic Experience*, 365–7. A revealing book on race and American Catholics is Stephen J. Ochs, *Desegregating the Altar: The Josephites and the Struggle for Black Priests, 1871–1960* (Baton Rouge, LA, 1990).

58. Tentler, *Seasons of Grace*, 497–514; Dolan, *American Catholic Experience*, 367–71.

59. Aristide R. Zolberg, 'How Many Exceptionalisms?', in Ira Katznelson and Aristide R. Zolberg, eds, *Working-Class Formation: Nineteenth-Century Patterns in Western Europe and the United States* (Princeton, 1986), 428.

8 Religion and the Formation of the Italian Working Class
John Pollard

> In the workshops, in the parched fields,
> we labour happily and contentedly,
> not like the turbulent plebeians,
> who drown out the wind with their insane accents:
> faithful labourers of the Gospel,
> as we work, we think of Paradise.
> (From the song of the Catholic Societies of Bergamo and Vicenza)[1]

The role which Catholicism played in the formation of the working class in Italy was profoundly different from that which it played in the US, whereas it presents many similarities with situations elswhere in Europe. Despite those similarities, however, the role which it played in Italy was predominantly determined by a number of factors peculiar to that country. The first was the nature of the working class itself: given the pattern of economic development in post-Unification Italy, the working class was essentially heterogeneous, consisting not only of an urban, industrial proletariat, not to mention a large residual artisan class, but a rural, agrarian proletariat of landless labourers, as well as various strata of peasant farmers. Indeed, it might make more sense to talk about the formation of the Italian working classes.

By comparison with the US and Britain, and even with other parts of Western Europe – such as Belgium, France and Germany – Italy was a latecomer to industrialisation.[2] Thus, at its unification in 1861, Italy was still an overwhelmingly rural, agrarian society with only a few small pockets of industry. The emergence of large-scale manufacturing industry was a phenomenon of the 1880s, 1890s and the early years of the twentieth century, hence the description of this period as that of the *prima industrializzazione*, the first industrialisation. It is with this period that we are concerned. Thereafter, Italian economic development went in a series of fits and starts, with the years of the First World War, the Fascist period and the late 1950s and early 1960s witnessing further major phases of economic growth.

The pattern of Italian economic development was also characterised by various forms of dualism, in the first place by the co-existence of a modern, industrial sector alongside 'backward' forms of production, i.e. the artisan sector. Dualism also developed on a geographical basis, the localisation of major centres of manufacturing industry in north-western Italy, the industrial 'triangle' of Milan, Turin and Genoa, as against the limited growth of industry in the Centre and extremely marginal development in the South. In the latter, the economy remained overwhelmingly agrarian, and that agriculture was often characterised by the survival of semi-feudal forms of landholding and backward methods of cultivation. Dualism also persisted within the agricultural sector itself, between small-scale subsistence farming virtually everywhere in Italy, and large-scale capitalist production, especially on the dairy farms of the Po Valley but also, exceptionally, in restricted areas of Apulia in the South.[3]

In these circumstances, during the period of the *prima industrializzazione*, the characteristically fragmented structure of the Italian working class quickly established itself. Alongside the burgeoning factory-based working class and workers in transport industries, large groups of artisans continued to survive and played an important role in the creation of the working-class movement. Of equal if not greater importance was the emergence of a rural, agrarian proletariat, most especially on the dairy farms of the Po Valley and in Apulia. This proletariat consisted of large numbers of *braccianti* (day labourers), *salariati* (labourers with more stable employment), and *mezzadri* (sharecroppers) whose standard of living was often as precarious as that of the *braccianti*. In addition, there was a bewildering variety of small tenant farmers, leaseholders and small landowners.[4]

It was also frequently the case that seasonal migration to towns, and seasonal or even permanent employment in manufacturing based in the countryside, especially of women, were essential to the family economy of the rural population.[5] To faithfully reflect the complexity and diversity of this picture, it needs to be emphasised that patterns of landholding, cultivation and employment not only varied widely between North and South, and from region to region, and province to province, but also within individual provinces. A final point, frequently made by Italian historians, is that most of the first generation of the industrial proletariat were inevitably recruited from a rural and largely agrarian background.[6] This was of considerable importance in determining the role which religion would play in the formation of the Italian working class.

A second important factor was the peculiarly Italian way in which the working-class movement, as it developed in the 1890s and early 1900s under Marxian ideological hegemony, elaborated and used the anticlerical traditions which it had inherited from its original Mazzinian and Garibaldian founding fathers and its more recent Anarchist precursors.

Also important was the complex and diverse nature of organised religion in Italy. Until recently, Catholicism has been nominally the religion of nearly 99 per cent of the population, thanks to the presence of the Papacy and its success in marginalising Protestant movements during the Counter-Reformation of the sixteenth century. But patterns of religious life, and the organisational effectiveness of the church, have varied enormously from North to South, from region to region and from countryside to town. The relationships between the clergy, the landowning and industrial classes and the poor has also varied markedly between regions. It should also be noted that the absence of any large organised Protestant denominations deprived the working class of a 'non-conformist' alternative to the 'established' church. On the other hand, the Catholic Church in Italy in this period was, in a legal sense at least, an established church. Despite the bitter conflict between the Papacy and the new Kingdom of Italy, provoked by the annexation of the Papal States and the implementation of anti-church legislation on the part of Cavour and the Moderate Liberal elite who unified Italy in 1861 and ruled it thereafter, Roman Catholicism remained, as the *Statuto* (constitution) of 1848 defined it, 'the sole religion of the State'. But establishment brought few advantages and many disadvantages, the most serious of the latter being the identification of the Church, in the eyes of many of the emerging proletarian masses, with the ruling class, despite the continuing hostility between large sections of that class and the Church authorities.

The other factor of great importance was the emergence of a Catholic movement in Italy, not only in the rural areas, and smaller industrial centres like Bergamo and Brescia, but also in the major industrial areas centring around Turin and Milan. Even if, as historians have frequently pointed out, the development of the economic and social associations of that movement were usually a response to the prior development of Socialist organisations, there is also plenty of evidence that, in its turn, the emergence of the Catholic movement conditioned the development of its Socialist rival.[7]

This analysis of the role religion played in the formation of the Italian working-class movement is essentially based on a synthesis of the results of existing macro and micro studies with which have been integrated the fruits of some, necessarily limited, research into primary source material.

In particular, it draws on studies of Milan and its hinterland, Turin, Bergamo and Brescia, and a few more isolated centres of economic development. Given the nature and diversity of these studies, it is important to take account of the varying approaches followed, in particular, the very different priorities of historians of the working-class movement as against those of its Catholic counterpart. What most members of both schools have had in common until recent years, however, has been a preoccupation with reconstructing the history of institutions rather than the history of the working class itself.

In analysing the role of religion in the formation of the Italian working class, three main issues will be explored:

1) The ways in which the processes of industrialisation, urbanisation, migration and proletarianisation affected the religious observance of the working masses and their allegiance to the institutional church.

2) The attitudes and strategies of the emerging working-class movement towards religion and the church, and the success of those policies in wresting working-class allegiance from the church and in establishing a secular counterculture.

3) The ideologies and strategies developed by the Catholic movement to recruit working-class support for its own economic and social organisations in competition with the Socialist-dominated working-class movement.

There are, unfortunately, no Italian equivalents of the Victorian census of Sunday church attendance in England which might provide some kind of statistical basis for a picture of the impact on religious practice of industrialisation, urbanisation, migration and proletarianisation. On the other hand, papal pronouncements, the deliberations of assemblies of the ecclesiastical provinces of bishops, diocesan synods and episcopal visitations of parishes provide considerable evidence of the effects of these processes in alienating the working classes from the church and of the reactions of the church authorities to this phenomenon.[8] Certainly, at the highest levels of the hierarchy there was a strong belief that such processes were having a deleterious effect on both religious practice and personal morality. Pius X (1903–14) in particular was deeply concerned about the effects of these changes, going so far as to make it policy to appoint bishops of northern extraction to southern dioceses in order to apprise the southern clergy of the perils of industrialisation.[9] In reality, the scope for industrial development in the South, apart from the Neapolitan hinterland and a few other areas, was minimal, despite the interventionist efforts of Giolitti's governments in the early 1900s. As we shall see, the only other area of the South in which economic and social changes posed a threat to church allegiance was Western Apulia.

In the industrialising cities of the North, such as Milan, Turin and Genoa, and minor centres of industry like Bergamo, Brescia and Vicenza, the clergy were quick to note any decline in the performance of religious duties. Research carried out on Turin and Milan in particular gives a clear picture of how the church sought to respond to this alienation of the working masses from religious life. In Turin, for example, the chief problem was seen to be a situation in which existing ecclesiastical structures and resources were being outstripped by rapid demographic change, particularly in new industrial suburbs. Immigration from the country areas of Turin province and the rest of Piedmont, with the consequent aggregation of large numbers of 'unchurched' poor, was perceived as being the major cause of the alienation of the industrial masses from religious practice: a situation which, in some ways, was not very different from that of industrial cities in either Britain or the US or the rest of Europe in the same period.

In the 1890s and early 1900s numerous requests were made by local parochial clergy and leading lay people for the building of new churches and the establishment of new parishes, the justification given being that the demographic changes consequent upon industrialisation were leaving workers 'without a moral guide and without a parish priest under whose direction two or three competent clergy might be able to preserve intact the treasury, the heritage of the faith'.[10] The Turin ecclesiastical authorities were slow to respond to these requests; in the period 1878–1906 only six new churches were built: another seven had been constructed by 1916.[11] The explanation for this slow and inadequate response appears to lie not only in the interminable bureaucratic delays of the diocesan curia, but also in the selfish, corporatist mentality of the city's parochial clergy, who tended to regard the parish more as a legal and financial entity than as the primary unit of ecclesial organisation: splitting parishes, therefore, meant a loss of revenue to incumbents from endowments, a loss which patrons were unwilling to make up.[12] Another explanation might lie in the attitude of the governmental authorities who, in Italy's complex system of ecclesiastical legislation, were responsible for giving legal effect to such changes.

A similar picture of a 'slow de-christianisation of factory workers' also emerges in the Milan area, but here a major obstacle to an effective response on the part of the ecclesiastical authorities to the problems thrown up by industrialisation and immigration lay in the lack of manpower.[13] Between 1805 and 1895 the numbers of parochial clergy in the Milan diocese declined from 2071 to 1895, and a similar decline was recorded for other industrialising Lombard dioceses such as Bergamo, Brescia and Como.[14] And this could be only partially offset by the activitiy of the regular clergy, i.e. those belonging to religious orders. Nevertheless, it should be noted that Milan was to see one of the first experiments in 'worker priests' in the history of the Catholic Church, the *Cappellani del Lavoro*.[15] How far Lombardy's clergy manpower problem was typical of a more general phenomenon in northern and central Italy is difficult to ascertain, but what was undeniably common to all these areas was a scarcity of means to pay the clergy, thanks to the partial expropriation of ecclesiastical property by Cavour and his successors.

The parochial clergy in industrialising areas (and also in some rural ones) often lamented the fact that due to the new patterns of work and production, many workers were unable to attend Sunday Mass: a phenomenon which was noted elsewhere in industrialising Europe.[16] Remonstrations with employers, often practising Catholics, about the need for the *riposo festivo* (Sabbath rest) were to no avail despite the pastoral letters of bishops and the sermons of parish priests. The gravity of the situation in Turin led to the founding of the *Pia Opera per la sanctificazione delle feste*, a sort of Italian Catholic equivalent of the Lord's Day Observance Society.[17] Also of concern to both bishops and local clergy were the alleged effects of industrialism upon personal morality: in particular, female and child labour were seen as posing a threat both to health and sexual mores.[18] Women's work was, of course, nothing new, but in rural, agrarian society it was largely carried out under the supervision of male family members. The sector of factory production in which women were most heavily employed was textiles, silk, cotton and wool, to which they had transferred so naturally and easily from domestic modes of production. In some areas, the solutions adopted involved the establishment of organisations specifically designed for the protection of female workers, the engagement of nuns to supervise the unmarried female factory workforce, and the provision of female residential hostels.[19]

In broader terms, clergy deplored the fact that the necessity of migration from countryside to town in search of work had destroyed the religious faith and habits, and the moral behaviour of the uprooted rural populations.[20] The perception of the city as a centre of decadence and degradation, in contrast to the healthiness and morality of the countryside (a myth that was later to bulk large in Mussolini's propaganda in favour of 'ruralisation') was a leitmotif of ecclesiastical discourse in this period.[21] Similar worries were evinced by the processes of immiseration and proletarianisation in a rural setting: the lamentations of rural priests about the degradation of members of their flocks who had lost their land – either owned or tenanted – and been reduced to the status of *braccianti*, the lowest of the low in the rural social hierarchy, were legion and usually evoked a charitable response on the part of the diocesan authorities and leaders of Catholic organisations.[22]

The starkest example of the effects of rural proletarianisation comes from the South. In his study of the rise of agrarian Socialism in the Apulian provinces of Foggia and west Bari, the rich agricultural lands of the Tavoliere, Snowden paints a picture of the alienation of the rural proletariat from the churches and outright hostility to the clergy.[23] The factors seen elsewhere, the brutal, inhuman demands made on the workforce by a ruthless new capitalist class, were all present, but this time in a rural, agrarian context. The abysmal levels of attendance at Mass which he records would have horrified the most besieged and desperate parish priest in the northern industrial towns.[24]

Part of the problem lay in the longstanding inadequacies of ecclesiastical organisation so common in the South – small, poor dioceses, much smaller than in the North and Centre of Italy – rather than in the results of demographic change.[25] In the areas that Snowden describes, the rural proletariat were concentrated in large 'agro-towns' that were not lacking in churches. What was lacking, however, was clergy: the national average of inhabitants per parish priest in the early 1900s was 1567; in the diocese of Trani, Nazaretto, Barletta and Bisceglie it was ten times that number.[26] A further problem was the abysmal quality of the clergy who were often poorly educated, semi-literate, superstitious, greedy and usurious.[27] These defects were in part the result of poor or non-existent seminary training, but Snowden also points to the heavy dependence of the clergy on the local elites as a factor in alienating the masses from the Church. In reality, this was largely the result of the *chiese ricettizie* system of paying local clergy which was peculiar to the South and had entered into crisis as a result of Liberal ecclesiastical legislation.[28]

This picture of the state of the church in some parts of the South is amply confirmed by other studies of the period and seems to have continued well into the Fascist era.[29] On the other hand, the diversity of rural society meant that in some provinces of Sicily, Calabria, and even Apulia itself, the relationships between clergy and peasantry were actually very close, so much so that during the great migration from the South to North America in the 1890s and early 1900s parish priests often accompanied their flocks to 'the promised land'.[30]

In northern and central provinces the parochial clergy were generally better educated, better behaved and less financially dependent on the local landowning class. Moreover, in large part they were recruited from the middle ranks of the peasantry itself and were thus natural leaders of their parishioners.[31] The fact that in some cases the parish priest himself cultivated his own 'glebe', alongside these rural proletarians, helped consolidate the relationship between clergy and parishioners. The burdens of the tithe did sometimes sour relations between the peasantry and their cure of souls, and the *diritti alla stola* – the fees which the parochial clergy charged for baptisms, marriages and funerals – were often resented by the poor, but in the end some form of balance between them was achieved.[32]

According to the nineteenth century Anarchist leader Michael Bakunin, Italian peasants were often superstitious and 'they loved the Church because of its dramatic dimension and because it interrupted the monotony and misery of country life with its theatrical and musical ceremonies'.[33] There is probably a great deal of truth in Bakunin's generalisation and it is very difficult to decide whether the decline in religious observance in Italian towns in the period of industrialisation and migration was an entirely new phenomenon or not. It is likely that the alienation of sectors of rural society from the church, so visible elsewhere in Europe, was not entirely absent in Italy. If so, given the overwhelmingly rural origins of the new urban, industrial proletariat it almost certainly contributed to the latter's loss of faith.

As bishops and parochial clergy regularly pointed out, a crucial factor in the decline of religious observance and loyalty to the church was the militant anticlericalism of the working-class movement which campaigned actively against religious belief and practice. Priests in Turin, for example, declared that, 'here the Socialist element has taken control' and claimed that they were facing 'a rising tide of Socialism' and in consequence that 'the religious spirit is being lost in local parishes'. In the Milan diocese the major justification for founding the *Cappellani del Lavoro* was given as the 'urgent need to protect religious faith from the Socialist propaganda that is spreading in this region'.[34]

The anticlericalism of the Italian working-class movement had its origins in Mazzinian republicanism and the Garibaldinian democratic movement, which had been its nursing mothers in the 1860s and 1870s.[35] While many Democrats, most notoriously Francesco Crispi, became conservative, even reactionary, in middle age, many others, like the followers of the *La Plebe* newspaper in the Lombard town of Lodi, passed over to Socialism, taking with them a lively anticlerical tradition.[36] In some parts of Emilia-Romagna and Le Marche, both formerly parts of the Papal States, the militantly anticlerical Republican movement enjoyed lingering working-class support down to the outbreak of the First World War.[37] Republican anticlericalism was also transmitted elsewhere through the culture and organisations of the artisans, an element which played a very important part in the creation of the working-class movement.[38] And the Italian experience of Anarchism ensured that anticlerical ideas would be planted in Liguria, Tuscany and even in remote areas of the South.[39] Thus the establishment of the ideological hegemony of Marxian Socialism over the Italian working-class movement in the early 1890s served to reinforce with atheistic materialism an already strong anticlerical culture.

The anticlerical line taken by Italian Socialism manifested itself in a number ways in the life of Italian workers. In some places it took the form of a purely nominal attendance of male workers at Sunday Mass: Rinaldo Rigola, one of the early leaders of the trade union movement, for example, remembered that during his youth artisans attended church but that they treated the proceedings in a perfunctory and sceptical manner:

> [During the Mass] . . . they remained standing at the back of the church, and spoke among themselves more or less as if they were in the piazza. At the end of the service they crossed themselves, and they departed fixing as they did so the place for the afternoon's festivities.[40]

Male abstention from religious practice also became common and at Biella, a northern Piedmontese textile town, at the end of the 1890s it was said that, 'Only the women go to mass.'[41] There thus developed what might be called the 'Berlinguer syndrome', that is working men accompanied their wives to Mass but remained outside the church to converse with comrades until it was over.[42] The religious sensibilities of women were a matter of great concern to the leaders of the working-class movement: in Cremona, for example, they urged the organisers of the peasant leagues to treat them kindly because 'in the confessional they are warned of the threat of family breakdown as a result of the introduction of new ideas'.[43] But working women were not always so passive in the face of clerical power as this passage suggests; in Cene, Bergamo, in 1895, several women textile workers hit back when both their bishop and and their parish priest excommunicated them for joining a Socialist trade union by denouncing them in an open letter to the local Socialist newspaper.[44]

The abandonment of religious duties never became universal. As in other parts of Europe, most working people continued to demand and to utilise the rites of baptism, marriage and burial, though as tensions arose between unionised workers and the church, refusal of the last rites became frequent.[45] Celebrations of religious rites by families of Socialist workers could also be divisive, especially funerals. At Bologna, in 1905, the police reported the case of a young member of the bricklayers' union, killed in an accident, who was given a religious funeral because he 'had always led a Christian life'.[46] When the priests arrived at the funeral parlour his Socialist comrades abandoned the procession and one of them delivered an oration outside the church in which he declared that 'the presence of the priests and of members of the young Catholic association had defiled the body of the worker'.[47]

As it consolidated its presence in Italian civil society the working-class movement began to institute secular equivalents of the services of the church in the matter of 'rites of passage'. In particular, as in France, there developed a veritable cult of the secular, civic funeral, modelled on the 'Republican' funeral already widespread in areas such as Emilia-Romagna and the Marche.[48] These 'celebrations of life rather than death' became the distinguishing mark of the new secular, Socialist culture and its leaders.[49] Working-class organisations in particularly strong Socialist centres sought to build a comprehensive counter-culture to that of the church, using the *Case del Popolo* and the *circoli operai*, social centres for workers and their families, to provide a whole range of facilities, including theatrical and musical associations, crèches and cheap restaurants, to serve the worker and his family in competition with the Catholic parish. In its definitive form, this culture was characterised by the adoption of all manner of secular events and heroes to contest the public demonstrations of Catholic piety and loyalty, particularly the celebration of local saints.[50]

The school became a major battleground between Catholics and Socialists in this period and the prize was the soul of Italian children. In the decades immediately following Unification, the battle had been between the Catholics and the anticlerical Liberal ruling elite, supported by radical and Republican elements, and in 1870 a victory of a kind had been secured by the 'lay' forces through the passage of a law which made the teaching of the catechism optional in primary schools.[51] But since the day-to-day administration of schools was the responsibility of local authorities, the effects of the law were extremely patchy. In the 1890s and early 1900s, the Socialists waged a powerful campaign to win control of local authorities and a key goal was to abolish the teaching of the catechism. At this point, in the face of the threat of a Socialist takeover, Catholics and Liberals joined together in clerico-moderate alliances. Whatever other interests were at stake for the Liberals, an important consideration was indeed the preservation of the catechism for, as Gramsci argued, the Italian ruling class never succeeded in elaborating 'a philosophy for the masses' and were thus forced to fall back on Catholic religious teaching as a means of insulating the masses against the 'virus' of Socialism,[52] implicitly accepting the Catholic claim that the catechism would teach children to 'obey their parents, to love them and to honour the family and the fatherland' and to 'respect other people and their property and to obey the authorities'.[53]

Whereas in the US the growing network of Catholic parochial schools was to play a key role in the formation of the immigrant working class, in Italy Catholic private schools remained only a tiny part of the total of all educational institutions – 2 per cent.[54] The important thing was that, as a result of the clerico-moderate alliances, the catechism continued to be taught in the overwhelming majority of state schools in industrialising areas.[55] So the Socialists had effectively lost the battle to secularise the primary schools before the First World War, and in consequence Catholicism remained the essential component in the culture of the emerging industrial and agrarian masses.

A characteristic feature of the handling of the religious question by the Italian working-class movement was the attempt by Socialist intellectuals to construct an alternative set of religious myths and values to Catholicism. This attempt, which was in part inspired by Garibaldi's concept of 'religion without the priests',[56] bore some resemblances to the ideas espoused by John Trevor's Labour Church and the 'ethical Socialism' of Keir Hardie.[57] The anticlericalism of Socialist intellectuals like Turati was seen to be too abstract, and that of Mussolini too crude and vulgar, to be an effective way of combating the residual Catholic values of the working population. Indeed some working-class leaders sought to avoid anticlerical propaganda altogether for fear of offending religious susceptibilities, like Antonio Labriola who, though forever warning of the use of religion as an instrument of repression by the ruling classes, argued that for tactical reasons it was probably best to treat it as a 'private matter'.[58] Others, like Prampolini, sought to construct a kind of de-mythologised, de-clericalised version of Christianity with which he hoped to attract the new proletariat. Appealing to a notional 'primitive' Christianity, Prampolini elaborated an evangelical Socialism which appropriated the values of charity and solidarity inherent in a perceived 'social gospel', built around the figure of Christ the Worker.[59] It is no accident that the rise of the modernist heresy in Italy caused alarm in some Socialist circles; not only because it was so closely associated with Romolo Murri and the Christian Democrats, the militantly reforming wing of the rival Catholic movement, but also because of its own tendency to de-mystify and de-clericalise the Catholic religion.[60]

Another prominent Socialist leader, Andrea Costa, also urged the necessity of offering a complete system of values to the working classes:

We should not believe that it will be enough to offer the people bread in order to make them revolt. The people are by nature idealistic and they will not rise until socialist ideas have the prestige and force of attraction religious faith once had.[61]

It is difficult to gauge the success of either Costa's or Prampolini's efforts but the iconographic evidence, that is the popularity of pictures of Christ the Worker and of Marx and the Madonna side by side in working-class homes, suggests that some workers at least arrived at a satisfactory synthesis of the old and new values.[62]

The attitude of the hierarchy and the parochial clergy to the rise of industrial capitalism in Italy was a broadly uniform but essentially ambivalent one. The social problems thrown up by the new industrial system were quickly denounced. Capitalism was seen to be the evil child of philosophical and political Liberalism and was condemned as the unfortunate result of the 'Manchester [School] of Economics'[63] and as the fruit of an 'unrestrained thirst for profit'.[64] Davis argues that, 'in denouncing the self-centred materialism of Liberal dogma, as the cause of these evils, the mainly Catholic conservative critics of the new Italy gave their imprimatur to the language of class'.[65] On the other hand, the 'language of class', and more particularly the Socialist concept of class struggle, were emphatically rejected by the ecclesiastical authorities who urged on the victims of the industrial system the virtues of accepting their social station, obeying their social superiors, and resigning themselves to their earthly destiny. Thus in 1899 Cardinal Ferrari, archbishop of Milan, and a noted Catholic leader in the social field, reiterated the message that the clergy, 'Should make the poor understand that everything is ordained by God, that it is God who makes some rich and some poor . . .'.[66] The constant reiteration of this message undoubtedly assisted industrial entrepreneurs in their efforts to transform the rural immigrants into a docile and disciplined industrial workforce.

The rise of Socialist working-class organisations in the 1880s and 1890s, with their explicit anticlericalism and their strategy of class struggle, ultimately determined the response of the Church for, as Bell points out, the creation of Catholic trade unions, peasant leagues and other economic and social organisations was almost entirely a response to previous Socialist organisational initiatives. Although there is some evidence of earlier Catholic activities in these fields, his thesis is endorsed by historians of the Catholic movement.[67] The first Catholic organisations for workers and peasants were erected in the 1880s and 1890s, essentially as charitable and philanthropic institutions, with a strong educational element for often illiterate young workers as well.[68]

In this new enterprise, the church disposed of two valuable assets. The first was the existing parochial structure. As Gabriele De Rosa has noted, the parish had long operated as a social centre, and provided a reference point for artisan groups in its confraternities and pious associations; as a result of industrialisation and the other processes of economic and social change, it became in many areas of Italy the heart of a new and vast network of Catholic lay associations.[69] So long, that is, as priests heeded the call of Leo XIII to 'come forth from the sacristy and go among the people'.[70] The second was the fact that in the existing Catholic movement – the *Opera Dei Congressi* – the Church already possessed a flourishing network of Catholic associations, and with it cadres of trained and combative lay leaders.[71] The *Opera* was essentially the product of Catholic intransigent opposition to the Liberal state and in particular to its abolition of the Temporal Power, the territorial sovereignty which the popes had exercised in central Italy. On the basis of these recreational and cultural associations it was soon possible to build specifically economic and social institutions.

On the other hand, two factors inhibited the early development of those institutions. The first was the established concentration of the efforts of the *Opera* on the 'Roman Question' – that is the struggle to restore the Temporal Power – and on battles against the anticlerical policies of the Liberal state. The crucial turning point came during the End of Century Crisis of the 1890s when Italy was wracked by economic difficulties, resulting social disorders such as the *fasci siciliani* (1893–5) and the Milan insurrection of 1898, and bitter conflicts within the political elite.[72] The emergence in precisely this same period of the working-class movement in the form of the Italian Socialist Party and the Socialist trade unions and peasant leagues prompted a change in the strategy of the *Opera*, the emphasis shifting away from the 'Roman Question' to the 'Social Question'. Socialism was identified as the new enemy. This change found its clearest expression in the formation of clerico-moderate electoral alliances between the Catholics and the Liberals at a local, and later national, level, which confirmed the Socialist claim that the Church was a part of the establishment.[73]

A further problem was the principles underlying Catholic action in the social field. As we have seen, the first Catholic organisations in the social field were essentially paternalistic and charitable in inspiration, most being of a 'mutual benefit' type, similar to the earliest organisations of the working-class movement. Like them, they were eventually to develop into *società di resistenza*, full-blooded trade union associations by category. Catholic paternalism also manifested itself in the activities of industrialists who in some areas, like Venetia, provided an array of facilities such as cheap canteens, crèches, hostel accommodation. This kind of paternalism was both a practical implementation of the Christian precept of charity and a method of maintaining a stable, contented, workforce.[74]

Paternalism was the essence of the solutions to the 'Social Question' proposed by the Pisan Catholic sociologist Giuseppe Toniolo, whose various social programmes were to have a formative influence on emerging social Catholicism in Italy.[75] Foreign influence – the examples of Catholic social movements in France, Belgium and Germany – also played an important part in the development of the Italian movement in the late nineteenth century.[76] Part and parcel of Toniolo's paternalism was the idea of the mixed unions of workers and employers, an essentially neo-Thomist re-evocation of the guilds of a mythical, medieval golden age of European Catholicism.[77] This idea was also to be found in *Rerum Novarum*, the great social encyclical of pope Leo XIII (1878–1903), published in 1891, which was taken as the official founding charter of social Catholicism and thus provided the main impetus to the creation of Catholic economic and social organisations throughout Europe.[78]

In practice paternalism, or inter-class 'solidarity' as it was officially described, meant that the first Catholic *unioni del lavoro* were dominated by wealthy Catholic notables and by the clergy, though the Turin experience suggests that Catholic industrialists were often unwilling to participate.[79] Paternalism also had the effect of initially discouraging the emergence of leadership cadres among the workers and peasants themselves; and the autocratic control of parish life by the clergy, sanctioned by both canon and civil law, ruled out an experience of democracy of the kind witnessed in the US.

It was the newly-emerging Christian Democracy movement of Don Romolo Murri, Don Luigi Sturzo and Filippo Meda, with its programme of radical economic, social and political reform, which gave impetus to the formation of true Catholic trade unions, especially in Milan and its industrial and agricultural hinterland. The effects of their recruiting activities were reinforced by all manner of Catholic charitable and welfare institutions operating among workers and peasants, including soup kitchens.[80] The success of these efforts may be judged by the rash of strikes of mainly agricultural workers in the 1890s and early 1900s, and it was also the Christian Democrats who provided much of the moral and material support for the *Cappellani del Lavoro* experiment referred to above.[81] But the election of Pius X signalled a setback in the development of Catholic trade unionism. Papa Sarto's innate social conservatism, coupled with his anxieties about the heretical tendencies of Murri and some of his followers, led him to dissolve the *Opera*, over which they had established such a strong influence, in 1904 and effectively outlaw the Christian Democrats.[82] For

the next ten years, the efforts of the local ecclesiastical authorities to protect their flocks from the modernist 'contagion' would cause bitter divisions
inside the Catholic movement and undermine the credibility of Catholic
peasant and trade union leaders.[83]

As several historians have pointed out, much time and effort was also
wasted by the Catholic movement in sterile controversies over the nature
of Catholic economic and social organisations: whether they should be
'mixed' or include only employees, and whether they should be 'confessional', requiring a declaration of religious allegiance (and often proof of
'good character' from a parish priest), or be open to all.[84] On the eve of
the outbreak of the First World War, organisations of all types continued
to exist – though the tendency was still towards confessional organisations
– but the overwhelming majority of unions were exclusively made up of
employees.[85] Another problem that exercised Catholics operating in the
trade union field was the morality of the use of the strike. It was permitted
by union rules, implicitly condoned by *Rerum Novarum* but still considered to be a weapon of last resort, and regarded with disapproval by the
ecclesiastical authorities.[86] It is significant in this regard that when the
bishop of Bergamo actually gave his moral and material support to a strike
of textile workers at Ranica in his diocese, in 1909, he did so without the
approval of the Vatican.[87]

The experience of the Ranica strike encapsulated so many of the difficulties facing Catholic trade unionism as it emerged in the early 1900s,
as well as exposing the internal contradictions from which most of these
difficulties sprang. A price was paid for the official support of the local
ecclesiastical authorities: the subordination of the union strike committee
to the diocesan leadership of the Catholic movement, in particular its
president Rezzara, who effectively took over the direction of negotiations
with the employers. Rezzara's moderation, and the increasing fears among
the clergy of the subversive effects of strike action, meant that the outcome of this long and bitter dispute fell far short of the workers' demands
and led to a decline in the Catholic union's position.[88] The fundamental
conflict within the Catholic trade union movement between the ideal of
interclass solidarity on the one hand, and the imperative of class struggle
on the other, was left unresolved.

Other important factors were the lack of co-operation with the local
Socialist unions (though these were sympathetic to the strike) and the
hostility of the Catholic middle class and aristocracy, the latter represented
by the very influential Count Medolago Albani.[89] Indeed, the Ranica incident highlights a general lack in the historiography of the Catholic movement, that is a clear understanding of the relationship between Catholic

trade unions and peasant leagues and the Catholic plutocracy, industrial manufacturers, large-scale farmers (mainly aristocratic) and financiers.[90]

Notwithstanding the problems outlined above, Catholic economic and social organisations grew rapidly in the 'Giolittian era' (1903–14), creating a network of not only trade unions and peasant leagues, but workers' mutual aid societies, *casse di risparmio* (credit unions) and workers' and peasant co-operatives as well. This development provoked the resentment and rivalry of the Socialists. In a speech to the CGL, the Socialist trade union confederation, in 1911, its secretary general, Rinaldo Rigola, denounced Catholic trade unionism as 'systematic blacklegging' and denied that the Catholic organisations were 'true unions'.[91] Catholic organisers hotly denied this, and even another Socialist trade union leader, Montemartini, declared that they were 'genuine class organisations'.[92] The rivalry deepened when Prime Minister Giolitti admitted representatives of the Socialist trade unions to his National Council of Labour in 1904, whilst excluding Catholics and discriminating against Catholic co-operatives in the awarding of government contracts.[93]

At the heart of the Catholic network was the *Ufficio del Lavoro*, an organism operating at a city, diocesan and provincial level to bring together Catholic workers in opposition to the Socialist *Camere del Lavoro* (modelled on the French *bourses du travail*). As Bell and others explain, every initiative on the part of the Socialists was matched by the Catholics, so that the Catholic movement quickly equipped itself with cultural and recreational organisations specifically aimed at the workers, including libraries, bands, concert halls and canteens.[94]

In 1910 the membership of the Socialist trade unions still outstripped that of their Catholic counterparts by a factor of six to one:

Socialists (reformists and syndicalists)	650 000
Catholics	104 000
Independents	60 000

The official surveys of organised labour carried out by the Ministry of Agriculture, Industry and Commerce at this time, and two years later, also confirm that the Socialist unions were very much stronger among the workers in heavy industry and among the *braccianti* than their Catholic counterparts. The latter's only major recruiting success in manufacturing industry was in textiles, and this was largely due to the support of women workers who formed two-thirds of the workforce. Membership of Catholic trade unions among metal and metal-mechanical workers, building trades workers, railwaymen and miners was slight by comparison with the Socialist unions. Equally, clerical workers were poorly represented in the ranks of Catholic trade unionists.[95] In agriculture, Catholic trade union membership was chiefly found among sharecroppers, small tenant farmers and even small landowners, but there were significant pockets of support among the *braccianti* and other labourers in Cremona, the stronghold of the Catholic deputy and peasant leader Guido Miglioli, and in other provinces in the Lombard plain.[96] The particular strength of the Catholic organisations in the agricultural sector may be attributed to a number of factors: the appeal of the Catholic ideal of the small peasant landowner to marginalised groups (as opposed to the Socialist aim of collectivisation); the idea of the 'co-management' of large farms adopted by Miglioli, and, possibly, the feeling that the Socialists were not fundamentally interested in the agrarian question.[97]

Lombardy was the stronghold of Catholic labour, with 62.5 per cent of the membership of its industrial unions and 42.33 per cent of the agricultural ones and 55 per cent of the total. Apart from Lombardy, the only other region with a significant proportion of Catholic unionised labour was Venetia with 18.2 per cent of total membership, and south of Rome, support for Catholic unions was exiguous.[98] These figures confirm that the phenomenon of a Catholic subculture was predominantly localised in the 'white provinces' of north-eastern Italy, whereas the Socialist subculture established itself in industrial cities like Turin and Milan (and industrial suburbs like Sesto San Giovanni) and in the 'Red Belt' of the Po Valley and central Italy among the rural proletariat of those areas.

Despite their minority role, the Catholic trade unions, peasant leagues and other economic and social organisations were now firmly established as a presence in Italian society and with the growth of the Catholic electorate due to the introduction of virtual universal adult male suffrage in 1912, they helped constitute the launching pad for the eventual emergence of a Catholic political party.

In his article 'Dechristianisation of the Working Class in Western Europe (1850–1900)' Hugh McLeod states:

there were several parts of Europe where the Roman Catholic Church had considerable success in resisting the movement towards Socialism and in building up its own network of political, trade union, social and benefit organisations.[99]

McLeod goes on to list Germany, the Netherlands and Flanders. Had his timescale extended to 1914, he would have been able to add Italy to that list. By then the church had clearly demonstrated its ability to maintain the allegiance of a substantial part of the working class that had emerged in the period of the first Italian industrial revolution, not only in the rural areas but also in the cities, and not only in the classically 'Catholic' provinces like Como, Milan, Bergamo, Brescia and Vicenza, but in nearly all the major industrial centres.

This success in creating a Catholic movement, a Catholic subculture alongside a working-class subculture, had the effect of splitting the Italian working class. Worker was divided against worker, and worker and peasant families were themselves sometimes split down the middle by religion according to generation and gender. This split in working-class loyalties was to have serious consequences in the early 1920s, opening the way to the rise of Fascism. In the period of working-class militancy known as the 'Red Two Years', that is from 1918 to 1920, the effectiveness of Socialist action in industrial and agricultural disputes was undermined by the almost total lack of co-operation with the Catholic trade unions and peasant leagues. Ironically, that part of the Catholic peasant leagues headed by Guido Miglioli often proved more militant than their Socialist rivals, leading to accusations of blacklegging against the latter.[100] And the 'white bolshevism' of Miglioli and his followers in Cremona, Bergamo and Verona drove many Catholic landowners to throw in their lot with the agrarian Fascist squads.[101]

Though Gramsci hailed the foundation of the Catholic *Partito Popolare Italiano* (PPI) in 1919 as 'the most important fact in Italian history since the Risorgimento', he was also quick to recognise that its emergence split the working-class vote and thus prevented a greater Socialist triumph in the elections of that year.[102] Furthermore, the anticlericalism of the working-class movement precluded the formation of a united front between the PPI and PSI which, as the two mass parties, with close to 50 per cent of the seats in Parliament, had a real opportunity to carry out a programme of radical economic, social and political reform in the post-war period. The fear of anticlericalism also led the Vatican to forbid the formation of a PSI/PPI-based coalition government in 1924, thus sabotaging the last-ditch attempt of the antifascist opposition to overthrow Mussolini. With the establishment of the Fascist dictatorship from 1925 onwards, both the Catholic and Socialist trade unions and peasant leagues were dissolved and would not be reconstituted for another twenty years.

NOTES

1. As quoted in G.B Guerri, *Gli italiani sotto la chiesa: Da San Pietro a Mussolini* (Milan, 1992), 320 (unless otherwise stated, all translations are by the author).

2. For a summary of the historiographical debate around the processes and timing of industrialisation, and the related issue of working-class formation, see J. A. Davis, 'Socialism and the Working Classes in Italy before 1914', in D. Geary, ed., *Labour and Socialist Movements in Europe before 1914* (London, 1989), 203–7.

3. V. Zamagni, *The Economic History of Italy: Recovery after Decline* (Oxford, 1993), 66–74.

4. Davis, 198–9, 216–7.

5. P. Corti and A. Lonni, 'Da Contadini a Operai', in A. De Clementi, ed., *La Società inafferabile: Protoindustria, città e classi sociali nell'Italia liberale* (Milan, 1986), 196, 243.

6. *Ibid.*, 243.

7. Davis, 221.

8. See, for example, F. Agostini, ed., *Le visite pastorali di Giuseppe Callegari nella Diocesi di Padova (1884–88/1893–1905)* (Rome, 1981); A. Lazzarretto, 'Parroci ed emigranti nel Vicentino del primo Novecento', in Various authors, *Studi di storia sociale e religiosa: Scritti in onore di Gabriele De Rosa* (Naples, 1980), 1091–112; and A. Monticone, 'L'Episcopato italiano dall'Unità al Concilio vaticano II', in M. Rosa, ed., *Clero e società nell'Italia contemporanea* (Rome-Bari, 1992).

9. Rosa, *Clero e società*, 278.

10. D. Menozzi, 'Le Nuove parrocchie nella Prima Industrializzazione Torinese (1900–1915)', in *Rivista di Storia e Letteratura Religiosa* 9 (1973), 70.

11. *Ibid.*, 85.

12. *Ibid.*, 85.

13. L. Bedeschi, *I Capellani del Lavoro: Aspetti religiosi e culturali della società lombarda negli anni della crisi modernista* (Milan, 1977), 211.

14. X. Toscani, *Secolarizzazione e frontiere sacerdotali* (Bologna, 1982), 55.

15. Bedeschi, 211–37.

16. H. McLeod, 'The Dechristianisation of the Working Class in Western Europe (1850–1900)', *Social Compass*, XXVII, 2/3 (1980), 191–214.

17. U. Lovato and A. Castellani, 'Il beato Leonardo Murialdo e il movimento operaio cristiano', in *Italia Sacra: Spiritualità e azione del laicato Cattolico* (Padova, 1969), 608; see also, F. Snowden, *Violence and Great Estates in Southern Italy; Apulia, 1900–1922* (Cambridge, 1986), 27.

18. A. Dewerpe, 'Cresciuta e ristagno proto-industriale nell'Italia meridionale', in A. De Clementi, ed., *La Società inafferabile*, 109.

19. A. Kelikian, 'Convitti operai cattolici e forza lavoro femminile', in A. Gigli Marchetti, ed., *Donna Lombarda* (Milan, 1992).

20. G. Battelli, 'Clero secolare e società italiana tra decennio napoleonico e primo novecento', in M. Rosa, *Clero e società*, 106–8.

21. Agostini, xcviii.

22. *Ibid.*, xcv.

23. Snowden, 79–110.

24. *Ibid.*, 80 .

25. Whereas the average southern diocese had a population of just under 100 000 (and many were much smaller), in the four northern regions the average was two to two and a half times that figure; see the *Annuario Pontificio* (Vatican City, 1948), 10–451. Monticone, 277 makes the point that no attempt was

made to adapt diocesan boundaries to the needs of industrialisation and urbanisation, as was done by the nineteenth-century Church of England, until the 1980s.

26. Snowden, 81.
27. *Ibid.*, 80: the picture painted by Snowden is curiously similar to that described by Antonio Gramsci in *La questione meridionale*, eds F. De Felice and V. Parlato (Rome, 1966), 151.
28. G. De Rosa, *Vescovi, popolo e magia nel Sud* (Naples, 1971), 262–7. The *chiese ricettizie* was a system of ecclesiastical patronage whereby churches were served by colleges of priests, often from the same family.
29. See Borzomati, *I giovani cattolici nel Mezzogiorno d'Italia dall'Unità al 1948* (Rome, 1970), 47–52 and C. Levi, *Christ Stopped at Eboli* (Harmondsworth, 1982), 191–6.
30. G. De Rosa, 'La parrocchia in Italia nell'età contemporanea', in Various authors, *La parrocchia in Italia nell'età contemporanea* (Naples, 1982), 19.
31. *Ibid.*, 25.
32. Faenza, *Communismo e Cattolicesimo* (Milan, 1959), 9 (this is a pioneering work, one of the first studies of the coexistence between Communism and Catholicism, in this instance in the Romagna) and F. Della Peruta, *Braccianti e contadini nella Valle Padana* (Rome, 1975), 29.
33. As quoted in G. De Rosa, *Vescovi, popolo e magia nel Sud*, 262.
34. As quoted in Menozzi, 79 (the Turin suburb of Borgo Vittoria) and Bedeschi, 216 (Milan).
35. A. De Grand, *The Italian Left in the Twentieth Century: A History of the Socialist and Communist Parties* (Bloomington, 1989), 6–7.
36. G. Camaiani, 'Valori religiosi e polemica anticlericale nella sinistra democratica e del primo socialismo', in *Rivista di Storia e Letteratura*, XX:2 (1984), 228.
37. C. Seton-Watson, *Italy from Liberalism to Fascism* (London, 1967), 67.
38. D. Howard Bell, *Sesto San Giovanni: Workers, Culture and Politics in an Italian Town, 1880–1922* (New Brunswick, 1986), 43–4, where he stresses the 'importance of pre-factory cultural traditions and their importance in the formation of the modern working class', and 'an attitude of anticlericalism which resulted in resistance to church influences in secular life'. Bell's work is of particular value to the present discussion because of his use of the diary of the parish priest of Sesto and its observations on the rise of the working-class movement there.
39. Davis, 185–6.
40. As quoted in D. Howard Bell, 244.
41. As quoted in S. Merli, ed., *Proletariato di fabbrica e capitalismo industriale: il caso italiano: 1880–1900*, vol. 2 (Florence, 1973), doc. CCLXXX, 645.
42. Enrico Berlinguer, Communist Party Secretary 1972–86, and author of the 'historic compromise': his wife was a devout Catholic. See D. Kertzer, *Comrades and Christians; Religion and Political Struggle in Communist Italy* (Cambridge, 1980), 200–4, for an account of religious practice among Communists in the post-war period.
43. As quoted in V. Romani Genzini, 'Il movimento contadino nel Cremonese all'inizio del'900', in Della Peruta, ed., *Braccianti e contadini nella Valle Padana* (Rome, 1975), 119.

44. Merli, doc. LXXXIX, 860.
45. McLeod, 62; see also Bell, 60.
46. Archivio Centrale Dello Stato (Rome), Ministero Dell'Interno, Direzione generale della Pubblica Sicurezza (henceforth ACS, MI, DGPS), fasc. 11, Bologna, 30.9.1905.
47. *Ibid.*.
48. Merli, 849, fn. 16 and Camaiani, 247.
49. Bell, 60 and Kertzer, 142 .
50. See, for example, Bell, 47 and Snowden, 86.
51. S. Pivato, *Movimento operaio e istruzione popolare nell'Italia liberale: Discussioni e ricerche* (Milan, 1986), 24.
52. *Ibid.*, 26.
53. *Ibid.*, 28.
54. *Ibid.*, 24.
55. G. Bonetta, 'Scuola e socializzazione fra '800 e '900', in G. Chittolini and G. Miccoli, eds, *Storia D'Italia, Annali 9, La Chiesa e il potere politico dal Medioevo all'età Moderna* (Turin, 1986), 509; where local authorities, Liberal or Socialist, succeeded in banishing religious education from schools, enormous efforts were made to replace it with evening catechism classes in churches and young people's *ricreatori*. See, for example, L. Barletta, 'Chiesa, Stato e città', in G. Galasso, ed., *Storia delle città italiane: Napoli* (Bari, 1987), 288.
56. For an analysis of Garibaldi's influence, see S. Pivato, *Clericalismo e laicismo nella cultura popolare italiana* (Milan, 1991), 77.
57. S. Yeo, 'A New Life: The Religion of Socialism in Britain', *History Workshop*, 4 (Autumn 1977), 27.
58. G. Zunino, *La questione cattolica nella sinistra italiana (1919–1939)* (Bologna, 1975), 12.
59. The most complete study of Prampolini's ideas is to be found in S. Pivato, *Clericalismo e laicismo*; see also E. Decleva, 'Anticlericalismo e religiosità laica nel socialismo italiano', in Various authors, *Prampolini e il socialismo riformista; atti del convegno di Reggio Emilia (27–29 Ottobre, 1978)* (Rome, 1979), 259–79. In English, see R. Hostetter, 'The Evangelical Socialism of Camillo Prampolini', *Italian Quarterly*, XVIII (1975).
60. Zunino, 20.
61. As quoted in A. Azzaroni, *Socialisti anticlericali* (Florence, 1961), 105.
62. Camaiani, 235 and G. Giarrizzo, 'Il Socialismo e la modernizzazione del Mezzogiorno', in C. Cingari and S. Fedele, eds, *Il socialismo nel Mezzogiorno d'Italia* (Bari, 1992), 6, where he says: 'The image of "Jesus the Socialist", both God and prophet, who rejected the church of the rich and the pharisees, appeared in the Southern countryside and spread widely.'
63. As quoted in, A. Gambasin, *Gerarchia e laicato in Italia nel secondo ottocento* (Padua, 1986), 151.
64. As quoted in F. Renda, *Socialisti e cattolici in Sicilia* (Palermo, 1972).
65. Davis, 220.
66. As quoted in C. Snider, *L'Episcopato di Cardinale Andrea Ferrari*, vol. 1 (Neri Pozza, 1981), 365.
67. Bell, 56.
68. Lovato and Castellani, 610.

69. G. De Rosa, 'La parrocchia in Italia', 25.
70. As quoted in C. Seton-Watson, 223.
71. For an account of the development of the Catholic movement in Italy see Richard A. Webster, *The Cross and the Fasces: Christian Democracy and Fascism in Italy* (Stanford, 1960), 3–26 and J.F. Pollard, 'Italy', in T. Buchanan and M. Conway, eds, *Political Catholicism in Europe* (Oxford, 1996), 69–77.
72. For an analysis of the crisis see John A. Davis, *Conflict and Control: Law and Order in Nineteenth Century Italy* (Basingstoke and London, 1988), 345–52.
73. Bell, 68–72.
74. Zamagni, 104–5 and L. Giuotto, *La fabbrica totale: Paternalismo industriale e Città sociali in Italia* (Milan, 1979), 81–2.
75. See Misner, *Social Catholicism in Europe: From the Onset of Industrialisation to the First World War* (London, 1991), 285–7.
76. *Ibid.*, 254, and U. Lovato and A. Castellani, 571.
77. Misner, 286.
78. Translation in C. Carlen, ed., *The Papal Encyclicals*, 5 vols (Wilmington NC, 1981).
79. Lovato and Castellani, 60.
80. Bedeschi, 217.
81. *Ibid.*, 226.
82. Webster, 13.
83. See ACS, MI, DGPS, busta 26, partito clericale, fasc. 11, Bologna, fasc. 17, Catania for evidence of these tensions.
84. See Snider, 245, and A. Caneva, *L'Azione sindacale in Italia dall'estraneità alla partecipazione*, vol. 1 (Brescia, 1979), 41.
85. Daniel D. Horowitz, *Storia del Movimento Sindacale in Italia* (Bologna, 1966), 186–7.
86. *Ibid.*, 187.
87. Hebblethwaite, *John XXIII: The Pope of the Council* (London, 1984), 63–4.
88. I. Lizzola and E. Manzoni, 'Proletariato Bergamasco e Organizzazioni Cattoliche: Lo Sciopero di Ranica (1909)', *Studi e Richerche di Storia Contemporanea*, 15 (May), 1981, 15–18.
89. *Ibid.*
90. For a study of the origins of this 'plutocracy' see M.G. Rossi, *Le origini del partito cattolicio in Italia: Movimento cattolico e lotta di classe nell'Italia liberale* (Rome, 1977), 281–310.
91. Caneva, 127.
92. *Ibid.* Local studies of Catholic trade unions and peasant leagues confirm this: see, for example, Valeria Romani Genzini, 'Il movimento contadino nel Cremonese all'inizio del' 1900', in F. Della Peruta, ed., *Braccianti e contadini nella Valle Padana*, 97.
93. Seton-Watson, 301–2.
94. Bell, 60.
95. The Ministry figures are quoted in Horowitz, 185–9.
96. A. Fappani, *Il Movimento Contadino Italiano*, (Rome, 1964), 156–62.
97. Horowitz, 186.

98. *Ibid.*
99. McLeod, 210.
100. See John Foot, '"White Bolshevism", the Catholic Right and the Fascists in Italy, 1920–1925', *Historical Journal* (forthcoming 1997).
101. J.F. Pollard, 'Conservative Catholics and Italian Fascism: The Clerico-Fascists', in M. Blinkhorn, ed., *Fascists and Conservatives: The Radical Right and the Establishment in Twentieth-Century Europe* (London, 1990), 40.
102. As quoted in John N. Molony, *The Emergence of Political Catholicism in Italy: Partito Popolare 1919–1926* (London, 1977), 47.

9 Inbetween Peoples: Race, Nationality and the New Immigrant Working Class*
James R. Barrett and David Roediger

> By the eastern European immigration the labor force has been cleft horizontally into two great divisions. The upper stratum includes what is known in Mill parlance as the 'English-speaking' men; the lower contains the 'Hunkies' or 'Ginnies'. Or, if you prefer, the former are the 'white men', the latter the 'foreigners'.
>
> John Fitch, *The Steel Workers* (1910)

In 1980, Joseph Loguidice, an elderly Italian-American from Chicago, sat down to give his life story to an interviewer. His first and most vivid childhood recollection was of a race riot that had occurred on the city's near north side. Wagons full of policemen with 'peculiar hats' streamed into his neighbourhood. But the 'one thing that stood out in my mind', Loguidice remembered after six decades, was 'a man running down the middle of the street hollering . . . "I'm White, I'm White!"' After first taking him for an African-American, Loguidice soon realised that the man was a white coal-handler covered in dust. He was screaming for his life, fearing that 'people would shoot him down'. He had, Loguidice concluded, 'got caught up in . . . this racial thing'.[1]

Joseph Loguidice's tale might be taken as a metaphor for the situation of millions of 'new immigrants' from eastern and southern Europe who arrived in the United States between the end of the nineteenth century and the early 1920s. The fact that this episode made such a profound impression is in itself significant, suggesting both that this was a strange, new situation and that thinking about race became an important part of the consciousness of immigrants like Loguidice. We are concerned here in part with the development of racial awareness and attitudes, and an increasingly racialised worldview among new immigrant workers themselves. Most did not arrive with conventional US attitudes regarding 'racial' difference, let alone its significance and implications in the context of industrial America. Yet most, it seems, 'got caught up in . . . this racial thing'. How did this happen? If race was indeed socially constructed, then what was the raw material that went into the process?

181

We are also concerned with how these immigrant workers were viewed in racial terms by others – employers, the state, reformers, and other workers. Like the coal-handler in Loguidice's story, their own ascribed racial identity was not always clear. A whole range of evidence – laws; court cases; formal racial ideology; social conventions; popular culture in the form of slang, songs, films, cartoons, ethnic jokes, and popular theatre – suggests that the native-born and older immigrants often placed the new immigrants not only *above* African- and Asian-Americans, for example, but also *below* 'white' people. Indeed, many of the older immigrants and particularly the Irish had themselves been perceived as 'nonwhite' just a generation earlier. As labour historians, we are interested in the ways in which Polish, Italian, and other European artisans and peasants became American workers, but we are equally concerned with the process by which they became 'white'. Indeed, in the US the two identities intertwined and this explains a great deal of the persistent divisions within the working-class population. How did immigrant workers wind up 'inbetween'?

Such questions are not typical of immigration history which has largely been the story of newcomers becoming American, of their holding out against becoming American or, at best, of their changing America in the process of discovering new identities. To the extent, and it is a very considerable extent, that theories of American exceptionalism intersect with the history of immigration, the emphasis falls on the difficulty of enlisting heterogeneous workers into class mobilisations or, alternatively, on the unique success of the US as a multi-ethnic democracy.[2] But the immigration history that Robert Orsi has recently called for, one which 'puts the issues and contests of racial identity and difference at its center', has only begun to be written. Proponents of race as an explanation for American exceptionalism have not focused on European immigrants, at best regarding their racialisation as a process completed by the 1890s.[3]

Even with the proliferation of scholarship on the social construction of race, we sometimes assume that such immigrants really were 'white', in a way that they were not initially American. And, being white, largely poor, and self-consciously part of imagined communities with roots in Europe, they were therefore 'ethnic'. If social scientists referred to 'national' groups as races (the 'Italian race') and to southern and east European pan-nationalities as races (Slavonic and Mediterranean 'races'), they did so because they used race promiscuously to mean other things. If the classic work on American exceptionalism, Werner Sombart's 1906 *Why Is There No Socialism in the United States?* has a whole section on 'racial' division with scarcely a mention of any group modern Americans would recognise as a racial minority, this is a matter of semantic confusion. If Robert Park centred his pioneering early twentieth-century sociological theory of assimilation on the 'race relations cycle', with the initial expectation that it would apply to African-Americans as well as European immigrants, he must not have sorted out the difference between race and ethnicity yet.[4] Indeed, so certain are some modern scholars of the ability of 'ethnicity' to explain immigrant experiences which contemporaries described largely in terms of race and nationality that a substantial literature seeks to describe even the African-American and Native American experiences as 'ethnic'.[5]

We make no brief for the consistency with which 'race' was used, by experts or popularly, to describe the 'new immigrant' southern and east Europeans who dominated the ranks of those coming to the US between 1895 and 1924 and who 'remade' the American working class in that period. We regard such inconsistency as important evidence of the 'inbetween'[6] racial status of such immigrants. The story of Americanisation is vital and compelling, but it took place in a nation also obsessed by race. For new immigrant workers the processes of 'becoming white' and 'becoming American' were intertwined at every turn. The 'American standard of living', which labour organisers alternately and simultaneously accused new immigrants of undermining and encouraged them to defend via class organisation, rested on 'white men's wages'. Political debate turned on whether new immigrants were fit to join the American nation and on whether they were fit to join the 'American race'. Nor do we argue that new immigrants from eastern and southern Europe were in the same situation as non-whites. Stark differences between the racialised status of African-Americans and that racial inbetween-ness of new immigrants meant that the latter *eventually* 'became ethnic' and that their trajectory was predictable. But their history was sloppier than their trajectory. From day to day they were, to borrow from E.P. Thompson, 'proto-nothing', reacting and acting in a highly racialised nation.[7]

Overly ambitious, this essay is also deliberately disorderly. It aims to destabilise modern categories of race and ethnicity and to capture the confusion, inbetween-ness and flux in the minds of native-born Americans and the immigrants themselves. Entangling the processes of Americanisation and of whitening, it treats a two-sided experience: new immigrants underwent racial categorising at the same time they developed new identities, and the two sides of the process cannot be understood one apart from the other. Similarly, the categories of state, class and immigrant self-activity, used here to explain how race is made and to structure the paper, can be separated at best arbitrarily and inconsistently. Expect therefore a bumpy ride, which begins at its bumpiest – with the vocabulary of race.

INBETWEEN IN THE POPULAR MIND

America's racial vocabulary had no agency of its own, but rather reflected material conditions and power relations – the situations that workers faced on a daily basis in their workplaces and communities. Yet the words themselves were important. They were not only the means by which native-born and elite people marked new immigrants as inferiors, but also the means by which immigrant workers came to locate themselves and those about them in the nation's racial hierarchy. In beginning to analyse the vocabulary of race, it makes little sense for historians to invest the words themselves with an agency that could be exercised only by real historical actors, or meanings that derived only from the particular historical contexts in which the language was developed and employed.

The word *guinea*, for example, had long referred to African slaves, particularly those from the continent's northwest coast, and to their descendants. But from the late 1890s, the term was increasingly applied to southern European migrants, first and especially to Sicilians and southern Italians who often came as contract labourers. At various times and places in the United States, *guinea* has been applied to mark Greeks, Jews, Portuguese, Puerto Ricans and perhaps any new immigrant.[8]

Likewise, *hunky*, which began life, probably in the early twentieth century, as a corruption of 'Hungarian', eventually became a pan-Slavic slur connected with perceived immigrant racial characteristics. By the First World War the term was frequently used to describe any immigrant steelworker, as in *mill hunky*. Opponents of the Great 1919 Steel Strike, including some native-born skilled workers, derided the struggle as a 'hunky strike'. Yet Josef Barton's work suggests that for Poles, Croats, Slovenians, and other immigrants who often worked together in difficult, dangerous situations, the term embraced a remarkable, if fragile, sense of prideful identity across ethnic lines. In *Out of this Furnace*, his 1941 epic novel based on the lives of Slavic steelworkers, Thomas Bell observed that the word hunky bespoke 'unconcealed racial prejudice' and a 'denial of social and racial equality'. Yet as these workers built the industrial unions of the late 1930s and took greater control over their own lives, the meaning of the term began to change. The pride with which second and third generation Slavic-American steelworkers, now women as well as men, wore the label in the early 1970s seemed to have far more to do with class than with ethnic identity. At about the same time the word *honky*, possibly a corruption of hunky, came into common use as black nationalism reemerged as a major ideological force in the African-American community.[9]

Words and phrases employed by social scientists to capture the inbetween identity of the new immigrants are a bit more descriptive, if a bit more cumbersome. As late as 1937, John Dollard wrote repeatedly of the immigrant working class as 'our temporary Negroes'. More precise, if less dramatic, is the designation 'not-yet-white ethnics' offered by immigration historian John Bukowczyk. The term not only reflects the popular perceptions and everyday experiences of such workers, but also conveys the dynamic quality of the process of racial formation.[10]

The examples of Greeks and Italians particularly underscore the new immigrants' ambiguous positions with regard to popular perceptions of race. When Greeks suffered as victims of an Omaha 'race' riot in 1909 and when eleven Italians died at the hands of lynchers in Louisiana in 1891, their less-than-white racial status mattered alongside their nationalities. Indeed, as in the case of Loguidice's coal-handler, their ambivalent racial status put their lives in jeopardy. As Gunther Peck shows in his fine study of copper-miners in Bingham, Utah, the Greek and Italian immigrants were 'nonwhite' before their tension-fraught co-operation with the Western Federation of Miners during a 1912 strike ensured that 'the category of Caucasian worker changed and expanded'. Indeed, the work of Dan Georgakas and Yvette Huginnie shows that Greeks and other southern Europeans often 'bivouacked' with other 'nonwhite' workers in Western mining towns. Pocatello, Idaho, Jim-Crowed Greeks in the early twentieth century and in Arizona they were not welcomed by white workers in 'white men's towns' or 'white men's jobs'. In Chicago during the Great Depression, a German-American wife expressed regret over marrying her 'half-nigger', Greek-American husband. African-American slang in the 1920s in South Carolina counted those of mixed American Indian, African-American and white heritage as *Greeks*. Greek-Americans in the Midwest showed great anxieties about race, and were perceived not only as Puerto Rican, mulatto, Mexican or Arab, but also as non-white *because of* being Greek.[11]

Italians, involved in a spectacular international diaspora in the early twentieth century, were racialised as the 'Chinese of Europe' in many lands.[12] But in the US their racialisation was pronounced and, as *guinea*'s evolution suggests, more likely to connect Italians with Africans. During the debate at the Louisiana state constitutional convention of 1898, over how to disfranchise blacks, and over which whites might lose the vote, some acknowledged that the Italian's skin 'happens to be white' even as they argued for his disfranchisement. But others held that 'according to the spirit of our meaning when we speak of "white man's government", [the Italians] are as black as the blackest negro in existence'.[13] More than metaphor intruded on this judgement. At the turn of the century, a West

Coast construction boss was asked, 'You don't call the Italian a white man?' The negative reply assured the questioner that the Italian was 'a dago'. Recent studies of Italian and Greek-Americans make a strong case that racial, not just ethnic, oppression long plagues 'nonwhite' immigrants from southern Europe.[14]

The racialisation of East Europeans was likewise striking. While racist jokes mocked the black servant who thought her child, fathered by a Chinese man, would be a Jew, racist folklore held that Jews, inside-out, were 'niggers'. In 1926 Serbo-Croatians ranked near the bottom of a list of forty 'ethnic' groups whom 'white American' respondents were asked to order according to the respondents' willingness to associate with members of each group. They were placed just above Negroes, Filipinos, and Japanese. Just above them were Poles, who were near the middle of the list. One sociologist has recently written that 'a good many groups on this color continuum [were] not considered white by a large number of Americans'.[15] The literal inbetween-ness of new immigrants on such a list suggests what popular speech affirms: the state of whiteness was approached gradually and controversially. The authority of the state itself both smoothed and complicated that approach.

WHITE CITIZENSHIP AND INBETWEEN AMERICANS: THE STATE OF RACE

The power of the national state gave new immigrants both their firmest claims to whiteness and their strongest leverage for enforcing those claims. The courts consistently allowed new immigrants, whose racial status was ambiguous in the larger culture, to be naturalised as 'white' citizens and almost as consistently turned down non-European applicants as 'nonwhite'. Political reformers therefore discussed the fitness for citizenship of new immigrants from two distinct angles. They produced, through the beginning of the First World War, a largely benign and hopeful discourse on how to Americanise (and win the votes of) those already here. But this period also saw a debate on fertility rates and immigration restriction which conjured up threats of 'race suicide' if this flow of migrants were not checked and the fertility of the native-born increased. A figure like Theodore Roosevelt could stand as both the Horatio warning of the imminent swamping of the 'old stock' racial elements in the US and as the optimistic Americaniser to whom the play which originated the assimilationist image of the 'melting pot' was dedicated.[16]

Such anomalies rested not only on a political economy which at times needed and at times shunned immigrant labour, but also on peculiarities of US naturalisation law. If the 'state apparatus' both told new immigrants that they were and were not white, it was clearly the judiciary which produced the most affirmative responses. Thus US law made citizenship racial as well as civil. Even when much of the citizenry doubted the racial status of European migrants, the courts almost always granted their whiteness in naturalisation cases. Thus, the often racially-based campaigns against Irish naturalisation in the 1840s and 1850s and against Italian naturalisation in the early twentieth century aimed to delay, not deny, citizenship. The lone case which appears exceptional in this regard is one in which US naturalisation attorneys in Minnesota attempted unsuccessfully to bar radical Finns from naturalisation on the ethnological grounds that they were not 'caucasian' and therefore not white.[17]

The legal equation of whiteness with fitness for citizenship significantly shaped the process by which race was made in the US. If new immigrants remained 'inbetween people' because of broad cultural perceptions, Asians were in case after case declared unambiguously non-white and therefore unfit for citizenship. This sustained pattern of denial of citizenship provides, as the sociologist Richard Williams argues, the best guide to who would be racialised in an ongoing way in the twentieth-century US. It applies, of course, in the case of Native Americans. Migrants from Africa, though nominally an exception in that Congress in 1870 allowed their naturalisation (with the full expectation that they would not be coming), of course experienced sweeping denials of civil status both in slavery and in Jim Crow. Nor were migrants from Mexico truly exceptional. Despite the naturalisability of such migrants by treaty and later court decisions, widespread denials of citizenship rights took place almost immediately – in one 1855 instance in California as a result of the 'Greaser Bill', as the Vagrancy Act was termed.[18]

Likewise, the equation between legal whiteness and fitness for naturalisable citizenship helps to predict which groups would *not* be made non-white in an ongoing way. Not only did the Irish, whose whiteness was under sharp question in the 1840s and 1850s, and later the new immigrants gain the powerful symbolic argument that the law declared them white and fit. They also had the power of significant numbers of votes, although naturalisation rates for new immigrants were not always high. During Louisiana's disfranchising constitutional convention of 1898, for example, the bitter debate over Italian whiteness ended with a provision passed extending to new immigrants protections comparable, even superior, to those which the 'grandfather clause' gave to native white voters. New Orleans' powerful Choctaw Club machine, already the beneficiary of Italian votes, led the

campaign for the plank.[19] When Thomas Hart Benton and Stephen Douglas
argued against Anglo-Saxon superiority for a pan-white 'American race'
in the 1850s, they did so before huge blocs of Irish voters. When Theodore
Roosevelt extolled the 'mixture of blood' making the American race a 'new
ethnic type in this meltingpot of the nations', he emphasised to new immigrant *voters* his conviction that each of their nationalities would enrich
America by adding 'its blood to the life of the nation'. Woodrow Wilson also
tailored his thinking about racial desirability of the European new immigrants in the context of an electoral campaign in which the 'foreign' vote
counted heavily.[20] In such a situation, Roosevelt's almost laughable proliferation of uses of the word *race* served him well, according to his various
needs as reformer, imperialist, debunker and romanticiser of the history of
the West, and political candidate. He sincerely undertook seemingly contradictory embraces of Darwin and of Lamarck's insistence on the here-
ditability of acquired characteristics, of melting pots and of race suicide,
of an adoring belief in Anglo-Saxon and Teutonic superiority and in the
grandeur of a 'mixed' American race. Roosevelt, like the Census Bureau,
thought in terms of the nation's biological 'stock' – the term by now called
forth images of Wall Street as well as the farm. That stock was directly
threatened by low birth rates among the nation's 'English-speaking race'.
But races could also progress over time and the very experience of mixing
and of clashing with other races would bring out, and improve, the best of
the 'racestock'. The 'American race' could absorb and permanently improve
the less desirable stock of '*all* white immigrants', perhaps in two generations, but only if its most desirable 'English-speaking' racial elements were
not swamped in an un-Americanised Slavic and southern European culture
and biology.[21]

   The neo-Lamarckianism which allowed Roosevelt to use such terms as
'English-speaking race' ran through much of Progressive racial thinking,
though it was sometimes underpinned by appeals to other authorities.[22] We
likely regard choosing between eating pasta or meat, between speaking
English or Italian, between living in ill-ventilated or healthy housing,
between taking of religious holidays or coming to work, between voting
Republican or Socialist as decisions based on environment, opportunity
and choice. But language loyalty, incidence of dying in epidemics, and
radicalism often defined *race* for late nineteenth- and early twentieth-
century thinkers, making distinctions between racial, religious and anti-
radical varieties of nativism messy. For many, Americanisation was not
simply a cultural process but an index of racial change which could fail
if the concentration of 'lower' races kept the 'alchemy' of racial transformation from occurring.[23] From its very start, the campaign for immigration

restriction directed against 'new' Europeans carried a strong implication that even something as ineluctable as 'moral tone' could be inherited. In deriding 'ignorant, brutal Italians and Hungarian labourers' during the 1885 debate over the Contract Labor Law, its sponsor framed his environmentalist arguments in terms of colour, holding that 'the introduction into a community of any considerable number of persons of a lower moral tone will cause general moral deterioration as sure as night follows day'. He added, 'The intermarriage of a lower with a higher type certainly does not improve the latter any more than does the breeding of cattle by blooded and common stock improve the blooded stock generally.' The restrictionist cause came to feature wings that saw mixing as always and everywhere disastrous. Madison Grant's *The Passing of the Great Race* (1916), a racist attack on new immigrants which defended the purity of 'Nordic' stock, the race of the 'white man par excellence', against 'Alpine', 'Mediterranean' and Semitic invaders, is a classic example.[24]

Professional Americanisers and national politicians appealing to immigrant constituencies for a time seemed able to marginalise those who racialised new immigrants. Corporate America generally gave firm support to relatively open immigration. Settlement house reformers and others taught and witnessed Americanisation. The best of them, Jane Addams, for example, learned from immigrants as well and extolled not only assimilation but the virtues of ongoing cultural differences among immigrant groups. Even progressive politicians showed potential to rein in their own most racially-charged tendencies. As a Southern academic, Woodrow Wilson wrote of the dire threat to 'our Saxon habits of government' by 'corruption of foreign blood' and characterised Italian and Polish immigrants as 'sordid and hapless'. But as a presidential candidate in 1912, he reassured immigrant leaders that 'We are all Americans', offered to rewrite sections on Polish-Americans in his *History of the American People* and found Italian-Americans 'one of the most interesting and admirable elements in our American life'.[25]

Yet Progressive Era assimilationism, and even its flirtations with cultural pluralism, could not save new immigrants from racial attacks. If racial prejudice against new immigrants was far more provisional and nuanced than anti-Irish bias in the ante-bellum period, political leaders also defended *hunkies* and *guineas* far more provisionally. Meanwhile the Progressive project of imperialism and the Progressive non-project of capitulation to Jim Crow ensured that race thinking would retain and increase its potency. If corporate leaders backed immigration and funded Americanisation projects, the corporate model emphasised standardisation, efficiency and immediate results. This led many Progressives to support reforms that called immigrant political power and voting rights into question, at least in the short run.[26] In the longer term, big business proved by the early 1920s an unreliable supporter of the melting pot. Worried about unemployment and about the possibility that new immigrants were proving 'revolutionary and communistic races', they equivocated on the openness of immigration, turned Americanising agencies into labour spy networks, and stopped funding for the corporate-sponsored umbrella group of professional Americanisers and conservative new immigrant leaders, the Inter-Racial Council.[27]

Reformers, too, lost heart. Since mixing was never regarded as an unmitigated good but as a matter of proportion with a number of possible outcomes, the new immigrants' record was constantly under scrutiny. The failure of Americanisation to deliver total loyalty during the First World War and during the post-war 'immigrant rebellion' within US labour made that record one of failure. The 'virility', 'manhood' and 'vigor' that reformers predicted race mixture would inject into the American stock had long coexisted with the emphasis on obedience and docility in Americanisation curricula.[28] At their most vigorous, in the 1919–20 strike wave, new immigrants were most suspect. Nationalists, and many Progressive reformers among them, were, according to John Higham, sure that they had done 'their best to bring the great mass of newcomers into the fold'. The failure was not theirs, but a reflection of the 'incorrigibly unassimilable nature of the material on which they had worked'.[29]

The triumph of immigration restriction in the 1920s was in large measure a triumph of *racism* against new immigrants. Congress and the Ku Klux Klan, the media and popular opinion all reinforced the inbetween, and even non-white, racial status of eastern and southern Europeans. Grant's *Passing of the Great Race* suddenly enjoyed a vogue which had eluded it in 1916. The best-selling US magazine *Saturday Evening Post* praised Grant and sponsored Kenneth Roberts' massively mounted fears that continued immigration would produce 'a hybrid race of people as worthless and futile as the good-for-nothing mongrels of Central America and Southeastern Europe'. When the National Industrial Conference Board met in 1923, its director allowed that restriction was 'essentially a race question'. Congress was deluged with letters of concern for preservation of a 'distinct American type' and of support for stopping the 'swamping' of the Nordic race. In basing itself on the first fear and setting quotas pegged squarely on the (alleged) origins of the current population, the 1924 restriction act also addressed the second fear, since US population as a whole came from northern and western parts of Europe to vastly a greater extent than had the immigrant population for the last three decades. At virtually the same time that the courts carefully drew a colour line between European new immigrants and non-white others, the Congress and reformers reaffirmed the racial inbetween-ness of southern and eastern Europeans.[30]

Americanisation therefore was never just about nation but always about race and nation. This truth stood out most clearly in the Americanising influences of popular culture, in which mass market films socialised new immigrants into a 'gunfighter nation' of Westerns and a vaudeville nation of blackface, in which popular music was both 'incontestably mulatto' and freighted with the hierarchical racial heritage of minstrelsy; in which the most advertised lures of Americanised mass consumption turned on the opportunity to harness the energies of black servants like the Gold Dust twins, Aunt Jemima and Rastus, the Cream of White chef, to household labour. Drawing on a range of anti-new immigrant stereotypes as well, popular entertainments and advertisements cast newcomers as nationally particular and racially inbetween, while teaching the all-important lesson that immigrants were never so white as when they wore blackface before audiences and cameras.[31]

Occasionally, professional Americanisers taught the same lesson. In a Polish and Bohemian neighbourhood on Chicago's lower west side, for example, social workers at Gads Hill Center counted their 1915 minstrel show a 'great success'. Organised by the Center's Young Men's Club, the event drew 350 people, many of whom at that point knew so little English that they could only 'enjoy the music' and 'appreciate the really attractive costumes'. Young performers with names like Kraszewski, Pletcha and Chimielewski sang 'Clare De Kitchen' and 'Gideon's Band'. Settlement houses generally practised Jim Crow, even in the North. Some of their leading theorists invoked a racial continuum which ended 'farthest in the rear' with African-Americans even as they goaded new immigrants toward giving up particular Old World cultures by branding the retention of such cultures as an atavistic clinging on to 'racial consciousness'.[32]

'INBETWEEN' JOBS: CAPITAL, CLASS AND THE NEW IMMIGRANT

Joseph Loguidice's reminiscence of the temporarily 'colored' coal-hauler compresses and dramatises a process that went on in far more workaday settings as well. Often while themselves begrimed by the nation's dirtiest jobs, new immigrants and their children quickly learned that the worst thing one could be in this Promised Land was 'colored'.[33] But if the world of work taught the importance of being 'not black', it also exposed new immigrants to frequent comparisons and close competition with African-Americans. The results of such clashes in the labour market did not instantly propel new immigrants into either the category or the consciousness of whiteness. Instead management created an economics of racial inbetween-ness which taught new immigrants the importance of racial hierarchy while leaving open their place in that hierarchy. At the same time the struggle for 'inbetween jobs' further emphasised the importance of national and religious ties among immigrants by giving those ties an important economic dimension.

The bitterness of job competition between new immigrants and African-Americans has rightly received emphasis in accounting for racial hostility, but that bitterness must be *historically* investigated. Before 1915, new immigrants competed with relatively small numbers of African-Americans for northern urban jobs. The new immigrants tended to be more recent arrivals than the black workers, and they came in such great numbers that, demographically speaking, they competed far more often with each other than with African-Americans. Moreover, given the much greater 'human capital' of black workers in terms of literacy, education and English language skills, new immigrants fared well in this competition.[34] After 1915, the decline of immigration resulting from the First World War and restrictive legislation in the 1920s combined with the Great Migration of Afro-Southerners to northern cities to create a situation in which a growing and newly-arrived black working class provided massive competition for a more settled but struggling immigrant population. Again, the results were not of a sort that would necessarily have brought bitter disappointment to those whom the economic historians term SCEs (Southern and Central Europeans).[35] The Sicilian immigrant, for example, certainly was at times locked in competition with African-Americans. But was that competition more bitter and meaningful than competition with, for example, northern Italian immigrants, 'hunkies', or white native-born workers, all of whom were at times said to be *racially* different from Sicilians?

The ways in which capital structured workplaces and labour markets contributed to the idea that competition should be both cut-throat and racialised. New immigrants suffered wage discrimination when compared to the white native-born. African-Americans were paid less for the same jobs than new immigrants. In the early twentieth century, employers preferred a labour force divided by race and national origins. As the labour economists Richard Edwards, Michael Reich and David Gordon have recently reaffirmed, work gangs segregated by nationality as well as by race could be and were made to compete against each other in a strategy designed not only to undermine labour unity and depress wages in the long run but to spur competition and productivity every day.[36]

On the other hand, management made broader hiring and promotion distinctions which brought pan-national and sometimes racial categories into play. In some workplaces and areas, the blast furnace was a 'Mexican job'; in others, it was a pan-Slavic 'hunky' job. 'Only hunkies', a steel industry investigator was told, worked blast furnace jobs which were 'too damn dirty and too damn hot for a white man'. Management at the nation's best-studied early twentieth-century factory divided the employees into 'white men' and 'kikes'. Such bizarre notions about the genetic '*fit*' between immigrants and certain types of work were buttressed by the 'scientific' judgements of scholars like the sociologist E.A. Ross who observed that Slavs were 'immune to certain kinds of dirt . . . that would kill a white man'. 'Scientific' managers in steel and in other industries designed elaborate ethnic classification systems to guide their hiring. In 1915 the personnel manager at one Pittsburgh plant analysed what he called the 'racial adaptability' of thirty-six different ethnic groups to twenty-four different kinds of work and twelve sets of conditions and plotted them all on a chart. Lumber companies in Louisiana built what they called 'the Quarters' for black workers and (separately) for Italians, using language very recently associated with African-American slavery. For white workers they built company housing and towns. The distinction between 'white' native-born workers and 'non-white' new immigrants, Mexicans and African-Americans in parts of the West, rested in large part on the presence of 'white man's camps' or 'white man's towns' in company housing in lumbering and mining. Native-born residents interviewed in the wake of a bitter 1915 strike by Polish oil refinery workers recognised only two classes of people in Bayonne, New Jersey: 'foreigners' and 'white men'. In generalising about early twentieth-century nativism, John Higham concludes: 'In all sections native-born and Northern European labourers called themselves "white men" to distinguish themselves from Southern Europeans whom they worked beside.' As late as the Second World War, new immigrants and their children, lumped together as 'racials', suffered employment discrimination in the defence industry.[37]

There was also substantial management interest in the specific comparison of new immigrants with African-Americans as workers. More concrete in the North and abstract in the South, these complex comparisons generally, but not always, favoured the former group. African-Americans' supposed undependability 'especially on Mondays', intolerance for cold, and incapacity of fast-paced work were all noted. But the comparisons were often nuanced. New immigrants, as Herbert Gutman long ago showed, were themselves counted as unreliable, 'especially on Mondays'. Some employers counted black workers as more apt and skilful 'in certain occupations' and cleaner and happier than 'the alien white races'. An occasional blanket preference for African-Americans over immigrants surfaced, as at Packard in Detroit in 1922. Moreover, comparisons carried a provisional quality, since ongoing competition was often desired. In 1905 the superintendent of Illinois Steel, threatening to fire all Slavic workers, reassured the immigrants that no 'race hatred' [against Slavs!] motivated the proposed decision, which was instead driven by a factor that the workers could change their tardiness in adopting the English language.[38]

The fact that the new immigrant was relatively inexperienced *vis-à-vis* African-American workers in the North in 1900 and relatively experienced by 1930 makes it difficult for economic historians to measure the extent to which new immigrant economic mobility in this period derived from employer discrimination. Clearly, timing and demographic change mattered alongside racism in a situation in which the new immigrant SCEs came to occupy spaces on the job ladder between African-Americans below and those who were fed into the economic historians' computers as NWNPs (native-born whites with native-born parents). Stanley Lieberson uses the image of a 'queue' to help explain the role of discrimination against African-Americans in leading to such results.[39] In the line-up of workers ordered by employer preference, as in so much else, new immigrants were inbetween.

In a society in which workers did in fact shape up in lines to seek jobs, the image of a queue is wonderfully apt. However, the Polish worker next to an African-American on one side and an Italian-American on the other as an NWNP manager hired unskilled labour did not know the statistics of current job competition, let alone what the results would be by the time of the 1930 census. Even if the Polish worker had known them, the patterns of mobility for his group would likely have differed as much from those of the Italian-Americans as from those of the African-Americans (who in some cities actually out-distanced Polish immigrants in intra-working-class mobility to better jobs from 1900 to 1930).[40] Racialised struggles over jobs were fed by the general experience of brutal, group-based competition, and by the knowledge that black workers were especially vulnerable competitors who fared far less well in the labour market than any other native-born American group. The young Croatian immigrant Stephan Mesaros was so struck by the abuse of a black co-worker that he asked a Serbian labourer for an explanation. 'You'll soon learn something about this country', came the reply, 'Negroes never get a fair chance.'

The exchange initiated a series of conversations which contributed to Mesaros becoming Steve Nelson, an influential radical organiser and an anti-racist. But for most immigrants, caught in a world of dog-eat-dog competition, the lesson would likely have been that African-Americans were among the eaten.[41]

If immigrants did not know the precise contours of the job queue, nor their prospects in it, they did have their own ideas about how to get on line, their own strategies about how to get ahead in it, and their own dreams for getting out of it. These tended to reinforce a sense of the advantage of being 'not nonwhite' but to also emphasise specific national and religious identifications rather than generalised white identity. Because of the presence of a small employing (or subcontracting) class in their communities, new immigrants were far more likely to work for one of 'their own' as an immediate boss. In New York City, in 1910, for example, almost half of the sample of Jewish workers studied by Suzanne Model had Jewish supervisors, as did about one Italian immigrant in seven. Meanwhile, 'the study sample unearthed only one industrial match between labourers and supervisors among Blacks'.[42]

In shrugging at being called *hunky*, Thomas Bell writes, Slovak immigrants took solace that they 'had come to America to find work and save money, not to make friends with the Irish'. But getting work and 'making friends with' Irish-American foremen, skilled workers, union leaders and politicians were often very much connected, and the relationships were hardly smooth. Petty bosses could always rearrange the queue.[43] But over the long run, a common Catholicism (and sometimes common political machine affiliations) gave new immigrant groups access to the fragile favour of Irish-Americans in positions to influence hiring which African-Americans could not achieve. Sometimes such favour was organised, as through the Knights of Columbus in Kansas City packinghouses. Over time, as second generation marriages across national lines but within the Catholic religion became a pattern, kin joined religion in shaping hiring in ways largely excluding African-Americans.[44]

Many of the new immigrant groups also had distinctive plans to move out of the US wage labour queue altogether. From 1880 to 1930, fully one-third of all Italian immigrants were 'birds of passage' who in many cases never intended to stay. This pattern likewise applied to 46 per cent of Greeks entering between 1908 and 1923 and to 40 per cent of Hungarians entering between 1899 and 1913.[45] Strong national (and sub-national) loyalties obviously persisted in such cases, with saving money to send or take home a far higher priority than sorting out the complexities of racial identity in the US. Similarly, those many new immigrants (especially among the Greeks,

Italians and Jews) who hoped to (and did) leave the working class by open-ing small businesses set great store in saving, and often catered to a clientele composed mainly of their own group.

But immigrant saving itself proved highly racialised, as did immigrant small business in many instances. Within US culture, African-Americans symbolised prodigal lack of savings as the Chinese, Italians and Jews did fanatical obsession with saving. Popular racist mythology held that, if paid a dollar and a quarter, Italians would spend only the quarter while African-Americans would spend a dollar and a half. Characteristically, racial com-mon sense case cast both patterns as pathological.[46]

Moreover, in many cases Jewish and Italian merchants sold to African-American customers. Their 'middleman minority' status revealingly identi-fies an inbetween position which, as aggrieved Southern 'white' merchants complained, rested on a more humane attitude toward black customers and on such cultural affinities as an eagerness to participate in bargaining over prices. Chinese merchants have traditionally, and Korean merchants more recently, occupied a similar position. Yet, as an 1897 New York City cor-respondent for *Harper's Weekly* captured in an article remarkable for its precise balancing of anti-black and anti-Semitic racism, the middleman's day-to-day position in the marketplace reinforced specific Jewish identity and distance from blacks. 'For a student of race characteristics', the reporter wrote, 'nothing could be more striking than to observe the stoic scorn of the Hebrew when he is made a disapproving witness of the happy-go-lucky joyousness of his dusky neighbor.'[47]

Other new immigrants, especially Slovaks and Poles, banked on hard labour, home ownership and slow intergenerational mobility for success. They too navigated in very tricky racial cross-currents. Coming from areas in which the dignity of hard, physical labour was established, both in the countryside and in cities, they arrived in the US eager to work, even if in jobs which did not take advantage of their skills. They often found, however, that in the Taylorising industries of the US, hard work was more driven and alienating.[48] It was, moreover, often typed and despised as 'nigger work' – or as 'dago work' or 'hunky work' in settings in which such categor-ies had been freighted with the prior meaning of 'nigger work'. The new immigrants' reputation for hard work and their unfamiliarity with English and with American culture generally tended to lead to their being hired as an almost abstract source of labour. *Hunky* was abbreviated to *hunk* and Slavic labourers in particular treated as mere pieces of work. This had its advantages, especially in comparison to black workers; Slavs could more often get hired in groups while skilled workers and petty bosses favoured individual 'good Negroes' with unskilled jobs, often requiring a familiarity and subservience from them not expected of new immigrants. But being seen as brute force also involved eastern Europeans in particularly brutal social relations on the shopfloor.[49]

Hard work, especially when closely bossed, was likewise not a badge of manliness in the US in the way that it had been in eastern Europe. Racialised, it was also demasculinised, especially since its extremely low pay and sporadic nature ensured that new immigrant males could not be breadwinners for a family. The idea of becoming a 'white man', unsullied by racially typed labour and capable of earning a family wage, was therefore extremely attractive in many ways, and the imperative of not letting one's job become 'nigger work' was swiftly learned.[50] Yet, no clear route ran from inbetween-ness to white manhood. 'White men's unions' often seemed the best path, but they also erected some of the most significant obstacles.

Historians are just beginning to understand this gendered quality of racial language, conventions and identity. It is apparent even in the sorts of public spheres privileged here – citizenship, the state, the union, the workplace. But we are *most* apt to find the conjunctions between gender and race at those points where more intimate relations intersected with the rule of law. The taboo against interracial sex and marriage, was one obvious boundary between low-status immigrant workers and people of colour with whom they often came in contact. As Peggy Pascoe has noted, 'although such marriages were infrequent throughout most of US history, an enormous amount of time and energy was spent in trying to prevent them from taking place . . . the history of interracial marriage provides rich evidence of the formulation of race and gender and of the connections between the two'. Yet we have little understanding of how this taboo was viewed by immigrant and African- or Asian-American workers. One obvious place to look is at laws governing interracial marriage and court cases aimed at enforcing such laws. Native-born women who became involved with immigrant men could lose their citizenship and, if the immigrant were categorised as non-white, they could be prosecuted for 'race-mixup'.[51]

WHITE MEN'S UNIONS AND NEW IMMIGRANT TRIAL MEMBERS

While organised labour exercised little control over hiring except for a few organised crafts, during most of the years from 1895 until 1924 and beyond, its racialised opposition to new immigrants did reinforce their inbetween-ness, both on the job and in politics. Yet the American Federation of Labor also provided an important venue in which 'old immigrant' workers inter-acted with new immigrants, teaching important lessons in both whiteness and Americanisation.

As an organisation devoted to closing skilled trades to any new com-petition, the craft union's reflex was to oppose outsiders. In this sense, most of the AFL unions were 'exclusionary by definition' and marshalled economic, and to a lesser extent political, arguments to exclude women, Chinese, Japanese, African-Americans, the illiterate, the non-citizen, and the new immigrants from organised workplaces, and, whenever possible, from the shores of the US. So clear was the craft logic of AFL restrictionism that historians are apt to regard it as simply materialistic and to note its racism only when direct assaults were made on groups traditionally re-garded as non-white. John Higham argues that only in the last moments of the major 1924 debates over whom to restrict did Gompers, on this view, reluctantly embrace 'the idea that European immigration endangered America's racial foundations'.[52]

Yet Gwendolyn Mink and Andrew Neather demonstrate that it is far more difficult to separate appeals based on craft or race in AFL campaigns to restrict European immigration than Higham implies. A great deal of trade unions' racist opposition to the Chinese stressed the connection between their 'slave-like' subservience and their status as coolie labourers, schooled and trapped in the Chinese social system and willing to settle for being 'cheap men'.[53] Dietary practices (rice and rats rather than meat) symbolised Chi-nese failure to seek the 'American standard of living'. All of these are cul-tural, historical and environmental matters. Yet none of them prevented the craft unions from declaring the Chinese 'race' unassimilable nor from sup-porting exclusionary legislation premised largely on racial grounds. The environmentalist possibility that over generations Asian 'cheap men' might improve was simply irrelevant. By that time the Chinese race would have polluted America.[54]

Much of anti-Chinese rhetoric was applied as well to Hungarians in the 1880s and was taken over in AFL anti-new immigration campaigns after 1890. Pasta, as Mink implies, joined rice as an 'un-American' and racialised food. Far from abjuring arguments based on 'stock', assimilability and homogeneity, the AFL's leaders supported literacy tests designed specifi-cally 'to reduce the numbers of Slavic and Mediterranean immigrants'. They blocked with the anti-new immigrant racism of the anti-labour Senator Henry Cabot Lodge, hoped anti-Japanese agitation could be made to con-tribute to anti-new immigrant restrictions, emphasised 'the incompatibility of the new immigrants with the very nature of American civilization', and both praised and reprinted works on 'race suicide'.[55] They opposed entry of 'the scum' from 'the least civilized countries of Europe' and 'the replacing of the independent and intelligent coal miners of Pennsylvania by the Huns and Slavs'. They feared that an 'American' miner in Pennsylvania could thrive only if he 'Latinizes' his name. They explicitly asked, well before the First World War: 'How much more [new] immigration can this country absorb and retain its homogeneity?' (Those wanting to know the dire answer were advised to study the 'racial history' of cities.)[56]

Robert Asher is undoubtedly correct in arguing both that labour movement reaction to new immigrants was 'qualitatively different from the response to Orientals' *and* that AFL rhetoric was 'redolent of a belief in racial inferiority' of Southern and Eastern Europeans. Neather is likewise on the mark in speaking of 'semi-racial' union arguments for restriction directed against new immigrants.[57] Gompers' characterisation of new immigrants as 'beaten men of beaten races' perfectly captures the tension between fearing that southern and eastern Europe was dumping its 'vomit' and 'scum' in the US and believing that Slavic and Mediterranean people were scummy. Labour sometimes cast its ideal as an 'Anglo-Saxon race . . . true to itself'. Gompers was more open, but equivocal. He found that the wonderful 'peculiarities of temperament such as patriotism, sympathy, etc.', which made labour unionism possible, were themselves 'peculiar to most of the Caucasian race'. In backing literacy tests for immigrants in 1902, he was more explicit. They would leave British, German, Irish, French and Scandinavian immigration intact but 'shut out a considerable number of Slavs and other[s] equally or more undesirable and injurious'.[58]

Such 'semi-racial' nativism shaped the AFL's politics and led to exclusion of new immigrants from many unions. When iron puddlers' poet Michael McGovern envisioned an ideal celebration for his union, he wrote: 'There were no men invited such as Slavs and "Tally Annes," / Hungarians and Chinamen with pigtail cues and fans.' The situation in the building trades was complicated. Some craft unions excluded Italians, Jews and other new immigrants. Among labourers organisation often began on an ethnic basis, though such immigrant locals were often eventually integrated into a national union. Even among craftsmen, separate organisations emerged among Jewish carpenters and painters and other recent immigrants. The hod carriers' union, according to Asher, 'appears to have been created to protect the jobs of native construction workers against competing foreigners'. The shoeworkers, pianomakers, barbers, hotel and restaurant workers and United Textile Workers likewise kept out new immigrants, whose lack of literacy, citizenship, English-language skills, apprenticeship opportunities and initiation fees also effectively barred them from many other craft locals. This 'internal protectionism' apparently had lasting results. Lieberson's research through 1950 shows new immigrants and their children having far less access to craft jobs in unionised sectors than did whites of north-western European origin.[59]

Yet new immigrants had more access to unionised work than African-Americans and unions never supported outright bans on their migration, as they did with Asians. Organised labour's opposition to the Italians as the 'white Chinese', or to new immigrants generally as 'white coolies' usually acknowledged and questioned whiteness at the same time, associating whites with non-whites while leaving open the possibility that contracted labour, and not race, was at issue. A strong emphasis on the 'brotherhood' of labour also complicated matters. Paeans to the 'International Fraternity of Labour' ran in the *American Federationist* within fifteen pages of anti-new immigrant hysteria such as A.A. Graham's 'The un-Americanizing of America'. Reports from Italian labour leaders and poems like 'Brotherhood of Man' ran hard by fearful predictions of race suicide.[60]

Moreover, the very things that the AFL warned about in its anti-new immigrant campaigns encouraged the unions to make tactical decisions to enrol southern and eastern Europeans as members. Able to legally enter the country in large numbers, secure work, and become voters, *hunkies* and *guineas* had social power which could be used to attack the craft unionism of the AFL from the right or, as was often feared, from the left. To restrict immigration, however desirable from Gompers' point of view, did not answer what to do about the majority of the working class which was by 1910 already of immigrant origins. Nor did it address what to do about the many new immigrants already joining unions, in the AFL, in language and national federations or under socialist auspices. If these new immigrants were not going to undermine the AFL's appeals to corporate leaders as an effective moderating force within the working class, the American Federation of Labor would have to consider becoming the Americanizing Federation of Labor.[61]

Most importantly, changes in machinery and Taylorising relations of production made real the threat that crafts could be undermined by expedited training of unskilled and semi-skilled immigrant labour. While this threat gave force to labour's nativist calls for immigration restriction, it also strengthened initiatives toward a 'new unionism' which crossed skill lines to organise new immigrants. Prodded by independent, dual-unionist initiatives like those by Italian socialists and the United Hebrew Trades, by the example of existing industrial unions in its own ranks, and by the left-wing multi-national, multi-racial unionism of the Industrial Workers of the World, the AFL increasingly got into the business of organising and

Americanising new immigrant workers in the early twentieth century. The logic, caught perfectly by a Lithuanian-American packinghouse worker in Chicago, was often quite utilitarian: 'because those sharp foremen are inventing new machines and the work is easier to learn, and so these slow Lithuanians and even green girls can learn to do it, and the Americans and Germans and Irish are put out and the employer saves money. . . . This was why the American labour unions began to organise us all.' Even so, especially in those where new immigrant women were the potential union members and skill dilution threatened mainly immigrant men, the Gompers' leadership at times refused either to incorporate dual unions or to initiate meaningful organising efforts under AFL auspices.[62]

However self-interested, wary and incomplete the AFL's increasing opening to new immigrant workers remained, it initiated a process which much transformed 'semi-racial' typing of already arrived new immigrants. Unions and their supporters at times treasured labour organisation as the most meaningful agent of democratic 'Americanization from the bottom up', what John R. Commons called 'The only effective Americanizing force for the southeastern European'.[63] In struggles, native-born unionists came to observe not only the common humanity, but also the heroism of new immigrants. Never quite giving up on biological/cultural explanations, labour leaders wondered which 'race' made the best strikers, with some comparisons favouring the recent arrivals over Anglo-Saxons. Industrial Workers of the World leader Covington Hall's reports from Louisiana remind us that we know little about how unionists, and workers generally, conceived of race. Hall took seriously the idea of a 'Latin race', including Italians, other southern Europeans *and Mexicans*, all of whom put southern whites to shame with their militancy.[64] In the rural west, a 'white man', labour investigator Peter Speek wrote, 'is an extreme individualist, busy with himself', a 'native or old-time immigrant' labourer, boarded by employers. 'A foreigner', he added, 'is more sociable and has a higher sense of comradeship' and of nationality. Embracing the very racial vocabulary to which he objected, one socialist plasterer criticised native-born unionists who described Italians as *guineas*. He pointed out that Italians' ancestors 'were the best and unsurpassable in manhood's glories; at a time when our dads were running about in paint and loincloth as ignorant savages'. To bring the argument up to the present, he added that Italian-Americans 'are as manly for trade union conditions as the best of us; and that while handicapped by our prejudice'.[65]

While such questioning of whiteness was rare, the 'new unionism' provided an economic logic for progressive unionists wishing to unite workers across ethnic and racial lines. With their own race less open to question, new immigrants were at times brought into class conscious coalitions, as whites and with African-Americans. The great success of the packinghouse unions in forging such unity during the First World War ended in a shining victory and spectacularly improved conditions. The diverse new immigrants and black workers at the victory celebration heard Chicago Federation of Labor leader John Fitzpatrick hail them as 'black and white together under God's sunshine'. If the Irish-American unionists had often been bearers of 'race hatred' against both new immigrants and blacks, they and other old immigrants also could convey the lesson that class unity transcended race and semi-race.[66]

But even at the height of openings toward new unionism and new immigrants, labour organisations taught very complex lessons regarding race. At times, overtures toward new immigrants coincided with renewed exclusion of non-white workers, underlining Du Bois' point that the former were mobbed to make them join unions and the latter to keep them out. Western Federation of Miners (WFM) activists, whose episodic radicalism coexisted with nativism and a consistent anti-Chinese and anti-Mexican racism, gradually developed a will and a strategy to organise Greek immigrants, but they reaffirmed exclusion of Japanese mine workers and undermined impressive existing solidarities between Greeks and Japanese, who often worked in similar jobs.[67] The fear of immigrant 'green hands', which the perceptive Lithuanian immigrant quoted above credited with first sparking the Butcher Workmen to organise new immigrants in 1904, was also a fear of black hands, so that one historian has suggested that the desire to limit black employment generated the willingness to organise new immigrants.[68]

In 1905, Gompers promised that 'caucasians are not going to let their standard of living be destroyed by negroes, Chinamen, Japs, or any others'.[69] Hearing this, new immigrant unionists might have reflected on what they as 'caucasians' had to learn regarding their newfound superiority to non-whites. Or they might have fretted that *guineas* and *hunkies* would be classified along with 'any others' undermining white standards. Either way, learning about race was an important part of new immigrants' labour education.

Teaching Americanism, the labour movement also taught whiteness. The scattered racist jokes in the labour and socialist press could not, of course, rival blackface entertainments or the 'coon songs' in the Sunday comics in teaching new immigrants the racial ropes of the US, but the movement did provide a large literature of popularised racist ethnology, editorial attacks on 'nigger equality' and, in Jack London, a major cultural figure who taught that it was possible and desirable to be 'first of all a white man and only then a socialist'.[70]

But the influence of organised labour and the left on race thinking was far more focused on language than on literature, on picket lines than lines on a page. Unions which opened to new immigrants more readily than to 'nonwhites' not only reinforced the 'inbetween' position of southern and eastern Europeans but attempted to teach immigrants intricate and spurious associations of race, strike-breaking and lack of manly pride. Even as AFL exclusionism ensured that there would be black strike-breakers and black suspicion of unions, the language of labour equated scabbing with 'turning nigger'. The unions organised much of their critique around a notion of 'slavish' behaviour which could be employed against ex-slaves or against Slavs, but indicted the former more often than the latter.[71] Warning all union men against 'slave-like' behaviour, unions familiarised new workers with the ways race and slavery had gone together to define a standard of unmanned servility. In objectively confusing situations, with scabs coming from the African-American, new immigrant and native-born working classes (and with craft unions routinely breaking each other's strikes), Booker T. Washington identified one firm rule of thumb: 'Strikers seem to consider it a much greater crime for a Negro who had been denied the opportunity to work at his trade to take the place of a striking employee than for a white man to do the same thing.'[72]

In such situations, whiteness had its definite appeals. But the left and labour movements could abruptly remind new immigrants that their whiteness was anything but secure. Jack London could turn from denunciations of the 'yellow peril' or of African-Americans to excoriations of 'the dark-pigmented things' coming in from Europe. The 1912 Socialist Party campaign book connected European immigration with 'race annihilation' and the 'possible degeneration of even the succeeding American type'. The prominence of black strike-breakers in several of the most important mass strikes after the First World War strengthened the grip of racism, perhaps even among recent immigrants, but the same years also brought renewed racial attacks on the immigrants themselves. In the wake of these failed strikes, the *American Federationist* featured disquisitions on 'Americanism and Immigration' by John Quinn, the National Commander of the nativist and anti-labour American Legion. New immigrants had unarguably proven the most loyal unionists in the most important of the strikes, yet the AFL now supported exclusion based on 'racial' quotas. Quinn brought together biology, environment and the racialised history of the US, defending American stock against Italian 'industrial slaves' particularly and the 'indigestion of immigration' generally.[73]

INBETWEEN AND INDIFFERENT: NEW IMMIGRANT RACIAL
CONSCIOUSNESS

One Italian-American informant interviewed by a Louisiana scholar remembered the early twentieth century as a time when 'he and his family
had been badly mistreated by a French plantation owner near New Roads
where he and his family were made to live among the Negroes and were
treated in the same manner. At first he did not mind because he did not
know any difference, but when he learned the position that the Negroes
occupied in this country, he demanded that his family be moved to a
different house and be given better treatment.' In denouncing all theories
of white supremacy, the Polish language Chicago-based newspaper *Dziennik
Chicagoski* editorialised, 'if the words "superior race" are replaced by the
words "Anglo-Saxon" and instead of "inferior races" such terms as Polish,
Italian, Russian and Slavs in general – not to mention the Negro, the
Chinese, and the Japanese – are applied, then we shall see the political
side of the racial problems in the United States in stark nakedness'.[74] In
the first instance, consciousness of an inbetween racial status leads to a
desire for literal distance from non-whites. In the second, inbetween-ness
leads to a sense of grievances shared in common with non-whites.

In moving from the racial categorisation of new immigrants to their
own racial consciousness, it is important to realise that 'Europeans were
hardly likely to have found racist ideologies an astounding new encounter
when they arrived in the US', though the salience of whiteness as a social
category in the US was exceptional. 'Civilized' northern Italians derided
those darker ones from Sicily and the *Mezzogiorno* as 'Turks' and 'Africans' long before arriving in Brooklyn or Chicago. And, once arrived, if
they spoke of 'little dark fellows', they were far more likely to be describing southern Italians than African-Americans. The strength of anti-Semitism,
firmly ingrained in Poland and other parts of eastern Europe meant that
many immigrants from these regions were accustomed to looking at a
whole 'race' of people as devious, degraded, dangerous. In the US, both
Jews and Poles spoke of riots involving attacks on African-Americans as
'pogroms'. In an era of imperialist expansion and sometimes strident nationalism, a preoccupation with race was characteristic not only of the
United States but also of many European regions experiencing heavy
emigration to the US.[75]

Both eager embraces of whiteness and, more rarely, flirtations with non-
whiteness, characterised new immigrant racial identity. But to assume that
new immigrants as a mass clearly saw their identity with non-whites or
clearly fastened on their differences is to miss the confusion of inbetween-

ness. The discussion of whiteness was an uncomfortable terrain for many reasons and even in separating themselves from African-Americans and Asian-Americans, immigrants did not necessarily become white. Indeed, often they were curiously indifferent to whiteness.

Models that fix on one extreme or the other of new immigrant racial consciousness – the quick choice of whiteness amidst brutal competition or the solidarity with non-white working people based on common oppression – capture parts of the new immigrant experience. At times southern and eastern Europeans were exceedingly apt, and not very critical, students of American racism. Greeks admitted to the Western Federation of Miners saw the advantage of their membership and did not rock the boat by demanding admission for the Japanese-American mine workers with whom they had previously allied. Greek-Americans sometimes battled for racial status fully within the terms of white supremacy, arguing that classical civilisation had established them as 'the highest type of the caucasian race'.[76] In the company town of Pullman and adjacent neighbourhoods, immigrants who sharply divided on national and religious lines coalesced impressively as whites in 1928 to keep out African-American residents.[77] Recently arrived Jewish immigrants on New York City's Lower East Side resented reformers who encouraged them to make a common cause with the 'schwartzes'. In New Bedford, 'white Portuguese' angrily reacted to perceived racial slights and sharply drew the colour line against 'black Portuguese' Cape Verdeans, especially when preference in jobs and housing hung in the balance.[78] Polish workers may have developed their very self-image and honed their reputation in more or less conscious counterpoint to the stereotypical 'niggerscab'. Theodore Radzialowski reasons that 'Poles who had so little going for them (except their white skin – certainly no mean advantage but more important later than earlier in their American experience), may have grasped this image of themselves as honest, honorable, non-scabbing workers and stressed the image of the black scab in order to distinguish themselves from . . . the blacks with whom they shared the bottom of American society.'[79]

Many new immigrants learned to deploy and manipulate white supremacist images from the vaudeville stage and the screens of Hollywood film where they saw 'their own kind' stepping out of conventional racial and gender roles through blackface and other forms of cross-dress. 'Facing nativist pressure that would assign them to the dark side of the racial divide', Michael Rogin argues provocatively, new immigrants and entertainers like Al Jolson, Sophie Tucker and Rudolph Valentino, 'Americanized themselves by crossing and recrossing the racial line'.[80]

At the same time, new immigrants sometimes hesitated to embrace a white identity. Houston's Greek-Americans developed, and retained, a language setting themselves apart from *i mavri* (the blacks), from *i aspri* (the whites) and from Mexican-Americans. In New England, Greeks worked in coalitions with Armenians, whom the courts were worriedly accepting as white, and Syrians, whom the courts found non-white. The large Greek-American sponge fishing industry based in Tarpon Springs, Florida, fought the Ku Klux Klan and employed black workers on an equal, share-the-catch system. Nor did Tarpon Springs practise Jim Crow in public transportation. In Louisiana and Mississippi, southern Italians learned Jim Crow tardily, even when legally accepted as whites, so much so that native whites fretted and black southerners 'made unabashed distinctions between Dagoes and white folks', treating the former with a 'friendly, first name familiarity'. In constructing an anti-Nordic supremacist history series based on 'gifts' of various peoples, the Knights of Columbus quickly and fully included African-Americans. Italian and Italian-American radicals 'consistently expressed horror at the barbaric treatment of blacks', in part because 'Italians were also regarded as an inferior race'. Denouncing not only lynchings but 'the republic of lynchings' and branding the rulers of the US as 'savages of the blue eyes', *Il Proletario* asked: 'What do they think they are as a race, these arrogant whites?' and ruthlessly wondered, 'and how many kisses have their women asked for from the strong and virile black servants?' Italian radicals knew exactly how to go for the jugular vein in US race relations. The Jewish press at times identified with both the suffering and the aspirations of African-Americans. In 1912, Chicago's *Daily Jewish Courier* concluded that 'In this world . . . the Jew is treated as a Negro and Negro as a Jew' and that the 'lynching of the Negroes in the South is similar to massacres on Jews in Russia'.[81]

Examples could, and should, be piled higher on both sides of the new immigrants' racial consciousness. But to see the matter largely in terms of which stack is higher misses the extent to which the exposed position of racial inbetween-ness could generate both positions at once, and sometimes a desire to avoid the issue of race entirely. The best frame of comparison for discussing new immigrant racial consciousness is that of the Irish-Americans in the mid-nineteenth century. Especially when not broadly accepted as such, Irish-Americans insisted that politicians acknowledge them as part of the dominant race. Changing the political subject from Americanness and religion to race whenever possible, they challenged anti-Celtic Anglo-Saxonism by becoming leaders in the cause of white supremacy.[82] New immigrant leaders never approximated that path. With a large segment of both parties willing to vouch for the possibility of speedy, orderly Americanisation and with neither party willing to vouch unequivocally for their racial character, southern and eastern Europeans generally tried to change the subject from whiteness to nationality and loyalty to American ideals.

One factor in such a desire not to be drawn into debates about whiteness was a strong national/cultural identification as Jews, Italians, Poles and so on. At times, the strongest tie might even be to a specific Sicilian or Slovakian village, but the first sustained contact between African-Americans and 'new immigrants' occurred during the First World War when many of these immigrants were mesmerised by the emergence of Poland and other new states throughout eastern and south-eastern Europe. Perhaps this is why new immigrants in Chicago and other riot-torn cities seem to have abstained from early twentieth-century race riots, to a far greater extent than theories connecting racial violence and job competition at 'the bottom' of society would predict. Important Polish spokespersons and newspapers emphasised that the Chicago riots were between the 'whites' and 'Negroes'. Polish immigrants had, and should have, no part in them. What might be termed an *abstention from whiteness* also characterised the practice of rank-and-file east Europeans. Slavic immigrants played little role in the racial violence which was spread by Irish-American gangs.[83]

Throughout the Chicago riots, so vital to the future of Slavic packinghouse workers and their union, Polish-American coverage was sparse and occurred only when editors 'could tear their attention away from their fascination with the momentous events attending the birth of the new Polish state'. And even then, comparisons with pogroms against Jews in Poland framed the discussion. That the defence of Poland was as important as analysing the realities in Chicago emerges starkly in the convoluted expression of sympathy for riot victims in the organ of the progressive, pro-labour Alliance of Polish Women, *Glos Polek*:

> The American Press has written at length about the alleged pogroms of Jews in Poland for over two months. Now it is writing about pogroms against Blacks in America. It wrote about the Jews in words full of sorrow and sympathy, why does it not show the same today to Negroes being burnt and killed without mercy?[84]

Both 'becoming American' and 'becoming white' could imply coercive threats to European national identities. The 1906 remarks of Luigi Villari, an Italian government official investigating Sicilian sharecroppers in Louisiana, illustrate the gravity and interrelation of both processes. Villari found that 'a majority of plantation owners cannot comprehend that . . . Italians are white', and instead considered the Sicilian migrant 'a white-skinned negro who is a better worker than the black-skinned negro'. He patiently explained the 'commonly held distinction . . . between "negroes," "Italians" and "whites" (that is, Americans)'. In the South, he added, the 'American will not engage in agricultural, manual labour, rather he leaves it to the negroes. Seeing that the Italians will do this work, naturally he concludes that Italians lack dignity. The only way an Italian can emancipate himself from this inferior state is to abandon all sense of national pride and to identify completely with the Americans.'[85]

One hundred per cent whiteness and one hundred per cent Americanism carried overlapping and confusing imperatives for new immigrants in and out of the South, but in several ways the former was even more uncomfortable terrain than the latter. The pursuit of white identity, so tied to competition for wage labour and to political citizenship, greatly privileged male perceptions. But identity formation, as Americanisers and immigrant leaders realised, rested in great part on the activities of immigrant mothers, who entered discussions of nationality and Americanisation more easily than those of race.[86] More cast in determinism, the discourse of race produced fewer openings to inject class demands, freedom and cultural pluralism than did the discourse of Americanism. The modest strength of *Herrenvolk* democracy, weakened even in the South at a time when huge numbers of the white poor were disfranchised, paled in comparison to the opportunities to try to give progressive spin to the idea of a particularly freedom-loving 'American race'.

In a fascinating quantified sociological study of Poles in Buffalo in the mid-1920s, Niles Carpenter and Daniel Katz concluded that their interviewees had been 'Americanized' without being 'de-Polandized'. Their data led to the conclusion that Polish immigrants displayed 'an absence of strong feeling so far as the Negro is concerned', a pattern 'certainly in contrast to the results which would be sure to follow the putting of similar questions to a typically American group'. The authors therefore argued for 'the inference that so-called race feeling in this country is much more a product of tensions and quasi-psychoses born of our own national experience than of any factors inherent in the relations of race to race'. Their intriguing characterisation of Buffalo's Polish community did not attempt to cast its racial views as 'pro-Negro' but instead pointed out that 'the bulk of its members express indifference towards him'. Such indifference, noted also by other scholars, was the product not of unfamiliarity with, or distance from, the US racial system, but of nationalism compounded by intense harrowing and contradictory experiences inbetween whiteness and non-whiteness.[87] Only after the racial threat of new immigration was defused by the racial restriction of the Johnson–Reed Act would new immigrants haltingly find a place in the ethnic wing of the white race.

This brief treatment of a particularly complicated issue necessarily leaves out a number of key episodes, especially in the latter stages of the story. One is a resolution of sorts in the ambiguous status of inbetween immigrant workers which came in the late thirties and the Second World War era. In some settings these years brought not only a greater emphasis on cultural pluralism and a new, broader language of Americanism that embraced working-class ethnics, but also a momentary lull in racial conflict. With the creation of strong, interracial industrial unions, African-American local officials and shop stewards fought for civil rights at the same time they led white 'ethnic' workers in important industrial struggles.[88] Yet in other settings, sometimes even in the same cities, the war years and the period immediately following brought riots and hate strikes over the racial integration of workplaces and, particularly, neighbourhoods. Most second-generation ethnics embraced their Americanness, but, as Gary Gerstle suggests, this 'may well have intensified their prejudice against Blacks, for many conceived of Americanization in racial terms: becoming American meant becoming white'.[89]

During the 1970s a later generation of white ethnics rediscovered their ethnic identities in the midst of a severe backlash against civil rights legislation and new movements for African-American liberation.[90] The relationship between this defensive mentality and more recent attacks on affirmative action programmes and civil rights legislation underscores the contemporary importance in understanding how and why these once inbetween immigrant workers became white.

NOTES

* Such a sprawling essay would be impossible without help from students and colleagues, especially regarding sources. Thanks go to David Montgomery, Steven Rosswurm, Susan Porter Benson, Randy McBee, Neil Gotanda, Peter Rachleff, Noel Ignatiev, the late Peter Tamony, Louise Edwards, Susan Hirsch, Isaias McCaffery, Rudolph Vecoli, Hyman Berman, Sal Salerno, Louise O'Brien, Liz Pleck, Mark Leff, Toby Higbie, Micaela di Leonardo and the Social History Group at the University of Illinois.

1. The epigraph is from John A. Fitch, *The Steel Workers* (New York, 1910), 147. Interview with Joseph Loguidice, 25 July 1980, Italians in Chicago Project, copy of transcript, Box 6, Immigration History Research Center, University of Minnesota, St. Paul, MN.

2. See, for example, Gerald Rosenblum, *Immigrant Workers: Their Impact on American Labor Radicalism* (New York, 1973); C.T. Husbands, 'Editor's

Introductory Essay', to Werner Sombart, *Why Is There No Socialism in the United States?* (White Plains, NY, 1976), xxix.

3. Robert Orsi, 'The Religious Boundaries of an Inbetween People: Street *Feste* and the Problem of the Dark-Skinned "Other" in Italian Harlem, 1920–1990', *American Quarterly*, 44 (September 1992), 335; Michael Omi and Howard Winant, *Racial Formation in the United States: From the 1960s to the 1980s* (New York and London, 1986), 64–5; Gary Gerstle, 'Working Class Racism: Broaden the Focus', *International Labor and Working Class History*, 44 (1993), 38–9.

4. Sombart, *No Socialism*, 27–28; Stanford M. Lyman, 'Race Relations as Social Process: Sociology's Resistance to a Civil Rights Orientation', in Herbert Hill and James E. Jones, Jr, *Race In America: The Struggle for Equality* (Madison, 1993), 374–83; see also Omi and Winant, *Racial Formation*, 15–17, for useful complications on this score; Thomas F. Gossett, *Race: The History of an Idea in America* (Dallas, 1963); Barbara Solomon, *Ancestors and Immigrants* (Cambridge, MA, 1956); Gloria A. Marshall, 'Racial Classification: Popular and Scientific', in Sandra Harding, ed., *The 'Racial' Economy of Science* (Bloomington and Indianapolis, IN, 1993), 123–4. On Park, race and ethnicity, see also Omi and Winant, *Racial Formation*, 15–17; Stow Persons, *Ethnic Studies at Chicago, 1905–1945* (Urbana, IL, 1987), 602.

5. For historical invocations of 'ethnicity' to explain situations experienced at the time as racial, in otherwise brilliant works, see Mary C. Waters, *Ethnic Options: Choosing Identities in America* (Berkeley, 1990), 79, and Werner Sollors, *Beyond Ethnicity; Consent and Descent in American Culture* (New York, 1986), 38–9. See also Michael Banton, *Racial Theories* (Cambridge, 1988), and David Theo Goldberg, 'The Semantics of Race', *Ethnic and Racial Studies*, 15 (October 1992), esp. 554–5. The most devastating critique of the 'cult of ethnicity' remains Alexander Saxton's review essay on Nathan Glazer's *Affirmative Discrimination*, in *Amerasia Journal*, 4 (1977), 141–50. See also Gwendolyn Mink, *Old Labor and New Immigrants in American Political Development* (Ithaca, NY, 1986), esp. 46, n. 1.

6. We borrow 'inbetween' from Orsi, 'Religious Boundaries of an Inbetween People', *passim*, and also from John Higham, *Strangers in the Land: Patterns of American Nativism, 1860–1925* (New York, 1974), 169. Herbert Gutman with Ira Berlin, 'Class Composition and the Development of the American Working Class, 1840–1890', in Gutman, Ira Berlin, eds, *Power and Culture: Essays on the American Working Class* (New York, 1987), 380–94, initiates vital debate on immigration and 'remaking' of the US working class over time.

7. Lawrence Glickman, 'Inventing the "American Standard of Living": Gender, Race and Working-Class Identity, 1880–1925', *Labor History*, 34 (Spring-Summer, 1993), 221–35; David Montgomery, *Beyond Equality: Labor and the Radical Republicans, 1862–1872* (Urbana, 1981), 254; Richard Williams, *Hierarchical Structures and Social Value: The Creation of Black and Irish Identities in the United States* (New York, 1990); Thompson, *Customs in Common: Studies in Traditional Popular Culture* (New York, 1993), 320.

8. On *guinea*'s history, see Roediger, '*Guineas, Wiggers* and the Dramas of Racialized Culture', *American Literary History* (forthcoming). On post-1890 usages, see William Harlen Gilbert, Jr, 'Memorandum Concerning the

Characteristics of the Larger Mixed-Blood Islands of the United States',
Social Forces, 24 (March 1946), 442; *Oxford English Dictionary*, 2nd edn
(Oxford, 1989), 6: 937–8; Frederic G. Cassidy and Joan Houston Hall, eds,
Dictionary of American Regional English (Cambridge and London, 1991),
2, 838; Harold Wentworth and Stuart Berg Flexner, *Dictionary of American
Slang* (New York, 1975), 234; and Peter J. Tamony, research notes on *guinea*,
Tamony Collection, Western Historical Manuscripts Collection, University
of Missouri, Columbia.

9. Tamony's notes on *hunky* (or *hunkie*) speculate on links to *honkie* (or *honky*)
and refer to the former as an 'old labor term'. By no means did *Hun* refer
unambiguously to Germans before the First World War. See e.g. Henry
White, 'Immigration Restriction as a Necessity', *American Federationist*, 4
(June 1897), 67; Paul Krause, *The Battle for Homestead, 1880–1892: Poli-
tics, Culture and Steel* (Pittsburgh, 1992), 216–17; Stan Kemp, *Boss Tom:
The Annals of an Anthracite Mining Village* (Akron, 1904), 258; Thames
Williamson, *Hunky* (New York, 1929), slipcover; Bell's *Out of this Furnace*
(Pittsburgh, 1976; originally 1941), 124–5; David Brody, *Steelworkers in
America* (New York, 1969), 120–1; Josef Barton, *Peasants and Strangers*
(Cambridge, MA, 1975), 20; Theodore Radzialowski, 'The Competition for
Jobs and Racial Stereotypes: Poles and Blacks in Chicago', *Polish Amer-
ican Studies*, 22 (Autumn, 1976): n. 7; Sinclair, *Singing Jailbirds* (Pasadena,
1924). Remarks regarding *Mill Hunky* in the 1970s are based on Barrett's
anecdotal observations in and around Pittsburgh at the time. See also the
Mill Hunk Herald, published in Pittsburgh throughout the late 1970s.

10. Dollard, *Caste and Class in a Southern Town* (Garden City, NY, 1949), 93;
John Bukowczyk, as cited in Barry Goldberg, 'Historical Reflections on
Transnationalism, Race, and the American Immigrant Saga' (unpublished
paper delivered at the Rethinking Migration, Race, Ethnicity, and Nationalism in Historical Perspective Conferences, New York Academy of the Sciences, May, 1990).

11. Albert S. Broussard, 'George Albert Flippin and Race Relations in a Western Rural Community', *The Midwest Review*, 12 (1990), 15 n.42; J. Alexander Karlin, 'The Italo-American Incident of 1891 and the Road to Reunion',
Journal of Southern History, 8 (1942); Gunther Peck, 'Padrones and Protest:
"Old" Radicals and "New" Immigrants in Bingham, Utah, 1905–1912',
Western Historical Quarterly (May 1993), 177; Georgakas, *Greek America
at Work* (New York, 1992), 12 and 16–17; Huginnie, *Strikitos: Race, Class,
and Work in the Arizona Copper Industry, 1870–1920* (forthcoming); Ruth
Shonle Cavan and Katherine Howland Ranck, *The Family and the Depres-
sion: A Study of One Hundred Chicago Families* (Chicago, 1938), 38–39;
Isaiah McCaffery, 'An Esteemed Minority? Greek Americans and Interethnic
Relations in the Plains Region' (unpublished paper, University of Kansas,
1993); see also Donna Misner Collins, *Ethnic Identification: The Greek
Americans of Houston, Texas* (New York, 1991), 201–11. For the African-
American slang, Clarence Major, ed., *From Juba to Jive: A Dictionary of
African-American Slang* (New York, 1994), 213.

12. Donna Gabaccia, 'The "Yellow Peril" and the "Chinese of Europe": Italian
and Chinese Labourers in an International Labour Market' (unpublished
paper, University of North Carolina at Charlotte, c. 1993).

13. George E. Cunningham, 'The Italian: A Hindrance to White Solidarity in Louisiana, 1890–1898', *Journal of Negro History*, 50 (January 1965), 34, includes the quotes.

14. Higham, *Strangers in the Land*, 66; Gary R. Mormino and George E. Pozzetta, *The Immigrant World of Ybor City: Italians and Their Latin Neighbors in Tampa, 1885–1985* (Urbana, 1987), 241; DiLeonardo, *The Varieties of Ethnic Experience* (Ithaca, 1984), 24 n.16; Georgakas, *Greek Americans at Work*, 16. See also Karen Brodkin Sacks' superb, 'How Did Jews Become White Folks?' in Steven Gregory and Roger Sanjek, eds, *Race* (forthcoming from Rutgers University Press).

15. Quoted in Brody, *Steelworkers*, 120; W. Lloyd Warner and J.O. Low, *The Social System of the Modern Factory, the Strike* (New Haven, 1947), 140; Gershon Legman, *The Horn Book* (New York, 1964), 486–7; *Anecdota Americana: Five Hundred Stories for the Amusement of Five Hundred Nations that Comprise America* (New York, 1933), 98; Nathan Hurvitz, 'Blacks and Jews in American Folklore', *Western Folklore*, 33 (October, 1974), 304–7; Emory S. Borgardus, 'Comparing Racial Distance in Ethiopia, South Africa, and the United States', *Sociology and Social Research*, 52 (January 1968), 149–56; F. James Davis, *Who is Black? One Nation's Definition* (University Park, PA, 1991), 161.

16. Thomas G. Dyer, *Theodore Roosevelt and the Idea of Race* (Baton Rouge, 1980), 131, 143–44; Mirian King and Steven Ruggles, 'American Immigration, Fertility and Race Suicide at the Turn of the Century', *Journal of Interdisciplinary History*, 20 (Winter, 1990), 347–69. On 'stock', see M.G. Smith's 'Ethnicity and Ethnic Groups in America: The View from Harvard', *Ethnic and Racial Studies*, 5 (January 1982), 17–18.

17. On race and naturalisation law, see David Roediger, '"Any Alien Being a Free White Person": Naturalization, the State and Racial Formation in the U.S., 1790–1952', in Ramon D. Gutierrez, ed., *The State and the Construction of Citizenship in the Americas* (forthcoming); D.O. McGovney, 'Race Discrimination in Naturalization, Parts I–III', *Iowa Law Bulletin*, 8 (March 1923); and 'Race Discrimination in Naturalization, Part IV', *Iowa Law Bulletin*, 8 (May 1923), 211–44; Charles Gordon, 'The Race Barrier to American Citizenship', *University of Pennsylvania Law Review*, 93 (March 1945), 237–58; Stanford Lyman, 'The Race Question and Liberalism', *International Journal of Politics, Culture, and Society*, 5 (Winter 1991), 203–25. On the racial status of Finns, A. William Hoglund, *Finnish Immigrants in America, 1908–1920* (Madison, 1960), 112–14; Peter Kivisto, *Immigrant Socialists in the United States; The Case of Finns and the Left* (Rutherford, NJ, 1984), 127–8. The whiteness of Armenians was also sometimes at issue, even if they lived on 'the west side of the Bosphorus'. See *In Re Halladjian et al*, C.C.D. Mass., 174 Fed. 834 (1909), and *U.S. v. Cartozian*, 6 Fed. (2nd) (1925), 919.

18. *U.S. v. Bhagat Singh Thind*, 261 U.S. 204; Joan M. Jensen, *Passage from India: Asian Indian Immigrants in North America* (New Haven, 1988), 246–69. On the now white status of Asians, see *ibid.*, and *In Re Ah Yup*, 1 Fed. Cas. 223 (1878); *In Re Saito*, C.C.D. Mass., 62 Fed. 126 (1894); *Ozawa v. U.S.*, 260 U.S. 178 (1922); Williams, *Hierarchical Structures*; David Montejano, *Anglos and Mexicans in the Making of Texas, 1836–1986*

(Austin, 1987); Sharon M. Lee, 'Racial Classifications in the U.S. Census, 1890–1990', *Ethnic and Racial Studies*, 16 (January 1993), 79; Almaguer, *Racial Faultlines*, 55–7; George Sanchez, *Becoming Mexican American; Ethnicity, Culture and Identity in Chicano Los Angeles, 1900–1945* (Oxford, 1993), 29–30.

19. Oscar Handlin, *Race and Nationality in American Life* (Boston, 1957), 205; Cunningham. 'Hindrance to White Solidarity', 33–5, and esp. Jean Scarpaci, 'A Tale of Selective Accommodation: Sicilians and Native Whites in Louisiana', *Journal of Ethnic Studies*, 3 (1977), 44–5 notes the use of 'dago clause' to describe the provision. For the Irish, see Roediger, *The Wages of Whiteness: Race and the Making of the American Working Class* (New York and London, 1991), 140–3, and Steven P. Erie, *Rainbow's End: Irish-Americans and the Dilemmas of Urban Machine Politics, 1840–1985* (Berkeley, 1988), 25–66 and 96, Table 10.

20. Reginald Horsman, *Race and Manifest Destiny: The Origins of American Racial Anglo-Saxonism* (Cambridge, MA, 1981), 250–3; Dyer, *Idea of Race*, 131; Mink, *Old Labor and New Immigrants*, 224–7.

21. Dyer, *Idea of Race*, 29–30 and 10–44, *passim*. Stephen Thernstrom, Ann Orlov and Oscar Handlin, eds, *Harvard Encyclopedia of Ethnic Groups* (Cambridge, MA, 1980), 379; quotations, Dyer, *Idea of Race*, 55, 66, 132.

22. Dyer, *Idea of Race*, 132; and for Roosevelt's revealing exchanges with Madison Grant, 17.

23. Higham, *Strangers in the Land*, 238–62.

24. Quoted in Mink, *Old Labor and New Immigrants*, 71–112, 109–10; Grant quote, Higham, *Strangers in the Land*, 156–7. In his *The Old World in the New* (New York, 1914), the reformer and sociologist E.A. Ross maintained that 'ethical endowment' was innate, and that southern Europeans lacked it.

25. Jane Addams, *Twenty Years at Hull House* (New York, 1910); Mink, *Old Labor and New Immigrants*, 223 and 226 for the quotes.

26. James Weinstein, *The Corporate Ideal in the Liberal State, 1900–1918* (Boston, 1968).

27. Stephen Meyer III, *The Five-Dollar Day: Labor Management and Social Control in the Ford Motor Company, 1908–1921* (Albany, 1981), 176–85; Higham, *Strangers in the Land*, 138, 261–2, and 316–17.

28. See also Dyer, *Idea of Race*, 42–4, 63, 130–1; Higham, *Strangers in the Land*, 317; John F. McClymer, 'The Americanization Movement and the Education of the Foreign-Born Adult, 1914–1925', in Bernard J. Weiss, ed., *American Education and the European Immigrant, 1840–1940* (Urbana, 1982), 96–116; Herbert Gutman, *Work, Culture and Society in Industrializing America: Essays in Working-class and Social History* (New York, 1976), 7–8 and 22–5. On the curricula in factory-based Americanization programmes, see Gerd Korman, 'Americanization at the Factory Gate', *Labor and Industrial Relations Review*, 18 (1965), 396–419.

29. Higham, *Strangers in the Land*, 263.

30. Quotes from *ibid.*, 273 and 321. See also 300–30, *passim*. On the triumph of terror and exclusion and the consequent turn by leading liberal intellectuals to a defeatism regarding 'race and ethnicity', see Gary Gerstle, 'The Protean Character of American Liberalism', *American Historical Review*, 99 (October 1994), 1055–67.

31.   Richard Slotkin, *Gunfighter Nation: The Myth of the Frontier in Twentieth-century America* (New York, 1992); Michael Rogin, ' "The Sword Became a Flashing Vision": D.W. Griffith's *The Birth of A Nation*', in *Ronald Reagan: The Movie and Other Essays in Political Demonology* (Berkeley, 1987), 190–235. 'Incontestably mulatto' comes from Albert Murray, *The Omni-Americans* (New York, 1983), 22; Zena Pearlstone, ed., *Seeds of Prejudice: Racial and Ethnic Stereotypes in American Popular Lithography, 1830–1918* (forthcoming). See esp. Michael Rogin, 'Blackface, White Noise: The Jewish Jazz Singer Finds His Voice', *Critical Inquiry*, 18 (Spring 1992), 417–53; Rogin, 'Making America Home: Racial Masquerade and Ethnic Assimilation in the Transition to Talking Pictures', *Journal of American History*, 79 (December 1992), 1050–77.

32.   Gads Hill Center, 'May Report' (1915) and 'Minstrel Concert' flyer. Thanks to Steven Rosswurm for identifying this source. See also Elisabeth Lasch-Quinn, *Black Neighbors: Race and the Limits of Reform in the American Settlement House Movement, 1890–1945* (Chapel Hill, 1993), esp. 14–30, quote 22; Lyman, 'Assimilation–Pluralism Debate', 191; Krause, *Battle for Homestead*, 218.

33.   Kathleen Neils Conzen, David A. Gerber, Ewa Morawska, George E. Pozzetta and Rudolph J. Vecoli, 'The Invention of Ethnicity: A Perspective from the U.S.A.', *Journal of American Ethnic History*, 12 (Fall 1992), 27.

34.   Stanley Lieberson, *A Piece of the Pie; Black and White Immigrants since 1880* (Berkeley, 1980), 301–59; Bodnar, Simon and Weber, *Lives of Their Own*, 141–49; Suzanne Model, 'The Effects of Ethnicity in the Workplace on Blacks, Italians, and Jews in 1910 New York', *Journal of Urban History*, 16 (November 1989), 33–39.

35.   See note 34. See also Sterling D. Spero and Abram L. Harris, *The Black Worker* (New York, 1969; orig. 1931), 149–81 and 221; and David Ward, *Poverty, Ethnicity and the American City, 1840–1925* (Cambridge, 1989), 211.

36.   Harold M. Baron, *The Demand for Black Labor* (Cambridge, MA, n.d.), 21–3; Spero and Harris, *Black Worker*, 174–7; Edward Greer, 'Racism and U.S. Steel', *Radical America*, 10 (September–October 1976), 45–68; Paul F. McGouldrick and Michael Tannen, 'Did American Manufacturers Discriminate against Immigrants before 1914?', *Journal of Economic History*, 37 (September 1977), 723–46; Allan Kent Powell, *The Next Time We Strike: Labor in Utah's Coal Fields, 1900–1933* (Logan, 1985), 92; John R. Commons, 'Introduction to Volumes III and IV', in Commons *et al.*, *History of Labor in the United States*, 4 vols (New York, 1966; orig. 1935), 3: xxv. Bodnar, Simon and Weber, *Lives of Their Own*, 5; quote, Montgomery, *Fall*, 243. See also Gordon, Edwards and Reich, *Segmented Work, Divided Workers: The Historical Transformation of Labor in the United States* (Cambridge, 1982), 141–3.

37.   Ross, as quoted in Lieberson, *A Piece of the Pie*, 25; Brody, *Steelworkers in America*, 120; Peter Speek, 'Report on Psychological Aspect of the Problem of Floating Laborers', United States Commission on Industrial Relations Papers (25 June 1915), 31. Thanks to Tobias Higbie for the citation. Huginnie, *Strikitos* (forthcoming); Georgakas, *Greek Americans at Work*, 17; John Bukowczyk, 'The Transformation of Working-Class Ethnicity: Corporate Control, Americanization, and the Polish Immigrant Middle Class

in Bayonne, New Jersey, 1915–1925', in Robert Asher and Charles Stephenson, eds, *Labor Divided: Race and Ethnicity in United States Labor Struggles, 1835–1960* (Albany, NY, 1990), 291; Higham, *Strangers in the Land*, 173. See also, Saxton, *Indispensable Enemy*, 281; Richard W. Steele, 'No Racials: Discrimination Against Ethnics in American Defense Industry, 1940–42', *Labor History*, 32 (Winter 1991), 66–90.

38. Jean Scarpaci, 'Immigrants in the New South: Italians in Louisiana's Sugar Parishes, 1880–1910', *Labor History*, 16 (Spring 1975); Lieberson, *Piece of the Pie*, 346–50. The judgement changed briefly in African-Americans' favour in the early 1920s. See Peter Gottlieb, *Making Their Own Way: Southern Blacks' Migration to Pittsburgh, 1916–30* (Urbana, 1987), 126 and 162; Baron, *Demand for Black Labor*, 22; quotes from Lieberson, *Piece of the Pie*, 348; Radzialowski, 'The Competition for Jobs', 16.

39. Lieberson, *Piece of the Pie*, 299–327; John Bodnar, Roger Simon and Michael Weber, 'Blacks and Poles in Pittsburgh, 1900–1930', *Journal of American History*, 66:3 (1979), 554.

40. Bodnar, Simon and Weber, *Lives of Their Own*, 141, Table 16.

41. Steve Nelson, James R. Barrett and Rob Ruck, *Steve Nelson, American Radical* (Pittsburgh, 1981), 16.

42. Model, 'Effects of Ethnicity', 41–2. See also Bodnar, Simon and Weber, *Lives of Their Own*, 141.

43. Bell, *Out of This Furnace*, 124; Attaway, *Blood on the Forge* (New York, 1941; reprint 1987), 122–3.

44. Roger Horowitz, ' "Without a Union, We're All Lost": Ethnicity, Race and Unionism Among Kansas City Packinghouse Workers, 1930–1941' (unpublished paper given at the 'Reworking American Labour History' conference, State Historical Society of Wisconsin, April 1992), 4. On marriage between Catholics but across 'ethnic' lines, see Paul Spickard, *Mixed Blood*, 8, 450. f.n. 70.

45. Mark Wyman, *Round Trip to America: The Immigrants Return to Europe, 1880–1930* (Ithaca, 1993), 10–12; see also Michael J. Piore, *Birds of Passage: Migrant Labor and Industrial Societies* (Ann Arbor, 1978), *passim*.

46. See Arnold Shankman, 'This Menacing Influx: Afro-Americans on Italian Immigration to the South', *Mississippi Quarterly*, 31 (Winter 1977–78), 82, 79–87; Scarpaci, 'Immigrants in the New South', 175; Robert Asher, 'Union Nativism and Immigrant Response', *Labor History*, 23 (Summer 1982), 328; Gabaccia, 'Chinese of Europe', 16–18; Scarpaci, 'Sicilians and Native Whites', 14.

47. See note 46, and, for the quotation, Harold David Brackman, 'The Ebb and Flow of Race Relations: A History of Black–Jewish Relations Through 1900' (PhD dissertation, University of California, Los Angeles, 1977), 450. See also Loewen, *Mississippi Chinese*, 58–72; Youn-Jin Kim, 'From Immigrants to Ethnics: The Life Worlds of Korean Immigrants in Chicago' (PhD dissertation, University of Illinois at Urbana-Champaign, 1991).

48. Adam Walaszek, ' "For in America Poles Work Like Cattle": Polish Peasant Immigrants and Work in America, 1880–1921', in Marianne Debouzy, ed., *In the Shadow of the Statue of Liberty: Immigrants, Workers and Citizens in the American Republic, 1880–1920* (Urbana, 1992), 86–8 and 90–1; Bodnar, Simon and Weber, *Lives of Their Own*, 5 and 60.

49. See note 48. Roediger, *Towards the Abolition of Whiteness: Essays on Race, Politics, and Working-class History* (London and New York, 1994), 163; Tamony Papers, on *hunkie*, excerpting *American Tramp and Underworld Slang*; Scarpaci, 'Immigrants in the New South', 174; Andrew Neather, 'Popular Republicanism, Americanism and the Roots of Anti-Communism, 1890–1925' (PhD dissertation, Duke University, 1993), 242; Model, 'Effects of Ethnicity', 33; Bodnar, Simon and Weber, *Lives of Their Own*, 60.

50. Neather, 'Roots of Anti-Communism', 138–223; James Barrett, 'Americanization from the Bottom Up: Immigration and the Remaking of the Working Class in the United States, 1880–1930', *Journal of American History*, 79 (December 1992), 1009.

51. Peggy Pascoe, 'Race, Gender, and Intercultural Relations: The Case of Interracial Marriage', *Frontiers: A Journal of Women's Studies*, 12 (1991), 5–17, quotes; Spickard, *Mixed Blood*, Appendix A, 374–5. In spite of all this, 'race mixing' occurred, of course. Chinese men who lived under particularly oppressive conditions because of restrictions on the immigration of Chinese women, tended to develop relationships with either African-Americans or Poles and other 'in-between' immigrant women. See Paul Siu, *The Chinese Laundryman: A Study of Social Isolation* (New York, 1987), 143, 250–71.

52. Barrett, 'From the Bottom Up', 1002. The classic recognition of this reality is found in DuBois, *The Philadelphia Negro*, 332–3. Higham, *Strangers in the Land*, 305 and 321–2.

53. Neather, 'Roots of Anti-Communism', 235–40; Mink, *Old Labor and New Immigrants*, 71–112; Messer-Kruse, 'Chinese Exclusion and the Eight-Hour Day: Ira Steward's Political Economy of Cheap Labor' (unpublished paper, Univ. of Wisconsin, Madison, 1994), 13 and *passim*. The classic expression of both the biological and cultural racism and much else, is Samuel Gompers and Herman Guttstadt, 'Meat vs. Rice: American Manhood Against Asiatic Coolieism: Which Shall Survive?' (San Francisco, 1902). On the distinction between opposition to coolies and to the Chinese 'race', see Andrew Gyory, 'Rolling in the Dirt: The Origins of the Chinese Exclusion Act and the Politics of Racism, 1870–1882' (PhD dissertation, University of Massachusetts at Amherst, 1991), esp. Ch. 4–6.

54. Gyory, 'Rolling in the Dirt', Ch. 4–6, and Glickman, 'American Standard', 221–35.

55. Krause, *Homestead*, 216.

56. Collomp, 'Unions, Civics, and National Identity: Organized Labor's Reaction to Immigration, 1881–1897', in Debouzy, ed., *Shadow of the Statue of Liberty*, 240, 242 and 246.

57. Neather, 'Roots of Anti-Communism', 242; White, 'Immigration Restriction as a Necessity', 67–69; A.A. Graham, 'The Un-Americanization of America', *American Federationist*, 17 (April 1910), 302, 303, 304.

58. Asher, 'Union Nativism', 328–72; Neather, 'Roots of Anti-Communism', 242, 267; Gompers as in Arthur Mann, 'Gompers and the Irony of Racism', *Antioch Review*, 13 (1953), 212; in Mink, *Old Labor and New Immigrants*, 97; and in David Brody, *In Labor's Cause: Main Themes on the History of the American Worker* (Oxford, 1993), 117. See also Prescott F. Hall, 'Immigration and the Education Test', *North American Review*, 165 (1897), 395; Lydia

Kingsmill Commander, 'Evil Effects of Immigration', *American Federationist*, 12 (October 1905).

59. McGovern, quoted in David Montgomery, *The Fall of the House of Labor: The Workplace, the State and American Labor Activism, 1865–1925* (Cambridge, 1987), 25; Asher, 'Union Nativism', 339 and 338–42. 'Internal protectionism' is Mink's term, from *Old Labor and New Immigrants*, 203; Lieberson, *Piece of the Pie*, 341–4. See also the explicit Anglo-Saxonism of *Railroad Trainmen's Journal*, discussed in Neather, 'Roots of Anti-Communism', 267–8.

60. Lieberson, *Piece of the Pie*, 342–3; Gabaccia, 'Chinese of Europe', 17–19; Mink, *Old Labor and New Immigrants*, 108. See also Lane, *Solidarity or Survival*. Graham, 'The Un-Americanizing of America', 302–4, runs in the same 1910 issue of the *American Federationist* as 'Where Yanks Meet Orientals' and 'The International Fraternity of Labor'. J.A. Edgerton's 'Brotherhood of Man', *American Federationist*, 12 (April 1905), 213, runs an issue before Augusta H. Pio's 'Exclude Japanese Labor'. On 'race suicide' see Lizzie M. Holmes' review of *The American Idea* in *American Federationist*, 14 (December 1907), 998.

61. Asher, 'Union Nativism', *passim*; Mink, *Old Labor and New Immigrants*, 198–203.

62. Asher, 'Union Nativism', 345, for the quote. See also *ibid.*, and Philip S. Foner, *History of the Labor Movement in the United States*, vol. 3 (New York, 1964), 256–81.

63. Barrett, 'From the Bottom Up', 1010 and *passim*; see also Brody, *In Labor's Cause*, 128.

64. Asher, 'Union Nativism', 330; Covington Hall, 'Labor Struggles in the Deep South' (unpublished ms., Labadie Collection, University of Michigan, 1951), 122, 138, 147–8, 183; *Voice of the People*, 5 March 1914; Roediger, *Abolition of Whiteness*, 149, 150, 175 n.75. See also Peck, 'Padrones and Protest', 172.

65. Speek, 'Floating Laborers', 31, 34, 36; plasterer quoted in Asher, 'Union Nativism', 330.

66. *New Majority*, 22 November 1919, 11. See John Howard Keiser, 'John Fitzpatrick and Progresssive Unionism, 1915–1925' (PhD dissertation, Northwestern University, 1965), 38–41; William D. Haywood, *Big Bill Haywood's Book* (New York, 1929), 241–2; James R. Barrett, *Work and Community in the Jungle: Chicago's Packinghouse Workers, 1894–1922* (Urbana, 1987), 138–42.

67. Du Bois, as quoted in Thomas Holt, 'The Political Uses of Alienation: W.E.B. Du Bois on Politics, Race and Culture', *American Quarterly*, 42 (June 1990), 313; Peck, 'Padrones and Protest', 173.

68. Dominic A. Pacyga, *Polish Immigrants and Industrial Chicago: Workers on the South Side, 1880–1930* (Columbus, 1991), 172; Barrett, *Work and Community in the Jungle*, 172–4. If newly-organised Poles read John Roach's 'Packingtown Conditions', *American Federationist*, 13 (August 1906), 534, they would have seen strike-breaking described as an activity in which 'the illiterate southern negro has held high carnival' and have wrongly learned that the stockyards strike was broken simply by black strike-breakers, 'ignorant and vicious, whose predominating trait was animalism'.

69. Gompers, 'Talks on Labor', *American Federationist*, 12 (September 1905), 636–7.

70. Quoted in Allen with Allen, *Reluctant Reformers*, 213; Mark Pittenger, *American Socialists and Evolutionary Thought, 1870–1920* (Madison, 1993); Higham, *Strangers in the Land*, 172; London's animus was characteristically directed against both 'racial' and 'semi-racial' groups, against 'Dagoes and Japs'. See his *The Valley of the Moon* (New York, 1913), 21–2.

71. Roediger, *Abolition of Whiteness*, 158–69; Powell, *Next Time We Strike*, 236 n.11; Barry Goldberg, '"Wage Slaves" and "White Niggers"', *New Politics* (Summer 1991), 64–83.

72. Warren C. Whatley, 'African-American Strikebreaking from the Civil War to the New Deal', *Social Science History*, 17:4 (1993), 525–58; Allen with Allen, *Reluctant Reformers*, 183; Roach, 'Packingtown Conditions', 534; Radzialowski, 'Competition for Jobs', 8 n.7, *passim*; Leslie Fishel, 'The North and the Negro, 1865–1900: A Study in Race Discrimination' (PhD dissertation, Harvard University, 1953), 454–71; Ray Ginger, 'Were Negroes Strikebreakers?', *Negro History Bulletin* (January 1952), 73–4; on the *niggerscab* image, see Roediger, *Abolition of Whiteness*, 150–3.

73. Higham, *Strangers in the Land*, 321–2; Mink, *Old Labor and New Immigrants*, 234; James R. Barrett, 'Defeat and Decline: Long Term Factors and Historical Conjunctures in the Decline of a Local Labor Movement, Chicago, 1900–1922', unpublished manuscript in Barrett's possession; Quinn, 'Americanism and Immigration', *American Federationist*, 31 (April 1924), 295; Gompers linked support for the 1924 restrictions to 'maintenance of racial purity and strength'. See Brody, *In Labor's Cause*, 117.

74. Scarpaci, 'Immigrants in the New South', 177; Radzialowski, 'Competition for Jobs', 17.

75. The first quote is from David Montgomery to Jim Barrett, 30 May 1995. On old-world prejudices, see Orsi, 'Inbetween People', 315; Mormino, *Immigrants on the Hill: Italian-Americans in St. Louis* (Urbana, 1986). For popular anti-Semitism in Poland in the era of massive Polish and East European Jewish immigration to the US, see Celia S. Heller, *On the Edge of Destruction: Jews of Poland between the Two World Wars* (New York, 1977), 38–76.

76. Ronald L. Lewis, *Black Coal Miners in America: Race, Class, and Community Conflict, 1780–1900* (Lexington, KY, 1987), 110; Allen with Allen, *Reluctant Reformers*, 180. For a recent expression of the common oppression argument, see Paul Berman, 'The Other and the Almost the Same', introducing Berman, ed., *Blacks and Jews* (New York, 1994), 11–30.

77. Peck, 'Padrones and Protest', 172–3; 'The Greatness of the Greek Spirit' (Chicago) *Saloniki* 15 February 1919; Georgakas, *Greek America*, 17; Kivisto, *Immigrant Socialists*, 127–8; Thomas Lee Philpott, *The Slum and the Ghetto: Middle-Class Reform, Chicago, 1880–1930* (New York, 1978), 193–4.

78. Brackman, 'Ebb and Flow of Conflict', 461–4; Marilyn Halter, *Between Race and Ethnicity: Cape Verdean American Immigrants, 1860–1965* (Urbana, 1993), 146–49; Mormino and Pozzetta, *Ybor City*, 241.

79. Radzialowski, 'Competition for Jobs', 14 n.20.

80. Rogin, 'Making America Home', 1053; Robert W. Snyder, *The Voice of the City: Vaudeville and Popular Culture in New York* (Oxford, 1989), 120;

Lewis Erenberg, *Steppin' Out: New York Nightlife and the Transformation of American Culture, 1890–1930* (Chicago, 1981), 195; Rogin, 'Blackface, White Noise', 420, 437–48; Brackman, 'Ebb and Flow of Conflict', 486.

81. Collins, *Ethnic Identification*, 210–11; Georgakas, *Greek Americans*, 9–12; Hodding Carter, *Southern Legacy*, 106; John B. Kennedy, 'The Knights of Columbus History Movement', *Current History*, 15 (December 1921), 441–43; Herbert Aptheker, introduction to W.E.B. Du Bois, *The Gift of Black Folk* (Millwood, NY, 1975; originally 1924), 7–8; Rudolph J. Vecoli, ' "Free Country": The American Republic Viewed by the Italian Left, 1880–1920', in Debouzy, ed., *Shadow of the Statue of Liberty*, 38, 33 and 34, for the quotes from the Italian-American press; and (Chicago) *Daily Jewish Courier* (August 1912).

82. See Noel Ignatiev, *How the Irish Became White* (London, 1996).

83. Barrett, *Work and Community*, 219–23; see also William M. Tuttle, Jr, *Race Riot: Chicago in the Red Summer of 1919* (New York, 1970); Roberta Senechal, *The Sociogenesis of a Race Riot* (Urbana, 1990).

84. Radzialowski, 'Competition for Jobs', 16; *Glos Polek* 31 July 1919; see also *Daily Jewish Courier* 22 April 1914; and *Narod Polski* 6 August 1919.

85. Luigi Villari, 'Relazione dell dott. Luigi Villari sugli Italiani nel Distretto Consolare di New Orleans', *Bolletino Dell' Emigrazione* (Italian Ministry of Foreign Affairs, Royal Commission on Emigration, 1907), 2439, 2499, and 2532. Thanks to Louise Edwards for the source and the translations.

86. Barrett, 'From the Bottom Up', esp. 1012–13; John McClymer, 'Gender and the "American Way of Life": Women in the Americanization Movement', *Journal of American Ethnic History*, 11 (Spring 1991), 5–6.

87. Niles Carpenter with Daniel Katz, 'The Cultural Adjustment of the Polish Group in the City of Buffalo: An Experiment in the Technique of Social Investigation', *Social Forces*, 6 (September 1927), 80–82. For further evidence of such 'indifference', see Scarpaci, 'Immigrants in the New South', 175, and Edward R. Kantowicz, *Polish American Politics in Chicago, 1888–1940* (Chicago, 1975), 149.

88. Gary Gerstle, *Working Class Americanism: The Politics of Labor in a Textile City, 1914–1960* (Cambridge, MA, 1989); Roger Horowitz, *'Negro and White, Unite and Fight!': A Social History of Industrial Unionism in Meatpacking* (forthcoming, University of Illinois Press, 1997); Rick Halpern, *Down on the Killing Floor: Black and White Workers in Chicago's Packinghouses, 1904–1954* (forthcoming, University of Illinois Press, 1997); Michael Goldfield, 'Race and the CIO: The Possibilities for Racial Egalitarianism in the 1930s and 1940s', *International Labor and Working Class History*, 44 (1993), 1–32.

89. Dominic Capeci, *Race Relations in Wartime Detroit* (Philadelphia, 1984); Gerstle, *Working-Class Americanism*, 290; Hirsch, *Second Ghetto*; see also Thomas Sugrue, 'The Structures of Poverty: The Reorganization of Space and Work in Three Periods of American History', in Michael B. Katz, ed., *The Underclass Debate: The View From History* (Princeton, 1993), 85–117; Russell A. Kazal, 'Revisiting Assimilation: The Rise, Fall, and Reappraisal of a Concept in American Ethnic History', *American Historical Review*, 100:2 (1995), 468–70. The little information we have on hate strikes suggests that they more likely involved recent southern white migrants than 'ethnics'.

See Nelson Lichtenstein, *Labor's War at Home: The CIO in World War II* (Cambridge, 1982), 125–6; Joshua Freeman, 'Delivering the Goods: Industrial Unionism in World War II', in Daniel J. Leab, ed., *The Labor History Reader* (Urbana, 1985), 398–400.

90.   David R. Colburn and George E. Pozzetta, 'Race, Ethnicity, and the Evolution of Political Legitimacy', in David Farber, *The Sixties: From Memory to History* (Chapel Hill, 1994), 130–8.

10 'Amiable Peasantry' or 'Social Burden': Constructing a Place for Black Southerners[*]

James R. Grossman

Booker T. Washington knew his white neighbours well. Southern employers and landlords might incessantly complain about their black labour force; various white southerners might repeatedly warn of the inability of African-Americans to reach the Anglo-Saxon level of civilisation; legislators might translate an ideology of racial hierarchy into spatial distance by mandating segregation. 'But when there is work to be done about the plantation, when it comes time to plant and pick the cotton the white man does not want the Negro so far away that he cannot reach him by the sound of his voice.'[1] During the half-century between emancipation and the publication of this insight in 1914, black southerners on the move tended to remain – at least metaphorically – within hailing distance. Two years later, however, a vast social movement known as the Great Migration signalled the beginning of very different, and less accommodating, patterns of African-American migration. White southerners responded in ways that reveal not only the extent of their dependence on black labour, but also the ideological, political and economic underpinnings of social relations and order in much of the South.

The roots of this inquiry lie in my attempt to understand the ambiguous and ambivalent response of white southerners to the Great Migration. At first there was little reaction, even as it began to appear that black southerners were leaving for the North in considerable numbers. Some whites blithely observed that only the riffraff were leaving. Others assumed that jobs in the North would become scarce, as northern employers grew dissatisfied with lazy black workers. The 'Negro's love of travel' abounds in the sources. The general tone tended to be either dismissive, or confident that the northern chill (meteorological and metaphorical) would send the migrants scampering home in no time.[2]

But they did not return. And as the magnitude of the exodus became clear, reassurances predicting the imminent return of 'our negroes' increasingly yielded to dire warnings about the threat to the labour supply. What soon emerged was a three-cornered debate whose positions can be summarised crudely: let the migrants go; stop them from leaving, using all repressive tools at hand; or institute reforms likely to convince blacks to stay.[3]

The content of this debate opens a window onto the very essence of social order in the South. Not all white southerners thought alike; but it is clear that among white southerners who exercised influence there existed a set of assumptions about community and order that defined a place for African-Americans in the New South. To understand that place is to understand the continuing salience of racial ideology as an integral element of social structure and relations of production rather than merely an artefact of class formation, a set of ideas, a psychological problem or a cultural flaw. In his recent presidential address to the American Historical Association, Thomas Holt argues that 'to re-think how race is made and thus might be un-made', we need to explore 'how racism is reproduced in American society'. This essay emerges from similar concerns, but is less ambitious, focusing only on the South in the late nineteenth and early twentieth centuries. It examines not how race was 'made' or 'unmade', but rather on how its reproduction might be understood through an exploration of its role as a force for order and stasis.[4]

Fixing our gaze on white southerners and listening to their responses to the threat of black 'emigration' impels us to interrogate a phrase that jumped out from the sources: white southerners did not want to lose their grip on what one Georgia cotton merchant referred to as 'a very amiable peasantry'.[5] His colloquial use of the term peasantry arouses as little curiosity now as it did then. But what does 'amiable' mean? That black southerners were willing to work under the particular conditions defined by their 'place' in the South? Or that they could be compelled to? Or a little bit of both? Recent historiography on tenant farmers, domestic servants and other African-American workers in the South teaches us that these people resisted conditions of labour and protocols of race. So why did white people think them 'amiable'? Why did this observer and so many others assume that only blacks could occupy this position in the southern economy?

The answers to these questions provide a framework for a much broader understanding of the fabric of southern society. In 1901 a delegate to Virginia's Constitutional Convention declared that to give 'the negro' the right to vote would mean 'unfitting him in every way for his station in life to which alone he can hope to aspire'. If the grammar is precise then it was the only station to which 'the negro' could aspire; if not, the speaker was declaring that only 'the negro' could aspire to that station.[6] The ambiguity points to a circular logic, but that circularity perhaps permits an almost seamless integration of race and class: tenants (and other African-American workers as well) were designated as particularly amiable because they were black; being black made them amiable because of both allegedly inherent racial characteristics and their peculiar relation to the legal system; the labour market itself was structured partly by the fact that racial discrimination limited their alternatives elsewhere; and their amiability was essential because of the particular nature of the southern economy. There were plenty of white workers and tenants; and a small black middle class occupied a central role in black communities. But the place of these two groups in the system could be accommodated without unravelling the essence of what made the South different from the North – a difference that historians have often understated in their dismissal of the North as equally racist and the South as equally capitalist. Anyone who has examined the Great Migration from the perspective of the migrants cannot privilege structure in this cavalier fashion; the difference mattered. The South depended not only on the presence of people a landlord or employer would call 'my niggers'. It depended on the idea of 'nigger' being more than a racial epithet – more like a description of a person's natural location as a man or woman in a social and economic order which had particular places for its 'niggers'. The South needed people who could fill those places; and only African-Americans could fill those places.

Attempts to understand post-Reconstruction southern society tend to cluster around two closely related historiographical controversies. One is a general attempt to disentangle the relationship between race and class in understanding social relations in a region where politics and culture have clearly divided along each of these fault lines. The other is more specific and is familiar through a classic text: C. Vann Woodward's *Origins of the New South*. Rejecting an insular regional history characterised by continuity, Woodward turned away from the Lost Cause of ante-bellum life and offered an essentially Beardian interpretation of the Civil War. The Old South, he declared, had not survived to reclaim its birthright. The planter class, ravaged by Civil War and emancipation, had been forced to adapt to a plantation system underpinned by capitalist principles of free labour. The New South, dominated by a new elite, located political and economic power in cities and industry. By the end of the nineteenth century, a regional bourgeoisie, newly risen and subservient to northern capital, dominated the South's political economy. Discontinuity was the central theme, with a capitalist class replacing what Eugene Genovese later described as a 'prebourgeois' slaveholding elite.[7]

Woodward's identification of a new ruling class and a new ideological foundation for class rule set the agenda for most of what has followed

– a plethora of explorations of the implications of a transforming process
(hence the discontinuity) defined by a transition from an agrarian society
based on non-wage labour to a wage economy dominated by merchants
and other capitalists. In this scheme race was 'a smokescreen', obscuring
the more fundamental class issues. Lynchings, discrimination and racist
rhetoric were instruments mobilised at various levels of society, but served
the hegemony of the new ruling class.[8]

Following in Woodward's substantial wake, one historiographical stream
encompasses a series of powerfully argued analyses of the relationship
between modes of production and ideologies of race. These scholars have
argued that the very category of race, as well as racism and its manifestations, is best understood as an evolutionary construct rooted in the
history of class relations. To understand the origins of slavery one should
look first not to English attitudes regarding race, nationality or physical
attributes, but rather to the implications of labour shortages and traditional
English assumptions about the likelihood of inducing the lower orders to
work without compulsion. 'Race' was invented as slaveholders gradually
sorted out the relationship between property, equality, liberty and production. It emerged as a vocabulary only when a generation of bourgeois revolu-
tionaries needed to resolve the contradictions between class exploitation
and radically new notions of universal liberty. As Barbara Fields succinctly
puts it, 'race explained why some people could rightly be denied what others
took for granted; namely liberty, supposedly a self-evident gift of nature's
God'.[9]

Subsequently, emancipation and Reconstruction were shaped less by the
dynamics of race relations than by the class experiences and imperatives
of various actors, North and South. Acknowledging their debt to W.E.B.
Du Bois's magisterial *Black Reconstruction*, Armstead Robinson and
others placed 'class development at the center of the study of Reconstruction'.[10] The drive for new methods of control initiated in the South towards
the end of the nineteenth century, including segregation and disfranchisement, was rooted in the changing imperatives of class hegemony in the
face of economic change and resistance on the part of black and white
farmers. Race and racism thus emerge as ideological constructs capable of
legitimising and buttressing the power of ruling elites, in part by obscuring
the objective reality of class relations. White farmers and workers shared
their oppression with blacks; their fear of sharing the degradation of
African-Americans provided fertile soil for what would become stereo-
typed condescendingly as redneck racism.[11] With a comparable orientation
toward the salience of capitalist development, labour historians interested
in black workers have begun looking at the early twentieth-century South

in terms of the process of proletarianisation, rather than focusing exclusively on racial discrimination in workplace and union hall.[12]

Class analysis, however, can be equally compatible with an emphasis on continuity. The 'New South' of the late nineteenth century, according to some historians, was itself more an ideological construct than a reality. This was simply one of a succession of New Souths proclaimed in the interest of an attempt to liberate the region (or at least the region's image) from its past, without changing fundamental relations of power. According to this argument, the planter class 'persisted'. This might mean that individuals maintained their land and their influence; it might refer to families. More convincingly it refers to a political culture and a social structure based on the plantation, which was the essence of continuity. The South's plantation society, this argument contends, looked more like its ante-bellum predecessor than any northern contemporary.[13]

The core of this pattern, argues Jon Wiener, lies in systems of labour relations, constituted in the South by what he calls 'labor repressive capitalism'. A distinctive political economy arose, based on a system of bound labour controlled by a remarkable corpus of legislation encompassing vagrancy laws, contract enforcement statutes, convict labour, enticement laws and emigrant laws. The levels of coercion and control, and the means of control, differed fundamentally from what northern capitalists had at their disposal. Alex Lichtenstein's study of convict labour takes this one step further to argue that because this particular mode of repressive labour relations was eagerly employed by 'some of the most prominent industrialists and financiers . . . the quintessential New South entrepreneurs', the continuity and regional distinctiveness posited by Wiener implies neither the hegemony of antibourgeois types nor hostility to industrial development. Premodern forms of class relations, based on dependence, isolated labour markets, and notorious levels of coercion existed within a modernising capitalist society.[14]

How could this mixture of continuity and discontinuity coexist? Wiener says that 'part of the answer . . . lies in the social origins of the postwar planter class – rooted in the slaveholding elite families, with a tradition and a way of life that committed them to a repressive racial order in agricultural labor'.[15] But his analysis says little about what white southerners actually thought about race, about how the content of their ideas about race affected how this system worked and flourished. Fields offers an explanation consistent with the vast literature emphasising the role of race as a legitimating ideology and mobilising force in the service of southern capital: the post-bellum South was in a 'transition period between one dominant mode of production [slavery] and another [capitalism]'. The result was a hybrid intermediate stage which seems less important historically than what came before and what followed.[16]

A look at the dynamics of southern labour relations suggests that Wiener is on the right track when he says that 'Southern distinctiveness arose out of the labor-repressive nature of Southern production and the direct participation of the state in enforcing restrictions on the mobility of labor.'[17] But the chemistry is incomplete without a more complete understanding of the racial component of this solution (not a *mixture*). What was continuous with the ante-bellum South in one way, and analogous to patterns elsewhere in the United States in another way, was the centrality of race to both labour markets and modes of labour management. The importance of race to labour markets and labour relations is not confined to the South; but it did operate differently in that region.

The tendency of some scholars to look to factors other than (or analytically prior to) race and racism is partly a reaction to historians who insist that despite the transformation of the southern economy, racism remained the central and overriding organising theme in southern history. This argument epitomises a long tradition in southern historiography and its resilience is readily comprehensible. The region's defining characteristics have rested on issues easily understood in racial terms. The formative experience was slavery, and for most of its life the slave regime defined a person's presumed status according to physical characteristics associated with African descent. For most of the present century, social, legal, and political distinctions based essentially on race continued to define for many the region's distinctiveness. A struggle for equality based on opposition to racial oppression occupied the nation's attention for a decade and fundamentally transformed southern life. Whether it is Ulrich B. Phillips seeking to justify both slavery and the plantation system of the early twentieth century by pointing to the value of 'race control', or the innumerable scholars who in recent decades have pilloried white supremacists, heroicised African-American resistance and written compassionately of the victims of racial oppression, race occupies centre stage.[18]

From a very different perspective, but with a similar view of race as the South's distinctive characteristic, economic historians working in neoclassical frameworks have identified racism as the single greatest barrier to southern economic development. Rejecting Woodward's jaundiced view of New South capitalists, these scholars have emphasised economic growth and pointed to impressive gains made by freed slaves and their children. The irrationality of racial discrimination, the tragic flaw of southern history, distorted markets and inhibited rational economically calculated behaviour, thereby impeding even more rapid progress.[19]

Historians of black workers have found it equally difficult to resist the explanatory power of racism: black workers have suffered discrimination at the expense of employers and unions; black and white workers have seldom lived, worked or organised together. Trade union history either comprises histories of exclusion and discrimination or laments the fate of interracial solidarity (or merely co-operation) crumbling under the force of corporate pandering to racial jealousies and suspicions.[20]

In general, the American obsession with race, combined with the visibility and codification of racial distinctions, has yielded primary sources more likely to underscore the ubiquity of racial discrimination than to highlight such factors as class and gender as salient social categories. Scholars working in the tradition of the 'caste/class' model popular among social scientists in the 1930s look first at racial ('caste') divisions, and then analyse class structure and its significance *within* each race.[21] Even historians who have tried to integrate class imperatives and racism have in the end frequently placed race on top: William Cohen's exhaustive study of labour markets, coercion, and black labour finds its bottom line in 'a society where the ideology of white supremacy reigned almost unchallenged . . . a world where white hegemony was complete'. As George Fredrickson has observed, 'when push came to shove, race-relations historians have assumed, this basic commitment to white supremacy was likely to take priority over economic or class interests'.[22]

All this adds up to two different ways of thinking about two concepts: race and class. To state it crudely, either the South's commitment to white supremacy structured its modes of production, stifled all change, dominated the world view of most of the population and defined its distinctive regional character, or, race is an ideology that exists because a capitalist mode of production requires inequality and an ideology that defines and justifies that inequality; as phenomena contingent on historical process, neither race nor racism can have independent historical impact. One approach too readily assumes the fundamental – if not primordial – nature of race as a basis of identity; the other denies a turn-of-the-century reality perhaps foreign to post-modern sensibilities: most southerners – both black and white – thought, acted, lived and worked in racial terms.[23]

To many white southerners at the beginning of the twentieth century white supremacy was a goal in and of itself. These individuals might not have known the origins of either their or their society's commitment to white supremacy, but they tied social order so closely to white supremacy that one seemingly could not exist without the other. Conversely, many black southerners identified white supremacy as the one overwhelming reality limiting their ability to 'better their condition'. Within this world, it did not matter whether or not race was a 'constructed' category. It had been reified; it had become part of the context within which people lived and made their history.[24]

Moreover, black and white southerners tied community to race: for black southerners, their historical experience and understanding of their own culture taught them that theirs was what Elsa Barkley Brown has called a 'community of struggle'. Brown is referring to the emergence of African-American communities after the Civil War, but her notion of what it takes to create and hold together a community has more general application. Brown insightfully argues that community does not require unity; difference can be accommodated within various commonalities, including common purpose or a common discourse. In the case of white southerners that common discourse was an ideology of race, one that assumed that blacks possessed certain characteristics and were naturally fitted to a particular role in economy, polity and society. In part because of black resistance, white southerners constantly worried that black people were, in fact, dangerous; did in fact, reject their place – and therefore constituted a threat to the community. The effort to keep blacks in their places constituted for whites a 'community of struggle' united by a common discourse. Maintaining the system – especially in the face of black resistance – was hard work, part of the 'social burden' borne by the white South.[25]

With race and class so embedded in both the sources and the historiography, scholars have recognised the dangers inherent in relegating either to a subordinate role in southern history. Research agendas point instead to an understanding of how race, class – and, increasingly gender – interact. But even studies that focus on the articulation of these factors tend (often implicitly) to situate them hierarchically, implying their existence as separable historical forces.

By the early twentieth century, however, racial ideology and a mode of production were intertwined in a particular form of social relations that cannot – even analytically – be disentangled to yield independent and comparable evaluations of the impact of class on the one hand, and the impact of race on the other.[26] White supremacy was neither merely a tool employed in the interest of class domination nor largely a discourse that obscured the real terrain of conflict. It formed an integral part of white southern elites' understanding of social order, and that social order both sustained and was sustained by systems of class relations which were themselves partly defined by ideas about particular characteristics imputed by race, class and gender. Rather than frame a hierarchy of historical influence, or establish one category of social relations as 'fundamental', it seems more useful to understand the peculiar imbrication of the material and the ideological. Race neither constituted the basis for relations of production nor was an artefact of those relations; race was part of the relations of production which in turn constituted an element of a broader social order understood by most southerners largely in terms of race. This was a society in which 'nigger' and 'place' not only constituted central components of a discourse of power; these terms also were essential to the operation of the system itself. Southerners, white and black, used the term 'place' to situate themselves and others within a framework of both social relations and individual relationships. Black southerners recognised that framework as that which they had to deal with culturally, economically, socially and politically. Their refusal to accept 'place' as normative placed an enormous burden on those white southerners who could not envision order without place (or without 'niggers').

Testing this approach leads first to the southern labour market, an economic institution so deeply influenced by ideologies of race that its functioning cannot be assessed independent of race. Whether distributed efficiently or inefficiently, labour had racially defined characteristics which skewed the market itself while contributing to the effects that the market had on southern society.

By the turn of the century the South was committed to a low wage economy. As Gavin Wright has shown, this commitment had multiple reverberations, from the need to restrict mobility within and out of the region, to the need to maintain a surplus based partly on household units. To some historians the message is clear: here lies an example of how an economic institution shaped social institutions and laid the foundations of black poverty. But why the depth of that commitment? And how was the market kept isolated?

To some scholars the obsession with the low wage economy stemmed from the imperative to maintain white supremacy. To keep blacks dependent, they had to be kept poor.[27] This begs the question of *why* they had to be kept dependent, an imperative whose relationship to white supremacy is inextricably entangled with gender and class. By nineteenth-century standards of manhood, dependent black men lacked the essential perquisite of independence. Their dangerous sexuality could be submerged in an image of dependence and docility, and their second class citizenship could be justified. And keeping entire black households dependent served the needs of the labour market: a surplus that could be mobilised according to the seasonal demands of the cotton cycle. Dependence on the employer rather than the market is also a characteristic of plantation systems in general. The relationship between a system of production (the plantation), the needs of a particular crop and the imperatives of race and gender

230 *American Exceptionalism?*

cannot be reduced to a prioritised scheme that measures the separate impact of race, class and gender.

The Great Migration introduced a complicating factor: once jobs opened up in the North the isolation of the South's labour market broke down. The repressive legislation was utterly ineffective, as were the various entreaties to the kinds of local and personal loyalties characteristic of plantation ideology. Still, some would argue, these were merely straightforward economic processes providing new alternatives which opened the market. But why had the market been relatively closed? Race. In the North an ideology of race had, for industrial managers, defined which European immigrants were likely to be proficient at which jobs. Lithuanians were 'good at trucking barrels or cases but mediocre at shoveling', and Ukrainians 'splendid under dusty and smoky conditions'. Italians were untidy, 'but not destructive'. Slavs were docile, bringing a 'habit of silent submission' to the strict supervision and long hours. Consigned to the lowest positions, southern and eastern Europeans were considered the bottom of the barrel. But they, at least, were in the barrel; northern industrialists assumed that African-Americans lacked not only 'the mechanical idea', but also the personal characteristics qualifying them for even the worst factory jobs. African-Americans were 'inefficient, unsuitable, and unstable', fit only for pushing a broom or a mop. As white southerners were fond of reiterating, in the North blacks had no 'place'.[28]

Moreover, the very functioning of the southern labour market was intertwined with race. White workers would seldom work with black workers. Planters often found that white farmers would not rent from landlords who also rented to blacks. Perhaps Steven Hahn is right to attribute what we call racism to the fear of poor whites that association with a degraded and dependent class of people would only accelerate their own immiseration and dependence – a condition actually rooted in incursions of the market economy. But by the turn of the century the association of race with dependence and degradation was deeply ingrained. It was so deeply ingrained, in fact, that it legitimated a system of legal and extralegal controls and limitations on black southerners. These constituted the extraordinary means by which blacks could be controlled so effectively that many southern landlords and employers considered them 'the best labor the South can get'. 'The Negro's redress is merely theoretical', recalled William Alexander Percy, whose father's Arkansas experiment with Italian sharecroppers had led to complaints that these immigrant labourers protested too much and were too 'enterprising'. As one Mississippi employer put it, 'when you just have Negroes, you can make them work by cussing and cuffing them ... But with whites you can't do that.'[29]

The reason northern employers did not share this assessment of black labour owed less to differences in ideologies of race than to differences in the institutionalisation of those differences. Northern foremen frequently cussed but they seldom cuffed. Nowhere outside the South did race sanction the kind of repressive apparatus available to southern employers.[30]

Indeed, despite their ready inclination to use whatever force at their disposal to crush unionisation, and their well-documented, heavy-handed methods of labour management, it is doubtful that northern employers considered managing as their contemporaries did in the South during this period. Midwestern agricultural employers rejected full-time workforces as too expensive, preferring to hire wage labourers at peak times for threshing and harvesting. But even seasonal workers could – and did – organise. They also were troublesome because their transience limited the types of informal community pressures likely to impel appropriate behaviour. Hence the concern with the social costs attached to sudden influxes of young, unmarried men, whose counterparts in the South were controlled through racial protocols.[31]

Midwestern farmers also worried about keeping their workers on hand through the harvest, often holding out pay until the crop was gathered. What one does not see, however, are coercive assumptions (or even a coercive discourse) comparable to the observation of a labour recruiter in the *Atlanta Constitution* around the turn of the century: 'there are farmers that would not hesitate to shoot their brother were he to come from Mississippi to get "his niggers," as he calls them, even though he had no contract with them'. Few northern farmers could realistically envision this level of proprietary claim over hired labour.[32]

Obviously there were many reasons why mechanisation proceeded more rapidly in the wheat belt; but the 'labor problem' clearly yielded solutions different from those found in the South. There, rural industry provided alternatives for men during agricultural lulls; and the assumption that black women and children constituted part of the labour force guaranteed extra harvest labour. Regionally recognised racial protocols governing the interactions of black men with white women minimised the threat that even transient black labour would pose to agricultural communities.[33]

Even in the West and Southwest, where racism and exclusions from citizenship rendered particular racialised groups subject to comparable levels of coercion, no system of social and economic relations so tightly bound together race, order and labour management. In the West (and to a lesser extent elsewhere in the nation), employers in the 1870s looked to the Chinese as a potential pool of casual labour who, as perpetual noncitizens, could be exploited almost at will. The Chinese, according to Ronald Takaki, seemed to offer a 'permanently degraded caste labor force . . . a unique "industrial reserve army" of migrant laborers forced to be foreigners forever, aliens ineligible for citizenship'. But no part of the nation's economy depended on them and they were new enough to the continent for racist movements to demand exclusion rather than massive instruments of control. In the Southwest, according to Josef Barton, Mexican-American farmers in the late nineteenth century 'found themselves bound by landowners and credit merchants in a knot of constraints'. Racism and citizenship issues left most Mexican-Americans little legal recourse. Yet extralegal resistance does not seem to have regularly provoked the levels of violence, hysteria and intimidation that were pervasive in the South. Barton points to a traditional 'weave of rights and obligations, a set of alliances and allegiances, on which was based a social order'. This foundation established a basis for the assertion of legal rights in addition to 'the placing of barriers across newly-cut roads to Anglo-American ranches; the destruction of new boundary markers . . . [and] the endemic rebellion of fence-cutting'. Moreover, there is little evidence that the existence of a Mexican-American middle class itself posed a threat to the system of social and economic relations.[34]

The isolation of southern management culture, both on and off the plantation, is most striking in comparison with trends in northern industry. Management culture was as isolated in the South as the region's labour market. The continued dominance of plantation-based assumptions about labour management was rooted in both a particular system of production and the heritage of dealing with a racially defined (and therefore readily marginalised legally) workforce. Historian Edward Ayers has recently referred to 'a lost plantation ideal' as more relevant to southern mill village paternalism than historians have suggested. But the notion of a lost ideal is somewhat misleading, masking an important degree of continuity; where African-Americans were involved the plantation constituted a cultural inheritance in the arena of labour relations, bequeathing assumptions about how to manage particular workers.

Turn-of-the-century northern managers operated from a different set of assumptions about their labour force. In company towns, the steel industry encouraged transiency as a defence against organisation. In contrast to the South where 'the more blacks strived, the more white anger they confronted', northern employers fed even the most unrealistic hopes of upward mobility as a means of encouraging loyalty and regularity. In the South the defence against organisation was more likely to emphasise the stasis of place. According to David Carlton, South Carolina's mill owners assumed that their white 'mill hands posed no threat to the social order because of their racial heritage'.[35] Their location in some place other than the bottom of southern society was guaranteed by dint of their race, which also held out the promise – if not the reality – of escaping their class. Those who did make noise were reminded of the dangers of associating with those who occupied a degraded place. The mobilisation of gendered familial metaphors tied them to a community defined essentially by its whiteness.[36]

African-Americans, on the other hand, were assumed to pose a threat more as dangerous individuals than as part of organised social movements. Ideas about racial characteristics bred assumptions (assumptions often at odds with reality) that organisation would happen only when outside agitators were involved; and if it did happen landlords and employers had access to a repressive apparatus that would have made most northern employers jealous. Unlike the manager of a northern factory or a northern farmer employing casual labour, a landlord could wipe out months of a tenant's investment through arbitrary eviction. The conventional shorthand is appropriate: black southerners had no rights that a white man need respect. In a local community a bad reputation had drastic implications in terms of credit. For a black southerner, 'being acceptable' carried enormous meaning. As Arthur Raper learned during his time in the Georgia black belt in the 1920s, 'it means that he is considered safe by local white people – he knows his place and stays in it'. Indeed, only blacks willing to accept this 'submerged status' were permitted to purchase land in that community.[37] Even if few black southerners accepted that status as just – or even inevitable – it is clear that many were pragmatically willing to operate within what one might describe as the discourse and etiquette of place.

Here was a different inflection in the use of the possibility of upward mobility as a means of control. The place of blacks in southern agriculture and in rural industry was permanent; education was useless and docility, rather than ambition, was rewarded. In mill towns, employers assumed that their legitimacy as paternalists required that they provide schools; even southern white mill workers might look to education as the next generation's path to the world beyond. Not so where black labour forces predominated. Schools were dangerous; they encouraged unrealistic expectations and could lead black labourers away from their work. Historian James Anderson, in his comprehensive study of southern black education, summarises the perspective of the 'southern white leadership': 'Any large-scale expansion of black education, even industrial education, would set in motion a revolution in race relations that would undermine the South's existing political and economic arrangements.' Where northern employers embraced education which would Americanise the workforce and imbue the proper habits of industry and lessons of citizenship, southern employers considered these very functions as not only irrelevant to black life but contradictory to the place blacks inevitably occupied in southern society.[38]

Equally important to an understanding of how deeply embedded race was in southern labour relations was a set of assumptions about black character. Surveys conducted in 1910 and 1912 revealed sentiments that had changed little since the Civil War: blacks would not respond to market incentives; they would not work except under compulsion. Give them a chance to earn too much money and they will lay off for a while. In Mississippi, an agricultural extension worker described as 'prevalent' the assumption that 'the negro must be kept ignorant and destitute in order to manage him safely'.[39]

These are, of course, familiar sentiments, recognisable in the literature on early industrial workforces in a variety of settings. And I sympathise with Thomas Holt's caution that although 'putative racial deficiencies provided a justification for maintaining a highly coercive labor discipline . . . the crux of the problem was the need for labor discipline regardless of the racial character of the work force'.[40] But racial perceptions affected how discipline was to be achieved and systems of race relations affected the boundaries of enforcement. Carrots, sticks or indoctrination? By the early twentieth century, northern capitalists increasingly were adding the kinds of incentives that even Frederick W. Taylor's ape-like shovel handler could appreciate. Welfare capitalism (which is very different from mill village paternalism) emerged as both a set of incentives and a mode of indoctrination. One finds little of this in the South, where a culture of management was shaped by a plantation culture and strategies to deal with black workers.[41] If northern industrial employers had embarked on a campaign to eliminate casual labour as dysfunctional, to be replaced with a 'state of mind' that emphasised thrift, regularity and initiative, southern employers remained wedded to a dependence on casual labour. This was not unusual in agriculture; what was different was the assumption that thrift and initiative could pose a threat. On the one hand it was widely advertised that blacks were incapable of thrift or initiative; on the other it was generally recognised that those who were thrifty threatened the system, and those who took initiative could be dangerous. The ability of black workers to respond to modern methods of management was considered questionable; the availability of coercive mechanisms provided cheaper and customary alternatives that would not threaten social order.[42]

This relatively isolated culture of management was most permeable in cases where corporations operated with labour forces within and outside the South, with African-Americans prominent among southern employees. A survey of employment practices on the Illinois Central Railroad suggests how a northern company modified its practices despite a commitment to uniform shop rules and personnel policies. Headquartered in Chicago, the Illinois Central took in more than a thousand black workers when in 1883 it formally absorbed southern lines that it had controlled for some years. Problems recurred in the southern units, attributable to 'local custom' and to assumptions about the capabilities of black workers. The response suggests an inclination to 'interpret' rules on an ad hoc basis; in other words to adapt to regional patterns. The general manager of these roads repeats a language common to the southern discourse on black labour, but irrelevant among northern employers at the time unwilling to hire black workers for anything other than service positions: 'We find them especially amiable, docile, and obedient . . . There is no better labor among any race in the world', he declared in 1883.[43]

African-Americans had a place that was defined not only by their role in the system of production, and their status as second class citizens, but also by a conventional wisdom – at least among whites – that attributed to them a set of characteristics that implied their acceptance of that place. On the plantation, in the railroad yard, black workers were available and pliable. More so than any other potential labour force possibly could be. 'The Negro is our ward . . . He will follow the white folks into the very jaws of hell if need be' declared a Mississippi newspaper in 1918.[44] A year after condemning peonage in 1903, one southern moderate declared that the Negro 'will accept in the white man's country the place assigned him by the white man'.[45] Given the actual levels of black resistance documented by historians, this seems a rather odd statement. But in many cases the 'hidden transcripts' recently described by scholars analysing such resistance were indeed hidden to whites, who read resistance as recalcitrance or some other form of collective racial deficiency (hence the burden endured by the South). Even if such sentiments might sound more like efforts at reassurance than deeply held beliefs, what matters is that they were considered plausible as reassurance. And their ubiquity cannot be discounted.

Thus for white southern landlords and employers African-Americans did indeed seem to constitute the perfect labour force. Joel Williamson, in his massive study of southern theories of race, has identified a widespread notion – especially among elites – that each race had its own essence; there was white soul and black soul. At best, white southerners acknowledged that blacks might not be inferior, while assuming that they would (and should) remain subordinate and have a place aside – on the farm, which was an especially suitable environment for Negroes because agriculture would cultivate virtues of thrift, morality and hard work. Blacks would grow the cotton; whites would process it.[46] African-Americans would perform the heavy tasks in sawmills and extractive industries that would otherwise require an influx of immigrants who would be less tractable than what southern journalists described as 'the best class of labor of its kind in the world'.[47] All was as it should be, and everybody supposedly knew their place in the system. Social order depended on it, and for those who needed to be reminded of the centrality of race to social order there was always a legend of Reconstruction familiar to us through the literature and historiography – and a central theme in hundreds of amateur local histories written in the late nineteenth-century South.

What threatened order – both the naturalised ideology of race and the operation of the labour market – were transgressions of place. A Louisiana newspaper understood what was at stake: 'a younger generation of negro bucks and wenches have lost that wholesome respect for the white man, without which two races, the one inferior, cannot live in peace and harmony together'. The behaviour signalling such a threat included servants addressing one another as 'Miss' or 'Mr'. Other dangerous young turks resisted being addressed as 'auntie' or 'uncle'.[48] It was not the content of the behaviour that mattered; it was the meaning, an implication of a refusal to accept the etiquette of place.

Given what was at stake, it is not surprising that transgressing place could incur consequences. The quickest route to a lynching was excessive ambition or a comparable challenge to subordination or dependence. Ida B. Wells stated it clearly – and dangerously: lynching was not the work of rabble; she found that men of property and standing were involved. Nor was lynching a response to threats to white womanhood. Less than one lynching in five involved even an accusation of rape. Even those could easily resemble the case of Robert Cromwell who in 1880 fell to a Texarkana lynch mob after allegedly attacking his white neighbour's wife; coincidentally the feisty Cromwell had recently had the temerity to sue that very same neighbour over a property dispute.[49] If historian Elliott Gorn is right that nineteenth-century southern white men affirmed their manhood by committing acts of violence against other men, then the obverse makes considerable sense: the manhood – and therefore the citizenship – of black men could be diminished through lynchings whose rituals could include accusations of sexual crimes and actual or symbolic castration of victims. In this sense lynching was less about sex than it was about gender; it cannot be separated from nineteenth-century assumptions about the relationship between manhood, citizenship and independence. The southern rape fantasy, Wells declared, was 'an excuse to get rid of Negroes who were acquiring wealth and property and thus keep the race terrorised'.[50] Not for the sake of terror itself, or out of loyalty to an idea: but to maintain order as they knew it. If, as one historian has recently put it, lynchings were 'communal' rather than 'aberrant' acts, they reaffirmed a community based partly on a discourse of place.[51]

But something else threatened the ideological underpinnings of the system. The Great Migration not only threatened the labour surplus that was central to the workings of the labour market, but it brought into question the very assumption that black southerners were by nature unambitious – that they envisioned any other place than their role in southern society and had the drive and initiative to act on that vision.

The southern economy, Booker T. Washington recognised in 1914, was 'based on the Negro and the mule'.[52] If there was an overriding theme that dominated southern white reactions to the Great Migration it implied agreement with the sage of Tuskegee. But the Negro and the mule each had a role, and dependence implied an assumption that each would continue to play that role. 'I know men who won't keep a horse', explained a member of the Tuskegee Institute staff in 1912. 'If they get one they will sell it. If you ask such a one why he sold his horse, he will very likely say: "white man see me 'n dat 'ere horse, he look hard at me. I make my min' a mule good 'nugh for a ole nigger like me."'[53]

Corollary to this relationship between dependence and the imperative of immobility was the relationship between dependence and subordination. Economic dependence might have been mutual but it was not equal; as long as white southerners lived in a plantation society and in a culture that took for granted particular definitions of racial categories it would be essential that blacks have a particular and subordinate place. Because blacks could occupy only that place, and nobody else seemed able to occupy that place, migration posed a threat. To render migration harmless it was necessary to define it as passive, to attribute it to outside forces rather than to dissatisfaction with place, and to limit its impact on the labour market. To do otherwise was to lose control over the labour force and over a potentially dangerous population that always sat at the brink of cultural regression. Indeed, one whole strain of thinking on these issues that lies outside the purview of this paper rejected the assumption that blacks were essential to social order and economic prosperity in the South. Arguing that the place occupied by blacks benefited only a small elite, and that the region as a whole could do without them, white southerners lacking ties to black labour markets cheered the Great Migration. But in the 'Black Belt', because of the way that 'place' had been defined, legitimated and enforced by the entanglement of class and race relations, white labour literally could not 'replace' black.

NOTES

* Too many people have read various incarnations of this essay to permit acknowledging all of my debts to colleagues. Earlier versions benefited from discussion at the Newberry Library Fellows' Seminar, the Emory University Seminar on Comparative Industrial Societies and the Social History Workshop at the University of Chicago. I am especially indebted to Elsa Barkley Brown and Laura Edwards for their patient and thorough criticism. I am grateful as well to James Barrett, Kathleen Conzen, Rick Halpern, Hannah Rosen and Nick Salvatore.

1. Booker T. Washington, 'The Rural Negro and the South', *Proceedings of the National Conference of Charities and Correction*, 41 (1914), 122.
2. Charles S. Johnson, 'Efforts to Check the Movement', 1, in folder marked 'Migration Study, Draft (Final)', Chapters 7–13, Box 86, Series 6, National Urban League Records, Library of Congress; Jackson *Daily Clarion-Ledger* quoted in Neil R. McMillen, *Dark Journey: Black Mississippians in the Age of Jim Crow* (Urbana, 1989), 262; Emmett J. Scott, *Negro Migration*, 72; Howard L. Clark, 'Growth of Negro Population in the U.S. and Trend of Migration from the South Since 1860', *Manufacturers Record*, 83:4 (25 January 1923), 61; Southerner, 'Exodus Without Its Canaan – But Not Without its Lessons', *Coal Age*, 11 (10 February 1917), 258; Baton Rouge *State Times*, quoted in Chicago *Whip*, 6 November 1920.
3. James R. Grossman, *Land of Hope: Chicago, Black Southerners, and the Great Migration* (Chicago, 1989), 38–56.
4. Thomas C. Holt, 'Marking: Race, Race-making, and the Writing of History', *American Historical Review*, 100:1 (February, 1995), 1–20; quotations are from 18. For the most powerful statement of the distinction between class as a material reality versus race as an ideological construction that is an artefact of class relations, see Barbara Jeanne Fields, 'Slavery, Race, and Ideology in the United States of America', *New Left Review*, 181 (May–June, 1990), 95–118; and Fields, 'Ideology and Race in American History', in J. Morgan Kousser and James M. McPherson, eds, *Region, Race and Reconstruction: Essays in Honor of C. Vann Woodward* (NY, 1982), 143–177. The literature on racial ideology as a psychological problem is as vast as it is outdated. An interesting place to begin is E. Franklin Frazier's pioneering essay, 'The Pathology of Race Prejudice', which characterised white racism as a form of paranoia. See G. Franklin Edwards, ed., *E. Franklin Frazier on Race Relations; Selected Writings* (Chicago, 1968). Social, psychological and political aspects of southern racism during this period are explored in Joel Williamson, *The Crucible of Race: Black White Relations in the American South Since Emancipation* (NY, 1984), 79–323, 414–482. Lawrence Goodwyn, *The Democratic Promise: The Populist Moment in America* (NY,

1976) maps out a progressive and broad-based democratic political culture in parts of the South during this period, with racism as the tragic flaw undermining this strand of populism. C. Vann Woodward's *Tom Watson, Agrarian Rebel* (NY, 1938) has a similarly tragic theme.

5. [Frank B. Stubbs], 'Memorandum of Southern Trip', 3 November 1923–5 December 1923, Folder 1006, Box 99, Laura Spelman Rockefeller Memorial, Rockefeller Archives Center, Tarrytown, NY.

6. Edward Ayers, *The Promise of the New South: Life After Reconstruction* (NY, 1992), 306.

7. C. Vann Woodward, *Origins of the New South, 1877–1913* (Baton Rouge, 1951); Eugene Genovese, *Roll, Jordan, Roll: The World the Slaves Made* (New York, 1974).

8. Ayers, *Promise*, 488.

9. Edmund S. Morgan, *American Slavery, American Freedom: The Ordeal of Colonial Virginia* (New York, 1975); Fields, 'Slavery, Race and Ideology in the United States'; Thomas C. Holt, '"An Empire Over the Mind": Emancipation, Race, and Ideology in the British West Indies and the American South', in Kousser and McPherson, eds, *Region, Race and Reconstruction*, 283–313. The quotation is from Fields, 'Slavery, Race and Ideology', 114. The most comprehensive treatise on the relationship between bourgeois liberalism and ideologies of race remains David Brion Davis, *The Problem of Slavery in the Age of Revolution, 1770–1883* (Ithaca, 1975). The classic text establishing the formative influence of English attitudes regarding race, nationality and physical attributes is Winthrop D. Jordan, *White over Black: American Attitudes toward the Negro, 1550–1812* (Chapel Hill, 1968).

10. Armstead Robinson, 'Beyond the Realm of Social Consensus: New Meanings of Reconstruction for American History', *Journal of American History*, 68:1 (June 1981), 297; W.E.B. Du Bois, *Black Reconstruction* (New York, 1935). See also Fields, 'Ideology and Race', 162–9; David Montgomery, *Beyond Equality: Labor and the Radical Republicans, 1862–1872* (New York, 1967). For some historians of this era, even when race seemed to be the central issue, as in the New York City draft riots, class tensions and imperatives lay underneath, finding expression through a language of race. See Iver Bernstein, *The New York City Draft Riots: Their Significance for American Society and Politics in the Age of the Civil War* (New York, 1990).

11. See Dwight B. Billings, *Planters and the Making of a 'New South': Class, Politics, and Development in North Carolina, 1865–1900* (Chapel Hill, 1979), 92; Steven Hahn, *The Roots of Southern Populism: Yeoman Farmers and the Transformation of the Georgia Upcountry, 1850–1890* (New York, 1983). See also George M. Fredrickson, *The Arrogance of Race: Historical Perspectives on Slavery, Racism, and Social Inequality* (Middletown, CT, 1988), 157–8. My purpose in this essay is less to debate the roots and implications of racial attitudes among the powerless (e.g. Hahn's yeomen) than to probe into the implications of racial ideology and class imperatives among the powerful (especially the planter class).

12. Particularly notable examples include Joe W. Trotter, *Coal, Class, and Color: Blacks in Southern West Virginia. 1915–32* (Urbana, 1990); Peter Gottlieb, *Making Their Own Way: Southern Blacks' Migration to Pittsburgh, 1916–30* (Urbana, 1987); Daniel Letwin, 'Race, Class, and Industrialization in the

New South: The Coal Miners of Alabama, 1871–1921' (PhD dissertation, Yale University, 1991).

13. Jonathan M. Wiener, *Social Origins of the New South: Alabama, 1860–1885* (Baton Rouge, 1978).

14. Alex Lichtenstein, *Twice the Work of Free Labor: The Political Economy of Convict Labor in the New South* (London, 1995). For a comprehensive examination of southern legislation designed to limit the mobility of black labour, see William Cohen, *At Freedom's Edge: Black Mobility and the Southern White Quest for Racial Control, 1861–1915* (Baton Rouge, 1991).

15. Jon Wiener, 'Reconsidering the Wiener Thesis', comments presented at the annual meeting of the Organization of American Historians, 1991, 13.

16. Fields, quoted in Lichtenstein, *Twice the Work of Free Labor*, 11.

17. Wiener, 'Reconsidering the Wiener Thesis', 15.

18. Whether one is inclined to conceptualise a 'ruling race' a 'ruling class', or some combination of these, what is clear is that both academic and popular history has tended to emphasise American slavery as a racial phenomenon. On Phillips see James Oakes, 'The Present Becomes the Past: The Planter Class in the Postbellum South', in Robert Abzug and Stephen Maislish, eds, *New Perspectives on Race and Slavery in America* (Lexington, KY, 1986), 158.

19. See e.g. Robert Higgs, *Competition and Coercion: Blacks in the American Economy, 1865–1914* (Chicago, 1977); Higgs, 'Race and Economy in the South, 1890–1915', in Robert Haws, ed., *The Age of Segregation: Race Relations in the South, 1890–1945* (Oxford, MS, 1987), 111–15; Stephen J. DeCanio, *Agriculture in the Postbellum South: The Economics of Production and Supply* (Cambridge, MA, 1974). Higgs ('Race and Economy', 90) argues that southern economic development 'solved' the 'race problem' because the system of race relations required continued isolation from the market. For a more complex analysis on the relationship between race and flawed economic institutions that relies on neoclassical models without apotheosising the market, see Roger Ransom and Richard Sutch, *One Kind of Freedom: The Economic Consequences of Emancipation* (Cambridge, 1977).

20. William H. Harris, *The Harder We Run: Black Workers since the Civil War* (New York, 1982); Robert J. Norrell, 'Caste in Steel: Jim Crow Careers in Birmingham Alabama', *Journal of American History*, 73:3 (December 1986), 669–694; Charles H. Wesley, *Negro Labor in the United States* (New York, 1927); Sterling Spero and Abram Harris, *The Black Worker: The Negro and the Labor Movement* (New York, 1931); Philip S. Foner, *Organized Labor and the Black Worker, 1619–1973* (New York, 1974).

21. The seminal texts include John Dollard, *Caste and Class in a Southern Town* (New York, 1937); Allison Davis, Burleigh B. Gardner, and Mary R. Gardner, *Deep South: A Social Anthropological Study of Caste and Class* (Chicago, 1941); and Gunnar Myrdal, *An American Dilemma* (New York, 1944). For more sophisticated applications of this model to northern cities see Allan H. Spear, *Black Chicago: The Making of a Negro Ghetto* (Chicago, 1967); David Katzman, *Before the Ghetto: Black Detroit in the Nineteenth Century* (Urbana, 1973); and Kenneth Kusmer, *A Ghetto Takes Shape: Black Cleveland, 1870–1930* (Urbana, 1976).

22. Cohen, *At Freedom's Edge*, 221; Fredrickson, *Arrogance of Race*, 155.
23. So did many other Americans. But given the distribution of population, most white Americans outside the South more often thought about what we would now call ethnicity when they thought about 'race'. And because race (however defined or categorised) was less important to social order outside the South, it is arguable that southerners thought in racial terms more often and more significantly than other Americans. They certainly thought more dichotomously.
24. On the importance of this idea among black southerners in the early twentieth-century South, see Grossman, *Land of Hope*, 34–37.
25. Elsa Barkley Brown, 'Uncle Ned's Children: Negotiating Community and Freedom in Postemancipation Richmond' (PhD dissertation, Kent State University, 1994), viii.
26. This is not to say that racial and class consciousness cannot be disentangled. Although these orientations toward social identity cannot be examined in isolation from one another, and most individuals perceive themselves in different ways at different times and in different contexts, there are occasions which require forms of behaviour or expression that imply a statement of the relative salience of various sources of identity. Moreover historians who have emphasised the salience of class as the structure of domination in the South have argued that race consciousness has been the very force impeding either effective African-American resistance or forms of class organisation against the white elite. See Genovese, *Roll, Jordan, Roll*; Robinson, 'Beyond the Realm of Social Consensus'; Goodwyn, *Democratic Promise*. On the problematic aspects of the search for interracial class consciousness see Leon F. Litwack, 'Trouble in Mind: The Bicentennial and the Afro-American Experience', *Journal of American History*, 74:2 (September 1987), 317; and Fredrickson, *Arrogance of Race*, 156–8.
27. See, for example, McMillen, *Dark Journey*.
28. David Montgomery, *The Fall of the House of Labor: The Workplace, the State, and American Labor Activism, 1865–1925* (Cambridge, 1987), 243; John Bodnar, Roger Simon, and Michael P. Weber, *Lives of Their Own: Blacks, Italians, and Poles in Pittsburgh, 1900–1960* (Urbana, 1982), 59; Gerd Korman, *Industrialization, Immigrants, and Americanizers: The View from Milwaukee* (Madison, 1967), 44–46, 65; John R. Commons, *Races and Immigrants in America* (New York, 1907), 46–49. See also Daniel Nelson, *Managers and Workers: The Origins of the Factory System in the United States, 1880–1920* (Madison, 1975), 81.
29. Columbia, SC *State*, 1917, quoted in Emmett J. Scott, *Negro Migration During the War* (New York, 1920), 156; Percy quoted in Lawrence J. Nelson, 'Welfare Capitalism on a Mississippi Plantation in the Great Depression', *Journal of Social History*, 50:2 (May 1984), 227. Leroy Percy quoted in Bertram Wyatt-Brown, 'Leroy Percy and Sunnyside: Planter Mentality and Italian Peonage in the Mississippi Delta', in *Shadows over Sunnyside: An Arkansas Plantation in Transition, 1830–1045* (Fayetteville, 1993), 88; Mississippi employer quoted in McMillen, *Dark Journey*, 159. See also Jones, *The Dispossessed*, 120. This sentiment outlasted the legal framework of Jim Crow. As late as 1971, a study of Mississippi could observe that 'even today many planters will admit they still prefer Negroes as tractor drivers and farm

workers to whites, for they are less troublesome and can be fired if necessary, with fewer repercussions'. See James Loewen, *The Mississippi Chinese: Between Black and White* (Cambridge, MA, 1971), 201.

30. Harold Woodman, 'Post-Civil War Southern Agriculture and the Law', *Agricultural History*, 53:1 (January 1979), 319–37.

31. Tobias Higbie, 'Indispensable Outcasts: Harvest Laborers in the Wheat Belt, 1895–1925', paper presented at Newberry Seminar in Rural History (1993), 20, 26.

32. Letter from Peg Leg Williams to *Atlanta Constitution*, quoted in Ray Stannard Baker, *Following the Color Line: American Negro Citizenship in the Progressive Era* (New York, 1964; orig. pub. 1906), 80. Landlords' sense of tenants as 'their niggers' is discussed in McMillen, *Dark Journey*, 125.

33. Jones, *The Dispossessed*, 89.

34. Ronald Takaki, *Iron Cages: Race and Culture in 19th-Century America* (New York, 1979), 236; Josef Barton, 'Capitalism and Community: Mexican Peasants and Southwestern Migrants, 1880–1930', paper presented at Newberry Seminar in American Social History (1992), 27–9.

35. David Brody, *Steelworkers in America: The Nonunion Era* (Cambridge, MA, 1960); David Carlton, *Mill and Town in South Carolina, 1880–1920* (Baton Rouge, 1982), 112. The quotation is from Ayers, *Promise*, 430.

36. Jacqueline Dowd Hall, James Leloudis, Robert Korstad, Mary Murphy, Lu Ann Jones, and Christopher B. Daly, *Like A Family: The Making of a Southern Cotton Mill World* (Chapel Hill, 1987).

37. Arthur Raper, *Preface to Peasantry: A Tale of Two Black Belt Counties* (Chapel Hill, 1936), 122.

38. Carlton, *Mill and Town*, 92–103; James P. Anderson, *The Education of Blacks in the South, 1880–1935* (Chapel Hill, 1988), 96; McMillen, *Dark Journey*, 93.

39. Charles Flynn Jr, *White Land, Black Labor: Caste and Class in Late Nineteenth-Century Georgia* (Baton Rouge, 1983); Mississippi State Extension Director R.S. Wilson quoted in McMillen, *Dark Journey*, 122.

40. Holt, 'An Empire Over the Mind', 298.

41. According to the historian of Birmingham's Sloss Furnace, what mattered about the management there around the turn of the century was that it came 'from a plantation background' and therefore was 'imbued with what can only be described as racist attitudes common at the time'. Lewis has correctly identified the culture of labour relations that influenced the management at Sloss, but has too readily attributed it merely to racism, rather than a combination of ideas about race and ideas about managing labour. W. David Lewis, 'Sloss Furnaces: The Heritage and the Future', paper presented at Sloss Furnaces National Historic Landmark, Birmingham, Alabama, 5 March 1992.

42. On management reform in the North see Montgomery, *Fall of the House of Labor*, 236; David Montgomery, 'Workers' Control of Machine Production in the Nineteenth Century' in *Workers' Control in America* (New York, 1979), 32–3.

43. James Clarke to T. Morris Chester, 29 April 1886, Illinois Central Archives, 1C 5.2, v. 9, Newberry Library, Chicago IL. For a similar perspective expressed in the 1930s by a transplanted northern manager adapting to southern

traditions of labour management, see Jones, *The Dispossessed*, 185–6. My understanding of Illinois Central policies has been enhanced by correspondence with Paul Taillon.

44. Gulfport and Biloxi *Daily Herald*, 11 April 1918.
45. Edgar Gardner Murphy, quoted in Fredrickson, *The Black Image in the White Mind: The Debate on Afro-American Character and Destiny,1817–1914* (New York, 1971), 287.
46. Williamson, *Crucible*, 439–42.
47. Tifton (GA) *Gazette*, reprinted (approvingly) in the *Atlanta Constitution*, 10 December 1916.
48. Lafayette (LA) *Gazette*, quoted in St Landry *Clarion*, 5 October 1895, quoted in Ayers, *Promise*, 133–34.
49. Little Rock *Gazette*, 1 June 1880.
50. Quoted in Thomas C. Holt, 'The Lonely Warrior: Ida B. Wells-Barnett and the Struggle for Black Leadership', in John Hope Franklin and August Meier, eds, *Black Leaders of the Twentieth Century* (Urbana, 1982), 47.
51. Stephen Whitfield, *A Death in the Delta: The Story of Emmett Till* (New York, 1988), 4.
52. Clark Wissler, 'Report of the Committee on the American Negro', Hanover [NH] Conference, 10–13 August 1926, 4, Folder 1020, Box 101, Laura Spelman Rockefeller Memorial Collection, Rockefeller Archives Center, Tarrytown NY; Booker T. Washington, 'Rural Negro and the South', 122. See also Jay R. Mandle, The *Roots of Black Poverty: The Southern Plantation Economy after the Civil War* (Durham, 1978), 69, 75.
53. Robert E. Park, 'The "Money Ralley" at Sweet Gum. The Story of a Visit to a Negro Church in the Black Belt, Ala.', typescript (ca. 1912), 11, Folder 10, Box 1, Robert E. Park Papers, Regenstein Library, University of Chicago, Chicago IL.

11 South African and US Labour in the Era of the Second World War: Similar Trends and Underlying Differences*

Peter Alexander

By imposing similar priorities on each of the belligerents, wars provide a valuable setting for cross-national comparison. Despite this, none of the fine comparative studies of the US and South Africa considered the period 1939–45 in any detail.[1] In addressing this weakness, an attempt will be made to justify two related conclusions. First, in the period under consideration, although there were important differences between the two countries' labour movements, similar trends were also apparent. More specifically, it was particularly in this period that, as a consequence of war-related industrialisation and resistance, black workers joined labour movements *en masse*. Secondly, the claims of exceptionalism that have been made for the working class of both countries are implicitly regarded as unhelpful (because they inhibit valuable comparative enquiry) and with respect to this period they are explicitly rejected as unwarranted.[2]

For South Africa, an exceptionalist case has been presented by both liberal and Communist writers; the former generally focusing on the heritage of the 'frontier', insisting that colour-bars were dysfunctional to capitalism, and the latter characterising pre-1994 political power as 'colonialism of a special type'.[3] In the 1970s, in the course of a broad revision of these orthodoxies by a generation of younger, mainly Marxist, scholars, key elements of South African exceptionalism were convincingly contested.[4] One important assumption, however, went unchallenged: that the class interests of white workers were always opposed to, or at least distinct from, those of the black majority.

The major comparative studies of the two countries appeared between 1980 and 1982 and, relying heavily on secondary sources, they were strongly influenced by this judgement. George Fredrickson supported a 'split labour market' account, but made no attempt to apply the theory to the 1930s and

1940s where, one suspects, it would have encountered considerable difficulties.[5] Stanley Greenberg's analysis was more subtle and impressively detailed, but he underestimated the extent of labour militancy and multiracial co-operation in the 1940s, and his conception of a 'bounded [white] working class' was too rigid to adequately accommodate the experience of racially mixed unionism (which, for instance, he himself outlined in the case of Alabama).[6] From the mid-1980s new research began to reveal a picture of white workers which was more complex and contradictory,[7] and it is this approach which will be further extended in the present account.

ECONOMY AND SOCIETY

Greenberg describes the US and South Africa as 'racial orders, societies where racial differences are formalized and socially pervasive'.[8] In both countries, capitalist development has involved colonial rule, dispossession and settlement, slavery, segregation, and working-class division; each of which has been defined, to a greater or lesser degree, in racial terms. Whilst it is these resemblances that provide a comparison with coherence and purpose, there are also contrasts that are no less significant. In particular, South Africa had a racially-designated system of cheap, migrant labour which was central to its development. Economic hardship and a battery of statutory instruments forced African men to migrate annually between rural homes and capitalist employment;[9] there was nothing similar in the US.

A number of factors contributed to this crucial difference. First, most black South Africans came from geographically separated reserves that preserved important aspects of pre-capitalist social organisation; subsistence production subsidised costs of reproduction, and notions of social necessity differed from those held by whites. By contrast, most black Americans, even those in rural areas, lived in relatively close proximity to whites, broadly sharing their lifestyles and expectations. Secondly, demographic differences would have made it impossible to apply the South African migrant labour system to the US. In 1946 blacks accounted for 80.9 per cent of the total South African population (Africans 68.7 per cent, coloureds and Indians 12.4 per cent). But in the US only 10.2 per cent of the population was black (African-Americans 9.8 per cent),[10] thus ensuring that most unskilled work would be performed by whites. Thirdly, the two states differed constitutionally and ideologically, reflecting different dominant class interests. Whereas the victors of the Anglo-South African War constructed a new 'gold and maize' state dedicated to supplying cheap labour to mines and farms,[11] the victors in the American Civil War institutionalised support for 'free labour', a key component in their triumph. Finally, South Africa's continuing dependence on gold mining and the relatively poor quality of its ore encouraged, or at least justified, reliance on unfree labour.[12] Moreover, the Chamber of Mines had considerable political influence; more so than the representatives of South Africa's secondary industry.[13] Partly this reflected gold's economic importance, partly divisions within manufacturing (much of which, being poorly mechanised, also benefited from the migrant labour system).[14] By comparison, the US economy was more variegated, and its industry more highly mechanised.

As a consequence of the migrant labour system and the factors from which it had arisen, the social gulf between black and white workers was generally much greater in South Africa than the US. For instance, it is probable that, at least at the beginning of the Second World War, the majority of urban Africans were migrants (as were nearly all African mine workers).[15] Unlike white workers and separated from them, most urban migrants lived in special single-sex accommodation, retaining a family and/or land rights in a rural area. Also, since few whites were fluent in an African language and only a minority of Africans spoke English or Afrikaans, there were difficulties communicating anything more than simple instructions across the racial divide. Significantly, the black/white wage gap was considerably larger in South Africa than the US. In 1939, within South African manufacturing, Africans received on average only 19 per cent as much pay as whites. Whilst, at the same date, the average African-American worker received something approaching 40 per cent of an average white worker's pay.[16]

Indeed, in significant respects, the position of African-Americans more closely resembled that of coloureds than Africans. As with African-Americans, most coloureds were descended from slaves or semi-slaves. Also, they lived in similar conditions to whites, and spoke one of the two white languages. Legally, as with African-Americans, but not Africans, they had full trade union rights, and in 1939, within manufacturing, coloured workers received on average 36 per cent as much pay as white workers.[17] Finally, in the Western Cape (where most coloureds lived) and in the US South, there were roughly equal numbers of, respectively, whites and coloureds and whites and African-Americans. However, for the purpose of this essay it would be too limiting to focus only on the coloured/African-American parallel. Crucially, whereas in the US African-Americans were generally at the bottom of job hierarchies and 'served as the lowest-ranking reference group for the society as a whole', in South Africa this was true of Africans rather than coloureds.[18]

A distinction should also be made between the South African primary sector, specifically gold mining, and its private manufacturing industry.[19] First, although even in private industry colour bars were ubiquitous, until 1956 they were non-statutory, permitting more flexibility than in mining. Secondly, unlike gold, manufactured goods were mostly sold on the home market where, especially after 1925, they benefited from tariff protection. This facilitated the employment of proportionately more whites than in the mines, and it made it possible for private industry's African labourers to be somewhat freer and better paid.[20] Thirdly, whilst the class position of private industry's white workers was similar to that of white workers in the US, South Africa's white miners were chiefly supervisors, and their income was determined by the productivity of their charges. As one Afrikaner nationalist put it, miners were 'not only workers – they [were] also bosses'.[21] Thus, there was almost no possibility of black/white unity in the mines; but the situation was somewhat different in private industry.

Moreover, the employment structure of South African private industry was changing. As a consequence of South Africa's 1932 withdrawal from the gold standard and the onset of world war, industry boomed; pressure to employ whites declined, and opportunities for black workers expanded.[22] During the war, a munitions industry developed; army requirements boosted the steel, clothing and food canning industries; and a range of import substitution industries began to flourish.[23] At the same time, because of prejudice against allowing black soldiers to carry arms, South Africa's Defence Forces enlisted only 125 000 blacks, compared with 225 000 whites.[24] As supplies of white male labour dried-up, white women were increasingly employed in previously male occupations, and the vacancies which they sometimes created were often filled by coloured and later African women. Numerically, the employment of much larger numbers of black men, particularly Africans, was even more significant, and in the six years after 1938–9 whites (including white women) declined from 37.2 per cent of private industry's workforce to 29.8 per cent.[25]

These changes in the employment structure of South Africa's secondary industry mirrored similar developments that occurred in the US under the impact of the New Deal and then war. In both countries, industrial growth was partly stimulated by government intervention. In both, this was coordinated by powerful new agencies, such as the War Production Board in the US and the Director-General of War Supplies in South Africa, and, in both, war-work contracts generally were awarded on a 'cost plus' basis, whilst wages and, to some extent, prices were controlled. In the US a greater proportion of the new, wartime workers were white women and rural whites, but the process and impact of industrial growth were comparable, and in both countries black urbanisation was marked. In South Africa, in the ten years before 1946, the urban black population increased by 48.9 per cent, while in the US, in the ten years to 1950, the urban non-white population grew by 43.5 per cent.[26] In both countries, there were also wartime housing shortages; with black urban residents experiencing racist resentment, particularly, perhaps, from those whites who felt most vulnerable, the newer settlers.[27] However, in both cases, there was also a significant improvement in black wages relative to those of white workers. In South African manufacturing, African incomes increased to 25 per cent of white incomes by 1945, and in the US, African-American wages were about 60 per cent of white wages by the early 1950s.[28]

Regarding urban segregation, the extent of difference between the two countries is far from clear, and the issue would benefit from detailed comparative study. Although there are statistics showing the extent to which 'races' were unevenly distributed across a city's census enumeration districts, they do not distinguish between black servants and black householders living within mainly white neighbourhoods. However, if anything, the data suggests that in the 1940s South African cities were rather less segregated than those of the US (where black ghettos were already well established).[29] With respect to workplace segregation, whilst US Executive Order 8802 of 1941 *prohibited* racist discrimination in war industries and government employment, the South African Factories Act of the same year *required* certain forms of workplace segregation. However, this stark contrast could be misleading. The executive order was, in part, an acknowledgement of widespread racial exclusion, and segregated workplaces could be found well after its promulgation.[30] Contrariwise, the Factories Act was partly a response to worries about the employment of white women alongside black men, and in 1944 there were still complaints about 'intermingling' (particularly in Cape Town, where segregation was often limited to separate benches).[31] Moreover, it is possible that African-Americans had almost as many difficulties obtaining skilled and semi-skilled work as black South Africans. In the US, the proportion of the black workforce not engaged in unskilled work increased from 12.6 per cent in 1930 to 23.8 per cent in 1950.[32] By comparison, among black South Africans affected by Wage Determinations made between 1937 and 1946, 26.9 per cent were considered skilled or semi-skilled (Africans 14.9 per cent, coloureds and Indians 51.9 per cent).[33]

It is necessary, then, to distinguish similar trends and underlying differences. There were similar trends in both countries, notably with regard to the war economies and their impact on working-class composition. But there were also significant differences; in particular, the South African economy was less developed and more reliant on forced labour.

LABOUR AND THE STATE

There was also a marked contrast between the structure of trade union organisation in the two countries. Whereas, in South Africa, unions were divided between the mainly-white South African Trades and Labour Council (SATLC) and mainly-African organisations (the most important of which established CNETU, the Council of Non-European Trade Unions, in 1941), in the US, unions were divided between a mainly-craft federation, the American Federation of Labour (AFL), and the industrially-based Congress of Industrial Organisations (CIO). This difference, between a racial and a craft divide, reproduced the two countries' divergent social structures, but it was also partly a consequence of legislation and the outcome of major conflicts.

South African labour organisation was shaped by the 1924 Industrial Conciliation Act, which was passed in the wake of the defeated 1922 general strike. The act encouraged a highly bureaucratic form of trade unionism (for instance, by banning most strikes). Moreover, the benefits of the act were only available to *registered* unions, and to obtain registration an organisation had to be composed of 'employees', where the definition of 'employee' excluded 'pass bearing natives'. In effect, the act reinforced existing racial divisions, with the main fault-line within the union movement reflecting the different interests of registered and non-registered unions. By contrast, in the US, the division between the AFL and CIO was a product of an upsurge in militancy and unionisation that occurred during the mid-1930s. The failure of the AFL's craftist leadership to involve the many thousands of workers who joined (or wanted to join) their affiliates, provided an opening for advocates of industrial unionism, who formed the CIO, first as a committee within the AFL and then as a separate organisation. Further, the 1935 National Labor Relations (or Wagner) Act tended to strengthen the position of trade unions, particularly perhaps the CIO unions, and unlike the Industrial Conciliation Act it was not concerned to reinforce racial discrimination.[34]

However, it would be a mistake to overstate the differences between the two countries' labour movements. First, the railway brotherhoods and at least 31 AFL affiliates barred African-Americans from membership (and other unions had segregated locals). Consequently, there were also unions, such as the Brotherhood of Sleeping Car Porters, which had a purely black

membership.[35] Secondly, until 1945 the South African Industrial Conciliation Act discouraged, but did not prohibit, registered organisations from
recruiting Africans, and Communist Party (CPSA) activists built a number
of successful multi-racial unions.[36] In addition, other unions, such as the
Garment Workers' Union (GWU), supported African parallel organisations, and the SATLC had a non-racial constitution and a handful of African
affiliates. Thirdly, in early 1943 Solly Sachs, leader of the GWU, was
arguing for a body similar to the American CIO, and during the next year
he discussed the idea with various CNETU leaders.[37]

During the war, labour leaders in both countries developed close collaborative relationships with their respective governments. These were
underpinned by two factors: a war-related shortage of workers, which
strengthened labour's hand, and a concern among union leaders to influence policy-making without recourse to strikes. Anti-war sentiment was
more widespread in South Africa,[38] and this may have further boosted its
labour leaders, but collaboration was broadly similar in both countries. In
South Africa, the Leader of the Labour Party (SALP), Walter Madeley,
became Minister of Labour, union leaders joined important government
committees, and a left-wing, ex-trade unionist was appointed to the powerful position of Controller of Manpower. In the US, a key figure in the
CIO, Sidney Hillman, headed the Labor Division of the National Defense
Administration, and union leaders participated in various government
committees, including the National War Labor Board (NWLB), an important body charged with resolving wartime disputes. There were, of course,
limitations to collaboration; so, for example, in both countries, demands
for increased union involvement in the management of industry were rejected. Moreover, collaboration was not an alternative to coercion; thus,
both governments, on occasion, mobilised troops against strikers.[39]

For the unions, collaboration did secure some improvements. In the US
maintenance of membership agreements helped assist an expansion of
trade unionism, and in South Africa various workers, ranging from engineering artisans to some African labourers, even were able to secure a
closed shop. There was, however, a price to pay. In the US, and certain
South African industries, notably engineering, unions had to accept a pay
freeze. Moreover, in the US unions had to provide a 'no strike' pledge in
return for membership deals, and in South Africa union leaders (including
most African leaders) accepted that they should prevent strikes. In both
countries, the combination of top-level collaboration, union membership
agreements and opposition to strikes tended to increase the gulf between
union leaders and their members. Also, at least in the US, the new workers
appear to have had little sympathy for old union leaders, and in South

Africa the organisers of African unions were typically better educated than their members, who were usually illiterate at least in English (the principal language of South African trade unionism). Thus, during the war, there was a substantial gap between union leaders and their members, and this may have contributed to subsequent militancy.[40]

Both wartime governments adopted more liberal policies towards black workers, but in South Africa racism was reasserted before the war's end. In the US, a threatened black people's March on Washington, mobilised by African-American trade unionist A. Philip Randolph, led to Executive Order 8802 and the creation of the Fair Employment Practices Committee (FEPC). Although the FEPC lacked teeth, its hearings and reports encouraged CIO activists and others to challenge racial discrimination, and partly because of this the proportion of blacks employed in war-related industries increased from under 3 per cent in March 1942 to over 8 per cent in November 1944.[41] Following an analogous trend, the South African Prime Minister, General Smuts, agreed that Africans should be included within the definition of 'employee'.[42] This decision, made in April 1942, followed advice from the Secretary for Native Affairs, who argued that it was necessary in order to exert a measure of 'control' over a rapidly expanding and increasingly confident African union movement. A proposed amendment to the Industrial Conciliation Act would have conceded the statutory recognition which African unions desired, and it would have provided a major boost to equal rights. But the government began to vacillate, and in December it announced that it would not proceed with the change; on the contrary, it promulgated War Measure 145, which, by banning all strikes by African workers, strengthened the racial divide.

Whilst the SATLC had frequently called for the kind of reform agreed in April, the policy of the Chamber of Mines was much more conservative, and the South African Federated Chamber of Industries (SAFCI) was non-committal.[43] Within the cabinet however, the argument was finely balanced, and new factors seem to have swung the scales to the side of repression. In particular, referring to a strike wave that occurred at the end of 1942, Smuts explained: 'Things are inconvenient now; there is a wave of [industrial] unrest.'[44] Statements by Madeley show that he was particularly disturbed by Indians combining with Africans in Durban and by the militancy of African strikers in Johannesburg, and comments by a third minister indicate that following a strike by Johannesburg sweet workers he was fearful of whites uniting with Africans. Thus, whilst a modicum of discontent had stimulated the government to contemplate change, the much sharper unrest of late 1942, involving an unprecedented level of multiracial unity, encouraged retreat. It is also possible that in April Smuts had agreed to the new policy because he feared a Japanese invasion and that once this threat had receded, as it had by the end of 1942, he returned to his old ways.[45]

Once again, one can discern important similarities between the US and South Africa. Notably, collaboration between labour leaders and the state was a significant feature of both countries' wartime industrial relations. Also, in a parallel and related development, there were specific improvements for black workers: in the US these included Executive Order 8802, and in South Africa wages were raised and, for a limited period, pass law administration was relaxed. However, War Measure 145 signalled a new and different trend, towards intensified attacks on Africans, and it demonstrated that on the 'race' issue there was still a big difference between the two countries. Ultimately, in South Africa, the weight of support for egalitarian change was relatively less than in the US. Crucially, perhaps, South Africa had the Chamber of Mines, with its reliance on coerced labour, and the US had a more confident, more racially integrated labour movement, exemplified by the CIO.

STRIKES, PAY AND UNION GROWTH

During and immediately after the war, both countries experienced record levels of strike action. Notwithstanding legal restrictions and union opposition, the stoppages – which generally were over pay – were often successful, and they probably contributed to the increase in trade union membership that occurred in both countries.

For South Africa, the official statistics understate the level of strike action that occurred between 1939 and 1945, and this was probably part of a conscious concern to downplay the extent of wartime disunity.[46] Using data culled from state archives, press reports and secondary sources it has been possible to reconstruct more accurate statistics, and these are presented below. The figure for 'days lost' during the war years, 439 919, might be compared with the Department of Labour's figure of 199 592. In general, the statistics demonstrate that from 1942 – when there were more strikers and more 'days lost' than in any year since 1922 – there was an upsurge in the level of industrial unrest. This peaked in 1946 and 1947 (when a record was established for 'days lost' that was not surpassed until 1987), before subsiding in 1948. Whilst it was rare for strikes involving white workers to end in defeat, from mid-1944, with the government adopting an even tougher stance against African workers, most black strikes were unsuccessful; including, in particular, the 1946 strike by 62 000 African miners, much the largest stoppage of the period. (See Table 11.1.)[47]

Table 11.1   Revised South African Strike Statistics, 1939–1948

Year	Strikes[a]	Black strikers	White strikers	Total strikers	Black days lost	White days lost	Total days lost
1939	23 (23)	4 894	104	4 998	4 351	128	4 479
1940	29 (27)	1 281	1 419	2 700	4 085	4 116	8 201
1941	43 (40)	5 142	733	5 875	25 078	7 232	32 310
1942	72 (69)	16 031	1 273	17 304	83 407	11 743	95 150
1943	64 (56)	10 097	8 887	18 984	51 861	62 825	114 686
1944	59 (56)	12 277	321	12 598	64 367	1 790	66 157
1945	66 (65)	13 963	2 326	16 289	110 500	8 436	118 936
Subtotal	356 (336)	63 685	15 063	78 748	343 649	96 270	439 919
1946	62 (58)	84 644	11 512	96 156	158 281	57 163	215 444
1947	68 (68)	6 734	22 268	29 002	684 026	694 945	1 378 971
1948	47 (46)	2 894	1 137	4 031	11 832	12 881	24 713
TOTAL	533 (508)	157 957	49 980	207 937	1 197 788	861 259	2 059 047

[a] Figures in brackets indicate the number of strikes upon which the data for 'strikers' and 'days lost' is based.
Source: Alexander, 'Industrial Conflict', Appendix 1.

The new data demonstrate that there was a much higher level of unrest among white workers than has previously been appreciated.[48] Specifically, three major white workers' strikes were excluded from the official schedules (and, hitherto, these went unrecorded in academic literature). First, in May 1943, there were sit-down strikes by white and coloured workers in 22 Transvaal clothing factories. This action was followed by a three-day lock-out of 9000 garment workers (more than 70 per cent of whom were women), who eventually won an impressive wage increase. Secondly, that September, 900 building artisans employed on defence contracts in Durban went on strike for three weeks; a pay cut was withdrawn, then, because of fears of generalised strike action, a threat of prosecution was removed. Finally, in March 1945, at least 1400 Durban engineering workers, mostly employed on urgent naval ship repairs, went on strike for five days over pay; in the end there was compromise following a direct appeal by the Controller of Manpower. In addition to these stoppages, there was the most disruptive strike of the war (in terms of 'days lost'); this was the 1943 shop workers' strike in Johannesburg and Cape Town, which mainly involved white women.[49] Also, in 1947, there was an even more disruptive action, the Transvaal building workers' strike, which, despite its scale and significance, has been ignored by those writers who assume that white working-class militancy terminated in 1922.[50]

In the US, during the three years and eight months that the country was at war, there were more strikes and more strikers than in any period of the same length.[51] Two groups were notably prominent: mine workers who, under the leadership of John L. Lewis, held a series of strikes in 1943, and auto workers, who were central to the unofficial strikes that were an important feature of these years. Between 1941 and 1946 about half of all strikers were CIO members (who comprised about two in five trade unionists).[52] As the war ended, strike action reached unprecedented levels. General Motors, steel, electrical, packinghouse, rail and, once again, mine workers all joined massive strikes, and in 1946 there were 4.6 million strikers (14.5 per cent of the workforce), who were responsible for 116 million 'days lost'.[53] On the other side of the world, the South African Department of Labour blamed these strikes, and those occurring in Britain, for disrupting local adjustment to post-war conditions.[54]

A number of factors may help to explain the high strike rate of both countries. First, because of army recruitment, economic expansion and a high turnover of labour, many workers were young and fairly new in their jobs, and, thus, commitment to the unions' anti-strike policies was probably less than it might otherwise have been. Secondly, as a consequence of the war, the labour market was relatively tight, making it more difficult for employers to take punitive action against union militants. Thirdly, again because of the war, there was a high level of inflation in both countries,[55] and this encouraged action over wages and hours. These two linked issues were raised as major concerns in 45.5 per cent of US strikes occurring between 1942 and 1945,[56] and they comprised 54.2 per cent of the demands that I have recorded for South African stoppages in the years 1939 to 1945. Fourthly, it is possible that the success of many wartime strikes encouraged further action. In both countries there was an increase in real wages, and, at least with regard to South Africa, militancy provides the main explanation.[57] There were numerous examples of wage-strike victories, and in manufacturing there was a definite correlation between the higher levels of strike action among Africans and their proportionately larger wage rises. Although much of the overall pay increase, especially for poorer workers, came from a statutory Cost of Living Allowance, this was introduced because, as Smuts put it, he was 'anxious to keep [his] workers in good temper'.[58]

Also, in both countries, there was a substantial expansion in the proportion of workers who were trade union members. In the US, membership increased from just under 9 million in 1939 and 1940 to just under 15 million in 1945 and 1946; that is, from about 27 per cent to about 36 per cent of the non-agricultural workforce.[59] In South Africa, the registered membership of registered unions increased from just over a quarter of a million in 1939 to more than a third of a million in 1946; the latter figure interestingly representing about 36 per cent of the non-African, non-agricultural workforce.[60] The wartime growth of African unions was even more impressive. At the outbreak of war it was estimated that the Johannesburg-based African unions had about 20 000 members, in June 1941 these unions claimed 37 655 members, and in February 1943 Gana Makabeni, the CNETU President, said that on the Witwatersrand there were 44 mainly-African unions with 80 000 members. Outside Johannesburg there were clusters of African unions in a number of towns, and in both Durban and Pretoria their membership probably exceeded 10 000.[61] At their peak, in late 1943 or early 1944, the African unions probably had between 100 000 and 150 000 members nationally. At this point, one in three or four Africans employed in industry and commerce was unionised (a density of membership not surpassed until the late 1980s).[62]

Unionisation occurred in two ways: passive (the product of, for instance, maintenance of membership agreements in the US or stop order provisions in South Africa) and active (workers voluntarily, personally paying dues to a union activist or official). Either way the process was linked, more or less directly, to the increased confidence of workers, demonstrated in particular by the level and character of strike action.[63] Whilst employer and government support for passive recruitment probably deterred unions from encouraging militancy, the original agreements and provisions arose from increased worries about the possibility of industrial action.

With South Africa's African unions, active recruitment (often at hostels) was always the main means of establishing and maintaining union membership. As with other workers, Africans joined unions in order to improve their wages and conditions, and if they achieved this and there was someone to collect their dues, they usually stayed in the union whilst they remained at the same workplace. However, partly because of migrancy, labour turnover was very high,[64] and if the union failed to secure further improvements, membership could decline rather rapidly. During the early war years, advances were being made and membership spiralled, but, as we have seen, from early 1943 and particularly after mid-1944 government policy made it much more difficult for Africans to better their wages. Also, the reluctance of many African leaders to take strike action may have made matters worse, and from late 1944 rising African unemployment probably dampened confidence. Eventually, the repression of the 1946 miners' strike led to the destruction of what had been the largest single African union, but African trade unionism was already in retreat by this stage.

So, both countries experienced an exceptional amount of strike action combined with a qualitative increase in union membership. The common experience of war probably contributed to this process in a variety of ways, including a young workforce, relative scarcity of labour and inflation. The one partial exception to the similarity between the two countries was, once again, African labour. Following the promulgation of War Measure 145, African unions encountered new obstacles to improving conditions and, by early 1944, they were in decline.

EGALITARIANISM AND WAR

But, what impact did war-related militancy and unionisation have on race relations among workers? This question takes us to two important controversies. For the US, the key issue concerns the extent to which the CIO was a positive force in the fight for racial equality. W.E.B. Du Bois, writing about the period 1917–47, concluded that the CIO was probably more successful than any other movement in 'softening race prejudice among the masses'.[65] By contrast, Herbert Hill has been highly critical, arguing that for white workers protection of privilege was the norm, and that where egalitarianism was espoused this was no more than rhetoric and expediency.[66] Regarding South Africa, debate has centred on the Nationalist victory of 1948. Whilst some writers have presented white workers as generally pro-apartheid, others have pointed to the non-racialism of the SATLC.[67]

In considering these questions, we might begin by observing racial aspects of strikes. For South Africa, if a mixed strike is defined as one involving at least a tenth black workers and a tenth white workers, 10.6 per cent of black strikers and 53.5 per cent of white strikers participated in mixed strikes during the war years. Although racial division was clearly extensive, it is unlikely that multiracial stoppages were as widespread at any other time in South African history, and it is reasonable to assume that a significant number of white workers gained a positive impression of black/white unity.[68] One example will serve to highlight this multiracialism and simultaneously illustrate its limitations. The 1942 sweet workers' strike involved about 400 members of the Sweet Workers' Union (SWU), mostly Afrikaner women, and about 300 African male labourers, members of the parallel African SWU. During the dispute, which lasted nearly five weeks, representatives of the African union attended the main strike committee, there were demonstrations involving both unions, and following a proposal from one of the Afrikaner women all strikers received £1 per week strike pay. However, because of worries about adverse publicity and a desire not to provoke the police, picketing was restricted to whites, and when the strikers celebrated the outcome of their action – a substantial pay rise for both groups – it was at separate functions. Thus, whilst economic pressures brought the workers together and created the basis for a famous victory, they were forced apart by social and legal pressures.[69]

For the US, attention has focused on hate strikes, stoppages by white workers protesting against the movement of black workers into all-white departments. Such events were appalling, but one wonders whether they have always been sufficiently contextualised by US writers. First, there is a matter of scale. Between March and June 1943, when these actions reached their peak, they were responsible for 100 000 'days lost'.[70] Although this is a large number, since there was a total of 6.9 million 'days lost' in the same period, there must have been many more instances of black and white workers striking in a common cause.[71] Secondly, in South Africa, there is little evidence of hate strikes, at least in this period.[72] Whilst this may, at first, seem rather surprising, it was probably because South African employers rarely challenged traditional job hierarchies. That is, hate strikes should be regarded as an unwelcome by-product of positive change. Thirdly, hate strikes generally failed, and in large measure this was because of opposition from organised labour. In particular, in Detroit, where the strikes were concentrated, the United Auto Workers (UAW) appears to have played an exemplary role (and this was also true of the union's response to the Detroit race riot of 1943, when 34 people were killed).[73] Overall, in the US, as in South Africa, wartime strikes probably had a directly beneficial impact on race relations.

Moreover, in both countries, wartime militancy was associated with other broadly positive trends, including greater involvement of black workers in labour and political movements, trade union federations becoming more overtly political, and some growth in support for left-wing politics. Regarding the first of these, in South Africa, in addition to the upsurge in African trade unionism, the registered unions were becoming blacker. To a large extent this reflected the changing composition of the workforce, a willingness (usually restricted in some way) to recruit black workers, and the general increase in union membership, but there were also new developments. First, trade unionism spread to previously unorganised industries, often ones dominated by black workers, and many of the new unions were eager to recruit all workers, including those who were not 'employees'. In Durban, where these new unions were a notably potent force, they were usually organised by Indians; in the Western Cape coloured workers were often prominent.[74] Secondly, in 1944, the Supreme Court accepted the GWU's contention that African women workers were 'employees' (because they were not 'pass bearing'), thus facilitating their recruitment by registered unions. Thirdly, among some craft unions, there was a continuation of an already existing tendency to expand the categories of workers who could become members; for instance, in Durban, the largest engineering and building unions both absorbed mainly-Indian unions. For the US, the CIO claimed that the African-American membership of the labour movement grew from less than 125 000 in 1935 to more than 500 000 in 1942 (most of whom were members of CIO unions).[75] Moreover, African-Americans played a key role in building the CIO, particularly in the South, and in a number of unions, including the UAW, black workers were elected or appointed to senior leadership positions.[76]

The wartime mood of black assertiveness was also expressed in political movements. In the US, membership of the principal civil rights organisation, the National Association for the Advancement of Colored People, soared from 50 000 in 1940 to nearly 450 000 six years later.[77] In South Africa, Johannesburg witnessed two 20 000-strong marches; first, in May 1944, by supporters of the Anti-Pass Campaign, and then the following year to join CNETU's Victory Day rally. The leadership of the African National Congress did respond to this new confidence, but slowly, and from 1943 three new organisations began attracting black supporters; these were the Non-European Unity Movement, the African Democratic Party, and the ANC's Youth League (which included Nelson Mandela among its leadership). Moreover, in both countries, labour and political mobilisation tended to reinforce each other. The CIO and NAACP often co-operated with each other (over desegregation campaigns and against strike-breaking, for example);[78] so too, to a more limited degree, did CNETU and the ANC (for instance, in support of the campaign to redefine 'employee' and against the pass laws). Although the SATLC was deeply divided and ineffective on key political issues, its local committees and affiliates (even some of its craft union affiliates) did provide valued practical assistance for African unions.

Also, with the possible exception of the AFL, the union federations became more involved in politics. It is likely that this was partly a response to the new mood of confidence among ordinary workers, but it was probably also a product of new challenges raised by wartime collaboration. In South Africa, although union leaders were less central to Labour Party affairs than their British counterparts, after the SATLC's 1942 Conference it and the SALP established a Collaboration Committee, and in 1945 the Mechanics' Unions' Joint Executive (which co-ordinated the work of the engineering unions) recognised the SALP as its representative in parliament. The party also experienced a mild leftward radicalisation and increased popularity during the war. In 1941, its conference called for

African workers to be accepted as 'employees', and although, following the government's volte-face there was some retreat from this position, an organised group of 'progressives' continued to push for change on this and other matters.[79] In October 1945, when the SALP won control of Johannesburg City Council, a leading 'progressive', Jessie McPherson, was elected as mayor, and the following year she became the party's national chairperson. In the US, the main development was the establishment of the CIO's Political Action Committee (PAC) in 1943. This was a double-edged move. On the one hand, the PAC helped stifle an impulse towards building a CIO-based labour party, on the other, it mobilised workers for political activity in a manner regarded as anathema by the AFL (including a special appeal to black workers).

Further, whatever Hill might say about the CIO's leadership, there was a genuine egalitarian tradition in the US, associated in part with United Mine Workers, but also, as in South Africa, with the Communist Party.[80] In both countries, the Communist Party was centrally involved in civil rights and union building activities during the war, and as a consequence it was able to extend its influence. In South Africa, where possible, it built multiracial unions, but, although slow off the mark, it was also involved in CNETU. Indeed, in 1945 a party member, J.B. Marks, the African miners' leader, defeated Makabeni for the CNETU presidency. Following a period of debilitating in-fighting during the 1930s, party membership rocketed from only 280 in 1940 to 2,700 in 1944 (by which time it is likely that most of its members were black).[81] In the US, the Communist Party was a dominant or significant influence in a number of unions, including the UAW, and membership was probably growing, at least until 1942, when there were 44 000 registered members, the most the party had ever recorded.[82] Also, in both countries, a minority of workers was drawn towards Trotskyism. In South Africa, although this tradition was small and poorly organised, one particular leader, Dan Koza, was the most effective African trade unionist of the period, and he led a sizeable left opposition within CNETU. In the US, the main organisation, the Socialist Workers' Party, grew to 1500 members before the end of the war (most of whom were industrial workers).[83]

During the war, union organisation became stronger, there was some radicalisation and real wages improved. Nevertheless, there were definite limits to the changes that occurred. The AFL and SATLC continued to accept affiliations from colour-bar unions; in the SATLC's case, at the end of 1946, 35 out of its 115 unions were exclusively white.[84] Moreover, the left-wing GWU excluded African men and it placed its black members in a separate branch with inferior status. Sachs was not a racist, but he felt, wrongly in my view, that it was necessary to make such concessions in order to avoid alienating the union's Afrikaner membership.[85] In the US South, the CIO usually accepted that segregated dances and dressing rooms could not be challenged (and, of course, social segregation was the norm in South Africa). Worse, once the war had started, the CIO abandoned its campaign to organise the South, and leading Communist Party trade unionists went along with this decision.[86] Furthermore, in the US, the Communist Party advocated 'no strike' pledges, and in South Africa it generally discouraged strikes, even among African labourers paid next to nothing.[87]

After the war, there was a rapid shift in the political mood of both countries.[88] This Cold War swing, which operated at both official and popular levels, would be a valuable subject for further comparative study. Briefly, although the post-war mood was foreshadowed by earlier developments, these did not represent the dominant trend, and even African South Africans were able to make some headway until near the end of hostilities. Then, in South Africa, drought and peace brought unemployment, particularly among Africans; the cabinet instructed registered unions to expel African male members; a split in the SALP leadership led to the loss of five of its nine MPs (including Madeley), and it rapidly lost electoral support; CPSA membership tumbled, and after the African miners had been crushed eight of its leaders were charged with sedition; then, in 1946 and 1947, members of the all-white Mine Workers' Union engaged in two strikes with strongly racist overtones. At the 1948 election, Smuts was defeated by the pro-apartheid National Party, and the new government proceeded to destroy the remnants of independent trade unionism. This was made easier by the fragmentation of the SATLC (partly a consequence of the CIO-provoked division of the international trade union movement). In the US, the key event was the strongly anti-union Labor-Management Relations (Taft-Hartley) Act passed in 1947. Before this, however, Harry Truman, a more conservative figure than Roosevelt, had become President, and in general the unions had failed to advance their position as a result of the 1946 strike wave. The NWLB, FEPC, PAC and NAACP membership were all casualties of the domestic Cold War, and in 1949–50 the CIO lost over one million members when it purged ten affiliates. In both countries, just as advances for the left and for black people had been intertwined, so too were the defeats.

During the war, an increased number of whites (as well as blacks) had been willing to support, in one way or another, the development of a more egalitarian society. There were a number of reasons why this should be so. For instance, in South Africa, the threat of fascism at home and abroad encouraged more people to become politically active; the announcement of the Atlantic Charter, the resistance of the Red Army and even the success of the British Labour Party provided inspiration; and within the army the liberal-minded Education Service and communist-led Springbok Legion contributed to the politicisation of young soldiers. In addition, it seems likely that successful strikes, many of them multiracial, and the growth of trade unions, among white and black workers, made a significant contribution. After the war, the process was reversed. Even then, however, on the eve of the 1948 election, Sachs, who was described as a 'Jew communist' by the Nationalists, became the single most influential leader within the SATLC. The response of white workers to their black fellow workers was complex, but it is likely that most rejected the party of apartheid in 1948. In wartime South Africa, as in the US, material interests had encouraged black and white workers to combine, and even in South Africa opposition to racial discrimination was encouraged by a small, but significant, egalitarian tradition among white workers.

CONCLUSION

In focusing on race and labour in South Africa and the US, this essay has sought to distinguish between similar wartime trends and underlying differences. Regarding similarities, in both countries, largely as a consequence of the war, this was a period of extensive industrial conflict and rising union membership. In both countries, the working class was transformed, becoming larger, younger, blacker and more female,[89] and, it would seem, less willing to accept admonishments not to strike. The war also tightened labour markets, thus promoting self-reliance among activists; and it also led to increased inflation, thereby creating pressure to improve wages. Moreover, since most strikes were successful, they tended to boost self-confidence. At the beginning of the war, labour leaders entered new collaborative arrangements with governments and employers, and although these were intended to reduce industrial stoppages they also encouraged unionisation, probably with contradictory effects. Whilst some militancy was racist in character, the vast majority was not; many strikes, even in South Africa, were multiracial. In both countries, there was improved organisation among black people (particularly workers) and an egalitarian tendency among whites (including white workers). Overall, it is likely that industrial militancy contributed to these trends. In general, workers benefited from stronger unions, improved wages and greater self-assurance. These features of the war years were especially marked among black workers. However, in both countries, with the end of the Second World War, the reformist drift was reversed as the Cold War made its mark.

There were also important differences between the two countries. During the war, these were highlighted in the contrast between US Executive Order 8802, banning racist hiring, and South African War Measure 145, reinforcing racial divisions. The latter signalled a shift towards harsher treatment of African workers, leading later to the quashing of the African miners' strike. In the process, African trade unionism was severely weakened and possibilities for multiracial working-class unity were substantially reduced. In South Africa, the balance of forces on questions of 'race' was more reactionary than in the US, and War Measure 145 reflected a reassertion of conservatism and the overwhelming of wartime liberalism. Compared with the US, South African capitalism was more dependent on forced labour, particularly within the dominant mining sector. Also, although South African trade unionists considered the CIO option, they rejected it. South Africa was less industrial than the US, the social gap between its black and white workers far greater, and its labour movement's record of struggle less successful. Finally, the key underlying differences were not merely ones of social structure, demography and economic development, but were also those related to the contrasting political settlements produced, on the one hand, by the US Civil War and, on the other, by the Anglo-South African War.

Nevertheless, at least during the war, on matters of race and labour, the similarities between the two countries were marked. Too marked, it seems to me, for it to be possible to claim that either country was exceptional. On the contrary, the comparison has illustrated that each was subject to processes which cannot adequately be explained in national terms. Without taking full account of the world economic system and the world war, it is not possible to adequately explain the unique history of either country.[90] Further, although exceptionalism, of whatever variety, embodies an *implicit* comparison (usually with an ideal type), there is a danger of exceptionalist conclusions discouraging *explicitly* comparative study, thereby stifling an assessment of the importance of international processes within national histories. Thus, this essay seeks both to challenge exceptionalist accounts within the specific context of the Second World War, and also to suggest that methodologically exceptionalism is unhelpful. Finally, on the basis of the account presented here, one might hypothesise that, confronted with similar circumstances (such as those produced by the war), workers and their rulers tend to respond in similar ways, regardless of nationality. To the extent that there were differences – notably with regard to race relations – they are perhaps best understood as a consequence of the relative underdevelopment of South African capitalism and by reference to the scars of its workers' defeats.

NOTES

* The author wishes to thank the following for comments on an earlier draft of this chapter: Simon Adams, Keith Flett, Rick Halpern, Baruch Hirson, Bruce Nelson, Hilary Sapire.

1. See Stanley B. Greenberg, *Race and State in Capitalist Development: South Africa in Comparative Perspective* (Johannesburg, 1980); George M. Fredrickson, *White Supremacy: a Comparative Study in American and South African History* (New York, 1981); Howard Lamar and Leonard Thompson, eds, *The Frontier in History: North America and South Africa Compared* (New Haven, 1981); John W. Cell, *The Highest Stage of White Supremacy* (Cambridge, 1982).
2. Whilst judgements about South Africa are based on my recent PhD dissertation, opinions about the US are drawn from a limited range of sources; thus conclusions should be regarded as suggestive rather than definitive. For further discussion and fuller references on South Africa, see Peter Alexander, 'Industrial Conflict, Race and the South African State, 1939–1948' (PhD thesis, University of London, 1994).
3. For a pioneering critique of the former, see Martin Legassick, 'The Frontier Tradition in South African Historiography' in Shula Marks and Anthony Atmore, eds, *Economy and Society in Pre-industrial South Africa* (London, 1980). For the latter view, see South African Communist Party, 'The Road to South African Freedom' in *South African Communists Speak: Documents from the History of the South African Communist Party, 1915–1980* (London, 1981), 297–307.
4. See, in particular, Stanley Trapido, 'South Africa in a Comparative Study of Industrialisation', *Journal of Development Studies*, 7:3 (1971).
5. Fredrickson, *White Supremacy*, 212–34.
6. Greenberg, *Race and State*, 273–355.
7. In particular, Jon Lewis, *Industrialisation and Trade Union Organisation in South Africa, 1924–55: the Rise and Fall of the South African Trades and Labour Council* (Cambridge, 1984); Eddie Webster, *Cast in a Racial Mould: Labour Process and Trade Unionism in Foundries* (Johannesburg, 1985); Robert Fine with Denis Davis, *Beyond Apartheid: Labour and Liberation in South Africa* (London, 1990); Iris Berger, *Threads of Solidarity: Women in South African Industry, 1900–1980* (Bloomington, 1992).
8. Greenberg, *Race and State*, 29.
9. See, for instance, Frederick A. Johnstone, *Class, Race and Gold: a Study of Class Relations and Racial Discrimination in South Africa* (London, 1976).
10. Bureau of the Census, *Historical Statistics of the US: Colonial Times to*

1970 (Washington, 1975), 1–12; Bureau of Census and Statistics, *Union Statistics for Fifty Years, 1910–60* (Pretoria, 1960).

11.   This formulation involves an explicit analogy with the German 'marriage of iron and rye'; Trapido, 'South Africa in a Comparative Study', 311.

12.   Gold was much the most important South African export (comprising 79 per cent of the total in 1941), and following the 1941 budget the mines provided 33 per cent of all government revenue. Although, from 1943, private industry contributed more to national income than mining, it was 1945 before the former began to employ more workers than the latter.

13.   Here I am at odds with Rob Davies, who argued that industrial capital was hegemonic in the early 1940s; R.H. Davies, *Capital, State and White Labour in South Africa 1900–1960: an Historical Materialist Analysis of Class Formation and Class Relations* (Brighton, 1979). See also, B. Fine and Z. Rustomjee, 'The Political Economy of South Africa in the Interwar Period', *Social Dynamics*, 18:2 (1992), who argue that mining capital was dominant.

14.   Indeed, largely because South Africa produced few machine tools and it became difficult to import them, wartime expansion led to even lower levels of capital intensity. My analysis of mechanisation and its industrial and political impact is at variance with other writers, notably Lewis, *Industrialisation and Trade Union Organisation*. For my response, see Peter Alexander, 'Collaboration and Control: Engineering Unions and the South African State, 1939–45', *South African Journal of Sociology*, 27:2 (1996).

15.   As late as 1948, 64 per cent of Africans employed in the Transvaal engineering industry were housed in compounds. See also, Doug Hindson, *Pass Controls and the Urban African Proletariat* (Johannesburg, 1987), 53–5; and Phillip Bonner, 'African Urbanisation on the Rand Between the 1930s and 1960s: Its Social Character and Political Consequences', *Journal of Southern African Studies*, 21:1 (1995), 118.

16.   For South Africa, Office of Census and Statistics, *Census of Industrial Establishments* 1941/2 (Pretoria), Tables 6 and 7. For the US, Department of Labor, *Negroes in the United States: Their Employment and Economic Status* (Washington, 1952), 24. In 1939, in manufacturing, the average white South African worker was paid £240 and the average US worker (including African-Americans) received £333.

17.   *Census of Industrial Establishments* 1941/2, Tables 6 and 7.

18.   Fredrickson, *White Supremacy*, esp. 256. In many ways the position of Indians in Natal, most of whom were descended from indentured labourers, was similar to that of coloureds in the Cape. In South Africa, as in the US, there were significant regional differences, but lack of space prevents me pursuing them. In addition to the demographic variation, to which I have alluded, nearly all of South Africa's gold mining and nearly half its manufacturing were concentrated in the Transvaal. Also, the Transvaal and Orange Free State had been Boer republics, whereas the Cape and Natal had been British colonies.

19.   The mining revolution of the late nineteenth century, which transformed South Africa, was based particularly on gold mining, and from 1930 mining contributed more to national income than agriculture. Publicly-owned industry, which in the 1940s was far less substantial than private industry, was more concerned than private industry with providing employment for white

workers. For a recent history of state industries, see Nancy L. Clark, *Manufacturing Apartheid: State Corporations in South Africa* (New Haven, 1994).

20. In 1939, whites comprised 37.2 per cent of the workforce in private industry, but only 11.3 per cent in mining. At the same date, on average, blacks in private industry received 24.4 per cent of white pay, but in mining the figure was only 9.0 per cent. Bureau of Census and Statistics, *Union Statistics*, G-5, G-6, G-20.

21. L. Naude (Albert Hertzog), *Die Nasionale Party en die Mynwerker* (Pretoria, 1969), 19, cited in Dan O'Meara, *Volkscapitalisme* (Johannesburg, 1983), 91.

22. *Union Statistics*, G-6.

23. Import substitution industries developed more rapidly after Pearl Harbor, which led to the allocation of allied shipping on the basis of 'end use'.

24. South Africa declared its opposition to Germany only a day after Britain, and its army made an important contribution to Commonwealth forces, particularly in Africa. As with the US, black soldiers were attached to segregated regiments; unlike African-Americans, black South Africans were regarded as non-combatants (although many acquired small arms for self-protection by the end of the war).

25. *Union Statistics*, G-6.

26. In 1946, 59.6 per cent of South Africa's urban population was black (42.2 per cent African), and in 1950 non-whites comprised 10.4 per cent of the US urban population. Native Laws Commission of Enquiry, *Report* (Pretoria, 1948), 6; Bureau of the Census, *Historical Statistics of the United States*, P 1–12.

27. For the US, see references to hate strikes below. For South Africa, see O'Meara, *Volkscapitalisme*, 242–3.

28. Office of Census and Statistics, *Census of Industrial Establishments* 1944/5, Tables 6 and 7. Department of Labor, *Negroes in the United States*, 24.

29. However, in both countries, levels of segregation were probably higher in the 1940s than the 1930s (partly because of rapid urbanisation), although lower than they became in the 1950s. Douglas S. Massey and Nancy A. Denton, *American Apartheid: Segregation and the Making of the Underclass* (Cambridge, MA., 1993); A.J. Christopher, 'Segregation Levels in South African Cities, 1911–1985', *The International Journal of African Historical Studies*, 25:3 (1992).

30. For instance, Manning Marable, *Black American Politics: From the Washington Marches to Jesse Jackson* (London, 1985), 86–7.

31. Jack and Ray Simons, *Class and Colour in South Africa 1850–1950* (London, 1983), 534; Department of Labour, 'Minutes of a Conference of Divisional Inspectors Held . . . 8th–9th November, 1944', ARB A181 pt 2, State Archives, Pretoria.

32. Dale T. Hiestand, *Economic Growth and Employment Opportunities for Minorities* (New York, 1964), 43, cited in Fredrickson, *White Supremacy*, 237.

33. Department of Labour, *Report* 1938, Table 1, 1940, Tables 4 and 9, 1946, Table 9. However, it is likely that this figure gives an exaggerated impression of the proportion of black workers engaged in skilled and semi-skilled work. It does not include wage determinations that applied only to unskilled workers. It also excludes industries covered by industrial agreements; these

tended to be more fully dominated by white workers, such as engineering, where in 1946 less than 6 per cent of Africans were not employed as labourers.

34. Robert H. Zieger, *American Workers, American Unions*, 2nd ed. (Baltimore, 1994), 26–46; Nelson Lichtenstein, *Labor's War at Home: the CIO in World War II* (Cambridge, 1982), 32–6.

35. Zieger, *American Workers*, 82; Philip S. Foner, *Organized Labor and the Black Worker 1619–1973* (New York, 1974); Eric Arnesen, ' "Like Banquo's Ghost, it Will not Down": the Race Question and the American Railroad Brotherhoods, 1880–1920', *American Historical Review* 99:5 (1994), 1601–33. In both countries, the railway unions were racially exclusive; by contrast, both countries' garment unions were racially inclusive.

36. For an insider's account of one of these unions, see Bettie du Toit, *Ukubamba Amadolo: Workers' Struggles in the South African Textile Industry* (London, 1978).

37. Although, partly perhaps because of opposition from the CPSA, no definite steps were taken. Bill Andrews, the party's national chair and a former SATLC general secretary, offered an alternative perspective. Like Sachs he was impressed with the CIO, but he was pessimistic about the possibility of involving key white workers, in a similar South African organisation, and he argued that, instead, the left should attempt to reform the SATLC. 'We Must Learn From the Workers of the USA', *Garment Worker* Jan./Feb. 1945; 'A CIO for S. Africa?', *Guardian*, 8 April 1943; Lewis, *Industrialization and Trade Union Organization*, 161. For an account of the GWU by its general secretary, see E.S. Sachs, *Rebels' Daughters* (London, 1957).

38. For instance, at the 1940 SATLC conference, an anti-war motion received 23 votes to 30 against. Following the German invasion of Russia, this left-wing opposition evaporated, but many Afrikaner and African workers still refused to support the war. For the US, which did not enter the war until late 1941, see Gary Gerstle, 'The Working Class Goes to War', *Mid-America*, 75:3 (1993), 303–22.

39. For South Africa, Alexander, 'Collaboration and Control'. For the US, Lichtenstein, *Labor's War at Home*, 51–85; Patrick Renshaw, *American Labour and Consensus Capitalism, 1935–1990* (Basingstoke, 1991), 50–7; Melvyn Dubofsky, *The State and Labor in Modern America* (Chapel Hill, 1995), 179.

40. For South Africa, particularly Baruch Hirson, *Revolutions in my Life* (Johannesburg, 1995), 175. For the US, Martin Glaberman, *Wartime Strikes: the Struggle Against the No-Strike Pledge in the UAW During World War II* (Detroit, 1980), 10, 34; Lichtenstein, *Labor's War at Home*, 73–4, 81; Gerstle, 'Working Class Goes to War', 305.

41. Philip S. Foner, *Organized Labor and the Black Worker, 1619–1973* (New York, 1974), 243.

42. Secretary for Native Affairs to Secretary for Labour, 10 April 1942, NTS 35/362/1 pt 2, State Archives, Pretoria. David Duncan, 'The State and African Trade Unions, 1918–1948', *Social Dynamics*, 18:2 (1992), 66, misrepresents the significance of this event.

43. At a government conference in October 1943 the SATLC's president and general secretary repudiated the SATLC's position, but it is unlikely that

this was decisive. I would certainly contest the claim that 'there was more support for African unions from white capital than from white labour'; Merle Lipton, *Capitalism and Apartheid* (Aldershot, 1986), 194.

44. *South African Outlook* 1 February 1943.

45. This argument is presented by Baruch Hirson, *Yours for the Union* (London, 1989), 96.

46. Alexander, 'Industrial Conflict', 67–71. US wartime strike statistics should also be questioned. See *Monthly Labor Review*, 57:3 (1943), 537; Glaberman, *Wartime Strikes*, 49.

47. The best account of the strike is that provided by T. Dunbar Moodie with Vivienne Ndatshe, *Going for Gold: Men, Mines, and Migration* (Johannesburg, 1994).

48. In general, both during and immediately after the war, white workers were no less militant than black workers.

49. See particularly, Norman Herd, *Counter Attack: the Story of the South African Shopworkers* (Cape Town, 1974).

50. For example, Davies, *Capital, State and White Labour*. The most detailed account of the strike is unpublished: Jon Lewis, 'The South African Labour Movement and the Building Workers' Strike' (Johannesburg, c.1980).

51. Art Preis, *Labor's Giant Step: the First Twenty Years of the CIO, 1936–1955* (New York, 1964), 236.

52. Lichtenstein, *Labor's War at Home*, 135; *Statistical Abstract of the United States* (Washington, 1950), Table 915.

53. Bureau of the Census, *Statistical Abstract of the United States* (Washington, 1950), Table 208. In general, US workers were probably more militant than their South African counterparts. For South African manufacturing, I estimate that an average of 20 workers per thousand joined strikes in the years 1944 to 1946; this figure is based on my own strike data and *Census of Industrial Establishments* 1946/7. It is possible that the comparable figure for the US was seven times as great; Lichtenstein, *Labor's War at Home*, 134.

54. Department of Labour, *Report* 1946 (Pretoria, 1948), 5.

55. Department of Labor, *Consumers' Prices in the United States 1942–48: Analysis of Changes in the Cost of Living* (Washington, 1949); 'Official Union and Foreign Statistics', *South African Journal of Economics*, various issues.

56. *Statistical Abstract of the United States* (Washington, 1945), Table 174, 1947, Table 240.

57. For other explanations, which I regard as unfounded, see Simons and Simons, *Class and Color*, 555; Lipton, *Capitalism and Apartheid*, 21, 196; Davies, *Capital, State and White Labour*, 292.

58. Smuts to M. Gillett, 24 July 1941, Smuts Papers, State Archives, Pretoria.

59. *Statistical Abstract of the United States* 1950, Table 915; Renshaw, *American Labour*, 73.

60. *Union Statistics*, G-18; *Census, 1946*.

61. For Durban unions, see David Hemson, 'Class Consciousness and Migrant Workers: Dock Workers of Durban' (PhD thesis, Warwick University, 1979), and Pauline Podbrey, *White Girl in Search of the Party* (Pietermaritzburg, 1993).

62. See also, Hirson, *Yours for the Union*, 192, 199. Some writers have been

misled by membership figures provided by CNETU and published in *Race Relations News* September 1945. This data – which gives a total membership for African unions (excluding Durban) of 158 000 – is unreliable.

63. For example, Glaberman, *Wartime Strikes*, 45.

64. According to an extensive survey of Johannesburg's 1936 to 1944 pass records, one half of jobs undertaken by Africans ended within six months; Industrial Research Section, Department of Commerce, 'Native Urban Employment: a Study of Johannesburg Employment Records' (University of the Witwatersrand, 1993), 759.

65. W.E.B. Du Bois, 'Race Relations in the United States, 1917–1947', *Phylon*, IX (1948), quoted in Michael Goldfield, 'Race and the CIO: the Possibilities for Racial Egalitarianism During the 1930s and 1940s', *International Labor and Working Class History*, 44 (1993), 2.

66. For valuable discussions of the CIO debate, see Goldfield, 'Race and the CIO', and Rick Halpern, 'Organized Labor, Black Workers, and the Twentieth Century South: the Emerging Revision', *Social History*, 19:3 (October 1994). See also, Herbert Hill, 'Black Labor and Affirmative Action: an Historical Perspective', in Steven Shulman and William Darity Jr, eds, *The Question of Discrimination* (Middletown, 1989). For recent contributions to the debate, see Bruce Nelson, 'Organized Labor and the Struggle for Black Equality in Mobile During World II', *The Journal of American History*, 80 (1993), and Rick Halpern, 'The CIO and the Limits of Labor-based Civil Rights Activism: the Case of Louisiana's Sugar Workers, 1947–1966', in Robert H. Zieger, ed., *Essays in Recent Southern Labor History* (Knoxville, 1997).

67. For the former position, see Davies, *Capital, State and White Labour*, and Lipton, *Capitalism and Apartheid*. For the latter, Lewis, *Industrialisation and Trade Union Organisation*.

68. This assumption is supported by oral testimony from activists involved in the sweet workers' strike of 1942 and the garment and shop workers' strikes of 1943.

69. See also, the account in Berger, *Threads of Solidarity*.

70. Marable, *Black American Politics*, 86. See also, Desmond King, *Separate and Unequal: Black Americans and the US Federal Government* (Oxford, 1995), Appendix 4.

71. *Monthly Labor Review*, 57:2 (1943), 290. In these months, most of the 'days lost' were a consequence of strikes by miners.

72. In 1942, 51 white building workers held a week-long strike in protest against the employment of a black general foreman. Then, in 1944, there was a short strike against the employment of a coloured women in a Germiston garment factory, but when the leaders of this action were sacked they were unable to mobilise a successful defence movement. To the best of my knowledge, these are the only wartime stoppages that might reasonably be called hate strikes.

73. For instance, Robert Korstad and Nelson Lichtenstein, 'Opportunities Found and Lost: Labor, Radicals, and the Early Civil Rights Movement', *Journal of American History*, 75:3 (1988), 798; Roger Keeran, *The Communist Party and the Auto Workers' Unions* (New York, 1980), 232.

74. For Durban, see, for instance, Bill Freund, *Insiders and Outsiders: the*

Indian Working Class of Durban, 1910–1990 (Pietermaritzburg, 1995), who, however, downplays the success of these unions.

75. Foner, *Organized Labor*, 253.
76. Halpern, 'Organized Labor, Black Workers', *passim*; Korstad and Lichtenstein, 'Opportunities Found and Lost', 794.
77. Korstad and Lichtenstein, 'Opportunities Found and Lost', 787.
78. Many of the CIO's anti-discrimination activities were organised through its Committee to Abolish Racial Discrimination; see Robert H. Zieger, *The CIO* (Chapel Hill, 1995), 155–61.
79. Although Sachs had initially supported the 'progressives' he left the SALP prior to the 1943 election. He founded the Independent Labour Party, and later he joined others in forming the Socialist Party, before returning to the SALP prior to the 1948 election.
80. Goldfield, 'Race and the CIO'. See especially Michael Honey, *Southern Labor and Black Civil Rights: Organizing Memphis Workers* (Urbana, 1993).
81. See also, Tom Lodge, 'Class Conflict, Communal Struggle and Patriotic Unity: the Communist Party of South Africa During the Second World War' (Seminar Paper, African Studies Institute, Witwatersrand, 1985); Dominic Fortescue, 'The Communist Party of South Africa and the African Working Class in the 1940s', *International Journal of African Historical Studies*, 24:3 (1991).
82. Glaberman, *Wartime Strikes*, 69.
83. For South Africa, D. Harries (Baruch Hirson), 'Daniel Koza: a Working Class Leader', *African Perspective*, 19 (1981); Baruch Hirson, 'The Trotskyists of South Africa, 1932–48', *Searchlight*, 10 (1993), 51–115. For the US, C.L.R. James *et al.*, *Fighting Racism in World War II* (New York, 1980), 23.
84. H.J. Simons, 'Trade Unions', in Ellen Hellmann, ed., *Handbook on Race Relations in South Africa* (Cape Town, 1949), 165–6.
85. See also, Les Witz, 'Support or Control: Children of the Garment Workers' Union, 1939–1945', in Alan Mabin, ed., *Organisation and Economic Change* (Johannesburg, 1989).
86. Preis, *Labor's Giant Step*, 376.
87. Arguably, the CPSA should also be criticised for opposing a move, supported by its leading black members in the Transvaal, to establish CNETU on a national basis. The party was worried that, if this were done, it would undermine the possibility of reforming the SATLC.
88. For South Africa, see, for instance, Miriam Basner, *Am I an African? The Political Memoirs of H.M. Basner* (Johannesburg, 1993), 177.
89. For the US, see Department of Labor, *Negroes in the United States*, 20.
90. Indeed, a good deal of my argument could be expanded to include Britain and much of the Commonwealth. See, for instance, Richard Croucher, *Engineers at War, 1939–1945* (Basingstoke, 1986); and Douglas Blackmur, *Strikes: Cause, Conduct and Consequences* (Sydney, 1993).

12 Apropos Exceptionalism: Imperial Location and Comparative Histories of South Africa and the United States*

Robert Gregg

[Stanley] wanted 'to punish Bumbireh with the power of a father punishing a stubborn and disobedient son.' The method he chose was to return to Bumbireh and empty box after box of Snider bullets into the ranks of the tribesmen while staying just out of range of their spears and arrows. He claimed to have shot down thirty-three men and wounded a hundred, many fatally. 'We had great cause to feel gratitude.' The 'victory' had put everyone into excellent heart. 'We made a brave show as we proceeded along the coast, the canoes thirty-seven in number containing 500 men paddling to the sound of sonorous drums and the cheering tones of the bugle, the English, the American and Zanzibar flags flying gaily in union with a most animating scene.'

> Thomas Pakenham, *The Scramble for Africa* (1991)

By St Mungo, is there any justice-giustizia in the Globe? Or, is it survival of the fittest and yet another man gone West?

> G.V. Desani, *All About H. Hatterr* (1986)

Artist and anti-apartheid activist Breyten Breytenbach has described his forebodings about the direction in which South Africa has been moving recently. In a nutshell, these stem from his fear that having concentrated their efforts on racial oppression radicals may now be unable or unwilling to combat the dangers of a centralised nation state. Breytenbach believes that the fight against apartheid and the hierarchical division of peoples on the basis of race and ethnicity in some ways allowed the notion of the state to go uncontested. The end of capturing the state from the National Party led anti-apartheid forces to overlook the negatives associated with the state itself. For Breytenbach it has become necessary 'to put in my plea for doubt and questioning, diversity, the maintenance of our "Ho Chi Minh trail" of underground tunnels of memory and resistance, tolerance, mixing, blending, crankiness, existentialism, humanism, anarchism . . . To avoid like the plague the tyranny of "being on the side of the angels."[1] Living in a moment of 'historical acceleration', as Breytenbach calls the present in South Africa, still requires that power and those who wield it continue to be opposed.

Breytenbach's comments represent a political shift made possible by the great transformation that has occurred in South Africa over the last ten years and in turn reflects the potential for a reinterpretation of the history of this region. On the basis of his fears, one could argue that if the next twenty or thirty years witness a struggle over federalism in the Republic and the pitting of new groups against the centralised state, then a new interpretation focusing on state formation may gain ascendancy over one founded solely on racial categorisation.[2] Certainly, the increasingly violent conflict between the African National Congress and Mangosuthu Gatsha Buthelezi's Inkatha movement, suggests that a more nuanced interpretation of racial division is required than one would expect given the centrality of the white/black division enshrined in apartheid.[3] As other political transformations occur in South Africa we can expect historiographical changes similar in magnitude to those witnessed in the United States over the last one hundred years in the interpretations of the Civil War and Reconstruction.[4]

The beginnings of a reassessment of South African history can be found in the analysis of the National Party's success in the Western Cape in the first democratic election of 1994.[5] William Finnegan has shown that this victory was not the result of shortsightedness among 'so-called coloureds' voting for their former oppressors simply because of their racial antipathy for black South Africans. Not only were the 'coloureds' political decisions made on the basis of National Party offerings and the failures of the African National Congress (so that their votes were as reasoned and sensible perhaps as any vote cast in the United States), there were important historical antecedents to the coalition refashioned between 'coloureds' and Afrikaners. Indeed, according to Finnegan, 'relations between the Afrikaners, the self-consciously "white" descendants of the early Dutch settlers, and the coloureds have for centuries been both tangled and intimate'. Drawing on the recent work of historian Hermann Giliomee, he continues:

There is even a vivid precedent for the National Party's recent interest in the coloured vote. . . . During the 1920s, in the relatively liberal Cape province, coloured and African men who met a property qualification had the right to vote . . . and 'non-whites' actually made up more than a quarter of the voters in the Cape Peninsula. The National Party, fearing an influx of immigrants from England who might eventually outnumber Afrikaans-speaking whites, embraced 'brown Afrikaners' as their natural allies, and succeeded in capturing enough of the coloured vote to win the 1924 election against the relatively pro-British South African Party of Jan Christian Smuts . . . The gesture turned out to be one of pure expediency, and the Nationalists soon abandoned their coloured supporters in their pursuit of white-supremacist Afrikaners of the northern provinces.[6]

The point is that such events, almost forgotten, can be dredged up from the deepest recesses of historical memory to explain current trends and form the basis of new interpretations.

Once such new interpretations gain ground and shifts occur in South African historiography the need for reappraisal of conclusions based on comparative analysis becomes imperative. Certain assumptions about change in the United States and the nature of American pluralism are founded in comparisons with nations that are believed incapable of such change. Radically transform the unchangeable and the extent of American pluralism may need reassessment. The belief that South Africa was incapable of change along the lines of race has been shown to be false and historians have been forced to discard the assumption that apartheid was so entrenched that only a bloody war, in which white people fought to the last ditch, or a nuclear weapon would bring about its demise (along with similar theories created to explain or keep vital the continuing conflicts in Northern Ireland and the Middle East, and to account for the immovable 'Iron Curtain' in Europe).[7] Historians like Hermann Giliomee are now looking for the roots of this transformation in South Africa, the weaknesses within the system of apartheid, and the system's failure to sustain its hold on the very party that had fashioned it.[8] Almost inevitably, the products of such work will lead to the reassessment of issues of race as they are understood and lived in the United States. After all, one of the most comforting things for many Americans ever since the civil rights transformation of the 1950s and 1960s, has been the fact that they were able to bring about a 'peaceful' reformation of racial practices when South Africa (which not coincidentally became a focus of black and white American political activity once social equality began to appear more difficult to achieve in the United States) seemed so incapable of embracing such liberal change.

With the potential for such interpretive shifts in mind, it is important to

note the re-emergence of notions of the 'unworthy poor', 'culture of poverty', and 'blaming the poor' (particularly single mothers), as organising
principles for distributing welfare in the United States.[9] For while South
Africa undergoes rapid change the United States seems increasingly entrenched on the issues of race, immigration and poverty. Alan Brinkley
has conveyed a clear sense of the mire in which ideas surrounding welfare
have always been stuck:

> even at moments of great optimism, unacknowledged preconceptions –
> about politics, about gender, and about morality – can shape and distort
> the boldest programs. Understanding the ways in which damaging and
> invidious distinctions have crept into our welfare system is a first step
> toward thinking about ways to remove them.[10]

When one remembers that such 'damaging and invidious distinctions' about
the poor are clearly delineated in Edmund Morgan's *American Slavery,
American Freedom*[11] and were very much a part of both the English colonial experience and the republican experiment, one can begin to comprehend
that for all the political shifts in the United States (Jacksonian democracy,
emancipation, women's suffrage, and civil rights to name a few) not much
has changed for some people. And now that the heady days of November
1992 – a time when many imagined that President Clinton might bring about
reform in health care and other social programmes – have been replaced by
November 1994's hangover, as Newt Gingrich and Co. (using history as
their most potent brew) proclaim a new war on those not welcome and those
'not pulling their weight', the endurance of pluralism and the potential for
liberal change in the United States appears less likely to be a rule of history than a luxury enjoyed by the lucky few.[12] Thus, the rhetoric of the War
on Drugs and 'the war on welfare', the respectable reception given to *The
Bell Curve*, the passage of California's Proposition 187, and the various
stages of the Rodney King incident – the beating, the initial acquittal of
the police involved, and the riots throughout South Central Los Angeles
– suggest that such pessimism about future political change and its impact
on poor inner-city dwellers and 'illegal' immigrants wherever they reside
is warranted.[13]

   A larger question arises from this awareness of contemporary political
and historiographical shifts: how is it that the comparative study of the
United States and South Africa never revealed the possibility of such
shifts? Much work has been undertaken comparing South Africa and the
United States, mainly concerned with their systems of slavery, segregation, and the nature of their discriminatory labour markets.[14] This literature
tends to dichotomise the two societies, emphasising the entrenched nature

of the racial system in South Africa as compared to the more malleable system of the United States.[15] While no one can be held accountable for their inability to predict the almost unforeseeable, the extent to which the two societies have been described as moving along different trajectories does suggest that comparative methodologies need to be reconsidered. Before turning the focus onto the United States and South Africa, therefore, some discussion of one of the limitations of this process of comparison is necessary.

COMPARATIVELY SPEAKING

> The many wars that have been fought in Europe since 1855, and are likely to be fought during the next twenty years, have or will have for one of their causes the discovery of Sanskrit. Though in itself this is by no means a very gratifying result, still I allude to it to simply show how deeply the Europeans have been influenced by the new ideas.
>
> R.G. Bhandarkar, 'The Critical, Comparative and
> Historical Method of Inquiry' (1888)

The most severe limitations of comparative literature have been its national and nationalist bent.[16] The unit of analysis under comparison is, generally speaking, the nation (or proxies thereof).[17] As such, there is a tendency among comparativists to compare large social structures, ideologies, or organisations to explain the nature of the American variant. The desire is to use some other nation's history to help explain 'American Slavery', 'American race relations', 'American working-class formation or class consciousness', and so on.[18] That there might be connections between these American forms and those others being compared is either ignored or not taken sufficiently into account; nor is the fact there might be differences within the United States that defy the label 'American' and lead one to reconsider its usage.[19]

Problems related to this national focus are compounded when nationalist assumptions are used to determine the ways in which another society is viewed. This can be explained most effectively by considering the two most common comparisons undertaken with the United States: those with Britain and South Africa – the former comparison made to highlight differences relating to class, the latter to reveal differences over race. This nation-based bifurcation of comparative analysis, with class on one side and race on the other, is particularly problematic here because for much of the period dealt with in these comparisons South Africa was a part of the British Empire. Consequently, any comparison with either Britain or South Africa ought to go beyond the boundaries of the nation state to understand the larger dimensions of the imperial system.

Comparisons with either metropolitan Britain or colonies like South Africa in isolation veil as much as they reveal. First, a comparison of the United States with Britain falls victim to a category of class that is so constructed (based on free white labour) as to hide both colonised labour in the British case and slaves and Indians (among others) in the American case.[20] Not surprisingly, the class system of Britain appears 'peculiar' for its absence of ethnic divisions, its 'Englishness', while that of the United States appears 'exceptional' for its constant addressing of racial and ethnic divisions (once slaves become freed people and levels of immigration rose).[21] Second, a comparison of the United States with places like South Africa, undertaken because the latter shared a system of slavery or other systems of racial discrimination, falls victim to a category of race that is so constructed as to hide free labour. Ignoring the manner in which understandings of racial slavery in both the US and the British Empire changed in relation to transformations in the experiences of 'free' white male labourers (and vice versa) leads to a reliance on static, nation-centred interpretations of race. As a result South African race relations appear unchanging and American race relations pluralistic, simply because the former society more closely resembles the rigid (and economically 'irrational') system believed to exist in slavery, while the latter society seems, for all its inequalities, to enshrine the doctrines of 'free labor'. The fact that the same assumptions about arduous and devalued labour (and who should perform it) prevail in both countries can be overlooked, even when the experiences for those who do this work and the assumptions about them (that they are somehow inferior) are similar. Finally, both kinds of comparisons (constructed as they are around racial/class questions) will overlook issues and connections relating to gender. The manner in which both class and race are categories with severe gender inflections will be deemed merely incidental to the larger comparative focus.[22]

When the United States is compared with former British colonies seen as part of an imperial framework, in other words when the existence of what C.A. Bayly calls an 'imperial meridian' is recognised, two things become apparent: American working-class formation around ethnicity, race, and gender is not exceptional and American institutions and ideologies have developed around their own 'imperial meridian'.[23] Bayly asserts that imperialist discourse was not confined to overseas ventures, so that the manner in which a large section of the British Isles was brought together into a single political unit was very much imperial.[24] In order to understand the ways in which people were incorporated into the society of London, or more generally of England, it is vital to look beyond 'the metropole'. Expatriate English, Scots and Welsh officials and settlers moved back and forth between 'periphery' and 'metropole', and along the way were influenced and sometimes accompanied by 'non-Britons' (Afrikaners, South Asians, Jews, and Africans to name a few). Moreover, as many Scots demonstrated, movement up the metropolitan social scale often could be accomplished most easily by being recognised for achievements at the periphery.[25] Further, understandings of empire helped to shape the ways people conceived of divisions in their locality and were evident in both their consumption patterns and what they read.[26]

If an imperial meridian is important for comprehension of British history, how much more so is it for the interpretation of the history of the United States? While the United States is seldom seen in imperial terms, imperialism has been as central to the development of the United States as a single, powerful nation state, as it was to the emergence of other imperial nation states – Great Britain, Spain, Japan, France, Belgium, Germany, the Netherlands, Denmark and Russia. All imperial nations bring together regionally and ethnically diverse peoples into political units according to a more or less hierarchical logic that privileges some sections of the state, while parcelling out benefits unevenly to other sections. The American analogue for the Scottish in the British Empire has been the Scotch-Irish, who very clearly saw 'the Birth of the American Nation' as a Scotch-Irish confection;[27] the 'frontier' and plantations provided locations that could be easily inflected with imperial and imperialist discourse; and similar consumption and reading patterns were to be found in the United States as those described by Edward Said for Britain.[28] When people, objects, and ideas are compared not in isolation, but in their imperial contexts, differences that may at first seem stark end up being shaded by an all-enveloping imperial fog.

Comparative studies, then, have not undermined exceptionalist arguments, and because they have generally compared two nations or two national types (American vs. South African slavery) they have shared an analytical frame with exceptionalist theories. Comparative studies of South Africa and the United States, like Cell's and Fredrickson's, have made explicit arguments that were already implicit because their authors have conformed to the presumption that national histories with clear, uncontested boundaries exist and should be compared.[29] Where national histories intersect and where those boundaries are contested (where they are themselves products of particular historical and historiographical conflicts) has often remained unexplored. Thus, while we can profit from comparing nations, such comparisons have to be undertaken in the knowledge that the nations may have histories that are intertwined (perhaps shaping the way their national histories have been conceived and written), that they may be part of larger imperial systems, and that regional and institutional differences or practices may be present in both countries that make comparison at another level of analysis besides the nation more appropriate. In short, comparativists must be careful not to reify and give transhistorical character to something that is, in spite of its ability to mobilise people, only historically contingent.

The remainder of this paper, then, attempts to use comparative history to broaden the outlines of American history and to move beyond the mire of nationalist exceptionalism. The comparative lens used is a variable one; now zoom, now wide-angled, never soft-focused, the lens can be altered according to the objects being observed. I am not attempting to disprove American exceptionalism by undertaking a systematic comparison of the United States and another nation, showing the similarities between the two histories. Doing so would merely reify the two narratives selected, and any similarities found would still beg the question whether or not the other nation was similar only because it was also exceptional. Instead, South African history is here appropriated or exploited selectively to reveal both the connections between some American and South African historical narratives (and by implication those of other countries and regions), and the ways in which nationalist narratives can be broken down into smaller units of analysis (individuals, organisations, cities, or regions) to produce different comparative results. The next section, then, will examine a few of the areas of overlap in American and Southern African histories, while the final section will examine similarities in the imperial locations of American populists and Afrikaner voortrekkers.

AFTER THE GOLD RUSH

> O, my shoes are Japanese
> These trousers are English, if you please
> On my head, red Russian hat –
> My heart's Indian for all that.
> (hit number 'Meera Joota Hia Japani' from the film *Shri 420*)[30]

In *Homelands, Harlem and Hollywood*, Rob Nixon insists 'on the wider links between the [South African] discourses of absolute rupture, authenticity, racial purity, and ethnic nationalism on the one hand and, on the other, the idioms of cosmopolitanism, transculturation, hybridity, and internationalism'. Nixon reveals the 'diverse ties between South African culture and the world beyond its borders' during the period between apartheid's implementation in 1948 and South Africa's first democratic elections in 1994, most especially the influence of Hollywood and American writers and musicians.[31] This intersection of South African and American histories can be seen going back well into the nineteenth century. Two linkages that come to mind immediately are the common origins (both in ideas and sometimes in personnel) of the two region's missionaries, and the overlapping of mining and prostitution capitalists in both countries.[32]

The common origins of the two regions' missionaries is not altogether surprising when one remembers that both Americans and British were captivated by David Livingstone's work in Africa, or at least Henry Morton Stanley's rendering of that work. It was Stanley, after all, who made the call for missionaries in his widely-circulated articles in the *Daily Telegraph* in Britain and James Gordon Bennett's *New York Herald* in the United States, and while this did not begin missionary work in Africa, it most certainly did contribute to its increase.[33]

In the process of describing contemporary views of segregation, John W. Cell has provided a very thought-provoking picture of the work of the African Methodist Episcopal Church in South Africa at the turn of the century.[34] Focusing on the work of Bishops Henry McNeil Turner and Levi J. Coppin in South Africa, Cell describes the attempts of the Philadelphia-based denomination to extend its missionary work to Southern Africa, after having previously worked only in the United States' own African project, Liberia. Understanding the nature of this work in South Africa requires knowing the degree to which it grew out of the very successful expansion of the AME Church throughout the American South during and after the Civil War – work that was also spearheaded by Turner. Coppin's and Turner's attitudes towards Africa's 'raw natives' replicated their view of Southern freed peoples, who needed to be 'uplifted' to the stage of civilisation reached by African-Americans in northeastern cities.[35] While there were clearly dimensions to this missionary work that made it different from similar work undertaken by white missionaries, the similarity of their attitudes to those held by white Christians should not be overlooked.

The AME Church's success in its Southern endeavours contributed to the belief that it could have the same impact outside the United States, not only in Africa but also Cuba and Haiti, winning over not just heathens but Catholics. Southern successes also contributed greatly to Turner's persuasiveness when he promoted the idea of repatriation to Africa, since the

Bishop could claim not only that African-Americans ought to leave the United States, but that if they did so, they would become leaders in the mission to 'uplift backward peoples', fulfilling God's original purpose in bringing Africans as slaves to America. Even when enthusiasm for leaving the United States waned in the late 1890s (coinciding, for a number of reasons, with the Spanish–American War), these ideas about employing the unique experience of African-Americans to give 'kindness and civilization' to their 'less fortunate' brethren remained strong.[36]

Further, the AME connection with South Africa was only one of many such linkages between African-Americans and South Africans. George Shepperson and Thomas Price's excellent biography of John Chilembwe shows the influence of both an English missionary and black church leaders in the United States in the lead up to the Nyasaland uprising of 1915.[37] Similarly, Brian Wilan's biography of Sol Plaatje reveals strong links between this early African Nationalist and leading African-Americans.[38] Such connections reinforced social developments that were occurring simultaneously on both sides of the Atlantic, an example of which was the 'moralizing of leisure time'.[39]

Indeed, contact with South Africa and Liberia helped African-Americans like Alexander Crummell develop an understanding of race that incorporated all 'Negroes' into one racial group, and allowed leaders like himself to 'speak for [the race]' and 'to plot its future'. Representing 'the race' was made problematic, however, by the fact that such leaders felt that African culture was, in Kwame Anthony Appiah's words, 'anarchic, unprincipled, ignorant, defined by the absence of all the positive traits of civilization as "savage"'.[40] Such impressions of race and Africa were shared by the leading African-American intellectuals of the day, from African Methodist bishops who served in Liberia and South Africa (like William Henry Heard, Levi J. Coppin, Robert R. Wright, Jr and John Gregg) to Edward Wilmot Blyden, Alexander Crummell, and even, with some modifications, W.E.B. Du Bois.[41] Race defined in this way could be employed to create a 'Black Atlantic' (as Paul Gilroy has suggested)[42] through Negritude and Pan-Africanism, or promote racial solidarity and Black Nationalism in the United States. But, such negative assumptions about African culture could also divide, 'establishing' the uniqueness of African-American experiences as compared to Africans, and of metropolitan African-Americans as compared to Southern 'greenhorns' (who, the urbanites maintained, had not travelled so far from their African condition).[43] Ironically, without connections and the commonality of experiences, arguing for exceptionalism with regard to the experiences of African-Americans would have been more difficult.

Capitalists in the nineteenth century were a transitory and diverse group of people, and they often traversed large sections of the globe carrying their imperial visions of capital and labour with them. This was particularly the case among mining folk. The story of Edward Hammond Hargreaves's return to Sydney from the California goldfields in January of 1851, followed by his discovery of gold in May of that year and the beginning of the New South Wales gold rush, is well known to most Australians.[44] Many other miners followed Hargreaves's example. According to Charles van Onselen, 'As the price of tin fell in Cornwall, and as some Australian goldfields faltered and failed, so many of the "hard rock men" set their sights on new targets and made their way to the Rand mines which, by [the 1890s], had been expanding for more than a decade.'[45] Migrating miners brought with them ideas and experience that would help shape economic and social developments in areas of the world from California, to Australia, the Yukon, and Witwatersrand.[46] The transitory nature of this population is revealed in the fact that in 1912, according to C.W. de Kiewiet, only 35 per cent of the white miners had been born in South Africa.[47]

Given the presence of these migrants among mining capitalists, it is not surprising that groups at the lower end of the opportunity scale faced similar experiences in places as far apart as California and Witwatersrand. There were important differences in the types of deposits in the world's goldfields that made for some significant variations in experience, but these were in the initial stages of mining. The California and Australian gold deposits were alluvial or surface deposits, so the independent miner with a pick, shovel, and prospecting pan could make a profit at first. Soon, however, these sources were exhausted and it became necessary for miners to blast away at rock and learn methods to extract the gold. These required capital investment and encouraged consolidation of businesses. In South Africa, however, there were no alluvial deposits. Mining development on the Witwatersrand occurred without the widespread experience of individuals staking their claim and then being replaced by larger corporate entities. Whether or not the leap to 'company mining' was entirely a result of the nature of the gold deposits, as de Kiewiet argued, or the result of the later discovery of South African gold during a time of emerging monopoly capitalism (particularly in the world's mining fields) as Duncan Innes argues, is not important here.[48] What is important is that Euro-American magnates were able to establish a firm foothold in the region and could establish tried-and-true labour practices.[49]

As such, attempts by more elite miners to push out the smaller mining enterprises, to rationalise the minefields, and consolidate power in their own hands, were very similar in both California and South Africa. In the process, many poor white Americans and Afrikaners (respectively) lost their footholds in this kind of production, as did the Chinese in California and Africans on the Witwatersrand. In both instances, the attempts to exclude these two 'races' were used to consolidate the power of a small minority of whites, increasing racial antipathy and competition among members of the lower classes, and leading to similar kinds of racial and nationalist politics in both regions with similar consequences. The Chinese Exclusion Act of 1881, pushed for (among others) by Californian working classes, and the South African Mines and Works Act of 1911, which established the colour bar in mining, were the two most significant legislative initiatives from these connected histories.[50]

That one of the most successful conglomerations to emerge from this series of gold and other mineral rushes, was the Anglo-American Corporation in South Africa, is a memorial to the intersectedness of these histories. Further, the manner in which the economic boycott of South Africa had such a significant impact over the last twenty years, where in many other instances boycotts have been ineffective, is also a testament to the way in which South African and American histories have overlapped.

Another view of such intersection can be found in the histories of prostitution. Van Onselen's *New Babylon* is particularly illuminating in this regard, and his stories of the Bowery Boys in South Africa are worth repeating at length here. From late 1898, according to van Onselen, 'hundreds of "undesirables"', 'including scores of Jewish pimps and prostitutes', abandoned the Bowery in New York City and made their way to England. London, however, proved to be a disappointment to these migrants, owing to the fact that a well-developed trade for prostitution already existed and profits were therefore limited.[51] Thus, according to van Onselen,

> when these well-travelled Russians and Poles heard of the exciting new opportunities developing in the southern hemisphere, they did not hesitate to move yet again. While some of their colleagues in the trade opted for South America, many of the former New York pimps and prostitutes decided to make their way to the goldfields of Kruger's republic.

An 'advance guard' of this American contingent was already involved in prostitution on the Witwatersrand as early as 1895, but over the next two years, 'their numbers were substantially augmented by the arrival of dozens of the more professional "white slavers" and their entourages from London'.[52]

Once they established themselves on the Witwatersrand, the Bowery Boys used intimidation in the form of 'blackmail, bribery and corruption, directed at the Morality Squad', to ensure that their brothels were protected while their competitors were plagued by law enforcement. In other words, tactics that had recently been so successful on the Bowery were now used to advantage in Johannesburg. Van Onselen goes on to describe the rise of Joe Silver, a Polish-American arriving from London in 1898, who became 'King of the Pimps in Johannesburg'. By ascending to the presidency of the American Club in 1898, Silver was able to maintain control of the Witwatersrand until his arrest and conviction a year later (when an English consortium took over prostitution). After his release from prison following the outbreak of the Boer War, he established his influence in other regions.

Beyond the similarities in personnel, there were also connections in labour markets. New York was not merely linked to Johannesburg, it was also connected with umpteen other cities around the globe. George J. Kneeland's study, *Commercialized Prostitution in New York City*, published in 1913, reveals this quite clearly. Appendix XIV, entitled 'Shipping Women', tells us of one person, 'X 47, alias X 47-a, who is part owner in X 46 West 25th Street'. According to Kneeland, '[He] has had his women in England, Russia, South Africa, Dallas, Texas, and Seattle, Washington. He travels back and forth between South Africa and New York.'[53] This man was just one of many who moved prostitutes from places all over the United States to Brazil, China, Argentina along with the places frequented by X 47-a's prostitute. Indeed, what is peculiar about the Bowery Boys locating themselves in Johannesburg, is not that Americans were profiting from prostitution among the mining populations, but the fact that, as a result of Progressive squeamishness in New York, pimps were being forced to migrate to the point of production. Once in Johannesburg, they were forced to compete with pimps chased out of London and Paris.

The common denominator among those places to which American pimps sent their prostitutes was fast economic growth occurring in a particular area which attracted disproportionately male populations of migrants (often indentured labourers) for whom some 'servicing' was believed necessary.[54] Consequently, it is no surprise to find that California and Witwatersrand developed very similar markets for prostitution. And just as the similarities between the mining capitalists gave rise to similar experiences for the labourers in the mines, so the similarity in methods and personnel among the pimps gave rise to similar experiences for the prostitutes.

A transformation is clearly evident at the end of the nineteenth century in the world of Johannesburg's prostitution. The early prostitutes, according to van Onselen, were 'daughters of South Africa's old proletariat', but soon, as the account of the Bowery Boys suggests, they would be outnumbered by new arrivals from Europe and America.[55] There is an air of the pre-industrial attached to the work habits of the early prostitutes, who 'chose to attach themselves to any one of the hundreds of canteens or hotels which abounded in the mining town'.[56] These work habits were gone by the time that (what we will call) 'company prostitution' took hold in the mid-1890s. There can be less disagreement about the origins of this 'company' system than in the case of monopoly capitalism in the mining industry. Louise White has asserted that 'men and male control enter prostitution only *after* the state does',[57] and it is clear that the increasing criminalisation and persecution of prostitutes forced women to seek 'protection' from pimps and brothels.[58] Before the Progressive purges of the 1890s in London and New York, pimps had bought off corrupt police officials, particularly those associated with Tammany Hall, thereby making it very difficult for the individual to ply her trade independently.[59] The profits that this system generated were such that the methods of corruption and intimidation could be transferred to 'frontier' towns with relative ease cementing an imperial labour market that resembled those found among the miners and plantation labourers.[60]

Even within this 'company' system experiences were wide-ranging for prostitutes (as experiences for labourers have been) ranging from the worst kinds of exploitation to experiences of empowerment. Van Onselen's description of Fanny Kreslo is clearly a case of the former, and one that Progressives dwelled on in their endeavours to bring 'morality' into the affairs of the city. Kreslo was a 15-year-old Lithuanian girl who, in 1898, was offered employment as a shop assistant in London, but on arriving in London learned that her employer had moved to the Rand. Having left Lithuania, and any people who might have advised her against following her employer to South Africa, she was easily persuaded to leave London. On arrival in Johannesburg, she was pressed into prostitution, until she was 'freed' in 1899 as a result of President Kruger's crackdown on the Bowery Boys.[61]

But van Onselen also describes incidences where women gained some sense of empowerment from prostitution, and it was not unusual for a woman to be running a brothel, working as a pimp, a 'madam', a pimp's 'prostitute/wife', a 'modiste', a 'procuress' or acting independently as 'streetwalkers' (who often were the women most despised, because they most obviously contested gender norms).[62] Historians have been reluctant to recognise these women as being empowered, even of being workers as such, but it is nevertheless the case that in the range of possibilities open to women at the *fin-de-siècle* prostitution was not necessarily uniquely exploitative.[63] And the stories of prostitutes in South Africa were linked to those of women outside the trade in sex, in paid and unpaid labour, and to other regions. Prostitutes' migration stories, from the most dismal to the most fortunate, were repeated for girls and young women drawn, or making their way, into prostitution all over the world.[64]

Here the limits of agency become readily apparent. If prostitution is sex labour then the prostitutes' resistance can be seen as similar to that of other labourers. And yet, as Philippa Levine has argued,

the woman's identity as prostitute or potential prostitute was constructed *through* resistance. A prostitute woman by definition lived in defiance, in resistance – of the proper sphere of Woman, of the male order, of respectability, exposing the threat of unordered female sexuality which led to codifications of female sexuality. In short, resistance invited containment which prompted resistance – and new definitions were born.[65]

As such, the very act of resistance, or the 'weapon of the weak', would be the very act or weapon that aided the social worker, government official, or other interested observer to find the woman in question guilty of the charge of 'looseness', 'coarseness', and so on. If this applies to the sex labourer, then so too can it apply to the labourer on the shop floor.[66] And where this is clear in the ordering of power in a city, it is even more so when the prostitute is located on the imperial terrain, and when ethnic groups endeavoured to situate themselves in relation to other groups according to the character of 'their women'.

The importance of prostitution in shaping migration experiences generally should not be underestimated. Not least, this was because so many migrants were engaged in prostitution. In San Francisco, for example, seven out of ten Chinese women were recorded as prostitutes in 1870, and until around 1907, there were believed to be 22.5 prostitutes to every 100 inhabitants in Chinatown.[67] If such numbers approximate the truth, then the fact of prostitution becomes central to Chinatown experience. And yet for those people who lived there prostitution may not have been considered a deviance of any sort, nor a life on the margins of respectability.[68] Once this is acknowledged, however, it becomes crucial to understand how normative experience was pushed to the margins so that it could become grist for the mills of moralising nationalisms. For one of the key features of nineteenth-century nationalism was the importance of women to its definition. Not only were women seen as the bearers and reproducers of culture, control over them was deemed central to determining the health and vitality of the group.[69] Du Bois's classic statement that the meaning of race lay in white 'ownership of women', which led to black men striving to reassert their control in this domain, can be applied to the way immigrant leaders saw 'their own' women.[70] Controlling 'one's women' was crucial in an environment like the United States where the 'vitality' of an ethnic group was believed to depend on those women choosing a man of the same ethnicity.[71]

If Anne McClintock is correct that 'All nations depend on powerful constructions of gender', then control of prostitutes and any women who might be considered of 'loose morals' would almost inevitably concern those who wished to advance the cause of particular nations.[72] Nationalists continually feared that the presence of such women reflected badly on their group as a whole. Thus, indentured labour migration from India to the British Caribbean and Africa was brought to an end once nationalists like Gopal Krishna Gokhale made the argument that national self-confidence and independence would never grow in India so long as the British maintained a system that led so many South Asian women into prostitution abroad.[73] Opposition to prostitution in California shows a similar appreciation among Chinese and Japanese nationalists of the inverse relationship between the 'success' of an ethnic group and the widespread association of that group with prostitution.[74] Often historians themselves have failed to see the contingent nature of this linkage and have readily accepted it as a barometer for determining immigrant fortunes in America. For example, Lynn Pan writes:

> Prostitution . . . is another matter. Along with opium, the organized traffic in prostitutes was what gave the overseas Chinese such a bad name; there was scarcely an American comment on Chinatown, rarely a description of the Chinese community, that missed the chance to bring up the subject.[75]

And, Pan continues, 'some of the American men really knew what they were talking about'. While it is unclear that such 'American' men could have had more than a one-sided impression of the lives and habits of Chinese prostitutes (and that controlled by the prostitute's ability to 'put something over on him'),[76] it is certainly clear from Pan that they were capable of basing assumptions about the Chinese as a whole on these partial transcripts. Thus an imperial bond could be cemented, that might otherwise have been difficult to forge, between Progressive reformer and ethnic nationalist.

The connections between histories that crossed the boundaries of the nation state often helped to define the ways in which those national histories would be perceived. African-American involvement in South Africa helped contribute to American ideas about the 'backwardness' of Africans; Anglo-American capitalists' investment in the Republic would contribute to imperial notions about development and modernisation; and the differential abilities of nationalists to control 'their' women abroad would contribute both to the way nations were perceived by Euro-American imperialists knocking at their doors and the way those migrants would be viewed by the communities around the world in which they settled. In short, determining exceptional status is most easy when one is involved, directly or indirectly, in the shaping of that other society to which one's own is to be compared. Provided, of course, one can remain out of the range of spears and arrows.

OMAHA, SOMEWHERE IN MIDDLE AMERICA

> Hey mister, if you're going to walk on water
> You know you're only going walk all over me.
>   Adam Duritz, *Counting Crows* (Geffen Records, 1993)

Introductory courses and textbooks on US history invariably give some attention to American Indians. In the section on westward expansion, which generally follows Reconstruction and Redemption, historians will often describe the experiences of American Indians, sometimes describing them as the ultimate victims of this expansion. The behaviour of Euro-Americans may or may not be described as genocidal, and, even if so, more weight will be given to the importance of disease and the loss of the buffalo herds (whether or not their decimation is described as being undertaken deliberately to weaken Indian communities) in determining the decline of the Indians.[77] With the massacre of the Dakota Sioux at Wounded Knee, South Dakota in 1890, the story of the Indians will generally come to a close.[78]

And with the end of this story, historians will turn to the plight of the farmers and the discussion of populism gets under way.[79] This story will be described as one of western farmers coming to terms with a nation now dominated by eastern capitalist interests. There is much disagreement among historians about the nature of populism. Were populists mid-westerners coming to terms with the closing frontier (Hicks), bigots fearful of blacks and Jews (Hofstadter), isolated rural dwellers in search of the camaraderie of populist rallies and picnics (Turner), creators of a democratic movement culture (Goodwyn), the generators of a class movement in opposition to capital (Pollack), or a pentecostal mix of all the above (McMath)?[80] There is enough disagreement here to provide some leeway for historians in introductory courses or text books to present their own view. But whatever it is, this view will never situate populists in relation to the American Indians. None of the above-mentioned historians spared a reference for Indians (even when in the case of Hofstadter doing so might have strengthened his argument); why should we expect this of the generalist?[81]

What is the significance of this omission and the invisibility of American Indians in discussions of mid-western populism? Surely, the presence or recent withdrawal of Indians from those areas that were building 'a movement culture', as Goodwyn would have it, influenced their demands and their political rhetoric.[82] While Goodwyn shrugs off the racism and anti-Semitism of Populists as something that they could not escape, rather than as something fundamental to their ideology, re-establishing the imperial location of Populists (in relation to Indians and the imperial expansion of the frontier) forces us to reassess some of the radical implications of their politics.

For, had Pierre-Joseph Proudhon been looking around in 1840 for proof of his famous axiom that 'Property is theft', he could have done no better than to observe the American frontier, where he would have seen the stripping of land from American Indians, followed by their relocation and the establishment of white American property in their place.[83] But, property's ultimate origins in displacement have been disguised in various legal transactions, in Constitutional practices, and in the process of history itself. Frederick Jackson Turner's claim that the frontier and the irrepressible American frontier spirit were to be found wherever there was 'free' land available, was just one part of this process of writing Indians out of the American narrative (and not coincidentally establishing the first systematic theory of American exceptionalism).[84]

That some mid-western populists endorsed ideas of imperial expansion is clear. Ignatius Donnelly, the 'Voice of Minnesota' and author of the preamble to the People's Party's most important manifesto (the Omaha Platform), and a man who amassed his wealth from land speculation, was a great supporter of the expansion of the United States into the far northern regions of the continent. In 1869, as he was completing a term in Congress, he addressed the St. Paul Chamber of Commerce about such expansion. Donnelly believed that the settlement of the Red and Saskatchewan Valleys by Americans was dictated by Minnesota's 'geographical necessities' (or 'Manifest Destiny'). Hoping to reorient President Grant's policy away from expansion into the Caribbean basin and towards the contested terrain of Canada, Donnelly proposed that the American government come to the aid of the population of the Red River that was resisting British domination. By supporting those fighting for independence (as President

McKinley would later do in Cuba and the Philippines in 1898), 'we may', Donnelly hoped, 'within a few years, perhaps months, see the Stars and Stripes wave from Fort Garry, from the waters of Puget Sound, and along the shores of Vancouver'. For, according to the future populist, 'This country [Rupert's Land] belongs to us, and God speed the Fenian movement or any other movement that will bring it to us!'[85] It is not surprising, then, to find that his preamble to the Omaha Platform was founded on fundamentally imperial assumptions about the nature and destiny of American history.[86]

Donnelly was also author of the Utopian novel *Caesar's Column*, written in 1890, in which Gabriel Welstein, a man of Swiss origin, returns to New York from East Africa in 1988 to find a society controlled by corrupt moneyed interests. After seeing thousands upon thousands killed in a worldwide revolt of the masses led by Caesar Lomellini (whose desire to destroy civilisation is perhaps accounted for by his not being of Anglo-Irish descent), in which gas was the weapon of choice, Welstein decides to fly back to his African home with a small group of friends. There, in Uganda, they hope to avoid the dangers of class struggle and to create a Utopian society centred around a town called . . . Stanley. Since Donnelly included no Africans in this Utopia, it is fair to say that these migrants carried with them their own American understanding of the frontier and the invisibility of indigenous people. It was only under such conditions, with the expansion of the European race around the world and the making invisible of indigenous peoples, that Utopian goals could be achieved and metropolitan corruption held at bay.[87]

This involvement of populists in the 'frontier' imperial project is further revealed in the comparison with the Southern African frontier.[88] Howard Lamar and Leonard Thompson, for example, have described the Americans who occupied Oregon, eastern Texas, the 'arid lands of the Great Basin', and pastoral Mexican California as 'voortrekkers'. Superficially, they say,

> the parallels to white occupation of the Orange Free State or the Transvaal are tantalizing, for in each of these regions the local Anglo-American population seized lands of both Indians and Spanish-Mexicans and practiced a doctrine of 'popular sovereignty' by establishing independent provinces or republics for a time. With the exception of the Mormons in Utah, however, these American trekkers were the cutting edge

of an aggressive American nationalism rather than a retreat from impe-rial or metropolitan authority.[89]

Whether or not this last statement is exactly correct, given the extent to which American pioneers saw themselves as escaping from the clutches of the metropole and Afrikaners were participating in a form of aggressive nationalism with imperial links of their own, clearly the aggressive nation-alism of the American 'voortrekkers' must have influenced the politics of the Populist movement.[90]

Lamar and Thompson argue that the alliance of the Federal Government with American pioneers, so different from the opposition facing Afrikaners from their Imperial Government, made for a different political situation on the two frontiers.[91] Moreover, as Christopher Saunders points out, Afrikaners faced a far larger African population than the Indian population facing American pioneers, and the Africans were to be used as a labour force while American Indians were pushed off to the distant reservation. In his chapter on the Great Trek, in *A History of South Africa to 1870*, Leonard Thompson notes that three main factors affected the course of the Great Trek: 'the qualities of the Voortrekkers as individuals and as a commun-ity; the environments into which they migrated; and the reactions of the British government and its local representatives'.[92] Such factors were evid-ent in all conditions of colonisation, from Fiji and New Zealand, eastward through Australia, India, Africa, the Caribbean, to the America Colonies. In the North American western 'frontier', these factors remained in place, the only change being that, for much of the region, the role of the Bri-tish government had been usurped by the US government and its local representatives.

Once gender is inserted into the experiences and imagery of the two 'frontiers', as inevitably it must be, the differences between South Africa and the United States continue to fade. Anne McClintock has written of South Africa:

> In the voluminous Afrikaner historiography, the history of the *volk* is organized around a male national narrative figured as an imperial journey into empty lands. The journey proceeds forwards in *geographical* space, but backwards in *racial* and *gender* time, to what is figured as a prehis-toric zone of linguistic, racial and gender 'degeneration'. The myth of the 'empty land' is simultaneously the myth of 'virgin land' – effecting a double erasure. Within the colonial narrative, to be 'virgin' is to be empty of desire, voided of sexual agency, and passively awaiting the thrusting, male insemination of European military history, language and 'reason'. The feminizing of 'virgin' colonial lands also effects a territorial

appropriation, for if the land is virgin, Africans cannot claim aboriginal territorial rights, and the white male patrimony can be violently assured.[93]

No wonder prostitutes would come to present such difficulties to nationalists! But more importantly, this passage could be transposed onto American colonial and imperial frontier without any difficulty whatsoever.

If any exceptionality arises from these 'frontier' comparisons, it clearly resides with the Afrikaners who, being of a different nationality from the government at the Cape, faced more significant opposition from their imperial power than was evident on other 'frontiers'. But this should not be overstated. Australian and New Zealand settlers often, for reasons of class, ethnicity, or presumed criminality, were restrained in their attempts to establish property rights. Moreover, the US government also entered into treaties with American Indian nations that, while usually discounted as not valid when it mattered, still needed to be confronted, and which sometimes placed them in positions of opposition to their settlers. With regard to the second of Thompson's factors, 'the environments into which they migrated', we must be careful not to exaggerate the degree to which the large African population made for a unique experience for Afrikaners. In the comparison with the United States this is portraying the 'frontier' in a single light. There were many different peoples with different political systems that presented a wide range of dilemmas for settlers. These tribes were capable of taking alternative political stances in relation to the federal government, eliciting a range of support among Europeans in the United States, and making alliances with other foreign powers which, in many cases, presented opposition as intractible to settlers as those met on the South African veld. Suffice it to say, if one examines the conditions in Texas and those in Minnesota, the stories are very different.

Finally, the idea that Africans would become the labour force for Afrikaners finds many parallels in the United States, where the migration of southern plantation capitalists to the southwestern states was made possible by their use of non-European slave labour, where the importance of labour importation would be seen as of paramount importance for development and labour control (internal slave trade, Chinese indentured labour), where such importation would lead to similar exclusion acts and racial job bars pushed for by white working classes, where the creation of reservations would be seen as appropriate, and where wars would be fought to determine which Europeans had authority over the territories.[94] Differences exist that make each situation unique, and each nation's 'frontier' a site of many ideologies and experiences. What we need to know, then, is not how different frontier movements differ, but how certain ideologies and experiences get privileged in the process of creating national narratives. In this instance we need to examine, not who the populists were (there were many strands to rural protest), but how it is that aspects of their disparate ideologies have been accentuated and others elided to produce one kind of movement, while the disparate elements of Southern African frontier movements have been given a different reading.

Actual or perceived differences in 'frontier' experiences may not be as important as the differences in the way historians and others have written about the ideologies that emerged from them. For example, American Populists have been valorised and the pioneer spirit has been seen as the backbone of their movement, while the same features found in Afrikaner nationalism have been vilified as products of their backwardness. While Populists can continue to be romanticised (through the invisibility of American Indians), only supporters of apartheid have done the same for the Voortrekkers, and the likelihood that this will continue uncontested even in Afrikaans-language South African historiography is slim. This difference is enshrined in Stanley's description of his massacre of Bumbireh Africans. Perhaps influenced by his reporting of fights against American Indians, Stanley revealed a certain relish at the massacre, and was shocked when his reports led to a great uproar at the British Foreign Office and the Royal Geographic Society.[95] The literary conventions that led to protest against such actions in Africa and acceptance of them on the American 'frontier' have been carried over into the historiography.

The comparison with the Southern African 'frontier' allows us to see the similarity between mid-Western Populists' predicament and those of Voortrekkers in Southern Africa. Although Afrikaners opposed the British imperial control, whether from Whitehall or Cape Town, they did not reject imperialism altogether; they shared many traditions that arose out from their Christianity, European background, and, with the opening up of diamond and gold mines, from a shared sense that the good society would be achieved by extracting minerals from the ground for themselves and not for the benefit of Africans. Theirs was a settler imperialism, that believed that more of the benefits of imperialism should accrue for those on the frontier, while those in the metropolitan centres should benefit less. The establishment of a government in the Transvaal, before and after the British occupation of 1877–80, gave concrete form to such aspirations. Many American populists would have endorsed similar beliefs. In their minds, it was they who 'won' the west; it was they who were carrying the benefits of western civilisation to the farthest corners of the North American continent. It should be they who benefited also. The *Spectator* of 1893, for example, observed: 'Almost everywhere, certainly in England, France, Germany, Italy, Scandinavia, and the United States, the agriculturalists, formerly so conservative, are becoming fiercely discontented, declare they gain less by civilization than the rest of the community, and are look-ing for remedies of a drastic nature.'[96] Clearly, the definition of 'civilisa-tion' had an imperial dimension, and in areas of expansion like Southern Africa and the American agrarian belt, would give rise to a particular kind of politics that opposed domination by the metropolitan centre.

Recognising the mid-Western Populists' location in the imperial middle is crucial to understanding their ideology. To suggest, as James Turner does, that they were isolated and confused, is implicitly to accept that the land which they had occupied really was 'free' and uncontested. Knowing that these people were linked to the militant expansion of American na-tionalism into the frontier regions and, to borrow from Takaki and Whitman, 'the masculine thrust towards Asia', provides us with an alternative source for their 'tendency to rely on scapegoats and panaceas'.[97] Rather than this tendency being the product of a 'sense of confusion' among farmers, it could have been the product of years of experience dividing the world into the forces of good (white Americans and civilisation) and evil (Indians) – essential if one was to participate in what Melville called 'the metaphysics of Indian hating'.[98] Incorporating eastern capitalists and Jews into this Manichean model was relatively easy, as William Jennings Bryan showed in his 1896 Cross of Gold Speech.

Clearly, important differences existed between frontier-informed Afri-kaner nationalism and frontier-informed American Populism – the degree to which Afrikaner nationalism was shaped by the Dutch Reform Church, for one thing. Moreover, Populists never took up arms against eastern industrialists as Afrikaners were to do against the British in the Anglo-Boer Wars. But such events, crucial as they may be, should not blind us to the similarities between the two. The manner in which Populism dissip-ated after 1896, when President McKinley turned 'the metaphysics of Indian hating' into a national obsession, only to be reborn in the Ku Klux Klan of the 1920s, highlights this imperial aspect. Further, while the terms within which Afrikaners and Populists would be incorporated into their respect-ive republics would differ, such incorporation would eventually take place.[99]

CONCLUSION

Indians are not historians; and they rarely show any critical ability. Even their most useful books, books full of research and information, exasperate with their repetitions and diffuseness, and lose effect by their uncritical enthusiasms. Such solid highways to scholarly esteem and approval as indexes and bibliographies are almost unknown to them.

Edward Thompson, *The Other Side of the Medal* (1926)

Exceptionalism is, in many respects, an imperial formulation. Those who have come to see themselves as exceptions to the rules of history, the British and Americans for example, have done so when their nations reached a position of world domination and when their interpretations of history (found in Whiggish and Progressive history, Orientalism and modernisation theory, to name a few) could prevail over others. More importantly, the idea of exceptionalism depends on a description of the nation that is defined by certain parameters and narratives that, however flexible and expansive, simultaneously elide or exclude others. This is an imposition on the historical record, the privileging of some over others, the accentuation of the peculiar, and the downplaying of similarities with other nations or peoples that are described in such a way so as to make them seem unexceptional or ordinary.

The kinds of narratives hinted at here – those formed around intersections with other societies and nation states, or based on the experiences of people who are generally deemed marginal (in other words, those people upon whom even social historians have had a difficulty conferring agency) – appear to contradict exceptionalist theories. Of course we will wish to impose order on the myriad narratives thrown up, we all strive towards synthesis. But as we perform this 'profoundly "worldly" activity' – creating worlds of 'first' and 'third' varieties, establishing nations of this and that kind – we do so in the political realm, shaped by our own imperial location and our own desire to protect a world that might be lost.[100]

Once this is recognised it becomes apparent that widespread acceptance of the exceptionalism of the United States depended to some degree on the fact that it had 'exceptional' historians: historians whose claims to 'objectivity' were never systematically dismissed as tainted on the basis of their social/imperial location, and who had the luxury to consider all other nations' historians so tainted. Like Henry Morton Stanley on Lake Victoria, Americanists were able to 'pick off the natives' while staying out of the range of any returning missiles. They could also choose those people with whom they would share their canoes.

NOTES

* The author has benefited from the advice and encouragement of numerous people among whom Antoinette Burton, Lee Cassanelli, Alan Dawley, Robert Engs, Gary Gerstle, Andy Gregg, Rick Halpern, Madhavi Kale, Ken Kusmer, David Ludden, Jonathan Morris, Carl Nightingale, Gyan Prakash, Dan Rodgers, Tom Sugrue, and

Mike Zuckerman have been most helpful. Antoinette Burton deserves special thanks for her insightful comments on an earlier draft and for essential references. Many of the arguments in this paper have developed over the years from conversations with Madhavi Kale and are, in some instances, founded on her research on indentured labour in the British Empire. My debt to her is great indeed. Finally, I am grateful for the questions and comments I received from the Commonwealth Fund Conference participants, particularly those of Shula Marks, Hilary Sapire, Ronald Mendel, and Peter Alexander.

1. Breyten Breytenbach, 'Dog's Bone', *New York Review of Books*, 26 May 1995, 4–5.

2. Stanley Greenberg, *Race and State in Capitalist Development: Comparative Perspectives* (New Haven, 1981), as the title suggests, analyses the role of the state in South African society. The main focus, however, is on the role of different social groups – mining and commercial capitalists, large farmers, and white labourers – in the creation of the apartheid state. It may be difficult to infer from this analysis how these different groups will act once apartheid is eradicated in a state that is perhaps even more centralised than before. See Michael Burawoy, 'State and Social Revolution in South Africa: Reflections on the Comparative Perspectives of Greenberg and Skocpol', *Kapitalistate*, 9 (1981), 93–122. Marxist historians, meanwhile, have argued that race has been manipulated primarily by capitalists who have retained their control over the state, and that race and class relations have merged. As such, they have used class analysis to understand the extreme racial divisions in South Africa. Whether or not their instrumentalist interpretation of the state is correct is beyond the scope of this paper, but questions remain about how different social groups have acted in the downfall of apartheid, whether these suggest different roles than were described by Marxist revisionists in the past, and so on. For Marxist revisionists, see (among others) H.J. and R.E. Simons, *Class and Colour in South Africa, 1850–1950* (Harmondsworth, 1969); Martin Legassick, 'South Africa: Capital Accumulation and Violence', *Economy and Society*, 3 (1974), 255–80; Frederick Johnstone, *Class, Race, and Gold: A Study of Class Relations and Racial Discrimination in South Africa* (London, 1976); Duncan Innes, *Anglo American and the Rise of Modern South Africa* (New York, 1984); and Robert H. Davies, 'Mining Capital, the State and Unskilled White Workers in South Africa, 1901–1913', *Journal of Southern African Studies*, 3 (1976), 41–69; and *Capital, State and White Labour in South Africa, 1900–1960* (Brighton, 1977). See also B.S. Kantor and H.F. Kenny, 'The Poverty of Neo-Marxism: the case of South Africa', *Journal of Southern African Studies*, 3 (1976), 20–40, and Harold Wolpe's response: 'A Comment on "The Poverty of Neo-Marxism"', *Journal of Southern African Studies* (1977), 240–56.

3. See Chris Lowe, 'Buthelezi, Inkatha, and the Problem of Ethnic Nationalism in South Africa', in Joshua Brown et al., *History from South Africa: Alternative Visions and Practices* (Philadelphia, 1991), 195–208.

4. See Colin Bundy, 'An Image of Its Own Past? Towards a Comparison of American and South African Historiography', *Radical History Review*, 46/7 (1990) for a discussion of historiographical shifts in both the United States and South Africa, as well as some discussion of future developments among radical historians of South Africa. National boundaries are not questioned

in this article in the ways proposed here. *Ibid.*, 82–104. For shifts in the historiography of Reconstruction in America, see Bernard Weisberger, 'The Dark and Bloody Ground of Reconstruction Historiography', *Journal of Southern History*, 25 (1959), 427–47.

5. William Finnegan, 'The Election Mandela Lost', *New York Review of Books*, 20 October 1994, 33–34.

6. *Ibid.*, 33.

7. Hermann Giliomee and Jannie Gagiano, eds, *The Elusive Search for Peace: South Africa, Israel and Northern Ireland* (Cape Town, 1990); Donald Harman Akinson, *God's People: Covenant and Land in South Africa, Israel and Ulster* (Ithaca, 1992). See also George M. Fredrickson, *Black Liberation: A Comparative History of Black Ideologies in the United States and South Africa* (New York, 1985), 319.

8. Giliomee stands at the forefront of such reinterpretation. See, for example, '"Survival in Justice": An Afrikaner Debate over Apartheid', *Comparative Studies in Society and History*, 36:3 (July 1994), 527–48; and 'Democratization in South Africa', *Political Science Quarterly*, 110:1 (1995), 83–104. Unlike other authors, however, Giliomee is pessimistic about the potential for the emergence of a liberal democracy in South Africa. More optimistic authors are: F. van Zyl Slabbert, *The Quest for Democracy: South Africa in Transition* (Johannesburg, 1992); Heribert Adam and Kogila Moodley, *The Opening of the Apartheid Mind: Options for the New South Africa* (Berkeley, 1993).

9. Michael B. Katz, *The Undeserving Poor: From the War on Poverty to the War on Welfare* (New York, 1989); Katz, ed., *The "Underclass" Debate: Views from History* (Princeton, 1993), 3–23; Linda Gordon, *Pitied but Not Entitled: Single Mothers and the History of Welfare* (New York, 1994). Nicholas Lemann's widely acclaimed *The Promised Land: The Great Black Migration and How it Changed America* (New York, 1991) revives the Frazier-Elkins-Moynihan thesis about the weak black family through his sharecropper thesis.

10. Alan Brinkley, 'For Their Own Good', *New York Review of Books* (26 May 1994), 43.

11. Edmund Morgan, *American Slavery, American Freedom: The Ordeal of Colonial Virginia* (New York, 1975), esp. 381–87.

12. Rob Gregg, 'The More Things Change . . .', *Chartist* (November–December 1992).

13. In *City of Quartz: Excavating the City of the Future in Los Angeles* (London, 1990), Mike Davis clearly shows at a structural level why it is that we should not be surprised by events that are occurring in Los Angeles, and how these are making their impact felt on California first, and the nation later.

14. The main book-length comparative studies of the United States and South Africa are: John W. Cell, *The Highest Stage of White Supremacy: The Origins of Segregation in South Africa and the American South* (New York, 1982); George M. Fredrickson, *White Supremacy: A Comparative Study in American and South African History* (New York, 1981); Howard Lamar and Leonard Thompson, eds, *The Frontier in History: North America and Southern Africa Compared* (New Haven, 1981); and, Stanley Greenberg, *Race*

and State in Capitalist Development. Debates between Edna Bonacich and Michael Burawoy over divided and split labour markets, while not explicitly comparative, extend to both countries and have comparative implications: Burawoy, 'The Capitalist State in South Africa: Marxist and Sociological Perspectives on Race and Class', *Political Power and Social Theory*, 2 (1981); Bonacich, 'Capitalism and Race in South Africa: A Split Market View', *ibid.* Similarly, William Julius Wilson's *The Declining Significance of Race: Blacks and Changing American Institutions* (Chicago, 1978), is implicitly comparative, founded in large measure on Pierre van den Berghe's typology in *Race and Racism: A Comparative Perspective* (New York, 1967).

15. George Fredrickson, for example, argues that the differences between Jim Crow in the South and 'native segregation' in South Africa 'are of such a degree as to cast doubt on the value of a detailed comparison of the unequal treatment of southern blacks during the Jim Crow era and the lot of Africans under segregation or apartheid since 1910'. *White Supremacy*, 241. Fredrickson nevertheless proceeds to make just such a 'detailed comparison' and finds differences between the two systems of segregation are 'too great, in terms of both underlying structures and patterns of historical development, to sustain comparison based on analogy'. *Ibid.* 250. While John Cell was able to build a book on this analogy, it is true that he too found substantial differences between the two countries' systems.

16. Ian Tyrell, 'American Exceptionalism in an Age of International History', *American Historical Review*, 96:4 (October 1991), 1031–55.

17. Where the nation state is not compared, a particular segment of the nation is taken as a proxy for the whole, or as a means to understand a national phenomenon. Thus, John Cell compares South Africa to the American South, and is critical of Stanley Greenberg for choosing to compare Alabama to South Africa: *The Highest Stage*, xii–xiii. In fact, this criticism highlights the nationalist bent, as taking Alabama (part of the American system) as a comparative focus for South Africa (part of the British imperial system) is justified on many levels. The assumption that there is just one system of segregation in the South and so also the United States may be invalid.

18. Tyrell, 'American Exceptionalism', 1035–36. Greg Cuthbertson, 'Racial Attraction: Tracing the Historiographical Alliances between South Africa and the United States', *Journal of American History*, 81:3 (December 1994), 1132. Fredrickson, 'Comparative History', in Michael Kammen, ed., *The Past Before Us* (Ithaca, 1986). Fredrickson attempts to move beyond this national focus in *The Arrogance of Race: Historical Perspectives on Slavery, Racism, and Social Inequality* (Middletown, 1988), but his Weberian typology of different societies, fulfils the same goal. Peter Kolchin, in 'Comparing American History', in Kutler and Katz, eds, *The Promise of American History* (Baltimore, 1982), 65, asserts that 'most historical judgments are implicitly comparative' and that 'comparative history constitutes the effort to do explicitly what most historians do most of the time'. He does not, however, question the national orientation of most historical judgements and his own comparative work, *Unfree Labor: American Slavery and Russian Serfdom* (Cambridge MA,1987) fits this model; see also, 'Reevaluating the Antebellum Slave Community: A Comparative Perspective', *Journal of*

American History, 70:3 (Dec. 1983). Other works on slavery typical of this focus are: Frank Tannenbaum, *Slave and Citizen: The Negro in the Americas* (New York, 1946); Stanley M. Elkins, *Slavery: A Problem in American Institutional and Intellectual Life* (Chicago, 1959); Herbert S. Klein, *Slavery in the Americas: A Comparative Study of Virginia and Cuba* (New York, 1967); Carl N. Degler, *Neither Black nor White: Slavery and Race Relations in Brazil and the United States* (New York, 1971); Richard R. Beeman, 'Labor Forces and Race Relations: A Comparative View of the Colonization of Brazil and Virginia', *Political Science Quarterly*, LXXXVI:4 (Dec. 1971); and Richard S. Dunn, 'A Tale of Two Plantations: Slave Life at Mesopotamia in Jamaica and Mount Airy in Virginia, 1799 to 1828', *William and Mary Quarterly*, XXXIV (January 1977). Ira Katznelson, *Black Men, White Cities: Race, Politics, and Migration in the United States, 1900–30, and Britain, 1948–68* (New York, 1973) reaches for national conclusions about race when a study of New York City and London might have different imperial stories to tell. In *City Trenches: Urban Politics and the Patterning of Class in the United States* (Chicago, 1981), he shows his affinity for the idea of American exceptionalism. Comparing the American city to the European he neglects to consider the possibility that while London, Paris and Stockholm may look different from New York, Chicago and Los Angeles, other cities like Bombay, Johannesburg and Manila may be structured very similarly to them. Eric Foner, in *Nothing But Freedom* (Baton Rouge, 1983), 2–3, endeavours to use comparative analysis 'to move beyond "American exceptionalism" to develop a more sophisticated understanding of the problem of emancipation and its aftermath'. And yet he arrives at a conclusion that 'sympathetic local and state governments during Reconstruction afforded American freedmen a form of political and economic leverage unmatched by their counterparts in other societies'. Generalising from South Carolinian experiences, and informed by the movement towards a 'Second Reconstruction', Foner's comparative study, too, falls foul of the nationalist tendency.

19. An interesting exception to this rule is the institution of slavery itself, which had to be considered 'peculiar' in order for it to be comfortably incorporated into the notion of 'American'. For further discussion of the intersectedness of histories, see Gyan Prakash, 'Subaltern Studies as Postcolonial Criticism', *American Historical Review*, 99:5 (December 1994), 1486. Sport which has been tied to colonialism and imperialism, and which has transnational histories has received insufficient attention from comparativists. For a compelling exception to this rule, see Ian Tyrell, 'The Emergence of Modern American Baseball c.1850–80', in Richard Cashman and Michael McKernan, eds, *Sport in History* (Queensland, 1979).

20. David Roediger, *The Wages of Whiteness: Race and the Making of the American Working Class* (London, 1991), 65–92. Ira Katznelson and Aristide R. Zolberg, eds, *Working-Class Formation: Nineteenth-century Patterns in Western Europe and the United States* (Princeton, 1986), makes no mention of slavery, abolitionism or empires generally.

21. E.P. Thompson, 'The Peculiarities of the English', in *The Poverty of Theory and Other Essays* (New York, 1978), 245–301. In *Towards the Abolition of Whiteness* (London, 1994), 27–33, David Roediger argues (contra Sean

Wilentz) that the existence of slavery and the prominence of race in the United States makes American labour exceptional when compared to European societies. Wilentz, 'Against Exceptionalism: Class Consciousness and the American Labor Movement', *International Labor and Working Class History,* 26 (1984), 1–36.

22. Joan W. Scott, *Gender and the Politics of History* (New York, 1988). See also, Gregg, 'Group Portrait with Lady', *Reviews in American History,* 20 (1992).

23. C.A. Bayly, *Imperial Meridian: The British Empire and the World, 1780–1830* (New York, 1989). For attempts to theorise empire in American studies, see William Appelman Williams, *Empire as a Way of Life* (New York, 1980); Amy Kaplan, 'Left Alone with America: The Absence of Empire in the Study of American Culture', in Kaplan and Donald E. Pease, eds, *Cultures of US Imperialism* (Durham, 1993).

24. Bayly, *Imperial Meridian,* 15. This important conceptualisation for British history has been further developed by Linda Colley in *Britons: Forging the Nation, 1707–1837* (New Haven, 1992). See also, Antoinette Burton, 'Rules of Thumb: British History and "Imperial Culture" in Nineteenth- and Twentieth-Century Britain', *Women's History Review,* 3:4 (1994); and Michael Hechter, *Internal Colonialism: The Celtic Fringe in British National Development, 1536–1966* (Berkeley, 1975). While being careful to see the imperial considerations in the political incorporation of Scotland, Ireland and Wales, we need also to be aware of the ways in which others besides Anglo-Saxons and Celts were incorporated into the imperial model. Moreover it is important to be aware that just because empire is significant this does not mean that *only* the history of the metropole is important, while histories of the peripheries should remain just that. This is an assumption that has been present to some extent in Eric Hobsbawm's work. As Tony Judt notes in his review of *The Age of Extremes: A History of the World, 1914–1991,* Eric Hobsbawm is 'unashamedly Eurocentric'. Building on this unashamedly eurocentric foundation, Judt notes: 'Any history of the world in our century is of necessity a history in large measure of the things Europeans (and North Americans) did to themselves and to others, and of how non-Europeans reacted to them and were (usually adversely) affected. That, after all, is what is wrong with the twentieth century, seen from a "third world" perspective, and to criticize Hobsbawm, as some reviewers have done, for understanding this and writing accordingly, seems to me incoherent.' 'Downhill all the Way', *The New York Review of Books* (25 May 1995), 21. Understanding that an imperial meridian exists should lead towards 'coherence' founded on the realisation that what non-Europeans did was in fact as important as, and in some cases more important than the actions of Europeans. An imperial perspective allows one to see how the actions of a Toussaint L'Ouverture in Saint Domingue could have an impact from Savannah to Moscow, a John Chilembwe in Nyasaland could affect people from South Africa to Edinburgh. The agency of all – white working classes, white elites, and non-Europeans alike – was limited by the imperial terrain, but that terrain was shaped by all, sometimes with minimal regard to the power relations within it. See Ranajit Guha, 'Dominance without Hegemony and its Historiography', in Guha, ed., *Subaltern Studies* VI (Delhi, 1992), in which he critiques the

'Cambridge approach' to South Asian history for 'writing up Indian history as a "portion of the British History"', 305. For the significance of Toussaint on Jefferson and Napoleon, see Michael Zuckerman, *Almost Chosen People: Oblique Biographies in the American Grain* (Berkeley, 1993).

25. Colley, *Britons*, 120–32.
26. Judith R. Walkowitz, for example, tells of the almost orientalist vision of East London when compared to West London; *City of Dreadful Delight: Narratives of Sexual Danger in Late-Victorian London* (Chicago, 1992), 19, 193. See also Ruth H. Lindborg, 'The "Asiatic" and the Boundaries of Victorian Englishness', *Victorian Studies* (Spring 1994); Edward Said, *Culture and Imperialism* (New York, 1993); Moira Ferguson, *Subject to Others: British Women Writers and Colonial Slavery, 1670–1834* (New York, 1992).
27. See Henry Jones Ford, *The Scotch-Irish in America* (Princeton, 1915).
28. Kaplan and Pease, eds, *Cultures of US Imperialism*.
29. Cell, *The Highest Stage*; Fredrickson, *White Supremacy*.
30. This number is used by Salman Rushdie in both *Imaginary Homelands: Essays and Criticism, 1981–1991* (London, 1991) and *The Satanic Verses* (New York, 1988). It also appears in the movie *Masala* (Canada, 1993), by director Srinivas Krishna.
31. Rob Nixon, *Homelands, Harlem and Hollywood: South African Culture and the World Beyond* (New York, 1994), 1, 5. Another attempt to make transnational linkages can be found in George M. Fredrickson, 'Resistance to White Supremacy: Nonviolence in the US South and South Africa', *Dissent* (Winter 1995), 61–70, which draws on the Gandhian influences in both American and South African resistance. The reliance on a national comparison is evident, and this leads to the rather predictable comparison being made between South African political violence and black-on-black violence in the United States. Since this comparison ends in the claim that 'in the short run, the need for more and better policing has become evident to many blacks' this national bias must certainly be considered a shortcoming; Fredrickson, 'Resistance', 70.
32. Ian Tyrell suggests other kinds of connections that can be made in, what he terms, 'transnational history', through regional analysis, environmental history, and the study of organisations, movements and ideologies; 'American Exceptionalism', 1038–53.
33. Mtesa, the Kabuka of Buganda, made the initial appeal for missionaries, which Stanley reported in November 1875. He added, according to Thomas Pakenham, that 'here was the most promising field for a mission in all the pagan world'; *The Scramble for Africa* (New York, 1991), 28.
34. Cell, *The Highest Stage*, 33–45. For an excellent book-length study of African Methodists in South Africa, see James T. Campbell, *Songs of Zion: The African Methodist Episcopal Church in the United States and South Africa* (New York, 1995).
35. For Turner's attitudes towards the freedpeople, see Leon Litwack, *Been in the Storm So Long: The Aftermath of Slavery* (New York, 1980), 458; for Coppin's views of Southerners, see Robert Gregg, *Sparks from the Anvil of Oppression: Philadelphia's African Methodists and Southern Migrants, 1890–1940* (Philadelphia, 1993), 94–95, 196; see also, Levi J. Coppin, *Observations of Persons and Things in South Africa, 1900–1904* (Philadelphia, 1905);

and, Adelaide Cromwell Hill and Martin Kilson, eds, *Apropos of Africa: Sentiments of Negro American Leaders on Africa from the 1800s to the 1950s* (London, 1969), 44–47.

36. Gregg, *Sparks*, 69–86; Cell, *The Highest Stage*, 41.

37. George Shepperson and Thomas Price, *Independent African: John Chilembwe and the Origins, Setting and Significance of the Nyasaland Native Rising of 1915* (Edinburgh, 1958).

38. Brian Wilan, *Sol Plaatje: South African Nationalist, 1876–1932* (Berkeley, 1984), 259–81. For additional connections between African-Americans and Africans, see Robin D.G. Kelley, 'Introduction' in C.L.R. James, *A History of Pan-African Revolt* (Chicago, 1995), 1–33.

39. Tim Couzens, '"Moralizing Leisure Time": The Transatlantic Connection and Black Johannesburg, 1918–1936', in Shula Marks and Richard Rathbone, eds, *Industrialisation and Social Change in South Africa: African Class Formation, Culture and Consciousness, 1870–1930* (Harlow, 1982).

40. Kwame Anthony Appiah, *In My Father's House: Africa in the Philosophy of Culture* (New York, 1992), 5, 21. Gregg, 'Beyond Boundaries, Beyond the Whale', *American Quarterly*, 45:4 (December 1993), 631–38.

41. Dennis C. Dickerson, *The Land of the Southern Cross: John A. Gregg and South Africa* (New Orleans, 1990); Levi J. Coppin, *Unwritten History* (New York, 1968); Robert R. Wright, Jr, *Eighty-Seven Years Behind the Black Curtain* (Philadelphia, 1968); William Henry Heard, *From Slavery to the Bishopric* (Philadelphia, 1924); Hollis R. Lynch, *Edward Wilmot Blyden: Pan-Negro Patriot* (New York, 1967); Wilson J. Moses, *Alexander Crummell: A Study of Civilization and Discontent* (New York, 1989) 179–95; Appiah, *In My Father's House*, 10–23 (Crummell) and 28–46 (Du Bois).

42. Paul Gilroy, *The Black Atlantic: Modernity and Double Consciousness* (London, 1993), 1–40. See Madhavi Kale, Review of *Black Atlantic*, in *Social History* (forthcoming).

43. Gilroy, *Small Acts: Thoughts on the Politics of Black Cultures* (London, 1993); Gregg, *Sparks*; James R. Grossman, *Land of Hope: Chicago, Black Southerners, and the Great Migration* (Chicago, 1989). For an example of assumptions about division within the African diaspora, see Clarence E. Walker's unfounded assertion that Americans could not have supported Marcus Garvey in the numbers some have claimed simply because he was Jamaican. *Deromanticizing Black History: Critical Essays and Reappraisals* (Knoxville, 1991), 34–55.

44. Manning Clark, *A Short History of Australia* (Victoria, 1986), 105–13.

45. Charles van Onselen, *Studies in the Social and Economic History of the Witwatersrand, 1886–1914*, vol. 1, *New Babylon* (Harlow, 1982), 108.

46. For one compelling example of Americans in South Africa and prospecting migrants, see Mary and Richard Bradford, eds, *An American Family on the African Frontier* (Colorado, 1993).

47. C.W. De Kiewiet, *A History of South Africa* (Oxford, 1978). James Campbell notes that more than half the mines on the Witwatersrand were managed by Americans ('one frustrated Rhodesian mining engineer complained that it was impossible to get a job without an American accent'); *Songs of Zion*, 126–7. Moreover, these transients did not merely stick to mining. Once the Australian gold rush ended, Pacific islands like Fiji were inundated with speculators looking for more gold and mineral deposits. When their efforts

to locate such deposits failed, and other opportunities appeared, they turned
to a wide range of capitalist endeavours. The emergence of the sugar plantation system in Fiji, for example, which drew on the Indian indentured
labour (a system established in the British Caribbean after emancipation),
was just one such development. No doubt others played important roles in
the coming of sugar and Chinese indentured labourers to Hawaii. I am
indebted to John D. Kelly for this information.

48. De Kiewiet, *A History of South Africa*, 166; Innes, *Anglo-American*, 47.
49. The antecedents to such labour practices were not, as might be expected, the
wage labouring systems of North America, but rather the indentured labour
systems developed by Anglo-American capitalists in the years after the end
of slavery. For an explanation of the process by which this occurred, see
Madhavi Kale, *Casting Labor: Empire and Indentured Labor Migration
from India to the British Caribbean* (forthcoming); 'Projecting Identities:
Empire and Indentured Labor Migration from India to Trinidad and British
Guiana, 1836–1885', in Peter van der Veer, ed., *Nation and Migration: The
Politics of Space in the South Asian Diaspora* (Philadelphia, 1995), 73–92;
'Opening Salvo: Making a Colonial Labor Shortage in Post-Abolition Brit-
ish Guiana and Trinidad, 1834–45', unpublished paper presented to the
Eleventh International Economic History Congress, Milan, September 1994;
and 'Casting Labor in the Imperial Mold: Indian Indentured Migration to
the British Caribbean, 1837–45', unpublished paper presented to the International Conference on Challenge and Change: The Indian Diaspora in its
Historical and Contemporary Contexts, Institute of Social and Economic
Research, University of the West Indies, St. Augustine, Trinidad, August
1995.
50. For a full description of the methods used to deprive the Chinese of access
to gold mines and then exclude them from the United States, see Connie
Young Yu, 'The Chinese in American Courts', *Bulletin of Concerned Asian
Scholars*, 4:3 (1972); and Alexander Saxton, *The Indispensable Enemy: Labor
and the Anti-Chinese Movement in California* (Berkeley, 1971). De Kiewiet,
A History of South Africa, 166. There was also, in South Africa, an exclusion
of Chinese indentured labourers ('celestials') in 1906; Philip Snow, *The
Star Raft: China's Encounter with Africa* (New York, 1988), 47–53.
51. Van Onselen, *New Babylon*, 110.
52. *Ibid.*, 111. In 1898, *The Standard and Diggers' News* had complained:
'There is a large and thriving colony of Americanised Russian women
engaged in the immoral traffic, who are controlled by an association of
macquereaus of pronounced Russian pedigree embellished by a twangy flashy
embroidery of style and speech acquired in the Bowery of NYC, where
most of them, with frequent excursions to London, have graduated in the
noble profession.'
53. George J. Kneeland, *Commercialized Prostitution in New York City* (Mont-
clair, NJ, 1969), 336.
54. In 1896, there were 25 282 white males and 14 172 white females living in
Johannesburg, a ratio of 1.78 men to every woman. For blacks the ratio was
even more skewed, with about ten men for every one woman in the city, and
in the nearby work compounds, a ratio of about twenty-four to one; van
Onselen, *New Babylon*, 104; Kale, 'Casting Labor'.
55. Van Onselen 107.

56.　*Ibid.*, 108.
57.　White, quoted in Philippa Levine, 'Rough Usage: Prostitution, Law and the Social Historian', in Adrian Wilson, ed., *Rethinking Social History: English Society 1570–1920 and its Interpretation* (Manchester, 1993), 276.
58.　Ruth Rosen, *Lost Sisterhood: Prostitution in America, 1900–1918* (Baltimore, 1982).
59.　The 'French Madam', Matilda Hermann, for example, paid about $5000 each year to the police. W.T. Stead, *Satan's Invisible World Displayed* (New York, 1974, orig. pub. 1898), 127.
60.　Levine, 'Rough Usage', 276. Levine writes: 'As we develop a better understanding of the complex relationship between state, law and work, a case may emerge for seeing large-scale prostitution (and its concomitant, a more attentive state) as the feminised auxiliary service industry to changing male work patterns, perhaps most particularly in "frontier" contexts such as the opening of the American West, the Europeanising of South Africa or the development of Australia.' The similarities between mining and prostitution labour markets was reinforced by the fact that when mining capitalists went to India, China and Japan to secure labour, members of the 'pimping fraternity' (so-called by Joe Silver) often shadowed them in pursuit of prostitutes. Van Onselen, *New Babylon*, 138.
61.　Van Onselen, *New Babylon*, 121. The Bowery Boys' methods in New York and the London East End, as described by their detractors at least, are described in full here. Van Onselen perhaps reads these sources uncritically and he conforms to a prostitution discourse which distances it from other labour, employing images from slavery that Progressives of the era also employed. Having seen capital move people and production from one region or country to others so readily in the last few decades this assumption of difference between slaves and prostitutes on the one hand, and free labourers on the other seems more tenuous.
62.　Other terms used by women were housekeeper, milliner, musician and florist. Van Onselen, *New Babylon*, 119–23. Philippa Levine, 'Women and Prostitution: Metaphor, Reality, History', *Canadian Journal of History*, XXVIII (December 1993), 484. Veena Talwar Oldenburg, 'Lifestyle as Resistance: The Case of the Courtesans of Lucknow', in Douglas Haynes and Gyan Prakash, eds, *Contesting Power: Resistance and Everyday Social Relations in South Asia* (Delhi, 1991), 23–61.
63.　Judith R. Walkowitz, *Prostitution and Victorian Society: Women, Class and the State* (New York, 1980); and, *City of Dreadful Delight: Narratives of Sexual Danger in Late-Victorian London* (Chicago, 1992), 21–22. Levine, 'Women and Prostitution', 482; 'Rough Usage', 266–92; and 'Consistent Contradictions: Prostitution and Protective Labour Legislation in Nineteenth-century England', *Social History*, 19 (January 1994), 17–35.
64.　See, for example, the experiences of Chinese and Japanese prostitutes described by Lucie Cheng, 'Free, Indentured, Enslaved: Chinese Prostitutes in Nineteenth-century America', in Cheng and Edna Bonacich, eds, *Labor Immigration under Capitalism: Asian Workers in the US before World War II* (Berkeley, 1984); Yuji Ichioka, 'Ameyuki-san: Japanese Prostitutes in Nineteenth-Century America', *Amerasia*, 4:1 (1977) 1–21, and *The Issei* (New York, 1988).

65. Levine, 'Women and Prostitution', 488; Walkowitz, *City of Dreadful Delight*.
66. Robin D.G. Kelley, 'We are Not What We Seem', *Journal of American History*, 80:1 (June 1993), 75–112; and 'An Archaeology of Resistance', *American Quarterly*, 44 (June 1992), 292–98. For a critique of Scott's work along these lines, see Haynes and Prakash, 'Introduction: The Entanglement of Power and Resistance', in *Contesting Power*, 2–4, 9–11; and Timothy Mitchell, 'Everyday Metaphors of Power', *Theory and Society*, 19 (1990).
67. Lynn Pan, *Sons of the Yellow Emperor: A History of the Chinese Diaspora* (Boston, 1990), 123; Tomas Almaguer, *Racial Fault Lines: The Historical Origins of White Supremacy in California* (Berkeley, 1994), 174–78.
68. Here note Darlene Clark Hine's critique of Roger Lane's estimates of prostitutes in Philadelphia's African-American population at the turn of the twentieth century. Hine is right to suggest that Lane's estimates are faulty and exaggerate the number of prostitutes. Lane argued that lower birthrates among African-Americans could be accounted for by the infertility caused by diseases associated with prostitution, and he suggested that as many as 25 per cent of all black women in the city had engaged in the 'trade'. Clark Hine prefers to see such lower birthrates arising from black women's sexual abstinence (in fact, the imbalanced sex ratios and the nature of domestic work were sufficient causes). Lane, *Roots of Violence in Black Philadelphia, 1860–1900* (Cambridge, 1986), 130–35, 158–59; Hine, 'Black Migration to the Urban Midwest: The Gender Dimension, 1915–45', in Joe William Trotter, Jr, ed., *The Great Migration in Historical Perspective* (Bloomington, 1991), 134–35. What is at stake for Clark Hine is the portrayal of women in the black community and whether or not historians can move beyond 'latent acceptance of the myths concerning the alleged unbridled passions and animalistic sexuality of black women'. And yet, if prostitution is such a common factor in all migrations, it need not tell us anything about passions and sexuality. In fact, both sides of the argument fall within Levine's category of 'rough usage' of prostitutes, failing to rise above the 'homogenous notions of prostitution as a category' and the moralistic arguments about prostitutes propagated by Progressive reformers and nationalists at the time; Levine, 'Rough Usage', 286.
69. Kale, 'Projecting Identities', 80–83.
70. Du Bois in Paula Giddings, *When and Where I Enter: The Impact of Black Women on Race and Sex in America* (New York, 1984), 61. See also, Dan Czitrom, 'Underworlds and Underdogs: Big Tim Sullivan and Metropolitan Politics in New York, 1889–1913', *Journal of American History*, 78:3 (1991), 548; and Irving Howe, *World of Our Fathers: The Journey of the East European Jews to America and the Life They Found and Made* (New York, 1976), 96–98. Howe devotes only two pages to prostitution, and claims that, along with crime, 'it was never at the center of Jewish immigrant life', 101. This claim perhaps shows the success Jewish leaders had struggling to disassociate their ethnic group from the taint of 'crime'. Defining 'the center' of immigrant life is problematic and is generally undertaken only when it is deemed important to push to the imagined periphery of one's own group behaviour considered common to other people.
71. Lisa Lowe, 'Heterogeneity, Hybridity, Multiplicity: Marking Asian American Differences', *Diaspora: A Journal of Transnational Studies*, 1 (Spring

1991). Evelyn Nakano Glenn, in *Issei, Nisei, War Bride: Three Generations of Japanese American Women in Domestic Service* (Philadelphia, 1986), 114, makes no mention of prostitution, and yet the manner in which many Japanese-American men resisted women's efforts to join the paid labour force (even under the direst economic conditions) provide examples of how men felt the behaviour of their spouses reflected badly on them and Japanese-Americans as a whole.

72. Anne McClintock, 'Family Feuds', 61.

73. Kale, 'Casting Labor in the Imperial Mold'. The other side of this nationalism coin, of course, is the anxiety whites in the United States and British Empire had that 'their women' might have been 'violated' by blacks and Indians respectively. Thus, any lynching and all the horrors perpetrated by the British in 1857 could be justified by claims (most often spurious) that white women had been in some way dishonoured. See Edward Thompson, *The Other Side of the Medal* (London, 1926), 38; and Gregg and Kale, 'The Empire and Mr. Thompson: The Making of Indian Princes and the English Working Class' (forthcoming).

74. Japanese nationalists and government officials, however, were far more successful in controlling access to prostitutes in America than were the Chinese. Cheng, 'Free, Indentured, Enslaved'; Ichioka, 'Ameyuiki-Sen', 16–17. In Bombay in 1911, the Turkish Consul, upset by the association between prostitution and 'Arabs', persuaded the Government of India to repatriate one brothel-keeper and many women to Baghdad. It is unknown whether the Japanese intervened on behalf of the many Japanese prostitutes: S.M. Edwardes, *Crime in India* (London, 1924), 87.

75. Pan, *Sons of the Yellow Emperor*, 123.

76. Oldenburg, 'Lifestyle as Resistance', 55.

77. This is based on a cursory study of several texts and syllabi. The texts include: Joseph R. Conlin, *The American Past: A Survey of American History* (New York, 1993); George Brown Tindall, *America: A Narrative History* (New York, 1988); James A. Henretta *et al.*, *America's History* (New York, 1993); John M. Blum *et al.*, *The National Experience: A History of the United States* (New York, 1993); Morison *et al.*, *A Concise History of the American Republic* (New York, 1977); and John A. Garraty, *The American Nation: A History of the United States* (New York, 1979). Nell Painter's, *Standing at Armageddon: The United States, 1877–1919* (New York, 1987) devotes one page to American Indians, though this is not included in an analysis of westward expansion but in a chapter on 'The White Man's Burden – Imperialism'. Even Alan Trachtenberg's *Incorporation of America* uses this layout, though for Trachtenberg the dichotomy established on the frontier between 'civilization' and 'savage' becomes central to the meaning of 'America' itself; 25–37.

78. Unless there is a brief mention of the American Indian Movement as an outgrowth of the Civil Rights movement in sections on the 1960s and 1970s.

79. This discussion focuses largely on mid-Western Populism. The analysis could be extended, with modifications, to Southern Populism.

80. John D. Hicks, *The Populist Revolt* (Minneapolis, 1931); Richard Hofstadter, *The Age of Reform* (New York, 1955); James Turner, 'Understanding the Populists', *Journal of American History*, 67:2 (1980), 354–73; Lawrence Goodwyn, *The Populist Moment: A Short History of the Agrarian Revolt in*

America (New York, 1978); Norman Pollack, *The Populist Response to Industrial America* (Cambridge, 1976); and, Robert C. McMath, Jr, *American Populism: A Social History* (New York, 1993).

81. This ignoring of the significance of American Indians is shared by other historians focusing on this period. In *Exodusters: Black Migration to Kansas after Reconstruction* (New York, 1976), 113, for example, Nell Painter mentions that the migrants were to relocate to former Cherokee land in Kansas. The significance of this is not commented upon. One of the latest overviews of populism, McMath's *American Populism*, even goes so far as to describe 'Populist Country Before Populism'. This background chapter makes no mention of the fact that Indians were either present or recently removed from this country.

82. Throughout the period of the populist movement Indians saw their territory reduced from 138 million to 78 million acres. Painter, *Standing at Armageddon*, 163. Moreover, this was a period of the commercialisation of the romanticised Wild West, both in dime novels and in Wild West shows. Trachtenberg, *Incorporation of America*, 22–25, and Alexander Saxton, *The Rise and Fall of the White Republic* (New York, 1990), 321–47.

83. This is not merely a condition for the mid-western and western states. Ward Churchill writes: 'No area within what are now the 48 contiguous states of the United States is exempt from having produced its own historical variant of the Sand Creek phenomenon. The very existence of the United States in its modern territorial and demographic configuration is contingent upon this fact. Racially-oriented invasion, conquest, genocide and subsequent denial are integral, constantly recurring and thus defining features of the Euroamerican make-up from the instant the first boatload of self-ordained colonists set foot in the New World.' *Fantasies of the Master Race: Literature, Cinema and the Colonization of American Indians* (Monroe, ME, 1992), 119.

84. Frederick Jackson Turner, *The Frontier in American History* (New York, 1920).

85. Joseph Howard, *Strange Empire: Louis Riel and the Metis People* (Toronto, 1974), 136–37.

86. See McMath, *American Populism*, 161–2.

87. Ignatius Donnelly, *Caesar's Column* (Cambridge, 1960); for the description of Stanley, see 209–309. Painter, *Standing at Armageddon*, 66; A.L. Morton, *The English Utopia* (London, 1978), 229–32. Morton notes that Theodor Hertzka, in *Freeland* (published in the same year as Donnelly's work), also located a Utopia in East Africa. According to Morton, 'Both books . . . were written in the very years in which the British East Africa Co. was preparing the way for the formal annexation of the whole region', 232. Donnelly did not pick Uganda at random; he must have followed events in Africa closely.

88. Kenneth P. Vickery, in '"Herrenvolk" Democracy and Egalitarianism in South Africa and the US South', *Comparative Studies in Society and History*, 16 (1974), 309–28, makes a similar comparison to that made here between Populists and Voortrekkers, though his argument is confined to the US South during slavery and Reconstruction.

89. Lamar and Thompson, *The Frontier in History*, 25.

90. Unfortunately, none of the essays in the Lamar and Thompson volume discuss the issue of the similarities in political ideologies thrown up by the

American and South African frontiers. Christopher Saunders does discuss the political conflict on the South African frontier, however, presenting some of the differences between Southern African and American frontiers. 'Political Processes in the Southern African Frontier Zones', 149–71.

91. *Ibid.*, 26.
92. Monica Wilson and Leonard Thompson, eds, *A History of South Africa to 1870* (London, 1982), 407. Fredrickson employs three 'crucial variables' – demography, geography and the role of imperial power in South Africa; *White Supremacy*, xxi.
93. Anne McClintock, 'Family Feuds', 69.
94. Snow, *The Star Raft*, 47–53.
95. Pakenham, *The Scramble for Africa*, 28. These American literary conventions were evident in Donnelly's efforts to write Africans out of Africa.
96. Hofstadter, *Age of Reform*, 50–1.
97. Turner, 'Understanding Populists', 368. Ronald Takaki, *Iron Cages* (New York, 1979), 253.
98. Trachtenberg, *Incorporation of America*, 27–34.
99. Thus, if we are to join Alan Brinkley in seeing continuities in republican political tradition from the populists to the followers of Father Coughlin and Huey Long in the 1930s, we must do so bearing in mind both the critique of capitalism and the status anxiety inherited from the days of frontier expansion. Brinkley, *Voices of Protest: Huey Long, Father Coughlin and the Great Depression* (New York, 1983), 143–68.
100. Prakash, 'Writing Post-Orientalist Histories of the Third World: Indian Historiography Is Good to Think', in Nicholas B. Dirks, ed., *Colonialism and Culture* (Ann Arbor, 1992), 353–88.

Index

Note: The Notes are only indexed where they give significant further information. **Bold** page numbers refer to Tables.

Index